"This collection, edited by Dr. Alsharif, offers a valuable cross-section of fresh perspectives on shifting patterns of immigration in one of the world's oldest and largest destination countries—now pursuing an ambitious vision of economic diversification beyond its traditional dependence on the oil sector."

Binod Khadria, Retired professor, Jawaharlal Nehru University, India, and President of the Global Research Forum on Diaspora and Transnationalism (GRFDT)

"This volume offers an insightful and balanced examination of labor migration in Saudi Arabia and the Gulf, grounded in rigorous scholarship and deep regional knowledge. It humanizes migration debates and provides timely analysis essential for policymakers and researchers engaging with the Kingdom's transformation under Vision 2030."

Dr. Abdulaziz Al Sager, Chairman of the Gulf Research Center (GRC)

Labor Migration Patterns in Saudi Arabia

Labor Migration Patterns in Saudi Arabia

Assessing Challenges and Opportunities for Vision 2030

Edited by Fahad Luwe Alghalib Alsharif

BLOOMSBURY ACADEMIC
LONDON • NEW YORK • OXFORD • NEW DELHI • SYDNEY

BLOOMSBURY ACADEMIC
Bloomsbury Publishing Plc, 50 Bedford Square, London, WC1B 3DP, UK
Bloomsbury Publishing Inc, 1359 Broadway, New York, NY 10018, USA
Bloomsbury Publishing Ireland, 29 Earlsfort Terrace, Dublin 2, D02 AY28, Ireland

BLOOMSBURY, BLOOMSBURY ACADEMIC and the Diana logo are trademarks of Bloomsbury Publishing Plc

First published in Great Britain 2026

Cover design: Adriana Brioso
Cover image © Drazen/Gettyimages.com

A catalogue record for this book is available from the British Library.

Names: Alsharif, Fahad (Fahad L.) editor
Title: Labor migration patterns in Saudi Arabia : assessing challenges and opportunities for Vision 2030 / edited by Fahad Luwe Alghalib Alsharif.
Description: London ; New York : Bloomsbury Academic, 2026. | Series: King Faisal Center for Research and Islamic studies series | Includes bibliographical references and index. | Summary: "Labor migration in Saudi Arabia is at a critical turning point. This open access book examines the consequences of four distinctive labor migration flows: international, internal, inter-gulf and undocumented. The 16 chapters offer in-depth discussion of Saudi Arabia's immigration plans, the intended and unforeseen repercussions of these four labor movement types, and the opportunities and challenges they present to Saudi and sending country government policymakers. This includes analysis of the complex relationships between economic, social, environmental and security factors that affect labor migration regulations, labor market developments, and long-term sustainability"– Provided by publisher.
Identifiers: LCCN 2026012521 (print) | LCCN 2026012522 (ebook) | ISBN 9781838606046 hardback | ISBN 9780755658602 paperback | ISBN 9781838606060 epub | ISBN 9781838606053 pdf
Subjects: LCSH: Labor market–Saudi Arabia | Employment forecasting–Saudi Arabia | Labor supply–Saudi Arabia | Manpower policy–Saudi Arabia | Migrant labor–Saudi Arabia | Skilled labor–Saudi Arabia | Foreign workers–Saudi Arabia | Labor mobility–Saudi Arabia | Saudi Arabia–Emigration and immigration–Economic aspects
Classification: LCC HD5812.35.A6 L33 2026 (print) | LCC HD5812.35.A6 (ebook)
LC record available at https://lccn.loc.gov/2026012521
LC ebook record available at https://lccn.loc.gov/2026012522

ISBN:	HB:	978-1-8386-0604-6
	ePDF:	978-1-8386-0605-3
	eBook:	978-1-8386-0606-0

Series: King Faisal Center for Research and Islamic Studies Series

Typeset by RefineCatch Limited, Bungay, Suffolk
Printed and bound in Great Britain

For product safety related questions contact productsafety@bloomsbury.com.

To find out more about our authors and books visit www.bloomsbury.com and sign up for our newsletters.

Contents

Foreword

Zahra R. Babar

Labor migration has long been central to the social, economic, and political architecture of the Arabian Peninsula, a reality that continues to shape the contemporary development trajectory of Saudi Arabia. This volume, through diverse yet complementary analyses, illuminates the complex interplay between migration, labor markets, and state transformation in the Kingdom, situating these processes both within the longue durée of regional history and the evolving imperatives of Saudi Arabia's Vision 2030. The chapters collected here demonstrate that understanding migration in Saudi Arabia requires more than conventional economic or demographic analysis; it demands attention to historical legacies, regional interdependencies, and the broader sociocultural contexts that have long defined mobility in the Gulf.

The historical depth of labor migration in the Kingdom reminds us that contemporary labor dynamics are neither exceptional nor merely a response to modern economic pressures. Long before the formal establishment of the Saudi state in 1932, the Hijaz attracted diverse populations through the pilgrimage economy, trade networks, and philanthropic activities that created enduring social and cultural ties across South Asia, the Horn of Africa, and the Levant. These historical networks facilitated not only the flow of people but also of knowledge, ideas, and skills, creating transregional linkages that continue to shape the social and economic fabric of the Arab Gulf.

The discovery of oil in Dhahran in 1938 marked a transformative moment, intensifying the demand for labor and accelerating the Kingdom's reliance on foreign workers. Workers from neighboring Arab countries and South Asia established patterns of structural dependence on foreign labor that endure today. These patterns were not merely a function of economic necessity; they were embedded in the Saudi state's broader project of nation-building, social development, and infrastructure expansion. By the 1970s and 1980s, remittance flows from Saudi Arabia had become a vital lifeline for many labor-sending countries, linking local labor markets to distant economies and positioning the Kingdom as a central node in transnational migration circuits.

These historical trajectories intersect with the current imperatives of Vision 2030, a program that seeks to diversify the Saudi economy, strengthen national identity, and reconfigure labor markets to reduce reliance on expatriate labor. Yet, as this volume makes clear, the transition is neither straightforward nor uniform. Skilled and semi-skilled migrants remain critical to sectors ranging from construction and services to tourism, entertainment, emerging green industries, and the broader "knowledge economy."

While the volume offers detailed analyses of migrant labor flows and their contributions to the Saudi economy, it is equally attentive to the experiences and aspirations of Saudi nationals themselves. Vision 2030 focuses not only on economic diversification but also on the imperative to cultivate a skilled, resilient, and dynamic citizen workforce. This has led to extensive reforms in education, vocational training, and higher education, designed to equip young Saudis with the knowledge, technical skills, and professional capacities required to participate meaningfully across various sectors.

Urban centers, particularly Riyadh, have become focal points for these demographic and labor transitions. The concentration of economic activity, government institutions, and private-sector opportunities in major cities has created both incentives and pressures for internal migration, with implications for social networks, family structures, and regional identities. As the Kingdom seeks to integrate more nationals into the workforce, it must grapple with the uneven distribution of educational and employment opportunities, ensuring that reforms do not merely benefit urban populations but also reach emerging regional hubs and peripheral communities.

In reflecting on the chapters in this volume, it becomes evident that the future of labor migration in Saudi Arabia cannot be disentangled from broader regional and global dynamics. Migration policies, remittance flows, and labor market reforms are situated within networks of political economy that span the Gulf, the Global South, and beyond. The Kingdom's efforts to balance nationalization objectives with the need for foreign talent exemplify a broader challenge facing many other states in the region seeking economic diversification while maintaining social and political cohesion.

This collection represents a significant contribution to our understanding of the contemporary labor landscape in Saudi Arabia and the Gulf more broadly. Readers will find in its pages both rigorous empirical analysis and thoughtful reflection on the meanings of work, mobility, and belonging in a rapidly transforming country. By combining historical depth, regional perspective, and attention to human experiences, this volume provides a comprehensive framework for engaging with one of the most consequential socio-economic phenomena shaping the Arabian Peninsula today.

Acknowledgments

Bringing this edited volume to life has been a deeply meaningful journey—both professionally and personally. My first experience serving as an editor has been filled with growth, reflection, and heartfelt appreciation for those who stood beside me throughout the process.

First and foremost, I am truly grateful to His Royal Highness Prince Turki Al-Faisal, Chairman of the King Faisal Center for Research and Islamic Studies (KFCRIS), whose steadfast support and lifelong commitment to knowledge have been a source of constant inspiration. I am also sincerely indebted to Her Royal Highness Princess Maha bint Mohammed Al-Faisal, Secretary-General of KFCRIS, and to Dr. Abdullah Hamidaddin, Assistant Secretary-General for Scientific Affairs. I am thankful to both of them for the trust they showed in me and in this project.

I'm especially indebted to my colleague and friend Mark C. Thompson for his generous advice, thoughtful insights, and encouragement along the way. I also extend heartfelt thanks to my colleagues at KFCRIS—Dr. Awad Albadi, Dr. Joseph Kechichian, Dr. Mohammed Subitli, Dr. Torki Alshubaiki, Dr. Yahya Alshamy, Mohnnad Alsaho, Tariq Al Mubarak, Tareq Alaqil, Abdulaziz Alhumaid, Dr. Mohammed Nusair, Subhan Ghani, Abdullah Hajar, and Rizwan Rafi, Suha Al-Bader, Aziz Alenazi, Mathal Almutairi, Mohammed Alorf and my friend Ahmad Alttarifi —each of whom played a vital role during different phases of this book's development.

This volume is lovingly dedicated to the memory of my late father, Alsharif Loay Alghalib—may God grant him the highest place in Paradise. His example continues to light my path. I also dedicate this work to my sons and daughters, Ahmed, Hossam, Raad, Majed, Dana, Jana, Maya, and Yara, and to my mother, Musbah—may God bless her with a long life and continued good health. Her strength and prayers have always been the foundation of everything I do.

To the incredible contributors of this volume: thank you. Your generosity with your time, ideas, and effort, especially those who traveled long distances to join our workshop, captured the collaborative spirit that shaped this book. Your commitment to engaging with Saudi institutions and local scholars infused this project with a unique energy, making it both globally minded and locally grounded. A special word of gratitude to you, Zahra R. Baber: I am delighted that you agreed to write such a fitting Foreword, connecting the discussion to the broader context.

I am equally grateful to the distinguished Saudi scholars, public servants, and institutional partners whose work aligns with Vision 2030's transformative goals. Special thanks to Her Excellency Dr. Monerah Almahmoud, Director of the Behavioral Science Department at the Human Resources Development Fund (HRDF), to Sarah Khan from the UNHCR's Regional Representation for the GCC in Riyadh, and to Dr. Manuel Schubert, Managing Director Behavia, Saudi Arabia. Their input and perspectives greatly contributed to this volume.

Finally, I extend my sincere appreciation to Sophie at Bloomsbury Publishing. Her professionalism, patience, and steady guidance helped shape this book into what it is today. Not least, I am immensely grateful to the three anonymous reviewers for their numerous constructive comments and suggestions, whose recommended revisions enhanced the quality and rigor of the book.

Of course, any mistakes that remain are mine alone. The views expressed in this volume are my own and should not be seen as representing the positions of KFCRIS or the Government of Saudi Arabia.

Contributors

Joseph A. Kéchichian is a senior fellow at the King Faisal Center for Research & Islamic Studies in Riyadh, Saudi Arabia. He held the position of Senior Writer at the Dubai-based Gulf News from 1995 to 2017. He served as the Honorary Consul of the Sultanate of Oman in Los Angeles, California, between 2006 and 2011. Kéchichian received his doctorate in foreign affairs from the University of Virginia in 1985, where he also taught (1986–1988) and assumed the assistant deanship in international studies (1988–1989). Between 1990 and 1996, he worked at the Santa Monica-based RAND Corporation as an associate political scientist and was a lecturer at the University of California, Los Angeles. The author of nineteen published books, his latest titles are *A Sultanate that Endures: Oman in the World from Qaboos bin Sa'id to Haitham bin Tariq* (Liverpool University Press, 2023) and *A Sacred Duty* (Sussex Academic Press, 2022 [Co-Author with Fahad L. Alsharif]).

Mark C. Thompson is a Senior Research Fellow and head of the Socioeconomics Program at King Faisal Center for Research and Islamic Studies (KFCRIS), Riyadh. His principal research areas are Saudi socioeconomic development, societal transformation, and youth issues. Mark's published books include: *Being Young Male and Saudi: Identity and Politics in a Globalized Kingdom* (Cambridge University Press, 2019), *Saudi Arabia and the Path to Political Change: National Dialogue and Civil Society* (Bloomsbury IB Tauris, 2014), co-editor of *Policymaking in the GCC: State, Citizens and Institutions* (Bloomsbury IB Tauris, 2017), *Domestic Policy Making and Governance in Saudi Arabia* (Bloomsbury IB Tauris, 2022), *Saudi Youth: Policies and Practices* (Springer, 2024), and sole editor of *Realizing Saudi Vision 2030: Governance, Institutions and Human Capital Development* (Bloomsbury IB Tauris, 2026).

Gerasimos Tsourapas is the 125th Anniversary Chair and Professor of International Relations at the University of Birmingham, where he leads the ERC-funded MIGDIPLO project on migration diplomacy. He is also a Jean Monnet Fellow at the European University Institute (2025–26) and Editor-in-Chief of *Migration Studies* (Oxford University Press). His research spans the international politics of migration, with particular focus on migration diplomacy, refugee governance, and transnational authoritarianism in the Middle East and the broader Global South. He is the author of *The Politics of Migration in Modern Egypt: Strategies for Regime Survival in Autocracies*

(Cambridge University Press, 2018), which received the 2020 ENMISA Distinguished Book Award of the International Studies Association, and *Migration Diplomacy in the Middle East and North Africa: Power, Mobility, and the State* (Manchester University Press, 2021). He has held fellowships at Harvard University, the London School of Economics and Political Science, and the American University in Cairo. He holds an undergraduate degree in economics and political science from Yale University, an MSc in international political economy from the London School of Economics and Political Science, and a PhD in politics from SOAS, University of London.

Françoise De Bel-Air, PhD, is a socio-demographer. She specializing in the Arab countries, especially the Middle East and Gulf region. Since 2013, she has been a senior fellow with the Gulf Labour Markets, Migration and Population (GLMM) Programme of the Gulf Research Center. Previously, she was a senior fellow at the French Institute for the Near East (IFPO) in Amman, Jordan, and a part-time professor at the Migration Policy Centre, European University Institute in Florence, Italy. Her research and expertise cover political demography, regional demographic dynamics, migration, data issues, and population policies. Her recent publications include *The Future of Migration to the GCC States. Migrants' Aspirations, Labour Reforms, and Politics*, Springer, 2025 (with Nasra Shah), and "The Politics of Migration in the Gulf States", in *Introduction to Gulf Politics*, Kh. Almezaini and K. Alexander (Eds). Cambridge: Cambridge University Press. https://orcid.org/0000-0002-2882-7304.

Sebastian Sons is a senior researcher at the Center for Applied Research in Partnership with the Orient (CARPO). He previously advised the GIZ Regional Programme "Cooperation with Arab Donors" and earned his PhD from Humboldt University Berlin, focusing on media discourses around labor migration from Pakistan to Saudi Arabia. He studied Middle Eastern studies, contemporary history, and political science in Berlin and Damascus, and was trained as a journalist at the Berlin School for Journalists. From 2009 to 2014, he served as head of research and editor-in-chief of Orient at the German Orient-Institute and later worked at the German Council on Foreign Relations (DGAP). As a political analyst, he advises international institutions and media on the Gulf monarchies. His expertise includes EU-GCC relations, Gulf foreign aid, migration policies, sport diplomacy, and Gulf engagement in Africa. He has published three books on political, economic, and cultural developments in the GCC region.

Cian Mulligan is a researcher specializing in labor market dynamics and the employment implications of energy transitions, with a regional focus on Saudi Arabia. His work integrates economic theory, occupational classification systems, and empirical modeling to assess the impacts of renewable energy deployment—particularly in the solar and wind sectors—on workforce composition and job creation. Cian's research also examines local content development, skill transformation, and the intersection of artificial intelligence and task-based labor exposure. He collaborates with think tanks and policy institutions to inform evidence-based strategies for sustainable economic development. His methodological expertise includes the use of full-time equivalent modelling, international employment factors, and granular labor force data.

Omar Bortolazzi holds a joint PhD in political science and history from Sciences Po – Université Paris I Panthéon Sorbonne and the Università degli Studi di Bologna. He joined the American University in Dubai (AUD) in January 2016 and serves as Associate Professor of Political Science and Program Director for the Master of Arts in International Affairs (MAIA). He teaches courses in political science, international relations, and cultural diplomacy at AUD. His scholarly work focuses on Middle Eastern politics, philanthropy in the Arab world, and soft power strategies. His recent research includes studies on economic diversification and public diplomacy in the UAE. His publications appear in academic journals and edited volumes from Springer and Routledge. He is the author of works on Islamic philanthropy and cultural diplomacy, including chapters on economic diversification and the Nasserist regime.

Mohammad Jalal Uddin Sikder is an Associate professor in the Department of Political Science and Sociology at North South University, Bangladesh. He has over twenty-five years of empirical research experience and a decade of professional engagement with international organizations, including the EU, SDC, FCDO, USAID, IOM, and ILO. His interdisciplinary research spans labor migration, irregular migration and trafficking, returnee reintegration, climate-induced displacement, Rohingya refugee issues, and labor rights in the RMG sector. A recipient of the NTS-Asia Fellowship (Nanyang Technological University), he has published widely and presented research in Asia, Europe, the Middle East, Africa, and North America. He serves on the Executive Committee of Asian Ethnicity and reviews for journals such as *Comparative Migration Studies*, *Migration and Development*, and *Asian and Pacific Migration Journal.*

Selim Reza is an associate professor of sociology at the Department of Political Science and Sociology and Coordinator of the Center for Migration Studies (CMS) at North South University in Bangladesh. His research specialisms include labor migration, exploitative recruitment practices, contingent employment practices, and individualized employment relationship issues, which are theoretically grounded in the field of the sociology of work. He is the author of the book *The Construction Precariat*, published by Taylor & Francis, which critically analyses systematic exploitation and slavery-like work conditions of the migrant construction workers. He holds a PhD in the sociology of labor migration, work, and employment from Flinders University, Australia. Before pursuing his PhD, he was a researcher at the Refugee and Migratory Movements Research Unit (RMMRU) of the University of Dhaka and worked on the UKAid-funded, multidisciplinary, multi-country Migrating out of Poverty Research Programme Consortium, based at the University of Sussex, UK.

Md Mizanur Rahman is a research associate professor at Qatar University and coordinator of research on society and culture in the Arabian Gulf. He holds a PhD in sociology from the National University of Singapore, where he received the NUS research scholar award and a doctoral fellowship from the SSRC. Dr. Mizan has worked at the Asia Research Institute and the Institute of South Asian Studies from 2004 to 2018 before joining Qatar University. He has published twelve books, over thirty journal articles, and twenty book chapters. Currently, he is a series editor for the Gulf Studies Series and the South-South Migration Book Series by Springer Nature, which has been indexed in Scopus. Dr. Mizan is also working on two book projects focused on families and marriages in the Arabian Gulf.

Sharique Umar is a PhD candidate in the Gulf Studies Program & Center at Qatar University, where he also works as a graduate assistant. Sharique's interdisciplinary research draws from international politics, migration, and economics to examine South-South migration in the Gulf Cooperation Council (GCC) countries. His current work explores temporary migration, migrant entrepreneurship, and the socio-economic dimension of migration flows in the region, while examining how the cultures and societies of the Gulf region shape these movements. Sharique has collaborated on various projects with organizations including Qatar Foundation, the Stimson Center in Washington, and the Schumacher Society in New Delhi.

Nasra M. Shah is a professor of migration and development at the Lahore School of Economics, Pakistan, and the scientific director of the Gulf Labor Markets & Migration Program. She was previously a professor of demographics at Kuwait University for over thirty years. Nasra earned her doctoral degree in Population Dynamics from Johns Hopkins University in 1974. Her research focuses on social factors in infant mortality, fertility predictors, women's roles, health service utilization, and the health of older persons. Labor migration from Asia to Gulf countries has been a key theme in her work. Her many publications include books on *Asian Labor Migration: Pipeline to the Middle East; Pakistani Women; Basic Needs, Women and development; Population of Kuwait: Structure and Dynamics; Skillful Survivals: Irregular Migration to the Gulf; Migration to the Gulf: Policies in Sending and Receiving Countries; Covid-19 and Asian Migration; and Social Remittances and Social Change: Focus on Asia and Middle East.*

Memoona Qazi is a Research and Policy Analyst at the Punjab SDGs Unit of the United Nations Development Programme (UNDP), where she supports the Planning & Development Board, Government of Punjab, on Health, Nutrition, and Population portfolios. She previously worked as a Research Associate at the Lahore School of Economics and contributed to the *Pakistan Migration Report 2024*. She has co-authored research on labor migration from Pakistan to the Gulf Cooperation Council (GCC), including a book chapter presented at the Gulf Research Meeting and a policy brief on highly skilled migration published by the Gulf Research Center (GRC) and Konrad-Adenauer-Stiftung (KAS). Her recent work also includes a cross-sectional study on son preference and fertility intentions in Pakistan. She has delivered a guest lecture at the Research Forum of the Doha Institute for Graduate Studies on "Competing for Skills in the Gulf: What Pakistan's Highly Skilled Migrants Reveal." She also serves as an Executive Council Member of the Population Association of Pakistan (PAP). Her research interests include demographic change, fertility preferences, labor migration, and sustainable development.

Shroug Saud Alotaibi is an Assistant Professor in the Department of Human Resources Management at King Abdulaziz University, Saudi Arabia. Her research focuses on the experiences of highly skilled migrants, particularly in relation to the role of human resource management in shaping their professional and social lives. She is especially interested in migrants' working experiences in business settings, and in the role of management and employers in influencing their employment conditions and wider experiences. Her work lies at the intersection of migration studies and HRM, with a focus on how workplace practices, institutional frameworks, and organizational policies shape migrants' integration and mobility.

AKM Ahsan Ullah is an associate professor of geography, environment, and development at the University of Brunei Darussalam (UBD). He has an extensive research portfolio and has worked with prestigious institutions such as the City University of Hong Kong, IPH at the University of Ottawa,

McMaster University, Saint Mary's University, Dalhousie University in Canada, the American University in Cairo (AUC), Osnabrück University, Germany, and the Asian Institute of Technology (AIT), Thailand. His research areas include migration and mobilities, international relations, intercultural encounters and development, with a geographic focus on the Asia-Pacific, Africa, and the Middle East, and a theoretical focus on globalization and neoliberalism, development and human rights, transnationalism, gender, intersectionality, and everyday life.

Lakshmi Venugopal Menon is a PhD graduate from Qatar University, with expertise in Gulf studies, cultural heritage protection, migration, and politics in the Gulf region. Her dissertation focused on the trafficking of cultural property in the GCC. She has held roles as a Qatar History instructor, research assistant at Qatar University, and research associate at the Indian Institute of Science. Her research focuses on the impact of migrant communities, social protection systems, and foreign policy in the Gulf region. Menon has authored numerous publications, including book chapters, journal articles, and online articles, addressing topics such as cultural interactions among Malayalee migrants, political influence in the Gulf, workforce nationalization, and regional security issues. Her work also explores Oman's foreign policy and Qatar's family law. Menon's publications are widely accessed, with thousands of downloads and views. She actively contributes to discussions on regional security, cultural heritage, and migration, providing insights through academic and media outlets. Her research aims to inform policy and promote understanding of Gulf socio-political dynamics, making her a notable scholar in her field.

Abbreviations

ACWA	Arabian Company for Water and Power Development
ASDA'A BCW	ASDA'A Burson-Marsteller (Arab Youth Survey Producer)
BBC	British Broadcasting Corporation
BDT	Bangladeshi Taka
BEOE	Bureau of Emigration and Overseas Employment (Pakistan)
BMET	Bureau of Manpower, Employment and Training (Bangladesh)
CAPMAS	Central Agency for Public Mobilization and Statistics (Egypt)
CMS	Center for Migration Studies
CREPS	Center of Research Excellence in Renewable Energy and Power Systems
ENTAG	Hail Non-Profit Organization
FDI	Foreign Direct Investment
FTE	Full-Time Equivalent
GA Stat / GASTAT	General Authority for Statistics (Saudi Arabia)
GCIM	Global Commission on International Migration
GDP	Gross Domestic Product
GLMM	Gulf Labor Markets and Migration Program
GoP	Government of Pakistan
Hajj	Annual Islamic Pilgrimage to Makkah
HCDP	Human Capability Development Program
HRM	Human Resource Management
HRW	Human Rights Watch

HSMWs	Highly Skilled Migrant Workers
ICESCO	Islamic World Educational, Scientific and Cultural Organization
ILO	International Labor Organization
IMF	International Monetary Fund
IOM	International Organization for Migration
IRENA	International Renewable Energy Agency
IRB	Institutional Review Board
ISCO-08	International Standard Classification of Occupations (2008)
ITCs	Integrated Tourism Complexes
KAUST	King Abdullah University of Science and Technology
KACARE	King Abdullah City for Atomic and Renewable Energy
KACST	King Abdulaziz City for Science and Technology
KAFD	King Abdullah Financial District
KAPSARC	King Abdullah Petroleum Studies and Research Center
KFCRIS	King Faisal Center for Research and Islamic Studies
KFUPM	King Fahd University of Petroleum and Minerals
KNOMAD	Global Knowledge Partnership on Migration and Development
KPK	Khyber Pakhtunkhwa
LMI	Labor Market Information
LMR	Labor Market Reforms
LSMWs	Low-Skilled Migrant Workers
MEMO	Middle East Monitor
MENA	Middle East and North Africa
MHRSD	Ministry of Human Resources and Social Development (Saudi Arabia)

MoFAE	Ministry of Foreign Affairs and Expatriates (Jordan)
MoL	Ministry of Labor (Saudi Arabia)
MOPHRD	Ministry of Overseas Pakistanis and Human Resource Development
NAVTTC	National Vocational and Technical Training Commission (Pakistan)
NETAQAT	Saudi National Employment Quota System
NEOM	North-West Saudi Arabia Mega Development Project
NGO	Non-Governmental Organization
NOC	Non-Objection Certificate
NRI	Non-Resident Indian
NSO	National Statistical Office
NTP	National Transformation Program
OECD	Organization for Economic Co-operation and Development
OEPs	Overseas Employment Promoters
PBS	Pakistan Bureau of Statistics
PIF	Public Investment Fund
PR	Permanent Residency
PRC	Premium Residency Card
QNV 2030	Qatar National Vision 2030
Qiwa	Saudi Labor Market Digital Platform
RBAS	Regional Bureau for Arab States (UNDP)
RCRC	Royal Commission for the City of Riyadh
RHQ	Regional Headquarters Program
SABIC	Saudi Basic Industries Corporation
SBP	State Bank of Pakistan
SDAIA	Saudi Data and Artificial Intelligence Authority
SDGs	Sustainable Development Goals

SETC	Sustainable Energy Technologies Center
SMEs	Small and Medium-Sized Enterprises
SPIRE	Saudi Polytechnic Institute for Renewable Energy
STEM	Science, Technology, Engineering, and Mathematics
SVP	Skills Verification Program
SYS	Saudi Youth for Sustainability
TIE	The Indus Entrepreneurs
TVET	Technical and Vocational Education and Training
TVTC	Technical and Vocational Training Corporation
UNB	United News of Bangladesh
UNDP	United Nations Development Program
UNESCO	United Nations Educational, Scientific and Cultural Organization
UIS	UNESCO Institute for Statistics
USCB	United States Census Bureau
WB	World Bank
WHO	World Health Organization
WTO	World Trade Organization
Vision 2030	Saudi Arabia's National Transformation Vision

Introduction

Labor Migration Patterns in Saudi Arabia and the Gulf

Fahad L. Alghalib Alsharif

Cultural contexts and the limits of Western frameworks

For decades, the movement of people across borders has been a key part of the development and evolution story of the Arabian Peninsula. However, in the context of Saudi Arabia, this phenomenon cannot be fully understood or adequately interpreted using Western theoretical lenses alone. Through my experiences with living, studying, and working in diverse cultural landscapes and settings, I firmly believe that only discerning scholars—those who combine deep academic insight with rigorous personal familiarity with Gulf societies—can truly unravel the understanding and complexities of labor migration in the Kingdom.[1] Attempting to apply Western models of social contracts to Gulf states, which are rooted in a distinct Islamic heritage and historical tradition, is not only straightjacketed by stereotypes but also risks overlooking the social realities and cultural elements that shape these societies today.

Nevertheless, labor migration in Saudi Arabia is not simply a reaction to economic pressures or demographic needs. It is part of a larger narrative about a nation undergoing significant transformation. Vision 2030 is not just a reform plan; it is a recalibration of national identity, economic diversification, and social progress, and a reimagination of national transformation (Alsharif, 2021a). Central to that vision is the question of labor: Who participates in formulating initiatives and suggests reasonable reforms, builds the roads, cares for the elderly, drives taxis, develops code, cleans homes?

Labor migration in Saudi Arabia, therefore, extends beyond responses or a sole reaction to economic pressures or demographic demands, reflecting a broader narrative of national transformation. Vision 2030 goes beyond reform and represents not merely a reform initiative but a strategic realignment of national identity, economic diversification, and social development. Central to this vision lies the question of labor: the individuals responsible for infrastructure development, care for the elderly, transportation, technological advancement, and domestic services.

Historically, surges in oil revenues driven by global shifts led to rising incomes among the Gulf households. This newfound affluence increased demand for a wide range of expatriate skills, particularly in domestic labor. Where families once managed household duties themselves—or, in wealthier households before the 1962 abolition of slavery by King Faisal, relied on enslaved labor —they now turned to housemaids, drivers, and cooks from abroad. Migration, in this context, becomes not only an economic mechanism but a deeply social one.

The modern migration landscape: Economic diversification and labor mobility

Saudi Arabia's efforts to diversify its economy, primarily through the Vision 2030 initiatives, have significantly influenced labor migration patterns. The influx of expatriate workers with qualifications and skills ranging from basic to highly sophisticated from South Asia, Southeast Asia, Africa, the Arab countries, the United States, the United Kingdom, and other European countries plays a crucial role in supporting sectors targeted for economic diversification, including tourism, entertainment, and renewable energy. Recent reports indicate that these diverse labor forces are key in reducing the Kingdom's dependence on oil revenues and promoting sustainable growth (Saudi Vision 2030, 2023; International Labour Organization, 2023). This migration trajectory has significantly shaped the demographic and labor structures of Saudi Arabia and the Gulf economies, with lasting implications for sustainable development, remittance economies, and bilateral relations. Saudi Arabia alone hosts millions of migrant workers from these countries, whose economic contributions are substantial.

Remittance economies: Gulf labor, global development, and economic contributions to sending countries

Remittance flows from Saudi Arabia and other Gulf Cooperation Council (GCC) countries—namely the United Arab Emirates, Qatar, Kuwait, Bahrain, and Oman—continue to represent a vital economic lifeline for many labor-sending countries, particularly across South Asia, Southeast Asia, and parts of Africa. These transfers play a crucial role in alleviating poverty, supporting household consumption, financing education and healthcare, and bolstering foreign exchange reserves in the recipients' home countries. According to recent World Bank data, Saudi Arabia ranks among the top five countries globally in terms of remittance sending. In 2023, it was estimated that remittances from Saudi Arabia totaled approximately US$35 billion, making it one of the most significant contributors globally, second only to the United States and the United Arab Emirates (UAE) (World Bank, 2023).

These transfers reduce pressure on national budgets, stabilize exchange rates, and often act as countercyclical buffers during economic downturns. They also contribute to financial inclusion by expanding access to banking services through remittance channels. Within Saudi Arabia, the implementation of labor nationalization policies (Saudization) has affected remittance volumes over the years. Although remittances dipped during the COVID-19 pandemic, the post-pandemic recovery and continued reliance on expatriate labor in specific sectors have stabilized outflows. Moreover, the Kingdom's Vision 2030 initiative, which aims to diversify the economy, still requires the employment of skilled and semi-skilled foreign labor, particularly in construction, services, and emerging sectors such as tourism and entertainment. This suggests that remittance flows will continue at significant levels in the medium term. In the wider GCC, the UAE remains a top remittance-sending country, with over US$48 billion sent in 2022, primarily to India, Pakistan, and the Philippines (World Bank, 2023).

In short, the remittance flows from Saudi Arabia and the GCC remain essential contributors to the socio-economic development of labor-sending countries. Despite policy shifts and labor market reforms within the Gulf, these transfers are likely to persist as long as migrant labor remains integral to the region's economies. Over the past several decades, Saudi Arabia has established itself as a key player in managing and reforming labor migration through a series of policies and regulatory frameworks that reflect its evolving economic priorities and demographic needs.[2]

Spiritual and civilizational dimensions of migration in Islam

The phenomenon of migration, however, is not only a modern construct but also a deeply embedded feature of human history. Within the Islamic tradition, migration holds profound theological and historical significance. The Prophet Muhammad's (PBUH) Hijrah (migration) from *Makkah* to *Madinah* is a foundational event in Islamic history, symbolizing both the pursuit of religious freedom and the reconfiguration of social order (Saadia, 2011; Levi, 2024). These narratives underscore the spiritual and civilizational dimensions of human mobility in Muslim thought.

Moreover, historical records indicate that for over a millennium, Muslim populations from the Indian subcontinent—particularly those from regions such as India (used here in its historical pre-Partition sense, referring broadly to the Indian subcontinent) and Sindh (a historic region in present-day southeastern Pakistan)—have regularly migrated to the Arabian Peninsula. These journeys, often taken for religious pilgrimages (Hajj and Umrah), trade, or settlement, predate modern state boundaries and reflect a long-standing transregional connectivity that underlies the cultural and spiritual ties between South Asia and the Arabian Peninsula.

These early journeys were far more than mere movements across borders—they were acts of faith, connection, and contribution. Over time, they gave rise to vibrant diasporic communities that became an integral part of the religious, cultural, and economic life of the Hijaz (the historic western region of the Arabian Peninsula, now part of present-day Saudi Arabia, including the two holy cities of Mecca and Medina). The pilgrimage routes were not only spiritual paths but also lively corridors of knowledge, where scholars, merchants, and Sufi mystics from the subcontinent brought with them ideas, wisdom, and traditions that left an enduring mark on *Makkah and Madinah* and Madinah. Through acts of generosity, South Asian Muslims also established charitable endowments and centers of learning, weaving together a legacy of care, scholarship, and shared spiritual heritage that continues to resonate between these regions today.

A historical snapshot of labor migration in Saudi Arabia: Pre-oil mobility and the historical roots of labor flows

Labor migration has been a defining characteristic of the Arabian Peninsula's sociopolitical and economic development, tracing back to the pre-modern era, long before the formal establishment of the modern Saudi state. Before the discovery of oil, the region's economy relied mainly on revenues from religious pilgrimages, subsistence agriculture, and maritime activities, including pearl diving. The cities of *Makkah and Madinah* attracted a diverse array of pilgrims, traders, and laborers from across the Muslim world. These early patterns of mobility established the groundwork for lasting transnational connections between the Hijaz and regions such as Yemen, India, the Horn of Africa, and the Levant (Ochenwald, 1984). The unification of Saudi Arabia under King Abdulaziz in 1932 marked a significant turning point, coinciding with the rapid expansion of the nascent oil industry. The 1938 discovery of oil in Dhahran catalyzed a profound economic transformation that intensified after the Second World War and reached new heights following the 1973 oil price boom during the Arab-Israeli War.

The sudden influx of oil revenues resulted in labor shortages in critical sectors, including infrastructure, construction, and services. To address this issue, the state actively recruited foreign labor, primarily from South Asia and neighboring Arab countries, initiating a structural dependence on expatriate labor that persists to this day (Hertog, 2012).

Historically, the territory also attracted non-wage migrants motivated by religious or philanthropic reasons. During the late Ottoman and early Saudi periods, Indian and Sindhi Muslims established charitable endowments (Awqaf) to support students and the poor in *Makkah and Madinah*. Notable among these were the "Egyptian Takkiya" (a charitable religious lodge supporting pilgrims, students, and people with low incomes) and "Shami Tekiya," institutions that provided food, shelter, and education, reflecting the long-standing spiritual and educational magnetism of the Hijaz (Peters, 1994; Al-Rasheed, 2010).

These charitable endowments not only served immediate humanitarian needs but also fostered intercultural ties, creating a sense of belonging and shared responsibility among diverse Muslim communities. By supporting religious scholarship and hosting students from various regions, these institutions played a key role in sustaining *Makkah and Madinah* as global centers of Islamic learning and piety. The presence of such philanthropic networks further illustrates how migration to the Hijaz was not solely driven by economic necessity, but was also deeply rooted in spiritual devotion, communal solidarity, and the desire to contribute to sacred causes.

Labor migration and regional cooperation: GCC frameworks

The establishment of the GCC in 1981 further institutionalized regional labor mobility, although the terms were heavily biased in favor of receiving states. In the contemporary era, Saudi Arabia's Vision 2030 initiative has introduced new dynamics into the migration policy landscape. As part of its broader goal to diversify the economy and reduce dependence on oil, Vision 2030 seeks to nationalize parts of the labor force (through programs like "Saudization") to lower the unemployment rates among Saudi nationals and transition toward a more knowledge-based economy (Vision 2030, 2016), which demands labor policies that attract talented foreign expatriates to assist in this vision of economic diversification. These reforms have spurred debates over the future of migrant labor in the Kingdom, raising questions about labor rights, skill composition, and long-term demographic sustainability (Ramady, 2010).[3]

Therefore, the historical trajectory of labor migration to Saudi Arabia reveals complex interplays among state-building, religious heritage, global economic shifts, and policy-driven labor dynamics. Understanding this evolution is crucial for comprehending the contemporary challenges and transformations in labor migration that this edited volume aims to address. The unification of Saudi Arabia under King Abdulaziz in 1932 was a pivotal moment in the nation's history, setting the stage for profound economic and social transformations. This unification coincided with the burgeoning discovery and exploitation of oil resources, which would eventually redefine the country's economic landscape.

The 1938 discovery of oil in Dhahran marked the beginning of a new era, catalyzing rapid economic growth and positioning Saudi Arabia as a key player in the global energy market. This growth accelerated in the period following the Second World War, reaching new heights following the 1973 oil price boom, which dramatically increased revenues and transformed the Kingdom's socio-economic fabric. As oil revenues surged, the Saudi government faced a critical challenge: a shortage of both skilled and unskilled labor necessary to develop infrastructure, build urban centers, and support the expansion of public services. To address this, the state actively recruited foreign labor, primarily from South Asia—India, Pakistan, and Bangladesh—as well as neighboring Arab countries such as Egypt and Jordan. This recruitment was driven by the need for a reliable workforce to sustain economic growth and development projects.

Over time, this reliance on expatriate labor has created a structural dependence that persists today, shaping the country's demographic and economic contours. The demographic composition of the labor force underwent significant changes during this period. By the 1970s, Saudi Arabia had become a major destination for migrant workers, with remittance flows to their home countries growing exponentially. For example, by 1983, remittances from Saudi Arabia alone exceeded US$4 billion, underscoring the Kingdom's vital role in regional and global labor migration circuits. These migrant workers made significant contributions to the economies of their home countries, supporting families and communities through remittances, which became a crucial source of foreign income for nations such as India, Pakistan, and Egypt. This migration pattern not only reflected economic opportunities but also highlighted the interconnectedness of regional economies and the importance of labor mobility in the Gulf's development trajectory, in general, and in Saudi Arabia, in particular.

Historically, the region also attracted non-wage migrants motivated by religious and philanthropic reasons. During the late Ottoman and early Saudi periods, Indian and Sindhi Muslims established charitable endowments, known as Awqaf, to support educational and social welfare initiatives in Mecca and Medina. These institutions, such as the Egyptian Tekiya and Shami Tekiya, provided food, shelter, and education, reflecting the long-standing spiritual and educational magnetism of the Hijaz region. These charitable activities underscored the deep historical ties between the Arabian Peninsula and South Asia, rooted in shared religious and cultural bonds that predate modern nation-states.

A complex interplay of push and pull factors has shaped migration patterns in the region. Economic disparity, political instability, and underemployment in the migrants' home countries served as push factors, compelling individuals to seek better opportunities abroad. Conversely, Saudi Arabia's oil-driven economic growth, tax-free incomes, and comprehensive state-led development projects acted as influential pull factors. The establishment of the GCC in 1981 further institutionalized regional labor mobility, although historically, the terms of migration were often heavily biased in favor of receiving states, limiting the rights and protections of migrant workers, in recent years and via the strategic objectives of the Saudi vision, many initiatives and reforms have taken place to remedy this shortcoming to attract the needed number of expatriates to be a partner in achieving the Saudi vision.

The future of migrant labor under Vision 2030: Migration, reform, and social justice principles

In recent years, Saudi Arabia's Vision 2030 initiative has introduced new dynamics into the migration landscape. As part of its broader goal to diversify the economy and reduce its dependence on oil revenues, the Kingdom has implemented policies aimed at increasing the participation of Saudi nationals in the workforce—a process known as Saudization. Programs like "Saudization" seek to reduce unemployment rates among Saudi citizens by replacing foreign workers with local talent, thereby promoting a more sustainable and inclusive labor market. However, this shift has sparked debates about the future of migrant labor, labor rights, skill composition, and demographic sustainability. Critics argue that reducing reliance on expatriates could impact economic growth and the availability of specialized skills, while proponents emphasize the importance of building a resilient, self-sufficient national workforce.

Understanding the historical evolution of labor migration to Saudi Arabia reveals a complex narrative intertwined with state-building, religious heritage, global economic shifts, and policy-driven labor dynamics. The reliance on foreign labor has been both a necessity and a strategic choice, shaping the social fabric and economic resilience of the Kingdom. As Saudi Arabia continues to navigate its development goals, the future of migrant labor remains a critical issue, raising questions about workers' rights, economic sustainability, and demographic balance. This ongoing transformation highlights the importance of developing nuanced policies that strike a balance between economic needs and social justice principles, ensuring that the benefits of growth are distributed equitably and that migrant workers are protected and effectively integrated into the national development agenda. This volume features chapters authored by distinguished scholars, each contributing insights and research on topics related to the economic and social dynamics of the Gulf states, with a particular focus on Saudi Arabia. As we were finishing up this book for its 2026 release, tensions between the US, Israel, and Iran suddenly rose in the region. This chaos changed the way people moved across the Gulf. After all the chapters were sent in and the book's structure was set, all of these adjustments happened. There was no way, and no good purpose, to go back and redo the various chapters for things that are continually changing. The editor instead inserted some short, forward-looking ideas to the end of the book to acknowledge the problems and show what they represent for future study. This remark is intended to inform readers that the chapters were written before the most recent storm and to assist them read with an understanding of how quickly the area is changing, without compromising the main idea of the original work.

The KFCRIS workshop

The King Faisal Center for Research and Islamic Studies (KFCRIS) hosted a two-day workshop in Riyadh in February 2023. The event brought together a wonderful mix of distinguished scholars, passionate researchers, and experts from Saudi Arabia and around the world, including those with extensive experience in Gulf countries and talented native Saudi researchers. The workshop's primary objective was to foster collaboration, facilitate access to the latest data, and inspire innovative new research projects on migration topics, all within a friendly and welcoming atmosphere.

The primary objective was to engage a diverse group of researchers in analyzing and assessing migration patterns through various theoretical frameworks and methods. The workshop focused on exploring the complex interactions of push and pull factors that influence migration decisions, covering social, cultural, economic, political, and environmental aspects. Key questions included the role of labor migration in supporting Saudi Arabia's economic diversification, the different migration patterns that emerge, and their respective benefits and challenges in achieving Vision 2030.

Furthermore, the workshop focused on strategic efforts to reduce expatriate numbers while maintaining a skilled workforce essential for economic growth. The discussions highlighted the challenges of balancing labor market needs with national employment goals, emphasizing the importance of attracting and retaining talented foreign professionals to support Saudi Arabia's broader development objectives. Additionally, the workshop examined Saudi labor policies, their alignment with expatriate expectations, and their role in national initiatives like the National Transformation Program.

Without setting limits, the workshop suggested addressing the following main questions:

- Is there a prospect for a permanent labor migration policy in Saudi Arabia? Under what circumstances and conditions might such a policy develop in the future?
- What is the role of labor migrants in the future of Saudi economic diversification and sustainable development?
- To what extent do the different labor migration patterns manifest in Saudi Arabia?
- What are the advantages and disadvantages of these various labor migration patterns regarding Saudi Arabia's sustainable development and economic diversification efforts?
- Which of the three labor migration patterns challenge Saudi policymakers, and which ones may provide opportunities for Saudi Vision 2030 to accomplish its objectives?
- What are the intended and unintended consequences of a family member's migration on those who stay behind?
- To what extent do social remittances of labor migrants in Saudi Arabia influence the lives of migrants and Saudi nationals?
- How do Saudi Arabia's migration patterns differ from those of its GCC neighbors, and how does that affect—positively or negatively—its effectiveness?

- How do Saudi labor policies and initiatives meet the expectations of expatriates with simple manual or semi-skilled to highly professional qualifications, and what is their role in supporting Vision 2030, the National Transformation Program (NTP), and the Kingdom's efforts to diversify its economy?
- Why did Saudi Arabia extensively pursue various strategies to reduce the number of expatriates in its labor market and increase the employment opportunities for Saudi nationals, since, despite initiatives like Ņitaqat, talented foreign expatriates are still necessary and need to be attracted and retained in the labor market?

Structure of the volume

The contributors, affiliated with reputable universities and research centers worldwide, employ rigorous methodologies and present comprehensive data, reflecting extensive expertise and scholarly dedication. The chapters collectively provide a detailed overview of the subject matter, highlighting diverse perspectives and in-depth analysis within this field of study. This book examines these dimensions through twelve chapters organized **into four interrelated parts.**

Part 1: Contextualizing migration patterns and policies in Aaudi Arabia

Chapter 1, "Demographic Changes and Migration into Saudi Arabia by 2030," written by Joseph Kéchichian, provides a comprehensive analysis of Saudi Arabia's demographic development and its implications for Vision 2030. The chapter focuses on labor markets, education, and infrastructure planning. As of 2022, the Kingdom's population was approximately 32.2 million, with expatriates accounting for the total population's 41.6 percent (around 13.4 million people). Projections anticipate a significant population increase to fifty–sixty million by 2030, with expatriates potentially rising to thirty million. These forecasts highlight two crucial challenges for Saudi Arabia: maintaining a large expatriate workforce and addressing the socio-economic needs of a growing, predominantly young population. The chapter raises critical questions about whether the Saudi education system can provide a sufficiently skilled national workforce to meet labor demands and reduce dependence on foreign labor. Despite massive investments in higher education—such as King Abdallah's $200 billion education expansion and the

King Abdallah Scholarship Program—the Saudi system has struggled to align graduate qualifications with labor market needs.

Since 2015, the vocational training sector, under the Technical and Vocational Training Corporation (TVTC), has made notable progress under the leadership of King Salman and Crown Prince Muhammad bin Salman. However, gaps persist in technical and high-skill areas. In this regard, Saudi labor market demographics show that male workers aged 20 to 60 dominate, while female participation, although improving, remains relatively low. With limited interest among Saudis in low-paid or vocational jobs, the Kingdom has historically relied on large numbers of migrant workers from India, Pakistan, Bangladesh, Egypt, and other countries. Discrepancies in migrant population figures indicate the need for more transparent and accurate labor data. Furthermore, high unemployment, particularly in peripheral regions like Al-Jouf and the Northern Borders (exceeding 23 percent), complicates labor planning. This situation urges the government to propose regional job centers and incentives for upskilling. Furthermore, urbanization exacerbates these issues, with projections indicating that by 2030, up to 97 percent of the population will reside in cities.

This trend necessitates investments not only in job creation but also in infrastructure for housing, transportation, water, and food. Kéchichian notes that resource management, especially water, emerges as another pressing challenge. The Kingdom faces severe water scarcity, with agriculture consuming more water than homes or industry. Although government efforts have included dam construction, desalination, and overseas agricultural investment (so-called virtual water), sustainability remains a concern. Additionally, energy consumption poses another challenge. Between 2008 and 2018, energy use increased by 60 percent, with demand projected to triple by 2030. While Vision 2030 established ambitious renewable energy targets (54–60 gigawatts), progress has been slow and inconsistent. The New Enterprise Operating Model (NEOM) and similar mega-projects depend on renewable capacity, which requires investments amounting to tens of billions of dollars. The author posits that migration policy reform represents a crucial development. Saudi Arabia has begun replacing its controversial kafalah (sponsorship) system with a more equitable, contract-based model, which offers expatriates increased labor mobility and protection. References throughout this volume to the kafala (sponsorship) system describe its operational features under the legacy framework that has been substantially reformed since 2021.

This aligns with broader objectives to balance the labor market, enhance productivity, and promote economic growth. The chapter contends that Saudi Arabia's demographic trends are experiencing significant transformations, with substantial implications for labor markets, infrastructure, education, and national policy. Successfully navigating these challenges, particularly labor market integration and sustainable resource management, will be crucial for achieving Vision 2030's ambitious goals. The Kingdom finds itself at a pivotal juncture, where strategic policy and effective implementation will shape its future socio-economic stability.

In **Chapter 2**, "Internal Migration Amongst Saudi Nationals: Issue and Challenges," drawing on extensive experience living, teaching, and working in Saudi Arabia, Mark C. Thompson provides a detailed examination of internal migration patterns within the Kingdom, with a particular focus on the surge towards Riyadh and other urban centers following the implementation of Saudi Vision 2030 in 2016. The analysis highlights multifaceted drivers of migration, which include demographic changes, economic opportunities, and social factors. Riyadh has emerged as the primary economic and employment hub, especially for young Saudis seeking improved livelihoods. This has accelerated urbanization and hyper-urbanization phenomena. Projections suggest Riyadh's population could reach fifteen million by 2030; however, recent policy adjustments aim for a more conservative target of ten million to address infrastructural and social challenges. Thompson contends that these challenges include housing shortages, rising living costs, traffic congestion, and a strain on infrastructure, all of which threaten the city's sustainability and the quality of life for its residents. To mitigate these issues, the chapter advocates for regional development strategies designed to distribute economic activities more evenly across the country. Initiatives such as the development of regional industries, including Sudair Industrial City, and policies promoting local content are aimed at diversifying the economy and creating employment opportunities outside Riyadh. These strategies aim to enhance regional capabilities, maintain economic value within localities, and preserve regional identities, all of which are vital for social cohesion.

The chapter also examines the social and cultural aspects of migration, highlighting the enduring presence of regional identities and the concept of "home." Despite urbanization, many Saudis continue to maintain strong ties to their hometowns and tribal roots, which influence their social behaviors and marriage choices. Resistance to migration in some regions is driven by a strong attachment to family, community, and a desire to uphold local traditions. The analysis concludes that internal migration to Riyadh is unlikely to diminish significantly in the near future. Consequently, policy measures should focus on improving urban living conditions through sustainable urban planning, infrastructure development, and environmental initiatives such as the Green Riyadh project. Simultaneously, fostering regional development by creating meaningful employment opportunities in the provinces can encourage Saudis to stay closer to their roots, balancing urban expansion with regional stability.

The chapter's insights contribute to a broader understanding of the complex dynamics of internal migration in Saudi Arabia, emphasizing the importance of integrated strategies that promote sustainable development and social cohesion in alignment with Vision 2030. Addressing urban challenges while strengthening regional economies is essential for the Kingdom's long-term stability and social fabric.

In **Chapter 3**, "Gulf Migration Interdependence and Saudi Arabia's Vision 2030," Gerasimos Tsourapas examines the complex dynamics of migration interdependence within the GCC and its strategic significance to Saudi Arabia's Vision 2030. Tsourapas introduces the concept of migration interdependence as a reciprocal political-economic relationship generated by cross-border mobility. While scholarship on migration has primarily focused on the coercive aspects of mobility—particularly in antagonistic contexts, such as Libya or Jordan—this chapter advocates for a broader understanding that includes positive-sum outcomes, especially within regional blocs such as the GCC. The core premise is that intra-GCC migration, though underexamined, plays a critical role in shaping the Gulf's economic integration, political cooperation, and social cohesion.

Tsourapas traces the evolution of the GCC's legal frameworks, such as the 1981 and 2001 Economic Agreements, which enshrine the principles of free movement, equal treatment, and cross-border labor rights. The author argues that these legal commitments have been translated into top-down initiatives that provide employment, residence, and social protections for GCC nationals, alongside efforts such as the GCC Common Market and the mutual recognition of qualifications. Notably, the chapter highlights the bottom-up aspects of migration interdependence. Gulf societies are historically interconnected through tribal and familial networks that transcend modern national borders. Policies facilitating intra-GCC labor mobility have allowed these networks not only to survive but also to thrive, reinforcing socio-cultural continuity and contributing to a sense of shared "Khaleeji" identity. Tsourapas, note that this social interdependence is further deepened through cross-border intermarriages and transnational kinship strategies, which sustain regional cohesion amid political uncertainty. The analysis further links migration interdependence to the strategic objectives of Vision 2030. By institutionalizing labor mobility, Saudi Arabia can harness regional human capital to drive economic diversification, innovation, and sustainability. Moreover, deeper migration ties reduce the likelihood of regional conflict by increasing the economic and social costs of antagonism—a dynamic exemplified during the 2017 Gulf Crisis.

As such, migration interdependence serves both as a stabilizing force and a vehicle for regional collaboration. Nonetheless, Tsourapas does not overlook challenges. Labor market segmentation, cultural norms that discourage relocation, wage and benefit disparities, and the lack of supranational infrastructure hinder the full realization of intra-GCC mobility. The author advocates enhanced policy coordination, improved data systems, and institutional innovations, like regional employment agencies, to facilitate labor mobility across borders. This chapter positions Gulf migration interdependence as a cornerstone of regional integration and a critical enabler of Saudi Arabia's long-term transformation agenda. It redefines the role of migration not merely as a demographic or economic phenomenon but as a strategic tool of regional politics and development. By providing a comprehensive and multilayered analysis, the author makes a significant contribution to the scholarship on migration diplomacy and regional governance in the Global South.

Part 2: Skilled migration, economic diversification, and sustainable development in Saudi Arabia

In **Chapter 4**, "The Working Experiences of Highly Skilled Migrants in the Kingdom of Saudi Arabia: A Relational Perspective," Shroug Saud Alotaibi provides an in-depth analysis of the working experiences of highly skilled migrant workers (HSMWs) in the Kingdom of Saudi Arabia (KSA), aligning with the national shift from an oil-based to a knowledge-based economy under Vision 2030. Using a relational framework that encompasses macro (national), meso (organizational), and micro (individual) levels, the study examines the dynamic role of HSMWs in bridging workforce skill gaps and sustaining economic diversification. Alotaibi, drawing on twenty-three qualitative interviews with skilled migrants and Saudi stakeholders (HR professionals, academics, and legal experts), highlights evolving patterns of employment, policy reforms, and workplace integration affecting HSMWs. At the macro level, findings underscore the persistent demand for skilled professionals in critical sectors—such as healthcare, technology, and higher education—despite efforts to localize the labor force through Saudization. While progress in national skill development is evident, gaps remain in areas requiring experiential expertise, prompting a continued reliance on foreign professionals. Notably, regional disparities exist, with urban areas exhibiting stronger institutional frameworks and a reduced dependence on migrants compared to rural settings. The author contends that Government reforms to the kafala (sponsorship) system—especially the shift toward contract-based employment and digital platforms like Qiwa—have been positively received by HSMWs. Migrants working in government positions, where HR departments have replaced individual sponsors (kafeel), report greater transparency, mobility, and improved work conditions. In contrast, private sector experiences remain varied, particularly when individual *kafeel* maintain considerable influence.

At the meso level, the author illustrates how empowered HR departments have emerged as key mediators between migrants and employers, often shaping workplace satisfaction and inclusion. HR professionals in large organizations often assume quasi-managerial roles, ensuring compliance with new labor laws and promoting supportive work environments. In contrast, smaller firms still exhibit variability in HR practices, with outcomes heavily dependent on individual HR personnel or residual kafeel control and at the micro-level analysis investigates the motivations and lived experiences of HSMWs. While financial incentives remain important, career advancement, professional fulfillment, religious proximity (especially for Muslim migrants), and a sense of belonging are key factors influencing migration decisions. Many migrants view Saudi Arabia not just as a workplace but as a long-term home, particularly second- and third-generation residents who feel deeply rooted in Saudi society. However, they continue to be legally foreign. The chapter also examines gender and nationality-based disparities, noting that Western and Arab migrants often receive preferential treatment, while others encounter structural and cultural barriers. Ultimately, Alotaibi concludes that skilled migration is not only essential for Saudi Arabia's economic aspirations but is also integrated within evolving governance systems and workplace practices.

The findings move beyond earlier characterizations of the migrant labor relationship by foregrounding a more nuanced, reform-oriented, and relational understanding of migrant work in the Kingdom. Future progress will rely on sustaining policy reforms, addressing structural inequalities, and fostering inclusive organizational cultures that support both local talent development and the integration of international expertise. The chapter makes a compelling case for HSMWs as co-architects of the Kingdom's transformation toward sustainable, knowledge-driven development.

In **Chapter 5**, "Current Drivers and Future Prospects for Arab Migration to Saudi Arabia," Françoise De Bel-Air offers a comprehensive analysis of the structural and policy-driven factors influencing contemporary Arab migration to Saudi Arabia, with a particular focus on skilled and highly skilled migrants from Egypt and Jordan. Historically, Arab migrants have constituted the backbone of Saudi Arabia's expatriate workforce, particularly since the oil boom of the 1950s. However, the migration landscape has evolved in response to socio-economic reforms in the GCC states, especially within the framework of Saudi Arabia's Vision 2030.

The chapter begins by outlining the transformation underway in Saudi Arabia's economy—from labor-intensive to knowledge-based—and the implications this shift holds for migration flows. While the Kingdom continues to attract Arab professionals, primarily due to wage differentials, cultural affinity, and proximity, nationalization policies such as Nitaqat and broader labor reforms have fostered a complex and occasionally contradictory environment for foreign workers. Françoise contends that Arab migration is driven by a mix of "push" factors in sending countries and "pull" factors in Saudi Arabia. Persistent youth unemployment, particularly among university graduates, is a prominent proximate driver.

The chapter presents detailed data showing alarmingly high unemployment rates among educated youth, especially women, in Egypt and Jordan. However, the author emphasizes that unemployment is often accompanied by broader structural issues, including limited job quality, wage stagnation, corruption, and the erosion of public services—factors that diminish domestic labor market attractiveness and fuel emigration. The chapter also examines the historical and political factors that underlie emigration policies in Arab states. In Egypt and Jordan, emigration serves not only as a socio-economic release valve but also as a political strategy to mitigate dissent and manage demographic pressures. This is supported by state-led efforts to institutionalize emigration, including job-matching programs, labor offices abroad, and formal strategies to boost remittances. On the receiving end, Saudi Arabia offers strong economic incentives, particularly for healthcare workers, engineers, and educators. Vision 2030's focus on developing sectors such as health, entertainment, sports, and tourism is generating new employment opportunities.

Moreover, reforms such as the relaxation of the kafala system and the introduction of premium residency schemes reflect an intention to attract and retain "high value-added" expatriates, which includes Arabs. Despite these opportunities, the author warns against excessive optimism. The effects of Saudization policies on Arab migrants remain largely unmeasured due to limited data transparency. Additionally, increasing quotas for nationals in skilled sectors could ultimately limit foreign professionals' opportunities. Geopolitical instability, particularly in the wake of the Arab uprisings and ongoing conflicts, further complicates the migration landscape.

In her conclusion, De Bel-Air emphasizes that although Saudi Arabia continues to present significant opportunities for Arab professionals amid regional instability and domestic labor market challenges in Arab sending states, the sustainability and accessibility of these migration channels rely on both domestic reforms and broader political dynamics. The future of Arab migration to Saudi Arabia remains ambiguous, requiring ongoing empirical monitoring and policy evaluation.

Part 3: Low-skilled migration and economic development within the Saudi Arabia–Asia migration corridor

Chapter 6, "Brain Circulation and Mobility of Talents: Indian Skilled Migration in the United Arab Emirates and Saudi Arabia," by Omar Bortolazzi, examines the evolving dynamics of Indian skilled migration within the GCC, particularly focusing on the UAE and Saudi Arabia. By utilizing the concept of "brain circulation," the chapter challenges traditional binaries, such as "brain drain" and "brain gain," instead emphasizing a cyclical, transnational flow of talent that simultaneously benefits both source and destination countries. Bortolazzi notes that India remains the largest source of skilled migration to the GCC, driven by economic disparities, structural unemployment, and the region's expanding economies. While prior scholarship has concentrated mainly on low-skilled laborers, Bortolazzi redirects the focus to highly skilled professionals, whose presence is increasingly vital to Gulf states' knowledge economies. He argues that these migrants act as conduits of knowledge transfer, entrepreneurship, and innovation, establishing robust links between home and host countries and facilitating the emergence of transnational professional networks.

The author contrasts South-to-North and South-to-South migration paradigms, assessing prevailing neoclassical and push-pull theories for their neglect of migrant agency and the complexities of return migration. Bortolazzi situates the India-Gulf migration within a broader "brain circulation" framework, where Indian professionals not only send remittances but also return with enhanced skills, found businesses, or form cross-border ventures. The chapter contends that this circulation of human capital supports both India's development and the GCC's economic diversification agendas.

The author notes that nationalization policies, such as Saudization and Emiratization, which aim to replace expatriate labor with locals, are viewed as both a challenge and a structural constraint. While these policies limit opportunities for expatriates, particularly in the public sector and leadership roles, they have not eliminated the demand for foreign expertise. Migrants often navigate regulatory frameworks, encounter limited career mobility, and face wage disparities. Despite these constraints, many Indian professionals turn to entrepreneurship as an alternative to wage labor, especially in sectors such as healthcare, construction, retail, and education.

Empirically, the chapter draws on demographic and labor market data, noting that Indian skilled workers comprise approximately 30 percent of the Indian migrant population in the Gulf. Their contributions are especially significant in sectors such as information technology, medicine, engineering, and finance. Case studies highlight the success stories of Indian entrepreneurs and the emergence of bilateral initiatives, such as the India-UAE skill harmonization program, which aligns vocational qualifications to meet the needs of the Gulf market, thereby enhancing labor mobility and productivity.

The author concludes that Indian skilled migration is a crucial aspect of the GCC's socio-economic transformation. He advocates for nuanced governance strategies that incorporate mobility, acknowledge transnational engagement, and foster mutual development.

The chapter emphasizes the importance of policy frameworks that facilitate talent mobility while addressing structural inequities. Ultimately, the Indian migration experience in the GCC provides a model for comprehending the broader impacts of skilled labor flows in a globalized, post-oil economic order.

In **Chapter 7**, entitled "Bridging Migration Challenges with Vision 2030: Exploring the Socio-Economic and Labor Conditions of Bangladeshi Migrants in Saudi Arabia," the authors critically examine the socio-economic realities of Bangladeshi migrant workers in Saudi Arabia within the broader context of the Kingdom's Vision 2030. Saudi Arabia remains one of the top destinations for Bangladeshi labor migrants, who significantly contribute to both the host country's economic aspirations and Bangladesh's development through substantial remittance inflows. Between 2014 and 2023, nearly 745,000 Bangladeshis migrated annually, with Saudi Arabia consistently receiving the largest number of migrants. In 2023 alone, remittances from Saudi-based workers totaled over US$3.2 billion, underscoring their pivotal role in sustaining Bangladesh's economy.

The chapter situates the migration experience within two theoretical lenses: Evans's "bounded agency" and de Haas's "aspirations-capabilities" frameworks. These perspectives illustrate how migrants' decisions are influenced by structural constraints, personal goals, and their ability to act. While many migrants aspire to improve their living standards and support their families, they often face high migration costs, exploitative recruitment practices, and limited labor protections.

Drawing on mixed-methods research conducted with sixty Bangladeshi migrants (divided between those holding work visas and those with free visas), the chapter identifies key push factors, such as poverty, unemployment, low agricultural returns, and environmental disruptions. Social networks and intermediaries play a pivotal role in facilitating migration, especially for those with free visas, who often rely on unofficial and costly channels. Migration expenses are notably higher for free visa holders, which exacerbates their financial vulnerability.

The authors contend that workplace conditions vary significantly by visa type. Work visa holders tend to be employed in structured environments with consistent access to benefits such as housing, healthcare, and paid leave. In contrast, free visa holders often experience irregular work, exploitative conditions, and delayed payments, despite having slightly higher earning potential due to employment flexibility. The burden of annual Iqama renewals, lack of employer sponsorship, and limited legal protection further worsen their precarity. Furthermore, the authors note that living conditions reflect similar disparities. While most migrants reside in shared employer-provided housing, overcrowding is common, and access to sufficient food and healthcare remains inconsistent. Free visa holders incur more out-of-pocket expenses for basic services, which diminishes their earnings and quality of life. Social dynamics in the workplace also reveal unequal treatment. Work visa holders typically experience more stability and respect from employers, while free visa holders report higher levels of discrimination and marginalization. Both groups, however, face a stratified labor environment influenced by nationality, visa type, and company hierarchy.

The authors conclude with policy recommendations designed to align labor practices with Vision 2030's objectives of fostering a more inclusive and efficient workforce. These recommendations include standardizing recruitment costs, expanding labor protections and benefits across all visa categories, providing opportunities for skill certification, and promoting workplace inclusion. By implementing these reforms and collaborating with Bangladesh, Saudi Arabia can better align its economic transformation with the rights and welfare of migrant workers. Overall, the chapter presents a nuanced, evidence-based account of how labor migration from Bangladesh intersects with the ambitions and limitations of Saudi Arabia's reform agenda, emphasizing the need for more equitable and transparent migration governance.

In **Chapter 8**, entitled "Most Favored Destination for Pakistani Migrants, Saudi Arabia: Trends, Patterns and Issues," Nasra Shah and Memoona Qazi explore the centrality of Saudi Arabia as the principal destination for Pakistani labor migrants, detailing the historical, economic, socio-cultural, and legal dimensions that shape this enduring migration corridor. The chapter begins with a contextual overview of the robust Pakistan-KSA bilateral relationship, founded on shared religious reverence, strong diplomatic ties, and economic interdependence, particularly through remittances and labor migration. In this regard, Migration from Pakistan to Saudi Arabia began in earnest during the 1970s, coinciding with the Gulf's oil-fueled development boom.

To manage the growing outflow, Pakistan established the Bureau of Emigration and Overseas Employment (BEOE) and implemented regulatory frameworks, including the Emigration Ordinance (1979). Most migrants register through nine protectorates, although many still depend on an extensive, often unregulated network of agents, which contributes to exploitation and high recruitment costs. According to the authors, the data indicates that out of 13.85 million labor migrants from Pakistan since 1971, over 50 percent headed to KSA. Though temporarily disrupted during the COVID-19 pandemic, KSA has remained the dominant destination, with nearly half of all migrants continuing to go there in 2023. The occupational profile of these migrants is predominantly unskilled or semi-skilled, with drivers and laborers forming the largest categories.

A notable decline in driver recruitment followed the Saudi reforms that allowed women to drive. Migrants primarily originate from Punjab and Khyber Pakhtunkhwa, driven in part by strong social networks that facilitate chain migration. However, the chapter outlines several pressing issues. First, high recruitment costs—averaging around $3,500, primarily due to informal visa fees—pose significant barriers, often forcing migrants to seek high-interest loans. Second, low skill levels among migrants hinder their competitiveness, particularly in light of Saudi Vision 2030, which aims to attract highly skilled workers. Despite initiatives such as the Skill Verification Program and vocational training programs in Pakistan, a persistent mismatch remains between supply and demand. Third, irregular migration continues due to overstaying pilgrimage visas or working outside the official sponsorship system, exposing migrants to detention and deportation. Fourth, rising incarceration and execution rates—particularly related to drug smuggling—highlight serious human rights concerns.

Pakistani detainees often lack legal support, face coercion, and endure systemic due process violations in KSA's opaque judicial system. The authors also highlight emerging concerns such as the trafficking of Pakistani beggars to KSA disguised as pilgrims, leading to diplomatic complaints and potential reputational damage. Injuries and a lack of worker protections further emphasize the vulnerability of this labor force. In their conclusion, the authors assert that while KSA will likely remain a major destination for labor migration from Pakistan, the long-term sustainability of this relationship depends on the alignment of workforce skills with Saudi development goals, enhancing migrant protections, reducing recruitment costs, and addressing irregular migration and human rights abuses. Skill certification, ethical recruitment practices, and strong consular support are considered essential for improving the safety, dignity, and effectiveness of Pakistani labor migration to the Gulf.

Part 4: Emerging trends in the Saudi migration-development nexus: Labor market transformation and the green hydrogen economy

In **Chapter 9**, entitled "Energy Diversification and a Shifting Labor Market in Saudi Arabia: Green Jobs and Education Potential in the Development of a Clean Hydrogen Sector," Cian Mulligan and Sebastian Sons argue that as Saudi Arabia accelerates its diversification agenda under Vision 2030, the connection between migration and development is being reshaped by significant economic and environmental reforms.

Central to these efforts is the Kingdom's goal of transitioning from a hydrocarbon-based economy to a green, knowledge-driven society. This transformation is supported by initiatives like the Saudi Green Initiative and the National Renewable Energy Program, which aim to decarbonize the economy, create new jobs, and develop human capital for emerging sectors, particularly clean hydrogen energy. One of the most important implications of this shift is the labor market's restructuring. Historically divided between high-paying public sector jobs for nationals and low-wage private sector roles for expatriates, the Saudi labor market has undergone significant reforms.

The authors note that the Nitaqat Saudization program and other targeted initiatives have increased the participation of Saudi nationals in private sector employment, especially women, whose labor force participation more than doubled from 17.5 percent in 2017 to 33.6 percent in 2022. Nevertheless, a dual labor market persists, with expatriates still constituting the majority in low-skill and technical roles, particularly in sectors where nationals are underrepresented. This segmentation becomes especially relevant as Saudi Arabia positions itself as a global leader in hydrogen production. The authors contend that with substantial investments in green and blue hydrogen technologies, including flagship projects in NEOM and collaborations with companies such as ACWA Power and Saudi Aramco, the Kingdom aims to be a major exporter of clean hydrogen by 2030. However, the labor market's readiness to support this ambition remains uneven. While clean hydrogen presents opportunities for high-skilled employment, the immediate demand is primarily in construction, metalwork, and plant operations—roles traditionally filled by migrant labor. At the same time, the Kingdom encounters critical gaps in hydrogen-specific education and training.

The authors contend that although institutions like King Saud University and King Fahd University of Petroleum and Minerals have launched academic and research programs, vocational and technical training in hydrogen remains limited. The Human Capability Development Program under Vision 2030 signals intent but lacks explicit emphasis on hydrogen education. Technical and Vocational Education Training uptake is growing, but cultural preferences for academic credentials over technical skills still constrain it.

The authors postulate that this skills mismatch highlights the ongoing reliance on expatriate labor, especially in the short to medium term. However, a simultaneous effort is being made to localize green jobs through curricular reforms, capacity building, and strategic international partnerships. Importantly, youth-led environmental organizations and female-led small and medium-sized enterprises (SMEs) are increasingly engaging with the sustainability agenda, indicating a cultural shift among younger Saudis towards environmentalism and green career paths.

In summary, according to the authors, the Kingdom's pivot to clean hydrogen exemplifies the broader dynamics of the migration-development nexus in the Gulf. Economic diversification strategies are creating new labor market demands that current national capacities cannot yet fully meet. As such, a dual approach is emerging—enhancing local skills through education reform while strategically recruiting international expertise. The success of this model will depend on aligning educational initiatives with labor market needs and striking a balance between Saudization and the realities of global labor mobility.

In **Chapter 10**, entitled "International Student Migration and Economic Diversification in Saudi Arabia," Md Mizanur Rahman and Sharique Umar examine the evolving role of international student migration within Saudi Arabia's broader economic diversification agenda under Vision 2030. As the Kingdom shifts away from oil dependence, it has increasingly positioned education and research as strategic pillars for fostering a knowledge-based economy. Central to this vision is the internationalization of higher education, with a growing emphasis on attracting global talent and cultivating a dynamic academic ecosystem. By 2023, the Saudi government had allocated over 17 percent of its national budget—approximately US$50.4 billion—to education and research, a move reflected in the rising prominence of Saudi universities in regional rankings. This investment has spurred a surge in international student enrollment, with over 64,000 international students accounting for 4 percent of tertiary education enrollments.

These students contribute not only to academic diversity and cultural exchange but also to the local economy through their skills, spending, and future potential in knowledge industries. The chapter argues that international student mobility operates as both a development strategy and a soft power tool. Inbound students are drawn by a combination of generous scholarships, relatively low living costs, religious and cultural affinity, and geographic proximity. Saudi Arabia's identity as the heartland of Islam significantly appeals to Muslim students globally, particularly in fields such as Islamic studies. Additionally, the scholarship ecosystem—comprising government initiatives, university-level aid, and contributions from international organizations like the Islamic Development Bank—has positioned the Kingdom as a cost-effective and spiritually meaningful study destination.

The authors note, however, that Saudi Arabia's policy landscape remains uneven. While visa procedures are streamlined and student support services are improving, the absence of a clear post-study work pathway undermines the full integration of international talent into the domestic labor market. Interviews with students and correspondence with universities reveal conflicting policies regarding the ability to transition from student to employment visas—highlighting a gap between the state's aspirations and its institutional frameworks. This contrasts with countries such as Canada, Qatar, and the UK, which offer structured post-study work opportunities that enhance their appeal to international students.

Methodologically, the chapter combines secondary data from the United Nations Educational, Scientific and Cultural Organization (UNESCO) and Saudi educational authorities with qualitative interviews conducted during field visits. The analysis reveals that student motivations to study in Saudi Arabia are driven by a complex interplay of push and pull factors—ranging from economic constraints at home to religious aspirations and career advancement opportunities. Cultural familiarity, the use of the Arabic language, and family ties in the Kingdom further facilitate student adjustment. The authors contend that while the presence of international students is a positive step toward building a globally connected higher education system, challenges such as language barriers, limited academic program diversity outside Islamic and Science, Technology, Engineering, and Mathematics (STEM) fields, and inadequate mental health support persist.

The authors note that the recent decline in international enrolments and competition from other Gulf states with more liberal education environments pose strategic concerns for the Kingdom. Ultimately, this chapter underscores the need for a more cohesive policy framework that integrates international student migration into Saudi Arabia's long-term development goals. By aligning educational strategies with labor market needs and social integration policies, Saudi Arabia can harness international student mobility as a powerful lever for sustainable economic diversification.

AKM Ahsan Ullah, in **Chapter 11**, "Labor Migration and the Sustainability of Saudi Arabia's Secondary Labor Market Sustainability," critically examines the intersection of labor migration, economic diversification, and sustainable development in Saudi Arabia, with a specific focus on the secondary labor market. This segment of the labor force—made up of low-skilled, low-paid jobs predominantly held by migrant workers from South Asia, Southeast Asia, and Africa—serves as the backbone of essential sectors such as construction, domestic work, and services. Despite their vital contribution, these workers frequently encounter structural disadvantages, including limited legal protection, restricted mobility, low wages, and social marginalization. In this regard, Ahsan Ullah highlights Saudi Arabia's dual labor market structure, where the primary sector, mainly reserved for Saudi nationals, provides better pay, job security, and upward mobility. Conversely, the secondary sector remains heavily dependent on migrant labor. The government's Saudization policies, including the Nitaqat program, seek to nationalize employment in the private sector.

However, the author argues that these policies encounter significant empirical and theoretical challenges. Low-skilled, routine jobs in the secondary sector often do not meet the aspirations or qualifications of the Saudi workforce, leading to a continuous demand for foreign labor. Vision 2030, the Kingdom's transformative national development strategy, aims to diversify the economy beyond oil and develop a skilled Saudi workforce. However, Ahsan Ullah emphasizes that completely replacing migrant labor is not feasible in the short to medium term. Migrant workers are structurally integrated into the economic system, especially in labor-intensive sectors. Sudden nationalization without sufficient vocational training and incentives risks disrupting economic productivity.

The author uses a case study of Bangladeshi migrant workers to illustrate their lived experiences and economic contributions. Despite facing hardships such as language barriers and exploitative conditions, these workers play a vital role in supporting Saudi economic sectors and sending substantial funds back to their home countries. Their experiences underscore the need to integrate migrant labor into national policy frameworks that strike a balance between economic needs and human rights. Furthermore, the chapter also addresses critical policy gaps, including the absence of trade unions for migrant workers, which hinders their ability to advocate for fair wages and better working conditions.

It emphasizes the necessity for bilateral cooperation with labor-sending countries, improved recruitment practices, and investment in skill development tailored to the demands of the secondary labor market. Policy recommendations, according to the author, involve enhancing cultural integration, expanding legal protections, and recognizing the contributions of migrant workers to Saudi Arabia's economic development. Notably, the author advocates for a balanced strategy that supports both local employment and the integration of migrant labor, aligning with Vision 2030's objectives of fostering a vibrant, diversified, and inclusive economy. In summary, this chapter presents labor migration not just as a temporary solution to labor shortages but as a vital component of Saudi Arabia's long-term development. It makes a strong case for strategically aligning migration policies with nationalization efforts, ensuring that migrant workers are recognized as essential contributors to the Kingdom's evolving economic landscape.

In **Chapter 12**, "Foreign Property Ownership in the Gulf," Lakshmi Venugopal Menon examines the changing landscape of foreign property ownership across three GCC countries—Saudi Arabia, the UAE, and Qatar—through the perspective of South Asian migrants, primarily Indians and Pakistanis. Menon's analysis is situated within the broader context of economic diversification, foreign direct investment (FDI), and national strategies, including Saudi Vision 2030 and Qatar National Vision 2030. By connecting foreign property ownership to migration and integration, the study addresses both structural policy changes and the real-life experiences of Gulf migrants. Using a mixed-methods approach that combines policy analysis with an empirical survey of 137 South Asian migrants, this chapter explores motivations, deterrents, and investment behaviors.

The UAE leads the region with its established freehold property policies in designated areas like the Palm Jumeirah and Business Bay. Qatar has followed suit by liberalizing its property laws, particularly in Lusail and Pearl Qatar, while also offering residency-linked investment incentives. Historically more conservative, Saudi Arabia has taken strategic steps under Vision 2030 to open its real estate sector through regulatory reforms, including the introduction of the White Land Tax, along with mega-projects such as NEOM and the Red Sea Project.

The findings reveal a nuanced picture: while 86 percent of respondents had not yet invested in property, nearly half expressed serious interest. Business owners were more likely than corporate employees or those in education to consider property investment, emphasizing economic self-reliance as a key enabler. The primary motivators included safety, a stable income, and cultural familiarity. In contrast, significant deterrents included a preference for investing in one's home country, unfavorable government policies, job insecurity, and a lack of permanent residency or citizenship options.

The chapter critically engages with both Real Estate Market Theory and the Theory of Planned Behavior to interpret these trends. It argues that market conditions, legal frameworks, and national incentives intersect with migrants' perceptions of social stability, belonging, and future security. Cultural integration and generational identity also play significant roles, as illustrated by survey responses in which some third-generation migrants identified the host country as their "home," influencing their decision to invest. Notably, Lakshmi Venugopal Menon emphasizes the implications of foreign property ownership for Gulf development strategies. For Saudi Arabia, easing property ownership restrictions for South Asians aligns with the Vision 2030 objectives of urbanization, economic diversification, private sector growth, and increased FDI. Property investments by long-term migrants could stimulate construction, legal, financial, and service sectors while fostering greater socio-economic inclusion. Ultimately, the study underscores the interconnection between migration, investment, and policy in shaping both migrant futures and national development trajectories in the Gulf. It calls for further research into the long-term integration potential of property ownership and recommends clear, consistent policies to attract stable investment from migrant communities.

A final remark

We hope this volume offers a comprehensive examination of labor migration to Saudi Arabia and the broader Gulf region, incorporating historical, economic, political, and policy perspectives. The twelve chapters together provide a layered analysis of how migration has evolved, adapted, and intersected with Saudi Arabia's national development goals, especially under Vision 2030. Chapter 1 lays the groundwork by tracing the historical development of labor migration in Saudi Arabia. Long before the discovery of oil, the region attracted diverse migrants driven by religious, commercial, and philanthropic motives. The post-1938 oil boom increased the Kingdom's dependence on foreign labor, mainly from South Asia and the Arab world. This volume highlights the transformation of Saudi labor markets, demographic changes, and the growing institutionalization of labor policies. As the nation moves toward a diversified, knowledge-based economy, labor migration remains both a strategic need and a point of debate. Together, these chapters create a layered narrative of migration as a dynamic force in Saudi Arabia's transformation. From internal migration to international student flows, from skilled professionals to construction workers, each group plays a crucial role in the Kingdom's pursuit of a diversified, knowledge-based, and inclusive economy. This book does more than just describe these changes; it immerses the reader in the discussions—inviting reflection, response, and reimagining of the future of labor migration in Saudi Arabia and the Gulf.

As the global discourse on labor mobility intensifies, this edited volume invites readers into the evolving landscape of migration in Saudi Arabia and the broader Gulf region. Tailored for academics, policymakers, and informed readers both within the Kingdom and globally. Its aim is not only to inform but also to provoke thoughtful engagement with the complexities, opportunities, and ongoing reforms that define labor migration today.

Migration is more than a policy challenge or an economic necessity; it is a human story woven through the tapestry of regional transformation. Saudi Arabia's labor migration journey mirrors its national evolution—from a land of pilgrimage and subsistence to a petrostate and now, ambitiously, a hub of innovation and knowledge under Vision 2030.

This volume, thoughtfully structured into four sections, provides an analytical yet accessible exploration of these shifts. In particular, the twelve chapters in this volume, when read together, weave a rich, multidimensional narrative of labor migration in Saudi Arabia and the wider Gulf—one that is historical, sociological, economic, and forward-looking. These contributions move beyond the static image of migrants as temporary laborers, revealing them instead as essential actors in the Kingdom's evolving national story.

From the demographic shifts explored in Chapter 1 to the institutional challenges of foreign property ownership in Chapter 12, the authors illuminate how migration is intricately tied to the region's development, diversification, and identity. The chapters collectively underscore that labor migration is not a singular phenomenon, but a dynamic ecosystem influenced by national policies, regional interdependence, global labor trends, and the aspirations of individuals. Internal migration patterns, as discussed in Chapter 2, highlight the spatial dimensions of labor and the socio-cultural negotiations that shape urbanization and regional inclusion.

Meanwhile, the analysis of migration interdependence in Chapter 3 presents mobility as a political and economic bridge within the Gulf, fostering stability and cohesion across national borders. Contributions on skilled and low-skilled migration offer nuanced insight into the real-life experiences of expatriates—from highly educated professionals navigating policy reforms and organizational culture, to construction workers and domestic laborers confronting legal and social precarity. These accounts challenge simplistic binaries of "sending" and "receiving" countries, instead revealing a deeply embedded transnationalism that links communities, economies, and institutions across continents.

Importantly, the volume situates these migration dynamics within the framework of Vision 2030, emphasizing that achieving the Kingdom's ambitions hinges on effectively managing labor flows, nurturing talent, and creating inclusive and equitable labor systems. Whether through fostering international student migration, expanding green job pathways, or enhancing bilateral cooperation with labor-sending countries, each chapter contributes a vital perspective to the national conversation. In sum, this book invites readers to reimagine labor migration not as a transient feature of Saudi Arabia's past but as a foundational element of its future. It encourages academics, policymakers, and practitioners to think critically about migration governance in a rapidly transforming region—one that is striving to balance national priorities with global realities, and economic growth with human dignity.

Notes

1 In Saudi Arabia and Gulf countries, labor migration is primarily a temporary work system involving migrant workers across various fields, from manual labor to professional roles. These workers join registered businesses under fixed-term contracts, with some systems offering pathways to citizenship or permanent residency under specific conditions.

2 COVID-19 magnified the structural vulnerabilities of Gulf migrant labor markets, exposing a lack of safety nets and amplifying uncertainties for communities in cities like Jeddah and Dubai (Alsharif and Malit, 2020).

3 The recent changes to the kafala system mark an important step toward increased labor mobility and independence for expatriate workers, but significant challenges still exist, particularly for domestic workers and low-wage migrants who remain excluded from certain protections (Alsharif, 2021b).

References

Al-Rasheed, M. (2010). *A History of Saudi Arabia* (2nd ed.). Cambridge: Cambridge University Press.

Alsharif, Fahad L. Alghalib (2021a). "Kafala Sponsorship Reforms in Saudi Arabia: Converging Toward International Labor Standards." Commentary. Riyadh: King Faisal Center for Research & Islamic Studies (KFCRIS). Available at: https://www.kfcris.com/en/view/post/332

Alsharif, Fahad L. Alghalib and F. Malit (2020). "Migration and the COVID-19 Pandemic in the Gulf: A Study of Foreign Expatriate Worker Communities'

Coping Attitudes, Practices, and Future Prospects in Dubai and Jeddah." Policy Report No. 15. Regional Programme Gulf States, Konrad-Adenauer-Stiftung. Available at: https://www.kas.de/en/web/rpg/detail/-/content/migration-and-the-covid-19-pandemic-in-the-gulf

Hertog, S. (2012). "A Comparative Assessment of Labor Market Nationalization Policies in the GCC." In M. al-Shamlan (Ed.), *National Employment in the GCC*, 65–6. Riyadh: Gulf Labour Markets and Migration.

International Labour Organization. (2023). *ILO Global Estimates on International Migrant Workers*. Geneva: ILO.

Levi, J. (2024). "Culture and Religion as Key Factors in the Migration of Muslims," *Migration & Development* 13, no. 1: 55–73.

Ochsenwald, W. (1984). *Religion, Society, and the State in Arabia: The Hijaz under Ottoman Control, 1840–1908*. Columbus: Ohio State University Press.

Peters, F. E. (1994). *The Hajj: The Muslim Pilgrimage to Mecca and the Holy Places*. Princeton, NJ: Princeton University Press.

Ramady, M. A. (2010). *The Saudi Arabian Economy: Policies, Achievements, and Challenges*. New York: Springer.

Saadia, Sh. J. (2011). "The Qur'anic Perspective on Immigrants: Prophet-Migration in Muslim Thought," *Journal for the Study of Religion* 24, no. 1: 23–42.

Vision 2030. (2016). Kingdom of Saudi Arabia. Riyadh: Council of Economic and Development Affairs.

World Bank. (2023). *Migration and Development Brief 38*. Washington, DC: World Bank.

Part One

Contextualizing Migration Patterns and Policies in Saudi Arabia

1

Demographic Changes and Migration into Saudi Arabia by 2030

Joseph A. Kéchichian

The Kingdom of Saudi Arabia boasted the fourth-largest Arab demographic mass in 2022, the last year for which official statistics are available as of this writing, with a reported population of 32,175,224.[1] An estimated 41.6 percent of these inhabitants were migrants, or roughly 13,384,893 expatriate workers, a figure that counted family members too. These were significant figures, as the country experienced a population explosion during the past forty years, which grew at a rate of 1.62 percent per year, and was poised to continue this development pattern well beyond 2030.[2] In fact, current projections anticipate a large population increase that may reach fifty to sixty million by 2030, of which an estimated twenty-five to thirty million would be expatriates. Speaking to reporters after unveiling the designs of The Line project in 2022, Heir Apparent Muhammad bin Salman predicted that the capital city alone could well accommodate a population of twenty-five million by 2030, while the overall NEOM projects may house about ten million.[3] According to the heir apparent, the first phase of NEOM may start welcoming 1.5 million residents by 2030, which would increase to 9 million by 2045.[4] Equally daunting figures were made by the United Nations, which projected the Saudi population at around 37.5 million in 2030, while the United States Census Bureau (USCB) forecast even higher data. In 2050, the USCB revealed, the Kingdom's crude birth rate per 1,000 persons would clock in at 10.800 NA (natalities per annum). While this recorded a decrease from the previous number of 10.900 NA for 2049, the updated yearly figures, which averaged 14.200 NA from June 1992 to 2050, had reached an all-time high of 34.000 natalities in 1992. The 10.800 NA in 2050 was still a relatively large figure that required attention by decision makers who prepared long-term national policies.[5]

All these figures confirmed that the Saudi population would reach unprecedented levels between 2030 and 2050, with two major consequences for Riyadh. First, a significant expatriate presence would continue to be present in the country well into 2050 and, perhaps, beyond that date. Second, these substantial population increases would also leave direct impacts on the

Kingdom's urban environment(s) that, in turn, would necessitate updated infrastructures at every imaginable level. Moreover, and given the fact that most residents may well be relatively young, the changing demographic scenes could impose fresh socio-economic, perhaps even political, requirements that will significantly drain basic available resources such as food, water, housing, education, and transportation. How Riyadh managed these two major challenges would largely determine whether Vision 2030 could be successfully implemented. Likewise, how Saudi authorities tackled a far more sophisticated migrant presence in the Kingdom (compared to past practices) and, in the process, maintained a demographic balance at home, illustrated the kind of challenges that few discussed. Given that Riyadh's myriad projects were intended to usher in fundamental transformations without upsetting society's fabric, were these objectives reachable and, in the affirmative, at what costs?

To better answer these questions, it was fair to ask what the implications of these significant demographic transformations were on Saudi society, and how the Saudi government planned to address various challenges. Ultimately, it was also useful to examine the role of recent demographic changes and their impact on the labor markets at two levels: first, by examining the number of Saudis entering the labor market and, second, by assessing the number of non-Saudis whose services may be required to fulfill various Vision 2030 objectives.

Towards that end, an effort is made to answer the following four questions:

1. What was the demographic reality of the Kingdom in 2024, and where was it expected to stand by 2030?
2. Was the Saudi education system graduating qualified, skilled, and vocational laborers to meet the country's needs? In the affirmative, in which fields, and in the adverse case, what were the political options available to decision-makers to remedy putative shortfalls?
3. What specific policies existed, were contemplated, or may be required to guarantee future labor needs?; and,
4. Would migrations (both the skilled and non-skilled varieties) provide the panacea that may ensure that Vision 2030 is implemented in full?

Demographics of the Kingdom in 2024

As discussed previously and illustrated in Figure 1.1, the Saudi Population Pyramid Projection for 2030 highlighted significant increases for citizens, which would presumably translate into a larger labor pool. Figure 1.1 projects a total population of nearly 37.5 million citizens based on an annual growth rate of 2.09 percent. The percentage of able-bodied Saudis aged 20 to 60 in the workforce was 41.3 for males and 22.9 for females, representing substantial assets for the economy. Notwithstanding these projections, it was unclear whether most eligible citizens would avail themselves of nascent opportunities and, equally important, whether they would prepare for their eventual retirements. As the figure further illustrates, a significant pool of Saudis aged under 20 (both males and females) would eventually rejoin the workforce with relatively positive outlooks. Yet, and even with a steady growth in female participation, specific shortages were likely to continue that, in practical terms, meant a need for expatriate workers. With an estimated 41.6 percent of the Saudi population in 2022, or roughly 13,384,893 expatriate workers (along with family members in many cases), the Kingdom could safely boast a long

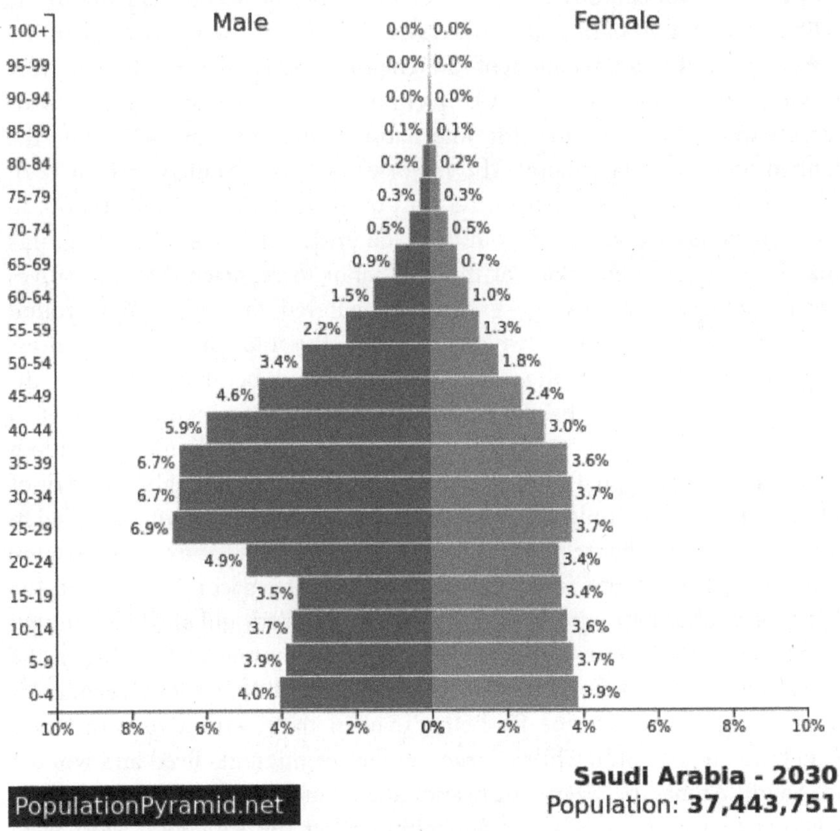

Figure 1.1. Saudi Arabia Population Pyramid Projection for 2030. https://www.populationpyramid.net/saudi-arabia/2030/

> tradition of hospitality as the overwhelming majority of these men and women played critical roles in the country's labor scene. In fact, and in the aftermath of the post-1974 oil boom economy, Saudi Arabia certainly attracted large numbers of foreign workers from a variety of countries throughout the world. Lest we overlook this fundamental point, it was important to remember that migration patterns on the Arabian Peninsula were centuries old, developed with the spread of Islam and, in the twentieth century, played critical roles in assisting the founder monarch with his manpower needs.[6]

As the Kingdom invested in developing its human resources, organized its economic policies, embarked on five-year plans to equip the country with core infrastructure facilities, and diversified post-oil boom visions starting in the mid-1970s, Riyadh encouraged skilled and semi-skilled workers to enter Saudi Arabia to meet a plethora of needs.[7] Starting in the 1970s, a steady flow of migrant workers headed to the Kingdom, transforming the country into a top recipient of foreign populations, currently hosting 13.4 million international workers, it is worth underscoring, making it the third-largest destination country for international migrants in 2022 after the United States and Germany.[8] The majority of Saudi Arabia's foreign-born population was males between the ages of 25 and 45, key contributors to labor markets that benefited from this vital presence. In fact, these migrants made up a larger percentage of the total labor force, given that the native-born population in this age group only entered the labor pool around the turn of the century, which reflected the indigenous population's demographic weight at the time. Moreover, and because young Saudis shunned poorly paid unskilled positions, the business community relied on expats from India (2.5 million), Pakistan (1.5 million), Bangladesh (1 million), and Egypt (1 million) for this critical pool, although hundreds of thousands of skilled Indian, Pakistanis, Bangladeshis and Egyptians toiled in important sectors that required skilled workers too.[9] As Figure 1.2 illustrates, estimates of migrants from a variety of countries confirmed that the Kingdom's labor requirements for skilled, semi-skilled, and unskilled foreign workers increased over the years. To be sure, many migrants toiling in the Kingdom endured difficult living and working conditions, though economic opportunities tended to be far better than in their respective homelands, which was telling. Still, while a large number of migrants lived and worked in Saudi Arabia between 2021 and 2022, and largely because of the COVID-19 pandemic, a significant number left the Kingdom. Most were replaced by fresh recruits whose presence was important for the burgeoning labor market.[10]

Continent: All | Region: All | Show Split by: Continent / Region / Detailed nationality | Show Table by: Absolute / Share

Full Data | PDF | This View | Metadata

Detailed nationality	Total	Male	Female
Bangladesh	2,116,192	1,950,943	165,249
India	1,884,476	1,712,780	171,696
Pakistan	1,814,678	1,647,704	166,974
Yemen	1,803,469	1,334,481	468,988
Egypt	1,471,382	1,181,180	290,202
Sudan	819,575	673,689	145,886
Philippines	725,893	274,305	451,588
Syrian Arab Republic	449,314	259,632	189,682
Nepal	297,561	293,049	4,512
Jordan	204,249	113,562	90,687
Indonesia	175,342	41,351	133,991
Myanmar	163,717	89,850	73,867
Ethiopia	159,221	44,154	115,067
Afghanistan	132,282	94,628	37,654
Palestine, State of	129,869	68,101	61,768
Uganda	127,932	8,157	119,775
Kenya	91,802	10,882	80,920
Sri Lanka	84,794	50,305	34,489
Nigeria	79,547	37,352	42,195
Lebanon	52,779	32,740	20,039
Kuwait	50,282	31,739	18,543
Morocco	48,796	18,363	30,433
Eritrea	47,258	22,167	25,091
Chad	46,193	20,527	25,666
Somalia	45,709	22,816	22,893
Mali	38,360	18,896	19,464

Non-Saudi Population

Saudi Census 2022, at https://portal.saudicensus.sa/portal/public/1/15/100659?type=TABLE

Figure 1.2. Migrant Populations from Selected Countries, 2022. Source: Kingdom of Saudi Arabia, census data for 2022, at https://portal.saudicensus.sa/static-assets/media/content/20230531_GASTAT_Population_Report.pdf?crafterSite=gastat-portal.

As the census data for 2022 illustrated, the latest available figures confirmed that the largest expatriate populations hailed from Bangladesh, (2.1 million), India (1.8 million), Pakistan (1.8 million) Yemen (1.8 million) and Egypt (1.4 million), although higher figures appeared in open sources not only for these five countries but also for many others (Table 1.1).[11] For example, while the census data for Indonesia counted 175,000 migrants from that country in the General Authority for Statistics database, an Indonesian source advanced the figure of 1.5 million.[12] Likewise, while the Census 2022 data for Lebanese expatriates in Saudi Arabia stood at 53,000, figures as high as 450,000 were routinely advanced by business community leaders. According to economist Ghazi Wazni, "[t]here [were] around 500,000 Lebanese working in Saudi Arabia and other Gulf states and nearly 15 percent of them [were] Shia" in 2016.[13] A Facebook Group, "Lebanese in Riyadh," listed that it had over 18,000 members in

Table 1.1. Selected Expatriate Populations, Saudi Arabia, 2022

Nationality	**Residents**
India	2,500,000
Syria	2,500,000
Yemen	>2,000,000
Pakistan	1,500,000
Indonesia	1,500,000
Bangladesh	1,000,000
Egypt	900,000
Philippines	900,000
Sudan	825,000
Myanmar	500,000 (Rohingya)
Lebanon	450,000
Jordan	430,000
Sri Lanka	400,000
Nepal	215,000

Source: Kingdom of Saudi Arabia, census data for 2022, at https://www.stats.gov.sa/en/w/الجنسية-2?category=127396&tab=436327

the capital city alone, which raised fresh questions about overall numbers while another source maintained that 269,000 Lebanese citizens resided in Saudi Arabia in 2021.[14] What these numbers highlighted was both the Saudi labor markets' dependence on expatriate workers as well as sharp disparities in actual figures. It was unclear why such disparities existed and whether appropriate measures were contemplated to reach definitive data as Riyadh adopted transparent methods to build confidence and ensure foreign direct investments.

Dilemmas of the Saudi Education System

Among the many challenges that confronted Saudi decision-makers was the level of education that its labor force acquired, both to meet local needs and, to a certain extent, compete with global enterprises that invested in the Kingdom. The question of whether the Saudi education system was graduating qualified, skilled, and vocational laborers to meet the country's needs was thus a fundamental concern. What were some of the dramatic changes that occurred over the course of the past two decades within the Saudi education world that advanced their effectiveness, and, if enough efforts were made, how could one determine whether improved education levels strengthened the political options that satisfied Vision 2030's long-term needs?

In August 2010, that is five years before King Salman acceded to the Kingdom's rulership, about 200 unemployed Saudi university graduates congregated in front of the Education Ministry in Riyadh to demand government jobs. This was a rare protest, but one that highlighted existing tensions and expectations that made higher education reforms a daunting prospect, notwithstanding significant expenditures on a sector that was critical for the welfare of the state. Regrettably, the Saudi education system did not assist the public sector with its needs, presumably because not every graduate could legitimately secure a lucrative administrative position. Simply stated, the country required young Saudis with "marketable" skills, including the vocational variety, something that was discussed but seldom met with satisfactory results. At the time, that is under King 'Abdallah's reign, a $200 billion budget was allocated to expand access to schools and universities, presumably to substantially increase vocational training by 2014. This was on top of the $36.5 billion for the King 'Abdallah Scholarship Program, which sent nearly 100,000 Saudis abroad to pursue graduate studies in leading Western institutions of higher learning. By 2014, the total number of university students in the Kingdom rose from 860,000 in 2009 to 1.7 million, which required attention, as these demographic changes reflected core socio-economic needs. As established institutions avowed, most Saudi university students continued to pursue non-scientific degrees, concentrating on social studies, religious studies, history, and literature, despite the labor market's requirements in technical training, engineering, science, and medical programs. New openings in administrative sciences and computer sciences, for example, were left vacant, often filled by expatriate workers from the Indian subcontinent. Incidentally, the August 2010 protest in front of the Education Ministry was organized by graduates of Arabic-language programs who demanded teaching jobs in government schools, which were already fully staffed.[15]

By 2015, when King Salman assumed rulership, about a third of the country's twenty-eight million residents filled most public sector jobs, and while Riyadh had imposed minimum quotas for Saudi employees on companies and decreed that certain businesses, like gold shops, travel firms, and car dealerships, be staffed with citizens, "Saudization" was not the panacea many contemplated. Limiting dependence on foreign labor, creating a more dynamic economy, and stanching rising unemployment required fresh ideas that necessitated well-trained Saudis for the kinds of jobs that Saudi markets demanded. High-skilled jobs in finance, engineering, and medicine, along with many service-sector positions, including taxi drivers or hotel receptionists, faced the same conundrum. Saudis expected higher salaries than those paid to expatriate workers, which could be secured for skilled jobs but could not be justified for unskilled ones. More than any other handicap, what many Saudis neglected to adopt were cultural habits that called for flexibility, adaptation, and a willingness to accept a prospective post at any price instead of joining the ranks of the unemployed. This was easier said than done, of course, which was why unemployment in 2015, while officially at almost 11 percent, was, in reality, at least twice as high, perhaps even at the 35 percent level among men in their early 20s with high school diplomas.

King ʿAbdallah's government called for the construction of twenty-five technology schools, twenty-eight technical institutes, and fifty industrial-training institutes, and was prepared to spend $240 million in grants for research projects each year, calling for the establishment of dozens of research centers and technology incubators at universities. Several of these projects were implemented in the post-2005 period, hoping to turn the Kingdom into a "knowledge economy" by early 2020, the most celebrated accomplishment being the 2009 establishment of the King ʿAbdallah University of Science and Technology, or KAUST, which was slated to "become one of the world's great institutions of research."[16]

To meet the country's needs, and soon after his accession, King Salman authorized Heir Apparent Muhammad bin Salman to embark on an ambitious reform agenda, better known as Vision 2030, which sought to usher in economic diversification and, an often-overlooked core objective, to improve living standards for Saudi citizens. Given that one of the main priorities of the Vision was/is to "enable the private sector to become a driver of job creation and enhance its contribution to the Saudi economy,"[17] Riyadh concentrated on increasing productivity and developing the full potential of the private sector by precisely adopting serious initiatives to encourage, train, and graduate technicians and vocational employees through the Technical and Vocational Training Corporation (TVTC). Vision 2030 emphasized the necessity to expand the Technical and Vocational Education Training (TVET) system and make smart investments in human capital for Saudi Arabia to gradually replace low-skilled foreign workers with its own subjects. Because the same challenges that confronted King ʿAbdallah existed in 2024, what were some of the key steps adopted by King Salman's government to remedy some of the traditionally low levels of participation among nationals in vocational jobs?

Riyadh intended to increase its capacity to enroll more students, including women, in TVET programs. Fresh investments in human capital, "improving curriculums, and developing more learning pathways by giving students more flexibility in transitioning between general and vocational education," were all backed to the hilt.[18] The goal was to expand the limited knowledge base of skills development in Saudi Arabia to better shape human capital decisions and policies, precisely to increase their effectiveness. Recent experiences confirmed that Saudis enrolled in TVET programs responded well to their training and job placements. In fact, TVTC graduates earned higher wages on average after graduation compared with before graduation, and most applicants actually found work in the private sector, which was the ultimate goal. If this trend continued, that is, if enough Saudis opted to forgo their traditional preferences for public sector employment, then there would indeed be hope for relative successes in Vision 2030 planks. According to a World Bank study that examined various developments over a five-year term between 2017 and 2022, "participation in TVET appear[ed] to increase students' likelihood of labor mobility, as well as enhance[ed] the mobility premiums of graduates during job transitions," which met initial objectives to provide higher private sector returns. Naturally, much more needed to be done, though the ice of reluctance was broken.

Future labor needs

Beyond vocational education, and because 80 percent of the Saudi population lived in urban settings, a figure that was expected to exceed the staggering figure of 97 percent by 2030, future labor needs required entirely different criteria. Acute urbanization meant that Saudi society would be far less engaged in agriculture, which would raise its own set of very serious concerns, as food dependence on manufactured goods (often imported) would require transportation and distribution labor skills. Will full-time employment be ensured in urban settings?

Recent figures confirmed that unemployment was relatively high in most cities, ranging from 8 percent to as high as 23 percent in some regions, which was yet another serious challenge to overcome. In fact, in 2018, the last year for which such statistics were available, unemployment stood at 7.0 percent in Najran, 7.8 percent in the Eastern Province, 9.4 percent in Makkah, 12.7 percent in Qassim, 13.9 percent in Riyadh, 14.0 percent in Hail, 14.8 percent in Al-Baha, 14.9 percent in Asir, 15.7 percent in Tabuk, 18.6 percent in Jizan, 19.8 percent in Madinah, 23.0 percent in the Northern Borders, and 27.3 percent in Al-Jouf.[19] These were high figures, and it was critical to promote regional development to avoid sustained unemployment in urban settings. What specific steps were required encompassed a broad range, including the establishment of Regional Job Placement Centers that would presumably provide appropriately tailored job search consultations, as well as specific programs to incentivize firms that would assist private companies to hire Saudis with additional incentives in upskilling programs.[20]

In addition to the challenge of unemployment among indigenous populations, future labor needs will probably require attention to several other areas, including food shortages that could impact perhaps 32 percent of Saudi Arabia's population by 2100, presumably because food would be diverted from animal feed and exports, which was shocking given that malnutrition was eliminated in the Kingdom decades ago.[21] Even worse were water conditions in the Kingdom, which experienced "very little rainfall, as Saudi Arabia's rain-fed water cycle provide[d] less than 90 cubic meters (m^3) per capita per annum" to support life.[22] These figures were well below the global average, amounts that could not sustain rivers or lakes, which were sorely needed to fulfill all of Vision 2030's projects. Moreover, it was important to bear in mind that with the considerable proportions of the limited quantities of rain that were lost in flash floods to the sea, precipitation failed to replenish subterranean aquifers, the all-important water-carrying rock formation that fed springs and wells. Notwithstanding this critical shortfall, Saudi Arabia developed a thriving agricultural sector after the mid-1970s oil boom that, in hindsight, was a double-edged sword. While investments in agriculture provided some food security, the excessive use of water drained aquifers that, logically, could not be replaced with ease, creating a different kind of insecurity. In 2015, for example, farming across the Kingdom consumed 14 million cubic meters of water, which was more than three times the combined amount consumed in the industrial sector (1.2 million m^3) or in private homes (3 million m^3).[23] According to one source, the overall demand for water in the Kingdom doubled between 1980 and 2010, and has been growing at an even faster pace ever since.[24]

In the past, Riyadh relied on four main methods to balance its water deficit, which could stand it in good stead even in the post-normal climate era, but there were no guarantees that these would be sufficient beyond 2030. To their credit, successive governments have constructed more than 200 dams since the 1980s, which captured flash floods in reservoirs feeding a network of irrigation conduits. This vital infrastructure remained in place and needed updates. Second, authorities invested in "fossil water," ancient non-renewable reservoirs hidden deep in sedimentary rock formations, even if drilling was very expensive and technically challenging. Such projects sifted the brackish liquid that emerged, often mixed with silty particles, which required technologically demanding filtering. Persistent efforts in this area, however, raised supplies by over two-thirds in 2005.[25] A third tactic in the Saudi water strategy is desalination, used primarily to provide water for domestic use in cities. Riyadh, for one example, gets desalinated water in a pipeline stretching 460 kilometers from the shores of the Arabian Gulf. Yet another approach has been to become a champion of "virtual water," which effectively meant leasing huge productive tracts in Africa and Southeast Asia to secure long-term procurement of imported staple foods, though fresh ideas were required to guarantee both food security and water availability. In all instances, many more laborers engaged in agriculture, water management, and critical transportation, which were necessary to fulfill Vision 2030 objectives.

Energy consumption and migration projections

Because Saudi Arabia's GDP leaped fiftyfold between 1973 and 2014, which reflected the "latecomer advantage" when contrasted with the United States (whose GDP grew only fourteenfold in the same period) or Germany (tenfold), two fundamental challenges confronted Riyadh in the years ahead: it's sustained energy consumption and the necessity to rely on expatriate workers to churn Vision 2030's development engine. Each deserved careful appraisal.

Between 2008 and 2018, the Kingdom saw energy consumption surge by 60 percent, with demand expected to triple by 2030.[26] The proportion of renewables in this projected growth, however, remained unclear. Although authorities pledged to do better, significant investments were required to sustain Vision 2030 projects. For example, a plan to install 54 gigawatts of renewable capacity by 2030, first announced in the late 2000s, was delayed to 2040 following the global financial downturn of 2008, then shelved for almost an entire decade.[27] Plans for renewables resurfaced in 2016 as Vision 2030 projects matured within the Kingdom's Plan for Economic Reforms. It was valuable to recall that under Vision 2030, key elements of the plan set a goal of 3.45 gigawatts of installed renewable capacity by 2020, though this barely materialized. The figure pledged for 2023 was 9.5 gigawatts, which could account for 10 percent of the country's projected electricity supply, again, with yet to be confirmed data. Under Vision 2030, $30–50 billion was to be invested in renewables, mainly in solar and wind, to ensure that all or most of the projects could be "powered." With the NEOM project, for example, the Kingdom's vision reached huge proportions, as NEOM was supposed to ensure 25 gigawatts of renewable capacity in five years, 60 gigawatts in ten years, and 200 gigawatts later this century, with investment forecasts ranging from $40 billion to $80 billion to make sure that these levels were reached.[28]

According to Wood Mackenzie, Saudi Arabia was on track to add 6.2 gigawatts of installed wind energy capacity by 2030. In 2019, a project for 850 megawatts that was scheduled for completion by 2022 under the leadership of the Renewable Energy Project Development Office was postponed. According to a Wood Mackenzie report titled "Middle East Wind Power Market Outlook, 2019–2028," developers were slated to build 6.2GW of wind capacity—46 percent of the region's total wind capacity addition—between 2019 and 2028, to further ensure that many of the mega projects could be powered appropriately.[29]

To be sure, Vision 2030 pledged 60 gigawatts worth of renewable capacity to be installed by 2030, though such an amount, which was equivalent to the entire quantity of power generated in the Kingdom in 2013, would bring the share of renewable capacity as a proportion of the country's overall power supply in 2030 to a third.[30] This was easier said than done, but progress was always slow in similar endeavors. How Riyadh envisioned its investments in energy consumption projects and how it remained steady in its approaches would probably illustrate whatever progress was achieved.

Likewise, a guarantee of its relative successes rested on its reliance on migrant workers, raised earlier in this chapter. Ambitious plans will require the availability of stable laborers that, in the context of Vision 2030, may even result in a shortage of workers. In this context, two types of potential employees will be recruited: unskilled workers who will engage for a limited period of time, and skilled workers who may extend their stays for longer stretches. As skilled expatriate employees reassess career paths in their respective countries for a variety of reasons, some changing sectors while others looking for jobs with more responsibilities, Saudi enterprises will confront potential worker shortages because the latter may well move around labor markets seeking better opportunities. Because the Kingdom's Vision 2030 projects required many more skilled employees than Saudi society could produce—at least between now and 2030—high-income workers will be in a good position to make higher salary claims. In fact, Saudi Arabia "is experiencing one of the most rapid transformations in the world, [with] Saudi nationals—particularly Saudi women—. . . joining the labor market at unprecedented rates, a trend likely sparked by recent reforms targeting female employment," which meant that those jobs that "disappeared since the start of the [COVID-19] pandemic," needed replacement.[31]

Saudi employees left their existing jobs in droves after 2021 ("roughly 270,000 workers—most of them citizens—quit their jobs in Q3 2021 compared with 134,000 in Q3 2020 and 152,000 in Q3 2019"), though this did not prevent private sector firms from hiring new workers. According to a recent Brookings study, this kind of "churning in the labor market" indicated that the labor markets were picking up strength, although few locals accepted the notion that shifting workers perhaps "to more productive jobs, firms, and sectors" was a sign of productivity enhancement and "therefore a positive development."[32] As stressed in the following Conclusion, such changes further highlighted significant improvements in the country's kafalah (now renamed United National program) sponsorship system, which allowed foreign workers to change employers without penalty.

By all accounts, the ongoing reshuffling, as well as the hiring of new expatriate workers, affirmed significantly better economic conditions. For the first time in a long time, Saudi Arabia confronted a tightening labor market, with burgeoning economic activities that were the result not only of rising oil prices but also solid growth in non-oil activities.[33] With decreasing unemployment among nationals (11.3 percent in 2023), employers faced many more difficulties finding qualified local labor to fill every available position. This was one of the reasons why average wages for Saudi workers were on the rise, particularly among educated Saudis who could easily lay claim to increasingly lucrative posts. The Brookings study cited previously revealed that "[r]oughly half of all new Saudi hires (51 percent) in the third quarter of 2021 joined employment in the professional or associate professional categories, compared to only 15 percent a year ago. Higher wages and the availability of more suitable work opportunities may be prompting Saudi workers to quit and seek better opportunities in new jobs," which was revealing indeed.[34] To be sure, Saudization and the role of the Nitaqat—a policy that obligated firms to hire a certain number of Saudis—played a key role in these improved statistics, but not only. Increased female participation in the workforce accounted for some of these changes, too, something that altered conditions on the ground despite negative assessments and, importantly, helped the Kingdom's economic outlook for the foreseeable future.[35]

Conclusion

When the United Nations General Assembly adopted the "International Convention on the Protection of the Rights of All Migrant Workers and Members of Their Families" on 18 December 1990, which earned the International Migrants Day label ever since, every effort was made to foster the rights of expatriate workers. As a host country with a significant international workforce, Saudi Arabia had devised the kafalah system, a sponsorship system that granted employers considerable countervailing powers over the migrants. Past abuses, including curtailments of the expatriates' rights to leave and re-enter the country, resign and move to another employer, or even contemplate raising objections to employment conditions, created a negative aura around it.[36] Mercifully, new reforms in the Kingdom—as well as in every Gulf Cooperation Council member-state—will permanently replace the system in place. In fact, one of the most important new laws introduced in Riyadh replaced the kafalah system with a contract-based mechanism that allowed and will henceforth permit most foreign workers to freely enter and exit the country, change employers a year after signing their first contract, and otherwise retain their passports.[37] This epochal reform effectively meant that the human rights of expatriate workers in the Kingdom were protected. Consequently, the Saudi economy was no longer burdened with the kind of handicap that prevented labor productivity from rising. Few should, therefore, be surprised by the dramatic enhancements in labor relations, as mobility and appropriate legislative changes will, inevitably, buttress the country's labor strategy.[38] Inevitably, one may well anticipate disruptions, though improved productivity will also translate into concrete economic benefits across the board. Henceforth, stable (and higher) wages would likely prevail, despite the Kingdom confronting serious environmental challenges. Equally important, businesses would be emboldened to accept financial risks as they allocate capital investments because, and this must be emphasized, they would most likely benefit from positive signs in productivity. Over time, even the significant wage gap between Saudis and non-Saudis would be gradually closing, something that would also benefit the Saudi worker.

To reiterate, while it might be too soon to fully appraise Saudi Arabia's demographic transformations, positive signs appeared on the horizon to: (1) introduce relatively stable demographic conditions; (2) ensure balanced labor collaboration between Saudis and expatriate workers; and (3) meet most, if not all, of Vision 2030's objectives. It was just a matter of time.

Notes

1 "Saudi Arabia's Population Crosses 32 Million, Census Results Show: 63% percent of population aged below 30; 41.6% are foreigners," *Saudi Gazette*, 31 May 2023, at https://www.saudigazette.com.sa/article/632956/SAUDI-ARABIA/Saudi-Arabias-population-crosses-32-million-census-results-show.

2 For additional details on census data, see the Saudi Census webpage at https://portal.saudicensus.sa/portal.

3 NEOM is a new urban area planned by the Kingdom in northwestern Tabuk Province. The site is north of the Red Sea, east of Egypt across the Gulf of Aqabah, and south of Jordan. The total planned area of NEOM is 26,500 km^2

(10,200 square miles, or the equivalent in size of Rwanda, Haiti, or Burundi). In addition to The Line, NEOM included several major projects, including Neom Bay, Oxagon, Trojena, Sindalah, Leyla, Epicon, Siranna, Utamo, and Norlana. Each of these projects was expected to house large numbers of residents. For details, see the dedicated webpage at https://www.neom.com/en-us.

4 "Crown Prince Expects Saudi Arabia's Population to Reach 50–60 million by 2030," *Argaam*, 26 July 2022, at https://www.argaam.com/en/article/articledetail/id/1576399.

5 CEIC (Circular Economy Indicators Coalition), "Saudi Arabia Demographic Projection," at https://www.ceicdata.com/en/saudi-arabia/demographic-projection.

6 David Long, *The Kingdom of Saudi Arabia*, 2nd edition, Gainesville, Florida: University Press of Florida, 2010, pp. 23–4.

7 Françoise De Bel-Air, "Demography, Migration and Labour Market in Saudi Arabia," Technical Report, Gulf Labour Markets and Migration (GLMM), Explanatory note, 1/2014, Florence, Italy: Migration Policy Centre, European University Institute and Riyadh, Saudi Arabia: Gulf Research Center, January 2014, at https://cadmus.eui.eu/handle/1814/32151.

8 United Nations, *International Migration Report 2022*, Geneva: International Organization for Migration, 2022, at https://publications.iom.int/books/world-migration-report-2022, pp. 24–5.

9 United Nations, International Migration Report 2022, ibid., p. 85.

10 "Expat Fee Pushes 1.05 Million Foreigners Out of Employment Market: Number of Saudis hired up by 179,000 in 45 months," *Saudi Gazette*, 18 January 2022, at https://saudigazette.com.sa/article/616000.

11 The data in Table 1 represent materials collected for the 2022 Census that reflect official figures. Those assembled in Table 2 represent materials described in various media sources. Both are presented here to highlight discrepancies. Census figures often underestimate population counts for a variety of reasons, including fear of repercussions in cases of irregular presence, while journalistic estimates tend to overestimate population counts because those tend to be based on anecdotal narratives or third-party data that are intended to inflate the foreign nationals' presence.

12 Almas Taqiyya, "Negara yang Banyak Orang Jawa, Nomor 1 Jumlahnya Lebih dari 1,5 Juta Jiwa" (Countries with lots of Javanese people, number 1, number more than 1.5 million people), *Sindo News*, 27 May 2022, at https://international.sindonews.com/newsread/781059/43/negara-yang-banyak-orang-jawa-nomor-1-jumlahnya-lebih-dari-15-juta-jiwa-1653635100.

13 Wazni was quoted in a *Daily Star* (Lebanon) report. See Karim Traboulsi, "Gulf Countries to Punish Beirut by Deporting Lebanese Expats," *The New Arab*, 26 February 2016, at https://www.newarab.com/news/gulf-countries-punish-beirut-deporting-lebanese-expats.

14 The dedicated page is accessible at https://www.facebook.com/groups/2530346313/. See also Joshua Project, "Lebanese Arab in Saudi

Arabia," at https://joshuaproject.net/people_groups/13017/SA. (The Joshua Project is a Christian ministry of Frontier Ventures based in Pasadena, California.) For its part, a reputable news outlet had claimed that in 2008, around a third of the Lebanese workforce, then estimated at about 350,000, lived in Saudi Arabia and the Gulf Cooperation Council states. See "Lebanon Starts to Feel the Pinch of Financial Crisis," Reuters, 6 December 2008, at https://gulfnews.com/business/lebanon-starts-to-feel-the-pinch-of-financial-crisis-1.148112.

15 "Jobless Arabic Teachers in Saudi Stage Protest," *ArabLit and ArabLit Quarterly*, 29 August 2010, at https://arablit.org/2010/08/29/jobless-arabic-teachers-in-saudi-stage-protest/.

16 Ursula Lindsey, "Saudi Arabia's Education Reforms Emphasize Training for Jobs," *The Chronicle of Higher Education*, 3 October 2010, at https://www.chronicle.com/article/saudi-arabias-education-reforms-emphasize-training-for-jobs/.

17 Nayib Rivera, Mehtabul Azam, and Mohamed Ihsan Ajwas, "Tracing Labor Market Outcomes of Technical and Vocational Training Graduates in Saudi Arabia: A Study on Graduates from the Technical and Vocational Training Corporation," *Social Protection & Jobs Discussion Paper*, Number 2202, Washington, D.C. World Bank Group, January 2022, at https://elibrary.worldbank.org/doi/epdf/10.1596/36863, p. 9.

18 Nayib Rivera et al., "Tracing Labor Market Outcomes," pp. 28–42.

19 Kingdom of Saudi Arabia, General Authority for Statistics, Statistical Database, at https://database.stats.gov.sa/home/indicator/999121.

20 Labor Market Q3 2018, General Authority for Statistics, at https://www.stats.gov.sa/sites/default/files/lm_2018_q4_en.pdf.

21 Met Office, *Climate Observations, Projections and Impacts: Saudi Arabia*, London: United Kingdom Department of Energy and Climate Change, 2011, at https://www.metoffice.gov.uk/binaries/content/assets/metofficegovuk/pdf/research/climate-science/climate-observations-projections-and-impacts/saudi_arabia.pdf, p. 2.

22 Erica DeNicola, Omar S. Aburizaiza, Azhar Siddique, Haider Khwaja and David O. Carpenter, "Climate Change and Water Scarcity: The Case of Saudi Arabia," *Annals of Global Health* 81:3, May–June 2015, pp. 342–53.

23 Khaled AbuZeid, Ahmad Wagdy, and Maged Ibrahim, *3rd State of the Water Report for the Arab Region 2015*, Cairo, Egypt: League of Arab States, Centre for Environment & Development for the Arab Region & Europe (CEDARE), OPEC Fund for International Development, and Arab Water Council (AWC), 2019, at https://www.arabwatercouncil.org/images/Arab-Water-Report/3rd%20Arab%20State%20of%20the%20Water%20Report%202015%20English.pdf, pp. 317–324.

24 Erica DeNicola et al., "Climate Change and Water Scarcity," p. 343.

25 Dan Rabinowitz, *The Power of Deserts: Climate Change, the Middle East, and the Promise of a Post-Oil Era*, Sanford, California: Stanford University Press, 2020, pp. 48–49.

26 "The plan to turn Saudi Arabia into a renewable energy leader," London: Oxford Business Group, 26 April 2019, at https://oxfordbusinessgroup.com/articles-interviews/the-plan-to-turn-saudi-arabia-into-a-renewable-energy-leader.
27 The International Renewable Energy Agency (IRENA), Abu Dhabi: IRENA, at https://www.irena.org/publications/2019/jan/renewable-energy-market-analysis-gcc-2019.
28 Fatehelrahman Yousif, "Saudi Arabia Plans to Invest $80 Bn in Renewable Energy," *Al-Sharq al-Awsat,* 5 March 2019, at https://english.aawsat.com/home/article/1619766/saudi-arabia-plans-invest-80-bn-renewable-energy.
29 "Saudi Arabia to become largest Middle East wind power market by early 2020s," Wood Mackenzie Power & Renewables, 8 April 2019, at https://www.woodmac.com/press-releases/saudi-arabia-to-become-largest-middle-east-wind-power-market-by-early-2020s/.
30 Hani A. Aldhubaib, "Electrical Energy Future of Saudi Arabia: Challenges and Opportunities," *Frontiers in Energy Research* 10, 2022, at https://www.frontiersin.org/articles/10.3389/fenrg.2022.1005081/full.
31 Nayib Rivera and Johannes Koettl, "Is Saudi Arabia entering a 'Great Reshuffle'?," Brookings, 24 January 2022, at https://www.brookings.edu/articles/is-saudi-arabia-entering-a-great-reshuffle/.
32 Ibid.
33 "Saudi Non-Oil Sector Thrives with 3.5% Growth, Private Sector's Positive Performance," Al-Sharq al-Awsat, 22 December 2023, at https://english.aawsat.com/business/4743951-saudi-non-oil-sector-thrives-35-growth-private-sector's-positive-performance#.
34 Rivera and Koettl, "Is Saudi Arabia entering a 'Great Reshuffle'?"
35 While it may be too soon to evaluate the important role that Saudi women are and will continue to play in the Kingdom's economy, anecdotal evidence suggests that rapid progress is under way, even if critics believe that the country's education system is poorly equipped to deal with improved economic conditions. See for example, Roula Baki, "Gender-Segregated Education in Saudi Arabia: Its Impact on Social Norms and the Saudi Labor Market," *Education Policy Analysis Archives* 12:28, 17 June 2004, at http://epaa.asu.edu/epaa/v12n28/.
36 Kali Robinson, What is the Kafala System?," Council on Foreign Relations, 18 November 2022, at https://www.cfr.org/backgrounder/what-kafala-system?utm_medium=social_share&utm_source=emailfwd.
37 Rawan Radwan Henshi Alshammari, "Saudi Arabia's labor reforms seen as big boost for private sector," *Arab News,* 4 November 2020, at https://www.arabnews.com/node/1758456/saudi-arabia.
38 Sharaf Abdul Salam, "Saudi Arabia's Labor Market Transitions to Thrive Vision 2030: A Demographic Appraisal," in Rajendra Baikady, S.M. Sajid, Jaroslaw Przeperski, Varoshini Nadesan, M. Rezaul Islam, and Jianguo Gao, eds., *The Palgrave Handbook of Global Social Problems,* Cham, Switzerland: Springer, 2022, pp. 1–22.

Bibliography

"9.5 million Egyptians live abroad, mostly in Saudi Arabia and Jordan," Al-Masry Al-Youm, October 1, 2017, at https://www.egyptindependent.com/9-5-million-egyptians-live-abroad-mostly-saudi-arabia-jordan/

Doanvo, Anhvinh. "Western Media's Miscount of Saudi Arabia's Syrian Refugees," *Huffington Post*, September 23, 2015, at https://www.huffingtonpost.com/anhvinh-doanvo/europes-crisis-refugees_b_8175924.html

"Dubai's Somali diaspora hope for change," CCTV.com, September 11, 2012, at https://web.archive.org/web/20150701165012/http:/english.cntv.cn/program/newsupdate/20120911/105653.shtml

International Nepal Fellowship, at http://www.inf.org/map/diaspora

Kaifee, Sib. "Over 2.7 million Pakistanis living in Saudi Arabia to benefit from new green card," Arab News Pakistan, May 14, 2019, at https://www.arabnews.pk/node/1496861/pakistan

Kingdom of Saudi Arabia, Ethnologue, at https://www.ethnologue.com/country/SA/

Md. Kamruzzaman, "Over 217 Bangladeshi workers deported from Saudi Arabia," Anadolou Agency, January 23, 2020, at https://www.aa.com.tr/en/asia-pacific/over-217-bangladeshi-workers-deported-from-saudi-arabia/1711803

"Myanmar Rohingya: What you need to know about the crisis, BBC News, January 23, 2020, at https://www.bbc.com/news/world-asia-41566561

Omari, Raed. "Saudi-Jordanian cooperation 'a role model' for the entire Middle East," Arab News, June 22, 2022, at https://www.arabnews.com/node/2108456/amp

Pukas, Anna. "Lebanese across the globe: How the country's international community came to be," Arab News, May 4, 2018, at https://www.arabnews.com/node/1296211/amp.Republic of the Philippines, "Distribution of Filipinos Overseas," June 2015, at http://www.dfa.gov.ph/distribution-of-filipinos-overseas

"Saudi Arabia," in International Religious Freedom Report 2007, Washington, D.C.: Department of State, Bureau of Democracy, Human Rights, and Labor, September 14, 2007, at https://2001-2009.state.gov/g/drl/rls/irf/2007/90220.htm

"Saudi Arabia: Yemeni Workers at Risk of Mass Forced Returns," *Human Rights Watch*, August 31, at https://www.hrw.org/news/2021/08/31/saudi-arabia-yemeni-workers-risk-mass-forced-returns

2

Internal Migration Amongst Saudi Nationals: Issues And Challenges

Mark C. Thompson

Introduction

As White and Lindstrom highlight, the study of internal migration involves an examination of two questions: "Who moves?" and "What places grow?" At the level of the individual or household, the answer to the question "Who moves?" is often found in a set of personal traits linked to economic activity, life cycle, sociocultural context, and policies that vary over space. Similarly, the answer to the question "What places grow?" is usually found in the comparative economic advantages across regions, demographic dynamics that shift either population composition or the number of those likely to migrate, and again, policy, intended or not, that shifts the costs and benefits of location for individuals and employers.[1] These two questions, and the answers White and Lindstrom provide, mirror patterns of internal migration in Saudi Arabia since the launch of Saudi Vision 2030 in April 2016.[2]

Unlike other Gulf Cooperation Council (GCC) States, Saudi Arabia has a relatively large, diverse population dispersed over a wide geographical area.[3] However, since the advent of the oil era, vast numbers of Saudis have relocated to cities due to more favorable economic conditions. The main population centers are located on the urban belt stretching from Jeddah in the west through the ever-expanding Riyadh to the Dammam-Khobar-Dhahran conurbation in the east.

Internal migration of Saudi nationals in the Kingdom involves principally movement from the regions to Riyadh for primarily economic reasons, especially employment. Riyadh has always played a key role in the development of Saudi Arabia; however, the launch of Saudi Vision 2030 in 2016 put a renewed emphasis on the capital's role in meeting national socioeconomic development goals.[4] For this reason, Riyadh has become an increasingly important economic activity hub and, even more significantly, in particular for young Saudis, the Kingdom's employment hub. Riyadh is where "everything happens," and younger and more ambitious Saudis comprehend that these days "all roads lead to Riyadh," as increasing numbers of younger nationals relocate to the capital looking for jobs and opportunities.[5] As a result, internal migration to the capital has been largely responsible for the population increasing to approximately eight and a half million.[6]

Yet since the launch of Saudi Vision 2030, the Kingdom has also experienced internal migration of Saudi nationals within and/or across regions to urban centers such as Abha-Khamis Mushait in Asir Province. Hence, this chapter considers firstly the significant increase in internal migration to the capital and to a lesser extent, regional examples. It reflects on the extent to which rapid internal migration within Saudi Arabia, in particular to the capital Riyadh, has affected social norms and regional identity narratives as families disperse and relocate. This chapter is based on a larger ongoing research project looking at youth narratives of everyday life and social transformation across Saudi Arabia, in the post-Saudi Vision 2030, post-pandemic eras. The chapter references the views of Saudis from across the Kingdom, gathered from the author's extensive, continuous travel around all of Saudi Arabia's regions between 2020 and 2026.[7]

Limitation

According to the 2022 census, the total population of Riyadh was 7 million, of which 3.35 million were Saudi nationals and 3.66 million were expats. The 2022 census revealed that the capital accounted for 21.8 percent of the entire population of Saudi Arabia, both Saudi and non-Saudi, and 17.8 percent of all Saudi nationals live in Riyadh. Of the population of Saudi nationals in Riyadh, 42 percent were under 20 years old and 62 percent were under 30.[8] However, at the time of writing, other sources provide different statistics, for example DataSaudi, which gives the 2022 population registered in Riyadh as 8,591,748 people, of whom 37.4 percent were females and 62.6 percent were males.[9] This anomaly could be attributed to the former focusing only on Riyadh city, and the latter on wider Riyadh Province. That said in 2025 the statistics for both the capital and province were out of date and while it is possible to reference Riyadh's population increase and differentiate between the numbers of Saudi and expatriate residents,[10] the data on internal migrants from each of the Kingdom's administrative regions who have relocated to the capital is unreliable and also out of date. For example, a 2019 book chapter, "Migration in Saudi Arabia: Present and Prospects,"[11] provides statistics on internal migration, but based on the General Authority of Statistics' (GASTAT) 2017 Demographic Survey. In addition, at the time of writing, a breakdown of current statistics on internal migration was not provided on either the

GASTAT or DataSaudi websites.[12] Therefore, at the time of writing, the understanding of this issue was based on local knowledge and anecdotal evidence, although it is a subject worthy of detailed research.

Background and context

Demographics

The 2022 census revealed the average age of Saudis and expatriates living in the Kingdom at 29, and excluding expatriates, the average age was 25, with Saudis under the age of 30 amounting to 51.1 percent.[13] The total population registered in 2024 was 35,300,280, with 62.1 percent male and 37.9 percent female,[14] with an annual growth rate of 4.7 percent compared to 2023.[15]

At the start of 2025, Saudi demographics were as shown in Figure 2.1. The key statistic is that approximately 60 percent of the population was under 34 years of age, and it is this demographic segment that was most likely to relocate to Riyadh in search of employment opportunities.[16] For example, in 2022, the female population in Riyadh was concentrated in the age group of 30–34 years, with 360,116 women, accounting for 11.2 percent of the total female population. Similarly, the male population was concentrated in the age group of 30–34 years, with 776,167 men, representing 14.4 percent of the total male population.[17] The 2022 census also documents another important statistic: 68 percent of the population was urban, residing in Riyadh, Jeddah/ Makkah, and the Dammam-Khobar-Dhahran conurbation in the Eastern Province,[18] although a 2026 statistic cites the urban population at 91.9 percent.[19]

7.8 percent was between the ages of 0 and 4.
12.7 percent was between the ages of 5 and 12.
7.4 percent was between the ages of 13 and 17.
10.7 percent was between the ages of 18 and 24.
21.6 percent was between the ages of 25 and 34.
20.1 percent was between the ages of 35 and 44.
11.0 percent was between the ages of 45 and 54.
5.7 percent was between the ages of 55 and 64.
3.1 percent was aged 65 and above.

Figure 2.1. Saudi demographics at the start of 2025. https://datareportal.com/ reports/digital-2025-saudi-arabia

Hyper-urbanization

Hyper-urbanization refers to the rapid and extreme growth of urban areas, often leading to the expansion of "megacities" that experience high population density and significant infrastructural challenges. This phenomenon is characterized by a migration influx, economic shifts, and the transformation of social dynamics as rural populations relocate to cities in search of better economic opportunities. However, the speed and intensity of this urban growth can outpace the ability of local governments to provide essential services and infrastructure.[20]

Globally, urbanization and urban growth, as Albarrak highlights, have reached unprecedented rates in cities.[21] Riyadh is no exception to the rapid urbanization and growth that has occurred in a sprawling and low-density pattern. According to an official announcement from the Royal Commission for the City of Riyadh (RCRC),[22] the capital's population will reach fifteen million people by 2030,[23] partly due to the attraction of events/factors such as the popular Riyadh Season and major projects including Qiddiya,[24] King Salman Park,[25] and Sports Boulevard.[26] The Saudi authorities emphasized the importance of making this growth sustainable.[27] Yet, in 2024, the government reduced this target as it reconfigured plans designed to support Crown Prince Mohammed bin Salman's multi-trillion-dollar agenda to diversify the Kingdom's economy. The RCRC maintained that the original target population of fifteen million was being reviewed, taking into account Riyadh City Strategy's targets and sectors, and in 2025, the Riyadh authorities said they were considering a reduced target of 10 million residents by the start of the next decade.[28]

Regardless of these goals, Riyadh's population is expected to comprise 4.1 million Saudis and 5.5 million expatriates by the end of this decade, marking a 38 percent increase driven by a compound annual growth rate of 4.1 percent.[29] The capital's workforce is forecast to expand by 39 percent by 2034, with the number of working-age Saudi nationals in Riyadh increasing by approximately a million over the next decade, reaching 4.2 million, corresponding to a compound annual growth rate of 2.8 percent. Significantly, as internal migrants relocate to Riyadh for work, this could add another 275,000, resulting in a total workforce growth of 36 percent.[30] Nonetheless, population growth comes with its own set of problems. For example, already, in 2025, housing was at a premium in Riyadh, with both land prices and rents skyrocketing, but additional population increases will drive a need for 305,000 additional housing units for Saudi nationals between 2024 and 2034, driven by household formation, increased homeownership, and, once again, internal migration from other Saudi regions.[31]

Demand for housing is especially high in August each year as internal migrants attempt to find accommodation before the start of the school year. As an example, during the summer of 2024, a real estate agent in the popular district of As Sulaymaniyah said that all of his available housing had been "snapped up" and he had "nothing on his books."[32] Indeed, Riyadh residents understand that if they complain to their landlords about rising rents and refuse to pay the increase, the landlord will simply ask the tenant to leave, as the landlord already has a replacement tenant to move in.[33] In response to societal concerns about soaring rents, in April 2025, the Saudi government announced that it was studying the implementation of a cap on residential and commercial rent increases to tackle spiraling prices.[34] Most significantly, in September 2025, under directives from Crown Prince Mohammed bin Salman, the Saudi government introduced sweeping rental market reforms in Riyadh, including a five-year freeze on annual rent increases for residential and commercial properties.[35] Needless to say, this development was welcomed by those renting property in Riyadh.[36]

Which Riyadh?

While there are regional variations within Saudi Arabia in terms of social norms and socioeconomic developments, there are also variations within cities and even within municipalities. For example, contemporary Riyadh is a huge sprawling city, and it is no longer correct to consider Riyadh as a homogenous unit, but rather we should ask "which Riyadh" because there are many "Riyadhs." For example, the more upmarket, fashionable, and expensive northern districts of Al Malqa and Hittin, the rapidly growing working-class district of Dhahrat Laban, the more "traditional" neighborhoods of Ash Shifa and As Suwaidi, and the Saudi Arabian National Guard (SANG) district of Khashm Al An, to name but a few. Therefore, how people perceive socioeconomic and societal transformations and the opportunities they provide depends on individual and/or family issues and concerns, as different people have different priorities depending on circumstances and/or their socioeconomic, family, or educational backgrounds.[37] Take employment as an example; it remains a top priority, especially for younger Saudis, but the way these priorities manifest themselves is dependent on individual circumstances: a female graduate in humanities from Al Jouf University in Sakaka, for example, could have very different employment priorities from a male graduate from Jizan Technical college. The challenge is to capture the nuances, the complexity, and the contradictions. which are inherent across Saudi Arabia's diverse societies and communities.

The concept of "home"

Despite Riyadh's population increase, for those Saudis who relocate to the capital for work, the city does not represent "home." Rather, this is considered a transient location, despite often being a long-term one, as "home" is always the family or tribal locality, frequently outside Riyadh.[38] Even children born in Riyadh to parents who moved to the capital do not consider Riyadh as home.[39] This phenomenon is most visible during the last ten days of Ramadan and the two Eid holidays when Riyadh empties and becomes extremely quiet as families and entire communities return to their hometowns for the celebrations. One Riyadh native jokes that it is the only time when someone can find parking in the capital.[40] For individuals or families whose hometowns are closer to Riyadh such as towns and villages in wider Riyadh Province such as Huraymila and Shaqra or localities in Al Qassim Province such as Onaizah, Ar Rass and AlMithnab (to name a few) the option of "going home" extends to weekends and for this reason, highways such as the Riyadh-Qassim one heading north, or the Riyadh-Dammam highway heading east, become extremely crowded on Thursday afternoons and evenings as people "head home."[41]

Furthermore, when young men working in Riyadh contemplate getting married, their choice of bride is frequently determined by their hometown relationships with other families in the locality. Their female relatives are tasked with looking for a suitable bride from their hometown, even if the prospective bride also works in Riyadh or another urban center. Finally, the marriage usually takes place in their hometown rather than Riyadh (where they are both employed).[42] Certainly, increased urbanization and relocating to a city for economic reasons is a universal phenomenon. However, the intensity of family and hometown ties is arguably greater in Saudi Arabia than in many other countries. It is also one of the reasons that the vast majority of Saudi scholarship students, if not all, return to Saudi Arabia upon completing their studies overseas.[43]

Identity narratives

As noted previously, rapid socioeconomic transformations post the launch of Vision 2030 have triggered an increase in migration to Saudi Arabia's main urban centers, principally to Riyadh.[44]

Still, there is a degree of concern amongst young Saudis from the regions about the need to protect and preserve regional identities, especially when they relocate from the provinces to Riyadh and/or other cities, because the specific characteristics associated with their regional hometowns can become subsumed into a bland, homogenous mass.[45] For instance, a Saudi academic from Tabuk who works in Riyadh points out that everything in the far north is different. The culture, rhythm of life, and the way people think are very different, and importantly, their concerns and expectations are also different from those of the more cosmopolitan Riyadh.[46] In truth, there is belief that local/regional identity narratives are essential to preserve the diversity of Saudi societies and communities, but this preservation should go in tandem with sociocultural normalization of the acceptance of others and/or strangers (by promoting tolerance) that is often found in large cities, but sometimes, according to survey participants, absent from regional towns and villages.[47] Thus, local/regional identities are important because they constitute not only an important part of individual identity, but also family, tribe, and community identities.[48] This was highly evident during the first "Founding Day" in 2022, when Saudis of all ages and from all walks of life donned their historical tribal and regional costumes to mark the event across the Kingdom, with many Riyadh residents wearing their regional 'hometown' dress in places such as the capital's Boulevard World.[49]

Still, some young Saudis surveyed for this chapter consider that in a vast Kingdom covering an area of approximately 2.25 million square kilometers, the imposition of uniform customs, in particular in the main urban centers where most of the population resides, has contributed to the undermining of different regional identities.[50] Thus, because diverse Saudi identities are closely tied to regional cultures, an individual who relocates to a large city might outwardly experience an identity change; however, the "local roots" inside the person will remain.[51] These local roots become highly evident when individuals return to their hometowns at weekends or for the Eid holidays, when identities associated with specific tribes, towns, and villages reassert themselves. A Jeddah resident tells a similar story, saying that when he and his relatives gather in their tribal home in Asir Province during the summer, he sees they all revert to their tribal roots in terms of behavior and language. Yet, as soon as they return to the main urban centers and take up their everyday lives, their clothes and even their voices revert to their "city lifestyles."[52]

Survey respondents maintain that when moving to a large city such as Riyadh, they usually highlight their place of origin when introducing themselves to new friends or colleagues (although some admit that they do not know why they do this).[53] Others contend that when moving to a large city, young nationals must take into account the fact that they might feel like "fish out of water."[54] However, rather than draw attention to their regional origins, some believe that if a young man from Jazan Province[55] moves to Riyadh, for example, he should not wear his "Jazani clothes" in public places as this will "highlight" his regional origins to others. Rather, it is better to assimilate according to the "general practices" of a particular location, for instance, reducing local dialect and/or slang vocabulary when interacting with people from other Saudi regions.[56]

An interesting example of simultaneous urban/regional identities comes from a young Saudi academic from Ad Dawadimi, a town in Riyadh Province east of the capital,[57] who remarks that although he obtained his doctorate from a British university in 2023, and now works for a major university in Riyadh, neither of his parents can read or write. Additionally, none of his many brothers attended tertiary education, and to his knowledge, do not have passports.[58] He observes that his brothers' lives are "very traditional and centered around Ad Dawadimi. They are very 'bedu,' they are only happy when they are out in the desert with their camels." This lifestyle suits them completely; they have "done very well" and all built large houses in the town for their families. However, one brother rejects this bedu lifestyle completely, preferring to live an "urban" life in Ad Dawadimi and Riyadh. Hence, the academic observes that it is almost as though he has a split of *hadar* and *bedu* within his own family.[59]

The academic says that before leaving Saudi Arabia to start his doctorate in Britain, he worked in Riyadh and found weekend visits to his hometown "extremely boring."[60] However, since returning to the Kingdom permanently, his attitude towards his hometown has changed completely. He now sees the "value of this traditional way of living," and in contrast to the hectic pace of life in Riyadh, he finds the time he spends in Ad Dawadimi to be "relaxing and meaningful." Furthermore, similar to the example cited previously, the academic notices how he behaves differently in his hometown from when he is in Riyadh, maintaining that "it is like having multiple identities that are dependent on context."[61]

The lure of Riyadh: Attraction and resistance

Attraction of relocating to Riyadh

In the course of conducting qualitative research across Saudi Arabia over many years, when asked to list the issues that concern them most, young nationals nearly always cite employment as the most important.[62] In truth, employment is a key issue because it is how many individuals judge the government, particularly those who believe that it is the government's duty to provide everyone with a job, preferably a public-sector one. In the past, many young Saudis, in particular young men and graduates, were looking for a "job for life," that is, a position in the public sector (or with a major corporation) whereby the individual was guaranteed a lifelong salary plus accompanying benefits such as healthcare for both himself and his family. However, the "job for life" situation has changed, and nowadays it is commonplace for young Saudis to change jobs sometimes with alarming regularity.[63] Still, many young nationals from across the regions continue to show a marked preference for public-sector employment, a great deal of which is located in Riyadh.

A Riyadh-based Saudi economic analyst maintains that the government's policy of centralization in Riyadh has been geared to encouraging talented young Saudis to relocate to the capital in order to boost economic growth. The plan is that economic growth in Riyadh will spill over, or trickle down, to other cities and regions of the Kingdom.[64] Of course, there are some who have reservations about this policy, not least because the capital's infrastructure is under strain due to the constant influx of migrants moving into Riyadh from the regions.

Furthermore, greater numbers of young Saudis of both genders are entering the labor market, and many enjoy higher disposable incomes than in previous eras. This is mainly the case in Riyadh, where, in recent years, ambitious young Saudis have been seeking positions in the public sector because of perceived higher salaries than in the private sector.[65] (However, as these young Saudis relocate to the capital in search of well-paid employment opportunities, this can be simultaneously understood as a potential "brain drain" from other parts of the Kingdom.) This is particularly true when considering the lure of public-sector employment, such as positions in the "fashionable" ministries (for example, the Ministry of Investment or Ministry of Culture) and/or jobs with foreign management consultancies that have been highly active in Saudi policymaking following the launch of Vision 2030. These include McKinsey and Boston Consultancy Group (BCG), as well as to a lesser degree local consultancy companies such as Strategic Gears.[66] In consequence, the "best and the brightest" from across Saudi Arabia are often drawn to these companies and institutions due to higher salaries, superior benefits, and the "cool" connotations associated with them.[67]

That said, in recent years, and as the Public Investment Fund's (PIF) role in Saudi Arabia has grown, for young, ambitious Saudis, the PIF has become a preferred employment option, with fierce competition for positions.[68] The PIF, Saudi Arabia's sovereign wealth fund, as Young explains, is best known internationally for investing in numerous large domestic infrastructure and tourism development projects that are central to the Vision 2030 agenda. These include giga-projects such as Neom,[69] Qiddiya,[70] and the Red Sea Global,[71] massive state development initiatives designed to modernize the Saudi economy and capitalize on untouched Saudi tourism and entertainment markets.[72]

The attractiveness of working for the PIF is highlighted by personal anecdotal evidence. When I was employed at KFUPM in the Eastern Province from 2012 to early 2020, most of my undergraduate students (who represent the Kingdom's academic elite), and during that period mainly engineering majors, expected (and hoped) to work in the oil and petrochemical sectors for entities such as Saudi Aramco and Saudi Basic Industries Corporation (SABIC) or with companies such as General Electric, Haliburton, or Schlumberger. However, post-pandemic, what is striking is that when I discuss employment options with current KFUPM students, they say that as a first choice they would prefer to join the PIF. In sum, the bottom line is that the majority of these jobs, whether with PIF, in the ministries, or with consultancy firms, are perceived to have higher salaries, wide-ranging benefits such as family health insurance coverage, and are located principally in Riyadh.[73]

Resistance to relocating to Riyadh

Many young Saudis from the regions face the dilemma of relocating to a big city for better employment opportunities or remaining in their hometowns to be close to family and friends.[74] A young man from Hafar Al Batin, for example, says he does not want to move away from his family, although he acknowledges that all the best opportunities are in Riyadh; "Unless you are in the capital you miss out, as you do not hear about these employment chances when you live outside Riyadh."[75] Still, as Bosbait and Wilson observed in 2005, "there is a marked preference for Saudis to work close to home,"[76] and it is unthinkable for some young nationals to move away from their extended families. This remains as true today as it was two decades ago. In fact, sometimes individuals remain unemployed (or underemployed) because they refuse to leave their hometowns even though there is little chance of finding reasonably paid work. For them, relocating away from their hometowns and families is never an option, a viewpoint I have encountered in places such as Wadi ad-Dawasir, Abu Arish and Az Zulfi.[77] For instance, in Az Zulfi, a young father asserts that nothing would make him relocate to Riyadh and away from his family, even though he does not have a full-time job in his hometown and survives financially on a variety of part-time positions.[78] This is a sentiment I have heard in multiple locations across Saudi Arabia over many years.[79]

There is frequently a feeling of "I do not want to move to Riyadh, but I must" due to a lack of viable employment opportunities in the regions, especially, in smaller towns and villages in, for example, Asir, Al Jouf, Al Qassim and Najran Provinces, where young Saudis complain of a lack of local job opportunities and/or job creation schemes away from the main urban centers.[80] In addition, visits to more remote localities, such as the Farasan Islands or the mountainous areas in Asir and Al Bahah, reveal limited job opportunities for local youth.[81] As an example, a young man who graduated from Al Jouf University with a degree in English language and literature managed to find a job at the university, but as a security guard, as it was the only job available in the area.[82] Thus, as documented in previous studies, in small regional towns or villages, many young men are obliged leave their hometowns to find work, mainly in Riyadh. To ameliorate the situation, a group of friends in AlMithnab contends that the government should create more well-paid employment opportunities in the regions, as they are often discouraged from working in their hometowns because of lower salaries than in the cities,[83] although the same individuals do not always factor in the higher cost of living in the main urban localities. These young men point out that local salaries are a lot less than those of public-sector jobs in Riyadh and/or with large state-owned enterprises such as SABIC[84] and Saudi Aramco.[85]

Even so, many younger men from the regions, many with only elementary and secondary education, continue to move to Riyadh in search of work. Very often, they find temporary or part-time employment in low-paying jobs such as in retail and hospitality, and more often than not as Uber or Careem taxi drivers.[86] At one point during 2022–2023, a large proportion of the Careem drivers I encountered were from Najran, and I have also met drivers from more remote places such as the Farasan Islands and Turaif.[87,88]

Rising cost of living in Riyadh

Another important issue is the rising cost of living in Riyadh. Since the end of the COVID-19 pandemic, land prices and rent have skyrocketed, resulting in individuals on medium to lower salaries struggling to manage financially.[89] The bottom line is that many of these people are only just "making ends meet" in an increasingly expensive Riyadh.[90] Furthermore, the rising cost of living in the capital, especially rents, which in many cases increased by 25 percent to 50 percent between 2023 and 2024, made it difficult for many young nationals (both male and female) to live alone, thus necessitating sharing accommodation with friends.[91] Certainly, among many youth constituencies, it is considered "cool" to work in Riyadh, but upon arriving in the capital, the realities of life in Riyadh, in particular the cost of living, become crystal clear.[92] A young man who works in Riyadh, but returns to his hometown of AlMithnab in Al Qassim Province every weekend, remarks, "When I am in Riyadh, I open my wallet, and it is always empty; it is as if the money flies away. When I am at home in Al Qassim I open my wallet, and all my money is still there !"[93]

Another example: three assistant professors at the University of Hail recall that upon completion of their PhDs overseas, they considered working at

Riyadh's King Saud University (KSU). However, they point out that a Saudi state university salary (and benefits) does not "go very far" in Riyadh due to the much higher cost of living in the capital (although university accommodation is usually provided as part of the contract). In comparison, the same salary at the University of Hail provides the individual with a "higher quality of life," and simultaneously, proximity to family and friends. One of the assistant professors says he accepted a position at KSU, but after a year, returned to his hometown away from the "stress of living in Riyadh and my salary not being able to cover the cost of living for myself and my family." In Hail, his quality of life is higher, far less stressful, and he has more disposal income.[94] This situation is mirrored by the views of similar individuals working at Jizan University, Al Jouf University, and Northern Borders University.[95]

Regional issues

Regional development and migration within regions

Despite significant internal migration to Riyadh, travel around Saudi Arabia reveals considerable regional development as well as population increases in places such as Abha, Hail, Najran, and Tabuk, within provinces such as Al Qassim and Jazan,[96] and also in the Holy Cities of Makkah and Al Madinah. Whilst precise and correct 2025 exact regional population statistics are not always available, the following are some examples:

- Najran population in 2025 was 450,000, a 1.81 percent increase from 2024.[97]
- Tabuk population in 2025 was 707,000, a 1.43 percent increase from 2024.[98]
- Makkah population in 2025 was 2,219,000, a 1.56 percent increase from 2024.[99]
- Madinah population in 2025 was 1,625,000, a 1.63 percent increase from 2024.[100]

These increases align with the national 1.38 percent increase in Saudi Arabia's population from 2024 to 2025.[101]

Regular visits to the regions over the years reveal the extent of development and related population increases.[102] The following are some examples:

- Similar to Dammam-Qatif-Dhahran-Khobar,[103] which in the past were separate places but subsequently merged into a single conurbation, the cities of Abha and Khamis Mushait in Asir have become one locality. Nowadays, the main highway linking the two cities is replete with new shopping malls, the increasingly popular "squares,"[104] hotels, coffee shops, and restaurants.[105]

- The presence of Neom (and the employment opportunities it has generated) near Tabuk has had an impact on the city's development, with, once again, new squares, restaurants, and entertainment venues being opened. Museums, including the one that houses the Hejaz Railway Exhibit, have undergone renovations.[106] Tabuk is also on the Chinese "tourist trail" as a follow-up destination to Al-Ula.[107]
- In Makkah, as well as the major developments to al-Masjid al-Haram (the Grand Mosque) and surrounding area, there are popular new squares located on the 4th Ring Road on the southeast side of the city near Mina. These squares comprise "lounges,"[108] where residents watch important football matches (the most popular places require a booking), as well as bowling alleys, games rooms, male and female gyms,[109] and a wide variety of restaurants offering international or Saudi cuisines. Yet, a young Saudi points out that just a few years ago, "there were only the old-fashioned type of shisha lounges on the outskirts of the cities; all of this is very new."[110]
- There are numerous economic, healthcare, and infrastructure projects in Al Madinah. The largest, Rua Al Madinah Holding, comprises current and future projects to develop a hotel and commercial system. It also aims to establish cultural, entertainment, and religious museums near al-Masjid an-Nabawi (The Prophet's Mosque), facilitating the accommodation of thirty million visitors to Madinah by 2030. The company also estimates that it will create 93,000 job opportunities in the city by 2030.[111]

Another example is the regional town of AlMithnab, in Al Qassim Province, situated just south of Onaizah. The 2022 census documented the population at approximately 43,000,[112] but 2025 statistics show an increase to 60,900.[113] On my first visit in early 2017, the opening of the Kudu fast-food restaurant branch was considered contentious.[114] Fast forward to 2026, and there are multiple fast-food outlets, as well as the brand-new Al Othaim Mall. According to the town's residents, the population increase is attributed to migration from small villages around AlMithnab. This is partly due to the closure of small health clinics and schools in these villages, considered economically unsustainable, thereby prompting local families to relocate to the larger town.[115]

The impact of internal migration on the regions

The oil-producing Eastern Province has traditionally been a job-creating region, and therefore, a magnet for both local and international investment.

A famous example is the prestigious KFUPM.[116] For decades, the rationale of the university has been to supply well-qualified graduates for the oil and petrochemical sectors located in the province. KFUPM also hosts the KFUPM AMAAD Business Park[117] and Dhahran Techno Valley.[118] However, as Riyadh grows in importance, businesses and job seekers have been leaving the Eastern Province for the capital.[119] Needless to say, there are misgivings about this development. A Saudi professor at KFUPM observes that a lot of Eastern Province businesses either relocated to Riyadh or closed.[120] Most famously, Saudi Aramco moved its Human Resources and Legal divisions to Riyadh as part of the Regional Headquarters Program (RHQ), although its operations will stay in the Eastern Province for obvious reasons.[121] A long-term Aramco employee claims there have been staff shortages across all Aramco divisions as younger Saudis leave in search of better job opportunities in Riyadh.[122] The exodus of businesses and workers is reflected in local malls such as the famous Al Rashid Mall in Al Khobar. Whereas the mall used to be crowded most of the time, nowadays a large number of retail outlets have closed, and areas of the mall are significantly quieter.[123] That said, the prominent Eastern Province Alfozan family[124] announced that it will not move any of its businesses to Riyadh, but rather invest heavily in new leisure/retail venues in the Eastern Province, such as Ajdan Walk square situated on the Al Khobar corniche.[125]

In addition, a young Saudi entrepreneur from Qatif emphasizes that there have been major investments in Qatif, such as the Ajdan Development Company's Al Ramis Al Awamiyah project,[126] as well as the Sharqia Development Authority's redevelopment of historic Dareen and Tarout Islands.[127] The idea is to attract tourists to Qatif, which until fairly recently was considered a "no-go" area for any non-Shia Saudis, a policy that appears to have been successful, as the police checkpoints in and out of Qatif have all but disappeared.[128] On a visit to a private museum on Tarout Island, the guestbook includes positive comments from three Saudi women from Al Qassim.[129] As the young entrepreneur points out, it would have been impossible just a few years ago for Qassimis to come to Qatif, let alone Qassimi women.[130]

Conclusion

Internal migration to Riyadh is unlikely to cease in the near future, although there is a growing comprehension that not everyone can or should live in the capital. However, accepting the current status quo requires considering two important options. Firstly, improving the quality of life for Riyadh residents (both current and future ones) and secondly, creating more viable employment opportunities in the regions, not only jobs, but also strong career paths for young Saudis.

Improving Riyadh's quality of life

As Riyadh expands rapidly, partly due to internal migration fueled by job seeking, policies are required that guide urban administrators in managing quality of life issues and challenges in the capital. These include the rising cost of living, especially housing, water, health, transportation, education, employment, and air quality.[131] To ensure that Riyadh remains an attractive work destination, the capital's development must be sustainable, with quality of life as a key component.[132]

A major issue for Riyadh's residents, especially when educational entities are open, is traffic congestion. As people move into Riyadh, they bring additional vehicles, at least two per family.[133] Consequently,, people living in the capital understand that a minimum of an hour is required for traveling from one destination in the city to another, frequently longer, and that, in all probability, parking will not be available at the end of the journey.[134] Thus, for Riyadh's residents, the golden rule is "live near your work" to avoid hours spent in traffic jams during rush hour.[135] For example, a young Saudi who works for the PIF in Riyadh's modern Digital City[136] remarks that as soon as PIF colleagues arrive at work, they start complaining about the traffic, all the time, every day. However, the problem is not just getting from home to Digital City; it is finding somewhere to park upon arrival. According to this young Saudi, the situation has been made worse by departments from various ministries, such as health and sections of the Royal Diwan, relocating to Digital City. That said, due to this overcrowding, certain institutions, including PIF, moved operations to King Abdullah Financial District (KAFD).[137] Still, there are reservations about relocating to KAFD, especially if employees are required to park on the district's outskirts and then be "bussed" to a number of pick-up points from where employees walk to their workplaces. As another Saudi public-sector employee says, "no one really wants to walk for 10 to 15 minutes during the height of the summer when the temperature is around 50 degrees."[138]

Rather than living in Riyadh, another option for employees is a daily commute into the capital from towns located in the wider Riyadh region (and sometimes beyond), such as Huraymila, Al Majmaah, Howtat Bani Tamim, or Al Kharj. Judging by traffic congestion on the main thoroughfares into and out of the capital during rush hour, the number of commuters doing this appears to be increasing.[139] Yet more savvy young Saudis have been buying land and/or property in these areas, knowing that as more people move to towns such as Huraymila, but commute into the city, land and property prices in these areas will increase increase.[140]

Certainly, increased availability of public transport is one way to ease traffic congestion, and this has started to become accessible in Riyadh. Public buses started running in March 2023 as part of the first phase of the King Abdulaziz Public Transport Project. This project, which consists of trains and buses and costs $22.5 billion, is considered the largest public transport project in the world.[141] In addition, the Riyadh Metro, the largest in the Middle East and the world's longest driverless train system serving 85 stations, including four major hubs across 176 kilometers, opened its doors in December 2024.[142] The launching of the metro was greeted with huge enthusiasm, especially by the capital's young Saudi residents.[143] Despite concerns that the metro would be underused, since it became operational, in 2025 RCRC announced that the metro has carried nearly eighteen million passengers across the city on over 162,000 trips. Stations such as KAFD are among the most popular destinations as they serve office workers in the busy financial district.[144]

Finally, the Green Riyadh project aims to improve the capital's livability, protect the environment, and make Riyadh a more attractive place to live. Launched in 2019, the project's goal is to ensure the capital's residents live happier, healthier, and more sustainable lives. The project's initiatives include creating green public spaces, improving air quality, decreasing power consumption, reducing temperatures, and enhancing the urban landscape of Riyadh.[145] One of Green Riyadh's largest initiatives is the rapidly developing King Salman Park in central Riyadh, which, among Saudi Arabia's mega-projects, receives scant attention outside the Kingdom even though the park will prove hugely beneficial to the capital's residents when it opens.[146] One of Riyadh's four mega-projects, the park sits on an area that spans more than 16 square kilometers. Strategically located, the park will be easily accessible to many with links to several main roads, as well as being connected to the Riyadh Metro and Riyadh bus network stations. In addition to the vast green areas that make up the largest share of its area, the park will include a wide range of artistic, cultural, and sporting attractions. At the time of writing, the park was expected to open in 2027.[147]

The need for Saudi Arabia and promoting regional content

As documented in this chapter, many young Saudis feel compelled to relocate to Riyadh in search of work even if they would prefer to remain in their hometowns. This situation raises important questions about how to create viable regional jobs and strong career paths for young Saudis in the regions, especially for those who do not want to move to the capital.[148]

One of the ways to address the requirements and aspirations of young Saudis in the Kingdom's regions as they attempt to enter the labor market is through the lens of localization and local content as applied to the internal Saudi context. Localization is a strategy focused on strengthening local/regional capability by empowering the workforce, businesses, and industries to drive job creation, economic growth, and sustainable development. This is achieved through developing labor skills, together with innovation promotion, technology transfer, capacity building, and establishing new local/regional capabilities.[149]

An excellent example establishing new local/regional capabilities that drive job creation is Sudair Industrial City (established in 2009), strategically located approximately 120 km north of Riyadh and 160 km south of Al Qassim Province on the highway that links central and northern Saudi Arabia to the capital.[150] At the time of writing, Sudair Industrial City hosted 302 factories, including those in operation and under construction, as well as managing 346 industrial and service contracts, and is expected to reach 400 tenants by 2030.[151] Companies operating in Sudair Industrial City have been providing employment opportunities for young Saudis from a variety of locations who commute to the city from places such as Al Majmaah, Az Zulfi, Sudair itself, and even northern Riyadh.[152] Some employees from farther afield rent apartments in Al Majmaah, for example, and commute to work from there, but then return home to their hometowns, for instance in Al Qassim, at the weekends. These young Saudis say that this arrangement offers them the best of both worlds and is far less expensive than renting accommodation in Riyadh. Furthermore, many jobs in the industrial city are well-paid and provide strong career paths that attract KFUPM graduates, among others.[153]

Linked to this is local/regional content, which plays an important role, placing focus on value retention and spending within local/regional economies.[154] To date, the Saudi government has been implementing local content requirements in various sectors, including energy, construction, and manufacturing, mandating that a certain percentage of goods, services, and labor be sourced locally. The rationale behind this is that strengthening and expanding local content policies can encourage the growth of local industries, create job opportunities, and nurture a competitive domestic market within localities.[155] I witnessed an example of successful local content on a December 2024 visit to Hail. The Association for Productive Families in Hail (ENTAG Hail) established a professional kitchen unit in the city for mainly local women entrepreneur chefs who were selling their produce locally, mainly sweets and cakes, on social media applications such as Snapchat and Instagram. This new facility not only provides business advice but also facilitates "scaling up" of the women's foodstuffs in a professional environment, as well as fostering a sense of community and self-worth. A measure of this venture's success is that previously local coffee/tea shops in the Hail area purchased their foodstuffs from Riyadh manufacturers, but nowadays many have switched to the local Hail content provided by this facility.[156]

The bottom line is that while internal migration to Riyadh, or to a lesser extent to other Saudi cities, cannot be halted, improvements in the capital's quality of life will alleviate some of the issues and challenges that Riyadh's residents currently face. In addition, creating long-term, viable job opportunities with strong career paths for young Saudis will lessen the need to relocate to the capital in search of employment. These jobs and careers must be worthwhile and sustainable, thereby assisting young nationals in the regions with personal development, fostering greater self-worth, and a sense of contributing to the national project, namely Vision 2030. Relying solely on filling quotas could lead to the danger of mistakenly creating under and/or phantom employment rather than meaningful and long-term employment opportunities.

Notes

1 Michael J. White and David P. Lindstrom, "Internal Migration," in: Poston, D.L., Micklin, M. (eds.) *Handbook of Population. Handbooks of Sociology and Social Research.* Springer, Boston, MA., 2005, https://doi.org/10.1007/0-387-23106-4_12, p. 341.

2 See: https://www.vision2030.gov.sa/en.

3 Saudi Arabia's thirteen administrative areas: Riyadh Region, Makkah Region, Eastern Province, Asir Region, Jazan Region, Al Madinah Region, Al Qassim Region, Hail Region, Tabuk Region, Najran Region, Al Jouf Region, Al Bahah Region, and the Northern Borders Region.

4 Ibid.

5 See, for example: Mark C. Thompson, "Saudi Vision 2030: The Importance of Being in Riyadh," *ISPI*, 9 September 2020, https://www.ispionline.it/en/publication/saudi-vision-2030-importance-being-riyadh-27323

6 See, for example: https://datasaudi.sa/en/region/al-riyadh. The website and app Saudi Data also provides demographic data for each region.

7 Author's interviews and observations across Saudi Arabia, 2020–2025.

8 See, for example: "How Population is Driving Development Riyadh's Near-Future," Frank Knight, October 2024, chrome-extension://efaidnbmnnnibpcajpcglclefindmkaj/https://content.knightfrank.com/research/2918/documents/en/riyadhs-near-future-how-population-is-driving-development-october-2024-11648.pdf.

9 https://datasaudi.sa/en.
10 Ibid.
11 Khraif, R.M., Salam, A.A., Nair, P.S., Elsegaey, I., "Migration in Saudi Arabia: Present and Prospects," in: Rajan, S.I., Saxena, P. (eds.) *India's Low-Skilled Migration to the Middle East*, Palgrave Macmillan, Singapore, 2019, https://doi.org/10.1007/978-981-13-9224-5_5, https://link.springer.com/chapter/10.1007/978-981-13-9224-5_5#citeas.
12 https://www.stats.gov.sa/en/home; https://datasaudi.sa/en.
13 "An Impactful Vision: The National Transformation Program's Achievements," *Annual Report 2023*, ww.vision2030.gov.sa/media/xqjbmpwg/english-ntp-anuual-report-2023.pdf, p. 43; Shujaa Albogmi, "Saudi Arabia's State-of-the-Art Census Reveals a Young Population," *Al Majalla*, 11 July 2023, en.majalla.com/node/295336/business-economy/saudi-arabia%E2%80%99s-state-art-census-reveals-young-population.
14 https://datasaudi.sa/en.
15 chrome-extension://efaidnbmnnnibpcajpcglclefindmkaj/https://www.stats.gov.sa/documents/20117/2435273/Population+Estimates+Publication+2024+EN.pdf/7d123c57-1626-7d2f-ba7f-8a719f928f28?t=1750142166351
16 Author's interviews and observations across Saudi Arabia, 2020–2025.
17 Ibid.
18 Shujaa Albogmi "Saudi Arabia's state-of-the-art census reveals a young population," *Al Majalla*, 11 July 2023, https://en.majalla.com/node/295336/business-economy/saudi-arabia%E2%80%99s-state-art-census-reveals-young-population.
19 https://www.worldometers.info/world-population/population-by-country/.
20 See, for example: https://library.fiveable.me/key-terms/hs-global-studies/hyper-urbanization.
21 Mohammed Abdulrahman Albarrak, "Managing Riyadh's Urban Growth: Assessing Resident Satisfaction in the Current Residential Neighborhoods and Examining Smart Growth Strategy Preferences for the Future Growth in the Context of Rapid Urbanization," *Virginia Tech*, 19 March 2025, https://vtechworks.lib.vt.edu/items/3dd3f526-131a-4e4c-bf7c-a6a1ef1ad581
22 https://www.rcrc.gov.sa/en/
23 Mohammed al-Mutairi, "Riyadh's Population Rise to 15 Million Helps Shift City towards Independent Economy," *Ash Sharq Al-Awsat*, 1 May 2024, https://english.aawsat.com/business/4994791-riyadh%E2%80%99s-population-rise-15-million-helps-shift-city-towards-independent-economy.
24 https://www.vision2030.gov.sa/en/explore/projects/qiddya.
25 https://kingsalmanpark.sa/en.
26 https://sportsboulevard.sa/en.
27 Mohammed al-Mutairi, "Riyadh's Population Rise to 15 Million Helps Shift City towards Independent Economy."
28 See, for example: Fahad Abuljadayel and Zainab Fattah, "Saudi Capital to Cut Population Goal as City Reviews Strategy," *Bloomberg*, 26 April 2024,

https://www.bloomberg.com/news/articles/2024-04-26/saudi-capital-to-cut-population-goal-as-city-reviews-strategy.

29 Dayan Abou Tine, "Riyadh's population to hit 9.6m by 2030, driving demand for 305k new homes: Knight Frank," *Arab News*, 25 October, https://www.arabnews.com/node/2576760/business-economy.

30 Ibid.

31 Ibid: Riyadh's new housing supply comes from four main sources, including the Ministry of Housing, which oversees affordable projects through the National Housing Company and private firms. There are also government developments led by the Public Investment Fund and Roshn, private sector initiatives from real estate companies, and self-development by families purchasing land for construction. Up to 2025, approximately 330,000 housing units have been announced by government-related entities. The projected demand from Saudi nationals is estimated at 220,000 units from 2024 to 2030 and 305,000 units from 2024 to 2034, suggesting that current construction efforts align with expected housing needs.

32 Author's interview, Riyadh, 2024.

33 Authors interviews and observations, Riyadh 2023–2025.

34 "Saudi Arabia considers rent cap as part of major real estate reforms," *Saudi Gazette Report*, 1 April 2025, https://www.saudigazette.com.sa/article/650592

35. Joanne Serrieh, "Saudi Arabia announces five-year rent freeze in Riyadh: Key rules explained", Al Arabiya, 25 September 2025, https://english.alarabiya.net/News/saudi-arabia/2025/09/25/saudi-arabia-announces-fiveyear-rent-freeze-in-riyadh-key-rules-explained-

36. Author's experience and observations, Riyadh 2025.

37 When it comes to Saudi Arabia, especially with the way Saudi Arabia is perceived from the West, there is this tendency to look at the Kingdom as a homogeneous entity and adopt a "one size fits all" approach to looking at Saudi Arabia, disregarding the huge internal diversity.

38 Very often an individual or family will rent in Riyadh but buy a property in their hometown with the plan to move back permanently at some point in the future. Author's interviews across Saudi Arabia 2020–2025.

39 Author's interviews and observations, Riyadh, 2020–2025.

40 Ibid.

41 Ibid.

42 Author's personal experiences of attending weddings across Saudi Arabia 2013–2025.

43 Naif Daifullah Z Alsulami, "Factors affecting the re-entry experiences of returning Saudi international students after studying abroad," *Journal of Education* 69 (January 2020), chrome-extension://efaidnbmnnnibpcajpcglclefindmkaj/https://edusohag.journals.ekb.eg/article_64547_37a4e50ba4daf586ad719c10da6f83b9.pdf, p. 102.

44 Author's regional identity survey.

45 Ibid.

46 Author's interview, Riyadh, 2022.
47 Ibid.
48 Ibid.
49 See, for example: Aziz El Yaakoubi, "Saudi Arabia for first time marks its founding, downplaying conservative roots," *Reuters*, 22 February 2022, https://www.reuters.com/world/middle-east/saudi-arabia-first-time-marks-its-founding-downplaying-conservative-roots-2022-02-22/#:~:text=A%20royal%20decree%20last%20month,of%20Saudi%20Arabia%20in%20193; Author's observations Riyadh 2022.
50 Author's regional identity survey.
51 Ibid.
52 Although I discussed this issue in 2019, it remains true in 2025. Mark C. Thompson, *Being Young Male and Saudi: Identity and Politics in a Globalized Kingdom*, Cambridge University Press, 2019, p. 29.
53 Author's regional identity survey.
54 Ibid.
55 Jizan is the city, Jazan the province.
56 Author's regional identity survey.
57 Ad Dawadimi has a population of 563,861 people (2022 census) and is located 320 kilometers by road west of Riyadh. The town is famous in Saudi Arabia as a hometown of the Al Otaibi tribe.
58 Author's interview Ad Dawadimi, January 2024.
59 Ibid.
60 Ibid.
61 Ibid. This is also discussed in Mark C. Thompson, *Being Young Male and Saudi: Identity and Politics in a Globalized Kingdom*, Cambridge University Press, 2019, p. 29.
62 See, for example: Multiple focus groups conducted across Saudi Arabia, 2016–2019, for Mark C. Thompson, *Being Young Male and Saudi: Identity and Politics in a Globalized Kingdom*.
63 Author's interviews and observations, Riyadh, 2020–2025.
64 Author's interview, Riyadh, 2024.
65 Mark C. Thompson and Neil Quilliam, "Saudi Vision 2030: Repurposing Ministries and Creating New Institutions" in John Sfakianakis (ed.) *The Economy of Saudi Arabia in the 21st Century: Realities and Prospects*, Oxford University Press, 2024, pp. 335–6.
66 See: https://strategicgears.com/; Author's observations 2012 to 2025.
67 Author's interviews and observations, Riyadh 2020–2025.
68 Author's interviews and observations, 2022–2025.
69 https://www.neom.com/en-us.
70 https://www.vision2030.gov.sa/en/explore/projects/qiddya.
71 https://www.vision2030.gov.sa/en/explore/projects/red-sea-global.
72 Karen E. Young, "Saudi State Capitalism" in John Sfakianakis (ed.) *The Economy of Saudi Arabia in the 21st Century: Realities and Prospects*, Oxford University Press, 2024, p. 155.

73 Ibid.
74 Author's interviews and observations across Saudi Arabia, 2020–2025.
75 Author's interview, Hafar Al Batin, November 2024.
76 M. Bosbait and R. Wilson, "Education, School to Work Transitions and Unemployment in Saudi Arabia," *Middle Eastern Studies*, 41, no. 4 (2005): 542.
77 Author's interviews in Wadi Ad Dawasir and Abu Arish, 2023.
78 Author's interview, Az Zulfi, April 2025.
79 Author's interviews and observations across Saudi Arabia, 2020–2025.
80 Author's interviews, Asir, Aljouf, Al Qassim, and Najran Provinces, 2020–2025. This was also discussed in Mark. C. Thompson, *Being Young Male and Saudi: Identity and Politics in a Globalized Kingdom*, p. 69.
81 Author's interviews, Farasan Islands, Al Namas, Baljurashi, and Al Bahah, 2021–2025.
82 Author's interview, Sakkaka, 2023.
83 Ibid. Although this topic was researched in 2017, it remains true today.
84 www.sabic.com/en.
85 Author's interviews, Asir, Aljouf, Al Qassim, and Najran Provinces, 2020–2025.
86 This lays to rest the persistent stereotype that Saudis will not do certain jobs, although construction work and barbering are still mostly "off-limits."
87. Turaif is a city and governorate in northern Saudi Arabia. It is part of the Northern Borders Province.
88 Author's interviews and observations, Riyadh 2020–2025.
89 Ibid. See, for example: https://wise.com/gb/cost-of-living/saudi-arabia/riyadh.
90 Rahaf Jambi, "Riyadh Rent Hike Drives Demand for Home Ownership," *Arab News*, 23 July 2024, www.arabnews.com/node/2555126/saudi-arabia. Author's interviews Riyadh 2021–2025.
91 The rent for the author's apartments, for example, increased by 30% between November 2023 and 2024. A colleague also said that in September 2024, "my boss went crazy when he suddenly received a text from his landlord telling him his annual rent was being increased by SAR 10,000."
92 Author's interviews and observations, Riyadh 2020–2025.
93 Author's interview, AlMithnab, December 2024.
94 Author's interview, Hail, December 2024.
95 Author's interviews, Jizan 2021–2025, Al Jouf and Ar'ar, December 2024.
96 According to the Saudi Census 2022, 1,404,997 people live in the province. Jazan Province is 13,000 km, covering 0.7 percent of Saudi Arabia's area. It is the most densely populated region, with a density rate of about 118 people per kmhttps://saudipedia.com/en/article/274/government-and-politics/emirates-of-provinces/the-emirate-of-jazan-province#:~:text=Area%20and%20population%20of%20Jazan,about%20118%20people%20per%20km.
97 https://www.macrotrends.net/global-metrics/cities/22429/najran/population
98 https://www.macrotrends.net/global-metrics/cities/22433/tabuk/population

99 https://www.macrotrends.net/global-metrics/cities/22426/mecca/population
100 https://www.macrotrends.net/global-metrics/cities/22427/medina/population
101 https://www.macrotrends.net/global-metrics/countries/sau/saudi-arabia/population
102 Multiple visits by the author to these localities, 2020–2025.
103 For instance, if you drive along the Damman Corniche, eventually you drive into Qatif, but if you do not know the area, you will not realize this.
104 The new Saudi squares comprise retail outlets, entertainment venues as well as restaurants and coffee shops in a single location, usually with parking. These new squares become "flavor of the month" for a short period, trending on social media platforms such as Snapchat, TikTok and Swarm, before another newer location goes viral on social media and "everyone moves on" to the new locale. Author's interviews, Makkah, 2025.
105 Author's visits and observations, 2020–2025.
106 Author's interviews at the museum, Tabuk, December 2024; https://www.visitsaudi.com/en/tabuk/attractions/tabuk-station-in-hejaz-railway.
107 Author's interviews and observations, Tabuk December 2024.
108 Lounges differ from coffee/tea shops in that they sell shisha. See: https://www.arabnews.com/node/1569011/saudi-arabia.
109 See, for example: https://www.fitnesstime.com.sa/en-us/
110 Author's observations, and interview with local Saudi youth, Makkah, Ramadan 2025.
111 https://ruaalmadinah.com/
112 https://www.citypopulation.de/en/saudiarabia/qasim/0404__al_midhnab/
113 https://kn.maptons.com/2436401
114 I discussed this in: Mark C. Thompson, *Being Young Male and Saudi: Identity and Politics in a Globalized Kingdom*, p. 28.
115 Author's interviews and observations, AlMithnab, 2017–2025.
116 https://www.kfupm.edu.sa/
117 https://www.stom.sa/en/kfupm-business-park-dhahransss.
118 https://www.dtvc.com.sa/
119 Author's interviews and observations, Easter Province 2020–2025.
120 Author's interview, Dhahran, 2023.
121 Ibid. See, for example: Nik Pratt, "Saudi law on regional HQ sees more than 120 relocations," *Funds Global MENA*, 4 June 2024, https://www.fundsglobalmena.com/saudi-law-on-regional-hq-sees-more-than-120-relocations/
122 Author's interview, Dhahran, 2023.
123 Ibid. The author worked at KFUPM for eight years, and nowadays, also finds Al Khobar much quieter than it used to be.
124 https://alfozan.com/press-releases/governor-eastern-province-opens-ajdan-walk-al-khobar-corniche#:~:text=AlOula%20Real%20Estate%20is%20the,more%20than%2017%2C000%20square%20meters.

125 Author's interview Al Kobar, 2023; https://ajdan.com/space/ajdan-walk.
126 https://alfozan.com/press-releases/ajdan-unveils-identity-downtown-al-awamiyah-project.
127 Author's interview, Qatif, 2023.
128 Author's observations, Qatif, 2008–2025.
129 Author's observation, Qatif, 2023.
130 Author's interview, Qatif, 2023; https://www.sda.gov.sa/program-details/73411?ltr=true.
131 Choguill, Charles. "Assessing the Urban Sustainability of Riyadh," *Journal of King Saud University* no. 2 (2008): 41–9.
132 Ibid.
133 Author's interviews, Riyadh 2024–2025.
134 Author's interviews and observations, Riyadh 2020–2025.
135 Ibid.; even worse when it rains.
136 Author's interview, Riyadh 2023; https://digitalcity.com.sa/
137 Author's interviews, Riyadh 2023–2024.
138 Ibid.
139 Author's interviews and observations, Riyadh 2020–2025.
140 Ibid.
141 "Riyadh public transport buses begin operation, with ticket charges set at SR4," *Saudi Gazette Report*, 19 March 2023, https://cdn.saudigazette.com.sa/article/630859/SAUDI-ARABIA/Riyadh-public-transport-buses-begin-operation-with-ticket-charges-set-at-SR4#:~:text=Riyadh%20public%20transport%20buses%20begin,transport%20project%20in%20the%20world.
142 "Riyadh Metro Opens Its Doors to the Public Today," *Saudi Press Agency*, 1 December 2024, https://www.spa.gov.sa/en/N2216717
143 Author's interviews and observations, Riyadh 2024–2025.
144 "The record-breaking numbers behind the Riyadh Metro: can you guess the busiest station?," *Time Out*, 19 February 2025, https://www.timeoutriyadh.com/news/riyadh-metro-popular-stations.
145 https://www.vision2030.gov.sa/en/explore/projects/green-riyadh.
146 https://kingsalmanpark.sa/en; The park is located at the end of the street where I live, so I can see the progress being made on a daily basis.
147 See, for example: "King Salman Park: World's Largest Urban Park in Riyadh," *Blackridge*, 12 February 2025, https://www.blackridgeresearch.com/project-profiles/latest-updated-details-king-salman-park-kspf-contractors-project-riyadh-saudi-arabia?srsltid=AfmBOopODJMzsrMr6tUMmt-Ad4zASdUoaEOvzLqi1bwcMQx1HdTS3N3k.
148 See: Mark C. Thompson, "Inherent contradictions in the Saudi rentier state: distributive capacity, youth employment preferences, and attitudes to education," *British Journal of Middle Eastern Studies* 47, no. 1 (2020): Revisiting Rentierism: The Changing Political Economy of Resource-Dependent States in the Gulf and Arabian Peninsula, January 2020.
149 https://www.efficioconsulting.com/en-gb/resources/reports/building-on-success-a-pathway-for-advancing-local-content-in-saudi-

150 https://modon.gov.sa/en/Cities/IndustrialCities/Pages/IndustrialCity.aspx?CityId=cbedec34-2138-4b40-9bf3-12ea1ce95a38; I drive past the industrial city on a regular basis and can verify that it is expanding.

151 Ibid.

152 Author's interviews Riyadh, Al Majmaah, Az Zulfi, and Sudair, 2022–2025.

153 Ibid.

154 https://www.efficioconsulting.com/en-gb/resources/reports/building-on-success-a-pathway-for-advancing-local-content-in-saudi-; Local content refers to the value being retained in a local/regional economy through the increased use of existing local/regional capabilities and capacities. It encompasses the proportion of spend on products and services that are procured from local/regional manufacturers and service providers, together with other key elements contributing towards the growth of the local/regional manpower and industries. Local content is calculated using different components carefully crafted to support a country's economic development agenda.

155 See, for example: https://acacialearning.com/sa/blog/human-resources/10-strategies-for-localisation-in-the-saudi-economy/

156 Author's interviews, Hail 2025.

3

Gulf Migration Interdependence and Saudi Arabia's Vision 2030

Gerasimos Tsourapas

Introduction

The political effects of cross-border human mobility on states' domestic and foreign policy priorities have been the subject of longstanding debate. While the field of international migration politics continues to grow, much of the focus remains on Europe and North America, with insufficient attention given to other regions, particularly in the context of labor migration. The Gulf Cooperation Council (GCC) states, historically among the world's major destinations for labor migrants, exemplify this gap. Existing literature predominantly examines international migration into the GCC, often overlooking the analytical significance and socio-economic impact of intra-GCC mobility. Intra-GCC migration flows are not only economically significant but may also play a crucial role in shaping regional political dynamics, fostering policy coordination among member states, and potentially promoting socio-cultural integration. This paper seeks to address this gap by fostering research on the mobility of citizens within the GCC and its specific implications for the Kingdom of Saudi Arabia. Specifically, how does intra-GCC mobility affect Saudi Arabia, and how might it align with the country's Vision 2030 agenda?

This study builds on the concept of interdependence, which posits that human mobility—like other cross-border economic activities—generates reciprocal political and economic effects for both sending and host states (Hirschman 1945, 194; Keohane and Nye 1987). In the Middle East, these dynamics have been explored primarily in the context of coercive migration diplomacy between antagonistic states in North Africa and the Levant, conceptualized as migration interdependence (Tsourapas 2018; 2019). However, little is known about how migration interdependence operates within the Gulf. Given the GCC's distinct economic and political configuration, understanding how migration interdependence functions in this context is crucial for a more comprehensive view of regional stability and integration. This paper uses the GCC's free movement regime as a case study to explore how migration interdependence fosters mutually beneficial relations and produces positive spillover effects.

The paper is structured as follows: it begins with a brief review of the relevant literature, followed by a discussion of the chosen methodology and methods. The analysis then traces the evolution of the Gulf's free movement regime under the GCC charter, with a particular focus on Saudi Arabia. It argues that GCC migration interdependence has led to two key outcomes: top-down cooperation and bottom-up opportunities for strengthening ties among transnational Gulf families. This dual dynamic not only enhances state-level collaboration but also reinforces social cohesion within the region, offering a unique model of migration-driven integration. The paper further examines the role of Gulf migration interdependence in advancing Saudi Vision 2030, highlighting its potential to increase the political and economic costs of regional antagonism, thereby reducing the likelihood of prolonged crises. Finally, the paper outlines the key challenges facing Gulf migration interdependence before concluding.

Understanding the international relations of migration and interdependence

The intersection of migration and foreign policymaking has long been a focus of international studies, as scholars have sought to apply insights from international relations (IR) to the international politics of migration, both globally as well as regionally (Hollifield, Martin, and Orrenius 2022; Geddes et al. 2019; Kechichian and Alsharif 2022). Migration, much like trade or security, has increasingly been recognized as a key factor in shaping bilateral and multilateral relations, with significant implications for state behavior and power dynamics. Early contributions by Weiner (1985) and Zolberg (1981) explored migration as a tool of statecraft, particularly within the Cold War context, where population flows were often weaponized to exert pressure or gain strategic advantage. This body of work introduced migration as a critical component of foreign policy, challenging traditional IR paradigms that viewed it as a secondary or "low politics" issue. As Hollifield later argues:

> International migration, like trade, is a fundamental feature of the postwar liberal order. But as states and societies have become more liberal and more open, migration has increased. Will this increase in migration be a virtuous or a vicious cycle? Will it be destabilising,

> leading the international system into greater anarchy, disorder, and war, or will it lead to greater openness, wealth, and human development?
> (Hollifield 2012, 372–3)

A close interaction, thus, traditionally exists between migration and political power (for a detailed discussion on migration power, see: Fernández-Molina and Tsourapas 2024), in which interstate relations and diplomacy feature heavily. Early work in this area focused on the coercive potential of migration, with Greenhill (2010) demonstrating how engineered migration crises can serve as tools of coercive diplomacy. Similarly, Tsourapas (2017) explored how migration diplomacy became a key instrument of Gaddafi's policymaking in Libya. Recent scholarship has sought to systematize these dynamics within a neorealist framework, emphasizing issue-linkage and bargaining strategies that range from zero-sum to positive-sum outcomes (Adamson and Tsourapas 2019). Migration diplomacy also encompasses softer forms of influence, such as fostering regional integration (Thiollet 2011) and shaping state-diaspora relations to advance foreign policy goals (Gamlen 2019). These studies highlight the dual nature of migration diplomacy, where states can employ migration as both a pressure tactic and a mechanism for enhancing international cooperation.

However, thinking critically through current scholarship on the interplay between migration and power reveals that, despite its strengths, the neorealist paradigm of migration diplomacy has concrete limitations (cf. Tolay 2023). Despite its emphasis on rationalism, it has yet to sufficiently incorporate findings from international political economy, particularly the liberal institutionalist thinking that emphasizes the centrality of institutions in explaining migration policy outcomes. One such avenue for thinking is the concept of *interdependence* (Cooper 1972), particularly in its application on international trade relations by Keohane and Nye (Keohane and Nye 1987). For the two scholars, the effects of interdependence work alongside multilateralism and international institutions to promote global cooperation. The rationale was that a new world economic order built alongside interdependence, trade, and investment would align with national interests while bringing states closer together.

Although Keohane and Nye did not discuss migration in their research, I have defined *migration interdependence* as "the reciprocal political economy effects arising from cross-border flows of people between a sending and host state" (Tsourapas 2018), developing an alternative argument around its coercive potential: focusing on the Middle East, I demonstrated how the concept of migration interdependence allows us to rethink power relations across Arab states—in fact, I demonstrated how two ostensibly-weaker states (Libya and Jordan) were able to apply pressure on an ostensibly-stronger state (Egypt) and force it into specific policy shifts. In short, this was due to Egypt's vulnerability to migration interdependence (in particular, the Egyptian economy's dependence on remittances from Libya and Jordan), which was exploited by two Arab countries of destination (Libya and Jordan). In a joint piece with Malit, we have further applied the concept of migration interdependence to the Gulf Cooperation Council (GCC) states (Malit and Tsourapas 2021): again, we demonstrated two strong Arab states, Kuwait and the United Arab Emirates, were vulnerable to migration intercedence vis-à-vis a weaker state, the Philippines, and how the latter exploited this vulnerability to force certain policy changes on Filipino domestic workers. Yet, beyond serving as a force of coercion and leverage, may migration interdependence also allow for cooperation across states, as Keohane and Nye originally envisaged?

The Gulf Cooperation Council as a case study in migration interdependence

We trace Gulf migration interdependence as taking place both top-down, in terms of a variety of legal and political initiatives, as well as bottom-up by Gulf citizens themselves. In terms of the former, freedom of movement across GCC nationals was included in the founding documents of the Council and constitutes one of the group's demonstrable successes in terms of regional integration. An analysis of the GCC Charter, in terms of the 1981 Unified Economic Agreement, demonstrate the six member states' commitment to "agree on executive principles to ensure that each member state shall grant the citizens of all other member states the same treatment as is granted to its own citizens without any discrimination of differentiation," with the first field in which this was applied being "freedom of movement, work and residence" (Article 8). The overarching goal of achieving "Gulf citizenship, including equality of treatment in the exercise of their rights to movement, residence, work, investment, education, health and social services," was reiterated in the 2001 New Economic Agreement, with Article 16 stating that:

> Member States shall undertake the policies necessary to develop and unify their labor rules and legislation, eliminate all obstacles restricting intra-GCC movement of national labor force. GCC citizens working in a member State other than their countries of citizenship shall be included within the percentages set for manpower nationalization.

The decision to facilitate freedom of movement, first implemented in 1981 and reinforced in 2001, has had profound implications for regional cooperation. It has not only strengthened ties among member states but also set the stage for further initiatives promoting intra-regional mobility. At the same time, as per the expectations of liberal understandings of migration interdependence, the opportunity of GCC citizens to engage in employment across the six states contributed to top-down coordination on labor, which is

Table 3.1. GCC-Wide Policy Agreements Regarding Citizens' Mobility (Ibrahim 2010)

1981	The GCC Council Economic Agreement	Similar regulations that guarantee equal treatment of movement, work, residence and inheritance
1993	The GCC Supreme Council Summit	Equal treatment of GCC citizens in the private sector
1995	The GCC Supreme Council	Statute to facilitate employment and free movement
1996	The GCC Supreme Council Announcement	Equal treatment of GCC nationals working in the private sector re-emphasized
1997	The Supreme Council Summit	Priorities in employment of GCC nationals
1998	The Supreme Council Summit	Mandate of the Supreme Council to conduct a study on the employment of national manpower and facilitate their intra-GCC movement
2001	The GCC Council unified Economic Agreement	Re-emphasize and extend the national treatment of GCC nationals in movement, residence and employment.
		Removal of national labor mobility barriers, GCC nationals are considered part of the nationalization targets
		No discrimination in pursuing professions among GCC nationals
		Coordination among GCC states to achieve Human Resource Development and employment
2002	The Supreme Council Summit	Equal GCC employment treatment stressed and implementation by 2005 at the latest
2003	The GCC Supreme Council Summit	Emphasized the timetable and the fields of equal treatment in both private and government sectors' employment and the full economic nationalization
2003	The Consultative Authority of the GCC Council	Study of the ways to ensure easy movement of national labor among GCC states.
2004	Announcement by GCC States	Measures announced to facilitate employment and movement of nationals such as ease of travel and border formalities
2004	The GCC Supreme Council Summit	Extension of umbrella of insurance protection to those GCC nationals working in other GCC states in both private and public sector in a more comprehensive way through a unified system from January 2005, optionally, and made obligatory from January 2006.

expected to produce spillover effects across other sectors. As per an earlier study on this by Ibrahim for the International Organization for Migration (2010), GCC states were tasked with coordinating policymaking across several issues related to mobility between 1981 and 2010 (Table 3.1).
Zahra Babar's (2011) analysis highlights the significant progress made in this area. For instance, GCC protocols have abolished visa requirements and entry permits for member-state citizens, allowing nationals to travel freely using only their national identification cards. Some states, like Bahrain and Qatar, have further streamlined this process by introducing multi-purpose smart cards that serve as travel documents at electronic gates in airports and border checkpoints. Future initiatives under discussion include a unified GCC passport and a joint tourist visa, which could enhance mobility for both nationals and expatriates.

Significant progress has also been made in ensuring equal employment rights across the region. In 1993, the GCC Supreme Council passed a resolution granting nationals equal access to private-sector employment across member states. By 2005, these rights were extended to the public sector, with directives urging governments to prioritize GCC nationals over non-GCC workers. Ministries of Labor and Social Affairs have actively implemented these policies, submitting annual progress reports to the Supreme Council to monitor advancements and identify challenges. A critical component of this integration is the assurance that GCC nationals working in other member states retain their social benefits. To this end, the GCC Supreme Council has developed mechanisms to extend social insurance and pension coverage across borders. A pivotal resolution passed in 2004 ensures that nationals employed in other GCC states receive the same social security benefits as they would at home, safeguarding their financial security and promoting labor mobility.

Over the years, the GCC has expanded the economic and professional opportunities available to its nationals, as would be expected from migration interdependence, producing multiple spillover effects. Early restrictions limited the types of businesses and professions that citizens could pursue outside their home countries. However, successive resolutions gradually lifted these barriers, culminating in the launch of the GCC Common Market (CM) in 2008, which institutionalized the principles of migration interdependence by providing a platform for the free movement of labor, goods, and capital. The CM underscores the importance of mutual economic reliance by allowing GCC citizens to work and invest in any member state under equal conditions. This liberalization enhances the region's collective economic resilience and bargaining power on the global stage, demonstrating how interdependent labor mobility can drive broader economic objectives. This market allows nearly unrestricted economic participation, enabling GCC nationals to own property, operate businesses, and practice professions across the region with minimal restrictions. The GCC has also made significant strides in education and professional accreditation. Protocols ensuring the mutual recognition of qualifications enable professionals to work seamlessly across member states without needing additional certification. Similarly, procedures for students to pursue higher education outside their home states have been simplified, fostering the development of a regionally integrated knowledge base (Fargues 2018). These initiatives collectively reflect the GCC's ongoing efforts to promote deeper economic and social integration, while ensuring that its citizens benefit from enhanced mobility and equal opportunities across the region.

By granting GCC nationals rights to freedom of movement, residence, and employment across borders, these agreements create a region-wide labor market. This legal infrastructure promotes mutual reliance, enabling member states to share and optimize human resources while addressing labor shortages in critical sectors. Migration interdependence fosters economic integration by facilitating the exchange of skills and labor, which enhances productivity and competitiveness across the region. Chapter 5 of the 2001 Economic Agreement outlines cooperative strategies for capacity building, emphasizing the collective responsibility to develop a skilled and adaptable workforce. These initiatives ensure that GCC nationals can leverage the opportunities afforded by the region's integrated labor market, thus reinforcing the economic interdependence between member states. Migration interdependence also plays a stabilizing role in the region by mitigating economic disparities among member states. By allowing labor to flow where it is most needed, the GCC reduces unemployment in labor-abundant states and fills critical skill gaps in labor-scarce states. This not only strengthens economic ties but also increases the political and economic costs of regional antagonism, fostering a cooperative environment conducive to sustained growth and stability. In sum, the GCC's approach to labor mobility exemplifies the productive potential of migration interdependence. By embedding mobility within its broader framework of economic integration, the region has crafted a model where the success of individual member states is deeply connected to the collective prosperity of the Gulf. Overall, Gulf migration interdependence serves as a cornerstone for achieving the GCC's long-term goals of economic diversification and resilience.

An often-overlooked aspect of GCC migration interdependence is its bottom-up dimension, where intra-national labor mobility serves as a mechanism to maintain and reinforce cross-border ties among large families and tribes (Lackner 1978). These networks have historically spanned the

Gulf region, with their social, economic, and cultural significance enduring despite the emergence of formal nation-states. The formation of Gulf states and the establishment of national borders in the mid-twentieth century, particularly following the independence of the Trucial States in the 1970s, marked a turning point in regional geopolitics (Gause 2009). However, these political boundaries often did not align with the historical realities of tribal and familial movements. As Vassiliev (1998) and Jureidini (2019) emphasize, the Gulf region has long been characterized by fluid borders, with tribes and families maintaining networks that extended across vast territories. These connections were vital for trade, labor exchange, and mutual support in the harsh environmental and economic conditions of the region.

The creation of new national boundaries meant that many tribal and family members suddenly found themselves citizens of different states. Yet, the social and economic functions of these networks remained unchanged, as mobility between states continued to be essential for preserving their cohesion and ensuring their livelihoods. The introduction of GCC-wide policies that prohibit discrimination among citizens across member states has played a crucial role in institutionalizing this historical mobility. By granting GCC nationals equal rights to live, work, and engage in economic activities in any member state, these policies have effectively preserved and even strengthened tribal and familial networks.

This legal framework aligns with the traditional norms of the Gulf, where kinship and tribal affiliations often supersede national identities. As Al-Etaibi (2022) highlights, tribal identities have historically functioned as transnational entities, capable of shaping regional politics and foreign policy. The resilience of these ties underscores their role as a form of transnational identity, bridging the political boundaries that emerged during state formation. The formal recognition of these ties through labor mobility rights has allowed tribal members to continue their historical patterns of cooperation, trade, and mutual support without being hindered by modern state boundaries.

The continuation of these cross-border networks through labor mobility has several important implications. Firstly, economic integration is fostered as tribal and familial ties facilitate the efficient distribution of labor across the Gulf. Members of the same tribe or family can seek employment in regions with the greatest demand, thereby contributing to the economic stability of both sending and receiving states. This movement helps balance labor market disparities within the GCC and supports the region's broader economic integration. Secondly, social cohesion also benefits, given that, beyond economics, these networks play a vital role in maintaining social ties. Tribal and familial bonds provide a support system that helps individuals navigate the challenges of living and working in different states. This cohesion is especially important in a region where tribal identity remains a cornerstone of social structure and cultural continuity. Finally, cultural continuity emerges as a result of such labor mobility. The preservation of these ties also ensures the transmission of cultural values and practices that have defined Gulf societies for generations. Mobility allows for the continued celebration of shared traditions, reinforcing a collective Gulf identity that transcends national borders.

While the institutional support for intra-GCC labor mobility strengthens tribal and familial ties, challenges remain. Economic disparities between member states and differences in living standards can sometimes hinder the full potential of these networks. Additionally, varying degrees of political and social stability across the Gulf may affect the willingness or ability of individuals to migrate. Nevertheless, the unique interplay between top-down policies and bottom-up tribal dynamics offers a powerful model for migration interdependence. It not only fosters economic and social integration but also highlights the resilience of traditional networks in adapting to modern political realities.

The bottom-up dimension of GCC migration interdependence underscores the enduring importance of tribal and familial networks in the Gulf. By institutionalizing these connections through policies that promote labor mobility, the GCC not only preserves its cultural heritage but also strengthens its economic and social fabric. This dynamic offers valuable insights into how regional cooperation can coexist with and enhance deeply rooted social structures.

Relatedly, a significant but underexamined aspect of GCC migration interdependence is its role in facilitating cross-border intermarriages, which serve as a vital mechanism for social and cultural integration. The ability of GCC citizens to freely reside and work in any member state not only strengthens economic ties but also fosters a sense of shared identity, commonly referred to as "Khaleeji" identity. Intermarriages between nationals of different GCC countries often act as a catalyst for cross-border mobility, both historically and currently. For Weiner,

> [t]he transnational nature of kinship groups also has important economic implications. In the pre-oil period, brothers from merchant families sometimes migrated to different cities in order to find good economic conditions. Today, these brothers and their descendants form a transnational network for economic collaboration. The existence of transnational family businesses integrates the regional Gulf economy, especially since many of these businesses are quite successful.
>
> (Weiner 2016)

For example, a Saudi man married to an Emirati woman may choose to settle in Dubai, where both partners are eligible to work and enjoy the same legal rights as local citizens. Similarly, an Omani woman married to a Bahraini man could move to Bahrain, where she can access employment and social services. These arrangements are facilitated by the GCC's freedom of mobility policies, which ensure that both partners can pursue career opportunities and access benefits such as healthcare and education in either state. Over time, such mobility contributes to the blending of national identities and promotes a stronger sense of regional belonging. Intermarried couples often establish family networks that span multiple countries, encouraging frequent travel and communication between their states of origin. This creates deeper interpersonal ties that transcend national borders, reinforcing the social fabric of the Gulf as a unified region. These cross-border family connections can also mitigate social divisions, as the next generation grows up identifying not just with one nation but with the broader Khaleeji identity. The intermingling of younger generations, facilitated by policies enabling labor mobility and intermarriage, plays a pivotal role in fostering a sense of shared identity. Younger GCC citizens often interact with peers from other member states through educational exchanges, regional sports, cultural festivals, and the workplace. These interactions can reshape how they perceive their national identity, encouraging them to see themselves as part of a larger Gulf community.

Furthermore, kinship networks demonstrate a remarkable adaptability to changing socio-economic contexts. In periods of economic uncertainty, they tend to emphasize broader tribal affiliations to maintain solidarity and access to shared resources, across borders. Conversely, during times of prosperity, they may highlight narrower familial identities to preserve exclusivity and consolidate power. As Weiner notes:

> Kinship groups adapt their tribal presentation in response to specific challenges. As groups grow more successful, powerful, or affluent, they tend to emphasize the smaller beit category to preserve exclusivity. In times of uncertainty, including with the current economic challenges facing the region, these same groups tend to emphasize belonging in the broader tribal group.
>
> (Weiner 2016)

This dual strategy reinforces their role as stabilizing agents in the region, capable of navigating both crises and opportunities.

While more research is needed to quantify the extent to which this phenomenon influences national identity, the cultural exchanges enabled by migration interdependence have the potential to dilute rigid national distinctions and nurture a more inclusive regional identity. Despite the advantages, challenges persist. Some GCC citizens may still experience subtle disadvantages when working in another member state, particularly in terms of career advancement or accessing state-specific benefits like favorable loans. However, the long-term benefits of fostering cross-border familial ties often outweigh these limitations. By facilitating intermarriage and mobility, GCC policies lay the groundwork for greater social cohesion and mutual understanding among Gulf nationals. Migration interdependence, particularly through the facilitation of intermarriage, is a key driver in the evolution of a shared Khaleeji identity. By enabling GCC nationals to live and work freely across borders, the region not only strengthens economic integration but also fosters deeper cultural and social ties. Over time, these dynamics could play a transformative role in shaping the collective identity of the Gulf as a more interconnected and cohesive entity.

Fostering Gulf migration interdependence and Saudi Vision 2030: A strategic nexus?

Saudi Vision 2030 seeks to position the Kingdom as a hub of economic innovation and sustainable development, with regional cooperation as a cornerstone. This contribution argues that, at the heart of this strategy is Gulf migration interdependence, which emphasizes the reciprocal benefits of labor and talent mobility across the Gulf. This form of interdependence aligns closely with Vision 2030's objectives, leveraging regional human and financial capital to drive Saudi Arabia's economic transformation and resilience. Gulf migration interdependence fosters economic diversification by creating a dynamic labor market that transcends national boundaries and complements Vision 2030's diversification goals. Sectors like technology, tourism, and finance rely on access to a highly skilled and adaptable workforce. By enhancing migration interdependence, Saudi Arabia can attract top talent from other GCC states, while simultaneously providing its citizens with opportunities to gain experience and skills abroad. This reciprocal flow of talent ensures that the Kingdom benefits from innovative ideas and practices across the region, accelerating its transition to a knowledge-based economy.

Vision 2030 emphasizes the development of human capital through advanced education and training programs. Migration interdependence facilitates the sharing of educational resources and workforce development initiatives across the GCC. For instance, Saudi nationals can access specialized training in neighboring countries, while professionals from the Gulf contribute to the Kingdom's growing demand for expertise in emerging industries. This interdependence also promotes the regional coordination of human resource strategies, ensuring that the collective Gulf workforce is equipped to meet future economic challenges.

A central tenet of migration interdependence is its role in fostering regional stability by embedding economic and labor ties among Gulf states. Vision 2030 recognizes that regional cooperation is vital for sustainable growth. By deepening migration interdependence, Saudi Arabia helps create a network of mutual economic reliance, which reduces the potential for conflict and enhances collective resilience to external shocks. This interconnectedness raises the economic costs of regional antagonism, promoting a cooperative environment that supports Vision 2030's broader goals of stability and prosperity. Migration interdependence also plays a crucial role in nurturing a vibrant ecosystem of innovation and entrepreneurship. Vision 2030 seeks to establish Saudi Arabia as a leader in technological advancement and business development. By facilitating the movement of entrepreneurs and investors across Gulf borders, the Kingdom benefits from a larger pool of creative and financial resources. Additionally, the integration of entrepreneurial activities across the region supports the growth of startups and small businesses, providing opportunities for collaboration and scaling within a unified market.

Finally, Saudi Vision 2030's commitment to sustainability is arguably reinforced by Gulf migration interdependence, which enables the pooling of expertise and labor for large-scale sustainable development projects. From renewable energy initiatives to advanced infrastructure and environmental management, the Kingdom can draw on the diverse capabilities of the Gulf workforce to meet its ambitious sustainability targets. The regional exchange of knowledge and resources, facilitated by migration interdependence, ensures that these projects benefit from the best practices and innovations available within the Gulf.

However, there remain unexplored possibilities: Gulf migration interdependence plays a crucial role in mitigating regional conflicts. By institutionalizing the free movement of labor, capital, and citizens across borders, the GCC has created a framework where the political economy costs of antagonism are significantly heightened. This interconnectedness acts as a stabilizing force, reducing the likelihood of prolonged regional crises. In the Gulf context, the liberalization of labor markets and cross-border economic activities has tightly woven the economies of member states together. This integration means that any political action disrupting the free flow of goods, services, or labor would have immediate and tangible economic repercussions. Transnational family businesses and cross-border investments, for example, could face significant losses in the event of a regional standoff. Thus, the economic incentives for maintaining cooperative relationships are greatly amplified.

Beyond economic considerations, the human cost of disrupting intra-GCC mobility further discourages sustained conflicts. As noted in instances such as the 2017 Gulf Crisis, measures like travel bans and expulsions of nationals not only severed business ties but also inflicted deep social wounds. Many GCC families have members spread across different states, and abrupt disruptions to their mobility imposed significant emotional and social strains. The resulting backlash underscored the value of maintaining open borders, not just for economic prosperity but for social cohesion. The institutional framework supporting intra-GCC mobility, including protocols on equal treatment in employment, social benefits, and mutual recognition of qualifications, also acts as a conflict deterrent. These agreements are rooted in collective decision-making, requiring cooperation at both the state and sub-state levels. Any attempt to unilaterally undermine these frameworks would risk eroding the trust and collaborative mechanisms that underpin the GCC as a regional bloc. Furthermore, the shared management of labor markets and social benefits, such as pension and insurance portability, means that member states have a vested interest in maintaining stable relationships. Disrupting these systems could lead to administrative chaos and financial losses, further disincentivizing confrontations.

By embedding economic and social ties within its institutional framework, the GCC has created a regional environment where the costs of antagonism outweigh potential gains. The ability of Gulf states to navigate political disputes without long-term disruption to their economic and social systems highlights the role of migration interdependence in conflict prevention. This model of integration not only strengthens the resilience of the GCC but also serves as a potential blueprint for other regions seeking to balance national sovereignty with economic and political cooperation. It underscores how deeply embedded ties—rooted in both policy and practice—can act as a stabilizing force in a politically volatile region. Despite its challenges, Gulf migration interdependence extends beyond fostering a shared identity; it plays a pivotal role in reducing the likelihood of sustained conflicts by increasing the economic and social costs of regional antagonism. Through its framework of open borders and institutionalized cooperation, the GCC has created a system where mutual reliance acts as a deterrent to conflict, promoting long-term regional stability.

Looking forward—challenges and opportunities in Gulf migration interdependence

Saudi Vision 2030 aims to transform the Kingdom into a diversified, sustainable economy with a dynamic and competitive labor market. Central to achieving this vision is the concept of migration interdependence, which emphasizes the reciprocal flow of labor and talent across the Gulf Cooperation Council (GCC). Still, despite these promising avenues for the interplay between migration and Vision 2030, questions remain about the effectiveness of policy implementation. The absence of robust supranational mechanisms for data collection and tracking the movement of GCC nationals complicates efforts to assess the true impact of these initiatives. Without comprehensive data, it is challenging to determine the extent to which citizens are leveraging these freedoms for employment, residence, and business purposes. This data gap poses a methodological constraint in evaluating the GCC's success in fostering regional integration. The GCC has made remarkable progress in removing barriers to intra-regional mobility, creating a framework that supports the free movement of citizens and equal access to economic opportunities. However, to fully capitalize on these initiatives, member states must address implementation challenges and establish more effective data collection systems. Strengthening these aspects will not only enhance regional integration but also ensure that the benefits of mobility are equitably realized across the Gulf.

For one, while Gul migration interdependence strengthens the evolution of a regional, "*khaleeji*" identity, in top-down and bottom-up manners, the numbers of GCC citizens that choose to relocate to another country continues to be relatively small compared to the number of non-GCC immigrants across the six states (see Table 3.2 on GCC citizens living in Saudi Arabia), a focus merely on migrant stock reveals a limited part of the picture: for instance, we are unable to currently estimate these 85,972 citizens' wages; wage differentials between citizens and non-citizens should feature into any attempt to understand the aggregate contribution of GCC citizens' contribution to the Saudi economy, which is much more significant than Table 3.2 suggests.

A critical challenge lies in the structural segmentation of GCC labor markets. While Vision 2030 emphasizes the development of a skilled and competitive Saudi workforce, the region continues to face a supply-demand mismatch. The majority of GCC nationals, including Saudis, graduate in fields like education, social sciences, and Islamic studies, leading to an oversupply in these areas. Meanwhile, technical fields such as engineering, healthcare, and information technology, which are vital for Vision 2030's diversification strategy, suffer from a shortage of qualified professionals. This mismatch limits the potential for labor mobility within the region and slows

Table 3.2. GCC Citizens Residing in Saudi Arabia (2023)

Kuwait	50,282
Bahrain	16,652
United Arab Emirates	8,317
Qatar	7,063
Oman	3,658
Total	85,972

Source: General Authority for Statistics (GASTAT). 2022. Saudi Census 2022. Riyadh: Kingdom of Saudi Arabia. https://perma.cc/JYR3-8PTF

down efforts to build a future-ready workforce. Vision 2030 seeks to foster greater mobility of talent within the region, yet deeply ingrained cultural norms present a significant barrier. Strong familial and social ties often discourage Saudi and other GCC nationals from seeking employment opportunities in neighboring states, even when such opportunities align with their skills and career goals. The importance of proximity to family and familiarity with local customs limits the willingness of individuals to relocate, thereby restricting the benefits of migration interdependence.

Economic considerations also complicate migration interdependence. Many Saudi nationals are reluctant to pursue opportunities in other GCC states due to the risk of losing valuable government benefits, such as subsidized housing, social insurance, and low-interest loans. Moreover, disparities in living costs across the GCC, particularly between high-cost states like Qatar and the UAE and more affordable regions such as Oman or Bahrain, further disincentivize cross-border mobility. These disparities undermine Vision 2030's objective of creating a seamless and integrated regional labor market. Despite the GCC's efforts to harmonize labor policies, regulatory and institutional differences persist. Vision 2030 aims to streamline labor market regulations to enhance mobility and economic efficiency. However, inconsistent wage structures, employment protections, and social benefits across member states complicate the movement of workers. Additionally, labor markets remain heavily influenced by government spending, which dampens the market-driven adjustments needed to foster regional labor mobility and adapt to economic changes.

Vision 2030 recognizes the importance of regional cooperation but is constrained by the absence of robust infrastructure to facilitate cross-border employment. Although GCC agreements provide for labor mobility, implementation has been weak. The establishment of supranational employment bureaus or manpower agencies, which could actively assist GCC nationals in finding jobs across borders, remains a critical yet unmet need. These agencies could provide essential services such as job matching, skills training, and relocation support, thus operationalizing the migration interdependence envisioned by Vision 2030. Vision 2030's success depends on creating a competitive environment that attracts and retains talent. However, variations in living standards and costs across GCC states present practical barriers. For example, while salaries in Qatar or the UAE may be attractive, higher costs of housing and services often negate the financial benefits of relocation. This imbalance discourages mobility and limits the regional integration necessary for Vision 2030's labor market goals.

The challenges of migration interdependence pose significant obstacles to Saudi Vision 2030. Overcoming these barriers requires coordinated regional efforts to align labor policies, enhance employment infrastructure, and address socio-cultural norms. By tackling these challenges, Saudi Arabia can unlock the full potential of migration interdependence, driving economic diversification, innovation, and sustainable growth across the Gulf region.

Conclusion

The analysis of Gulf migration interdependence reveals its dual role in fostering both economic integration and socio-political stability within the GCC. By institutionalizing labor mobility through a robust legal framework, the GCC has created a dynamic environment where member states mutually benefit from shared resources and expertise. This interdependence supports economic diversification, enhances human capital, and mitigates labor market disparities, aligning closely with Saudi Vision 2030's objectives. Beyond economic advantages, migration interdependence strengthens regional cohesion, as intra-GCC mobility fosters cultural continuity and reinforces transnational family and tribal networks. These connections not only support social integration but also serve as a stabilizing force in the face of political tensions. The cooperative framework arguably underpins a collective resilience that enhances the Gulf's capacity to navigate external shocks and sustain long-term growth.

However, realizing the full potential of migration interdependence requires addressing key challenges, including disparities in labor policies, cultural norms that discourage mobility, and economic inequalities among member states. Enhanced data collection and the establishment of supranational employment bureaus could further streamline labor mobility, while targeted reforms could reduce regulatory inconsistencies. Additionally, fostering a shared regional identity through increased mobility and cross-border integration will be crucial for sustaining cooperation. As Saudi Arabia continues to advance its Vision 2030 agenda, leveraging migration interdependence offers a strategic pathway to achieve its goals of economic transformation and regional leadership. By building on the foundation of mutual reliance, the Kingdom can position itself as a central player in promoting a more integrated, resilient, and prosperous Gulf.

Bibliography

Adamson, Fiona B., and Gerasimos Tsourapas. 2019. "Migration Diplomacy in World Politics." *International Studies Perspectives* 20 (2): 113–28.

Al-Etaibi, Abdulla. 2022. "Transnational Identity and Foreign Policy: Tribal Identity and the Gulf Crisis." *Journal of Arabian Studies* 12 (1): 84–102. https://doi.org/10.1080/21534764.2022.2225669.

Babar, Zahra. 2011. "Free Mobility within the Gulf Cooperation Council." *CIRS Occasional Papers*.

Cooper, Richard N. 1972. "Economic Interdependence and Foreign Policy in the Seventies." *World Politics* 24 (2): 159–81. https://doi.org/10.2307/2009735.

Fargues, Philippe. 2018. "Shaping Smart Societies: How Migration and Education Policies Meet in the Gulf States." In *Migration to the Gulf: Policies in Sending and Receiving Countries*, edited by Philippe Fargues and Nasra M. Shah. Cambridge: Gulf Research Centre.

Fernández-Molina, Irene, and Gerasimos Tsourapas. 2024. "Understanding Migration Power in International Studies." *International Affairs* 100 (6): 2461–79. https://doi.org/10.1093/ia/iiae230.

Gamlen, Alan. 2019. *Human Geopolitics: States, Emigrants, and the Rise of Diaspora Institutions*. Oxford: Oxford University Press.

Gause, F. Gregory III. 2009. *The International Relations of the Persian Gulf*. Cambridge: Cambridge University Press. https://doi.org/10.1017/CBO9780511818264.

Geddes, Andrew, Marcia Vera Espinoza, Leila Hadj Abdou, and Leiza Brumat. 2019. *The Dynamics of Regional Migration Governance*. Cheltenham: Edward Elgar Publishing.

Greenhill, Kelly M. 2010. *Weapons of Mass Migration - Forced Displacement, Coercion, and Foreign Policy*. Ithaca, NY: Cornell University Press.

Hirschman, Albert O. 1945. *National Power and the Structure of Foreign Trade*. Berkeley: University of California Press.

Hollifield, James F. 2012. "Migration and International Relations." In *The Oxford Handbook of The Politics of International Migration*, edited by Marc R. Rosenblum and Daniel J. Tichenor, 345–82. Oxford: Oxford University Press.

Hollifield, James F., Philip Martin, and Pia Orrenius, eds. 2022. *Controlling Immigration: A Global Perspective*. 4th ed. Stanford: Stanford University Press.

Ibrahim, Badr El Din A. 2010. "Intra-National Labour Mobility among the Arab Gulf Cooperation Council States in the Context of the Financial Crisis And the Gulf Monetary Union." In *Intra-Regional Labour Mobility in the Arab World*. Cairo: International Organization for Migration.

Jureidini, R. 2019. "Global Governance and Labour Migration in the GCC." In *Global Governance and Muslim Organizations*, edited by L.A. Pal and M.E. Tok, International Political Economy Series. Cham: Palgrave Macmillan. https://doi.org/10.1007/978-3-319-92561-5_14

Kechichian, Joseph A., and Fahad Alsharif. 2022. *Sa'udi Policies Towards Migrants and Refugees: A Sacred Duty*. Chicago, IL: Sussex Academic Press.

Keohane, Robert Owen, and Joseph S. Nye. 1987. "Power and Interdependence Revisited." *International Organization* 41 (4): 725–53.

Lackner, Helen. 1978. *A House Built on Sand: A Political Economy of Saudi Arabia*. London: Ithaca Press.

Malit, Froilan T, and Gerasimos Tsourapas. 2021. "Weapons of the Weak? South–South Migration and Power Politics in the Philippines–GCC Corridor." *Global Studies Quarterly* 1 (3): ksab010. https://doi.org/10.1093/isagsq/ksab010.

Thiollet, Hélène. 2011. "Migration as Diplomacy: Labor Migrants, Refugees, and Arab Regional Politics in the Oil-Rich Countries." *International Labor and Working-Class History* 79 (1): 103–21.

Tolay, Juliette. 2023. "Interrogating and Broadening the Emerging Narrative on Migration Diplomacy: A Critical Assessment." *Millennium: Journal of International Studies*, March. http://journals.sagepub.com/doi/10.1177/03058298221139589.

Tsourapas, Gerasimos. 2017. "Migration Diplomacy in the Global South: Cooperation, Coercion and Issue Linkage in Gaddafi's Libya." *Third World Quarterly* 38 (10): 2367–85.

Tsourapas, Gerasimos. 2018. "Labor Migrants as Political Leverage: Migration Interdependence and Coercion in the Mediterranean." *International Studies Quarterly* 62 (2): 383–95.

Tsourapas, Gerasimos. 2019. "Migration Interdependence in the Post-Arab Spring Middle East." In *The Dynamics of Regional Migration Governance*, edited by Andrew Geddes, Marcia Vera Espinoza, Leila Hadj-Abdou, and Leiza Brumat, 128–46. Northampton, MA: Edward Elgar Publishing.

Vassiliev, Alexei. 1998. *The History of Saudi Arabia*. London: Saqi Press.

Weiner, Myron. 1985. "On International Migration and International Relations." *Population and Development Review*, 441–55.

Weiner, Scott J. 2016. *Kinship Politics in the Gulf Arab States*. Washington, DC: The Arab Gulf States Institute in Washington.

Zolberg, Aristide R. 1981. "International Migrations in Political Perspective." In *Global Trends in Migration: Theory and Research on International Population Movements*, edited by Mary M. Kritz, Charles B. Keely, and Silvano M. Tomasi, 3–27. New York: Center for Migration Studies.

Part Two

Skilled Migration, Economic Diversification, and Sustainable Development in Saudi Arabia

4

The Working Experiences of Highly Skilled Migrants in the Kingdom of Saudi Arabia: A Relational Perspective

Shroug Saud Alotaibi

Introduction

The Kingdom of Saudi Arabia (KSA) is an economy in transition and diversification, driven by its ambitious national Vision 2030 strategy. National prosperity, once based on oil dependency, will be replaced by a knowledge-based economy. Central to this transformation is the human capital of Saudi nationals and the supplemented skills of high-skilled migrant workers (HSMWs) to close the well-known KSA workforce skills gaps. As the country invests in new services, innovation, and technology, the demand for skilled professionals across all "knowledge" sectors becomes increasingly critical (Saudi Vision 2030, 2016).

The global competition for talent, and persistent labor shortages, has intensified the policies to attract skilled workers to the region (Michaels et al., 2001), whilst KSA investments have been made to develop national talent to meet skills gaps (domestic expertise), but this is a slower process than recruiting from international talent pools to fill immediate needs. HSMWs are now essential to the Kingdom's pursuit of economic diversification and long-term sustainable growth (Guo and Al Ariss, 2015), yet studies in this subject are few and largely dominated by unskilled migrant experiences (Khraif et al., 2019).

The Gulf Cooperation Council (GCC) countries have traditionally relied on migrant labor (construction and domestic work), but these roles are nearly redundant in a knowledge-driven economy, where workers with "know-how," tertiary education, and specialized skills are critical to national innovation and competitiveness. Such workers, due to excessive demand and restricted supply, can be more selective in which regions they choose to relocate to (in 2013, the OECD estimated a 70 percent increase in demand for such migrants between 2001 and 2010, showing the imbalance of demand to supply). However, it is important to note that the Global Commission on

International Migration (GCIM, 2005) emphasized that both high-skilled and low-skilled workers remain essential for the production of goods and services.[1] The Saudi Vision 2030 identifies the substantial development of education, healthcare, and technology to support the knowledge economy transition and address key gaps in the national workforce skill sets (Tharenou and Kulik, 2020).

Despite the increasing significance of skilled migrants, research on their experiences in the KSA remains limited in comparison to major host nations (the United States, Australia, and Germany; Almeida et al., 2015). Existing literature, from unskilled labor accounts (Adham, 2023; Alogla, 1990), portrays the traditional kafala system (sponsorship system) as imbalanced, where a national sponsor "feels" and migrant workers have an unequal and potentially exploitative relationship (Alshahrani and Morley, 2015). Such exploitation for HSMWs is unviable as they can simply relocate to other economies that will value their skills and provide better work-life conditions.

This chapter addresses the academic knowledge gap, using Syed and Özbilgin (2009) and a relational framework, to examine the macro-national, meso-organizational, and micro-level influences that shape the modern employment context for HSMWs in the KSA. The pioneering and holistic approach explores migrant working experiences and professional contributions to the Saudi economy. Table 4.1 provides a summary of the holistic influences addressed by the research. The chapter will explore the key question of "What are the experiences of HSMWs working in the KSA?"

Methodology

An inductive epistemology of qualitative and context-rich methods was designed for this perceptual study of HSMWs. The research gap emerged from a traditional literature review (Crowley⊠Henry et al., 2018; Tharenou and Kulik, 2020) and exposed a significant void of studies involving HSMWs (internationally) and also in the context of the KSA. Purposively selected KSA/international professional and academic experts validated the focus and methods of the study. Twenty-three interviews (fifteen HSMW and eight Saudi HRM professionals/academics/ employment lawyers) were conducted. Semi-structured interviews (in Arabic and English) were used to capture informant perceptions, which were audio-recorded, transcribed, and analysed.

Table 4.2 shows the demographic characteristics of the interview informants. The responses were analysed using thematic analysis (NVivo software) and analysed in both the Arabic and English languages by the researcher (fluent in both), so nuances could be detected and explored.

Table 4.1. The Holistic and Relational Approach to HSMWs in the KSA

Level of Study	Definition	Existing Knowledge	New Insights of the Study and the KSA
Macro-level	National policies, relevant employment laws that shape the working and living experiences of HSMWs. Socio-cultural and religious norms, including practices, are also included. Islamic values and principles of strict family and tribal networks.	(Alshahrani and Morley, 2015; AlShehabi, 2021; Dito, 2015)	– HSMWs and the modern kafala sponsorship system. – Perception of migrants prior to and during employment. – Saudisation and dependent fees.
Meso-level	Organizational level focus on corporate identities, structures and procedures, including the role of HRM / practices for HSMWs integration.	(Afiouni et al., 2014; Farashah & Blomquist, 2020; Zikic, 2015)	– The interaction of the kafeel/HRM specialist and the HSMWs.
Micro-level	Work and life experiences for the individual HSMWs, including differences between groups of migrants (nationality, gender, skills, motivation to migrate).	(Alghadir et al., 2020; Cerdin et al., 2014; Rahman, 2018)	– Multifaceted Motivations Beyond Economic Gain. – Nationality-based Experience and Integration.

Source: The author (2024)

Findings

The three tiers of analysis (macro, meso, and micro) were framed using existing categorizations (Syed and Özbilgin, 2009) and new additions by the author.

Macro findings: Demand for HSMWs

The findings show the KSA skills gap has decreased (over the last five years), but HSMWs' dependency remains high. Whilst nationals seek employment

Table 4.2. The Demographics of Informants

No.	Professional Expertise	Gender	Nationality
1	Nurse	Female	Philippines
2	Nurse	Female	Indian
3	HR Associate Professor	Female	Pakistani
4	Business IT	Female	Yemeni
5	Accountant	Male	Sudanese
6	HR Consultant	Female	Egyptian
7	Public Relation	Female	Lebanese
8	HR Associate Professor	Female	Indian
9	Nurse	Female	Indian
10	Business Consultant	Male	Lebanese
11	Marketing Manager	Male	British
12	IT Manager	Male	Pakistani
13	Logistic Officer, Airforce	Male	British
14	Information System Assistant Professor	Male	Egyptian
15	Business Assistant Professor	Male	Gordini
Saudi	National Informants		
16	Business Assistant Professor	Male	Saudi
17	Law Consultant	Male	Saudi
18	Financial Manager	Female	Saudi
19	HR Associate Professor	Male	Saudi
20	Business Associate Professor	Male	Saudi
21	Innovation Manager	Male	Saudi
22	HR Associate Professor	Male	Saudi
23	Business Assistant Professor	Female	Saudi

Source: The author (2024).

in educational and medical establishments. IT, software development, programming, robotics, data analytics, operations and supply chain management, and project management are more typical for HSMWs. The finding shows there is demand, but in very specific employment settings for migrants where "mastery" of employment expertise is long and subject to significant tacit and explicit knowledge (Interviewee 13). The skills gap was confirmed by the interviews, and healthcare emerged as a sector of high demand (midwives and emergency department professionals in particular). Exploring nurse perceptions (Jeddah) unearthed a contradictory low perceived demand and exposed "location" as a potential modifier of attitudes. This study offers evidence that "local" supply conditions have regional differences and reliance levels on HSMWs. Further, urban locations (major conurbations where employers co-locate) and locations of government-owned health and care facilities suffered fewer HSMWs shortages and were prioritized as desired employers.

The study also found that certain migrant skillsets were generally perceived as "low demand," especially general nursing, where a competent national supply and nationals' preferences for employment in this sector existed. The finding reveals the "Saudization" rebalancing of the supply of nationals with competence (and career opportunities in the sector) has displaced HSMWs. The focus on educational and medical fields among Saudi nationals has consequently created shortages in other essential areas. Migrants, therefore, are required for increasingly specialized job contracts, which Participant 22 (an academic with HR specialist knowledge) summarized as "Saudis are concentrated on educational and medical jobs, and they left a gap on some jobs such as in factories, production, supply chain manager, and medical roles, so there is still a need for these skilled migrants."

Technology and IT sectors were also a contested professional field where both skilled migrants and Saudi specialists perceived demand-driven shortages (programmers, software developers, robotic engineers, IT developers, and data analysts). Shortages of national labor in these professions are recognized in the national Vision 2030. Informants proposed "convenient" migrant supply was being used to allow national skills and experienced professionals to develop and increase domestic availability. One Saudi expert participant proposed that the supply of KSA professionals remains "weak" and insufficient. This was a common pattern among all informants.

Experts in higher education with backgrounds in computer science, physics, and mathematics are currently experiencing significant demand. A Saudi HR academic noted, "Higher education institutes have the biggest skills gaps in the country." This informant hails from a rural city in the KSA.

Essentially, the Saudi experts commonly identified skills gaps that matched the Vision 2030 priorities in technology, veterinary medicine, manufacturing, and supply chains. In conclusion, the experts evidenced local talent shortages, pressure to meet the Vision 2030 framework and its goals, causing a reliance on skilled migrants and deficiencies in the regions rather than large metropolitan centers. The latter finding cannot be totally divorced from the intentions of migrants (city locations are often attractive places where formalized "best practice" HR management is practiced), whereas regions remain dominated by the kafeel (in the absence of HR specialists) who may not be so familiar with HR "best practices."

Participant 7 summarized the state of the nation by arguing that "There's always a need. You never stop needing those people ... they have different perceptions. They have different work skills, different visions. It is always good to have a diverse workplace and people who are creative to encourage good and healthy competition [in the country]."

With unanimous support, the interviewees supported the return of highly skilled Saudis from abroad (reintroduction of Saudis back to the KSA) and the proposed investments in education and training programs to enhance domestic workforce capabilities (increasing domestic supply and making migrants less economically attractive to employers). The explicit agreement for a reverse flow of migration is an interesting insight that foresees a growing pool of Saudi professionals who are well-equipped to meet the demands of domestic employers, as Participant 9 stated, "... when I came to Saudi Arabia, at that time, there was a lot of difference than today actually. Before, when I used to, there were not many bachelor's degree professionals. But now it's almost all [employees] everywhere, holding bachelor's degrees. So, I think they [employers] will not need more skilled migrants because they are already skilled and available."

The quote (from a nurse specialist) shows progress has been made in reducing HSMWs reliance, and they viewed this as a transitional period, as Saudi graduates may possess the knowledge, even though lacking in the experience needed for certain roles, which is a function of experiential time lag for the country. The finding shows that significant effort has been made on a national level to increase the skills pool of key professionals supplied by the national educational establishments, in areas that were traditional targets for migrants but now filled by trained Saudis with career promotions to senior positions from within their employer organizations. The finding is significant because it exposes a fundamental dimension of migrant work that is missing in modern research on the KSA—that is, the time lag between the training of nationals and these skilled nationals adopting key roles in the management structures of organizations. Such a temporal dimension has not been addressed widely by other studies (which focused on case studies) or research on short-term demand/supply contractions by a single employer rather than the deliberate actions of the government, national institution investments, and their consequences on the labor market and skills shortages. The vacuum of studies on training and education versus practical leadership and workplace experience was exposed by Participant 8, who contended, "Saudi PhD holders—they have the knowledge. But, as far as experience is concerned, they are lacking it. So, they need time to develop or to gain that experience ... So currently, [and] in the next five to six years, they do need the expats. But after that, when the local market is developed, they would fulfil the requirements. So, by that time, maybe they won't need all those expats."

Government regulations: Saudization and family fees

Interviews with both Saudi nationals and HSMWs frequently highlighted that the "Saudization" program faced limitations in effectively reducing the demand for migrant labor. Participants noted that the program was also perceived as excessively bureaucratic and costly. For instance, an increase in visa fee revenue (al-Rusoom) placed a financial burden on business owners, who are legally responsible for covering such fees. As a result, some employers reduced their demand for migrant workers, making the hiring of Saudi nationals a comparatively more affordable option. Additionally, the Human Resources Development Fund supports employers by subsidizing a portion of Saudi employees' salaries, further incentivizing local hiring (as explained by a Saudi legal consultant in an interview with participant 17).

The "Saudization" policy has significantly affected the employment landscape, particularly for HSMWs. Historically, prior to Saudization, migrant workers in HR posts contributed to the migrant inflow and frequently brought their families with them. Participant 17 argued, "The reason why Saudi hosted a huge number of migrants before is because HR positions were dominantly for migrants, so they used to bring their children and family and hire their relatives". This is one of the few studies to identify the Human Resources profession as directly linked to migration.

Some large "Saudi" companies operated with HR departments and managerial roles predominantly held by non-Saudis, and these, the informants identified, created barriers for Saudi citizens to access key positions. Participant 5 noted these dynamics and proposed, "Now, only Saudi citizens can work in HR management. There have been varied experiences, especially when these departments, many of which were filled with non-Saudis who showed favoritism towards certain nationalities or those in power."

The finding is an important insight into the skilled migrant system and shows that historically local discrimination often occurred when a certain nationality bias affected employment and controlled the recruitment processes even to the detriment of nationals. These actions are now forbidden under the "Saudization" process, yet informants (mainly second and third generation immigrants) still held this view. The current changes have therefore liberalized the employment system and allowed nationals to enter and, at the very least, challenge unfair and discriminatory HR practice. The informants also suggested that the nationals could and did now hold significant HR roles, and the system had become fairer but still had a potential for bias this time in favor of the national skilled applicants. The author reflected that this could lead to a form of retribution, but this was not possible to test. The requirement that all HR employees should be Saudi nationals limits the options available to qualified and experienced skilled migrants. The informants claimed that migrants with HR degrees (even from reputable Universities in the KSA) were unsuccessful applicants because of their nationality, which underscores the structural difficulties the non-Saudis face when trying to work in HR. Nonetheless, others have indicated a readiness to assist with HR tasks in an unofficial capacity, demonstrating a commitment to help in spite of legal restrictions. The latter would appear as a manipulation of the regulations, such that the person performs an HR task and process but does not enjoy the formal job title associated with the role.[2] The informant went further to warn that the practice was undertaken and the informant had experience of this but that careful attention was paid to ensure the practice was not detected by others and external auditors.

Another inconsistency was detected in the NETAQAT policy,[3] which demanded that a specific proportion of the national workforce must be nationals, thereby limiting the HSMWs. With reference to NETAQAT, the lack of domestic skills was a concern voiced by the majority of interviewees. Another Saudization paradox concerns Saudi-born, second and third-generation residents who still must pay visa fees despite their longstanding commitment to the KSA. These migrants perceived themselves as Saudi in essence but migrants by definition. Interviewee 6 stated, "I feel it is my country, the people around me are my people. Even if I went to my own country I wouldn't feel fit as much as I fit here."

The new kafala sponsorship system

The kafala sponsorship system elicits a wide range of perceptions among migrants. Previous studies primarily focused on low-skilled migrant workers (LSMWs) and often reported negative experiences (Khraif et al., 2019). However, this study explores the views of HSMWs, who are crucial to the country's shift towards knowledge-based sectors. The findings indicate a significant difference in attitudes based on contract type: those with government contracts viewed the system more positively than those in private sector roles. Government organizations, characterized by higher formalization, have shifted from individual kafeels to corporate HR departments, leading to more standardized and professional processes. In contrast, private organizations often rely on individual kafeels, who may lack specialized knowledge in HR, resulting in a more inconsistent experience for migrants. Both migrants and nationals declared a preference for government employment status over private employment, which is a new finding that has previously been undetected by studies.

Notably, the second- and third-generation migrants expressed negative views (equating the system to modern slavery by dependence on kafeels), particularly in private sector jobs. For instance, Pakistani Participant 12, with a neutral stance, remarked: "The kafala is one of those things which I had to accept the day I came over here. Alright, you can call it modern slavery." Other migrants argue that kafala functions similarly to the visa agent systems in other countries, serving under a necessary regulatory framework. The diverse interpretations of kafala range from facilitation of administrative tasks to a covert mechanism of control. They highlight the diversity of migrant experiences and expose (again) greater private sector employment variability and a greater presence of the kafeel as an actor in this setting (especially if the company is a private manufacturer operating in a rural location). This finding shows new nuances and system challenges that other research has not detected.

Recent changes to the kafala system revealed that traditionally, the kafeel held autocratic power over the migrant and could exercise their rights to prevent migrant travel or expulsion from the country. Informants believed that deliberate weakening of this autocratic power has been "proceduralized" and weakened by bureaucracy (expulsion requires justification, and HSMWs have been awarded rights to contest kafeel decisions). A new Saudi labor force information system allows migrants to bypass kafeels and request travel permission online from a company, not an individual. The company must give reasons to prevent travel, or the decision will be overturned (Interviewee 7). The easing of traditional system rigidities has consequences, and online platforms still cause fear amongst migrants that challenges would be digitally recorded, made visible to employers, and potentially trigger retaliation, including contract non-renewal, workplace marginalization, or other indirect forms of sanction.

Significant reforms, aimed at increasing fairness and protecting migrant workers' rights, have been enacted, and participants overwhelmingly viewed these changes positively. The new system seeks to balance power between kafeels and migrants, offering greater autonomy and improving working conditions. Although some legacy practices persist, the reforms (in areas like employment flexibility and exit requests) are seen as beneficial. One notable change is the provision allowing workers to seek alternative employment at the end of their contracts, which eases job transitions and retains talent. This significant departure from the previous "dependency model" grants more agency in career decisions to HSMWs. However, participants emphasized these changes did not obviate the need for kafeel relationship compatibility (especially in the private sector).

Efforts to reduce "abuse of power" (by overt regulations requiring sponsors to justify actions) now extend to dispute resolution and redressing personal bias in decisions. Participant 5 explained: "If my company refuses an exit visa, I can raise the request . . . they [the government] will issue the visa if there are no sufficient reasons to prevent travel."

The new contract-based framework, where legal agreements take precedence over personal relationships, is a major change under "new kafala," and this promotes greater accountability and transparency. Participant 12 highlighted "My father used to need permission to travel, but now the process has changed ... these changes are phenomenal!" Government reforms now ensure salary payments are timely and reduce the power of the kafeel to withhold salaries.

Meso factors

The meso-level analysis focuses on the organizational factors and specifically the role of the HRM department and its impact on HSMWs.

HR and kafeel power dynamics

The interviews revealed significant changes to the role of HR and a shifting power dynamic from the kafeel (sponsor) to HR specialists as a result of modifications to the kafala system. These findings confirm that HR specialists are reshaping the employment experience of skilled migrants, particularly in government-related roles, and these professionals are determining the rate of change in national working practices. The result is a retrenchment of the powerful kafeel to the private employment sector, where less formalized processes exist.

One of the key patterns that emerged is the expanding authority of HR specialists to holistically manage operational issues for and with migrants (employment contracts, daily work-related issues, and employee welfare). The nursing and academic sectors demonstrated significant power of HR specialists, who functioned as the main point of contact for HSMWs. This shift reduces the direct involvement of the kafeel in managing the professional lives of migrants—a notable departure from the traditional kafala system. Participant 4 proposed, "The HR function holds considerable authority and is akin to the CEO," and the general sentiment was that HR professionals, in smaller organizations, held significant influence over the design of the work environment.

Participants consistently repeated that the relationship of the HSMWs with the HR specialist enhanced or hindered the migrant experience. A proactive and empathetic HR relationship was highly cherished by HSMWs, and the specialist was seen as a partner in the workplace. Participant 5 exposed the two modes of HR, stating, "They can make the workplace either 'heaven or hell' for employees." The informant responses show HR professionals are moving beyond managing administrative tasks, but are highly involved in fostering a supportive and nurturing workplace and providing a protective role, acting as an intermediary between employees and management, to ensure employee rights are respected.

In smaller companies, the HR professional's personality and approach to the role were frequently cited as decisive factors in shaping the employee experience and which companies the migrant would want to work for. Participant 4 described their HR manager as a champion and "first-class fighter" for employee rights, regardless of nationality and a person who espoused a family-like atmosphere at work. She continued, "He fights for everything we need in front of the owners ... it's like we are family." This common pattern of findings signifies the role of HR professionals as interpreting kafala system changes and balancing organizational policies with a person-centered approach, which is empathetic, positive, and engaged with HSMWs employees.

However, the power dynamics between HR and the kafeel represent a more complex relationship—especially in the private sector and smaller company contexts. While HR departments are present, their influence can be overshadowed by the kafeel, who often retains substantial control over key aspects of employment (e.g., job mobility, visa renewals, and job security). Participant 6 described the HR role as a "bridge between the employee and the sponsor" but emphasized that the kafeel's authority often undermined the HR specialist, including the employees' personal and professional lives. "Having an HR in the middle is like having a mother in the family," Participant 6 explained in a way that portrays the HR specialist as an empathetic nurturer of HSMWs skills and working life. Nevertheless, this study detects a significant dual power structure, where the kafeel's position-based authority can overshadow the expert power of HR when the kafeel remains active with employee management.

The introduction of formal work contracts (a new addition to the traditional kafala system) has necessitated the greater and proactive use of HR specialists to manage the continued compliance of HSMWs, and Participant 17, a legal consultant, noted the shift, stating, "It is a work contract, not kafala anymore." The latter comment demonstrates a more standardized and formal employment relationship approach of the modern system that is led by HR specialists for the benefit of the HSMWs.

Despite these advancements, challenges remain, particularly in organizations where the HR role is more reactive and focused on administrative compliance rather than employee advocacy and development. Participant 4 contrasted their current company's rigid, regulation-driven HR approach with their previous employer, where HR took a more flexible and familial stance. They remarked, "Here in my company, they are less flexible ... like meticulous ... taking the regulations line by line, which is absolutely right." This rigid adherence to formal policies, while legally sound, can result in a less personalized approach to employee well-being, limiting HR's ability to foster a supportive work environment. The researcher reflected that this binary, compliance-driven approach, while efficient, lacks the relational empathy necessary to build stronger, more enduring employer-employee bonds.

Importantly, the findings show that HR's role is not heterogenous (across sectors or organizations), and in government employment, HR is a vital intermediary and empathetic leadership role that ensures fair treatment and resolves employee concerns. Participant 6 noted, "HR is the bridge between the employee and the sponsor or the employer ... if that bridge is ethical, stable, and knowledgeable about the rights of the employee, then 50 percent of the work environment and lifestyle of the employee will be stable." The findings show the HR role supports stable and harmonious work environments, where employees feel their rights are respected and upheld.

In conclusion, while the role of HR in the KSA's evolving kafala system is becoming increasingly prominent, the power dynamics between HR professionals and kafeels remain complex. HR departments are recognized as crucial actors in ensuring compliance with labor laws, promoting employee welfare, and fostering positive work environments. However, the continued influence of kafeels, particularly in the private sector, underscores the need for further reforms to balance power and fully realize the benefits of the new and standardized kafala system. Ultimately, this research shows that the quality of the migrant experience is heavily influenced by the personal empathy and proactive stance of HR professionals, as well as the broader organizational culture in which they operate.

Skilled migrants' experience in the KSA: Emotions and feelings about the workplace

The informants believed individuals from diverse cultural backgrounds, including British, Indians, Philippines enjoyed high satisfaction with their KSA employment experiences (Participant 7). Many participants, regardless of nationality or religion, shared positive opinions of Saudi culture and work environments and felt embedded in the national culture. Participant 7 remarked, "A lot of people enjoyed Saudi culture, especially around important holidays like Ramadan," highlighting the sense of inclusion and solidarity with coworkers (reduced working hours during Ramadan offered participation and experience of cultural traditions, which were seen as beneficial). Migrants also appreciated opportunities to visit locations of national pride, especially HSMWs from Pakistan and the UK who called their cultural experiences transformative for their lives and careers. Participant 12 termed the KSA as "a godsend" and proposed that it had changed their life for the better in all aspects.

The researcher explored personality traits and workplace satisfaction to find that extroverts (who embraced adventure and cultural discovery) reported higher levels of happiness in both their work and social lives (enjoying camping, hiking, and exploring tourist spots like the Al Wahbah crater and Al Baha). These individuals were more likely to positively engage with Saudi culture and show a contrast to the historical image of migrants living in isolated compounds with limited social engagement. The study finds that embracing the local culture positively impacts the workplace experience for HSMWs.

Micro factors: The micro level addresses the individual level of analysis

Motivation to migrate to the KSA

The interview findings showed HSMWs have complex motivations that determine their decisions to relocate to the KSA. The decision to migrate is therefore both strategic and multifaceted, where long-term career benefits and a deeper sense of fulfilment presented the key motivators. A contrast to the image of LSMWs being exclusively economically motivated.

Professional growth

The opportunity for professional growth and career advancement is qualitatively different from contract work and the KSA (and its ambitious national projects) offers significant opportunities for continued work for HSMWs. The Kingdom's Vision 2030 plan includes numerous large-scale projects (especially infrastructure, technology, and national transformation projects) that suit HSMWs' talents. These projects are vast in scope and are unmatched in many of the migrants' home countries. Participant 12 articulated the appeal of the KSA's evolving economic landscape, stating, "Saudi is still a land of opportunities ... one of the few countries which is growing and developing." This sentiment was confirmed by almost all participants, who viewed the Kingdom as a place where their skills could be fully utilized and where they could achieve substantial career milestones. Participant 10 proposed, "The projects here are super new. And the scale that you find here, you don't find that anywhere else in the world." The experience of transformational projects (and skills development in such settings) increases the value of the HSMWs post-employment in the KSA. Thus, the appeal of these future opportunities extends beyond immediate job prospects and were firmly regarded as an investment in their future. By working on such prestigious projects, they enhance their résumés, positioning themselves for better roles either within the Kingdom or in other international markets upon completion of their contracts.

In parallel, the stability and long-term nature of employment in the KSA was also a significant factor for many migrants who saw the KSA as a long-term destination where they could work for extended periods through successive contracts. Participant 7 remarked, "There are plenty of opportunities here and higher positions than our home country." This sentiment underscores the KSA's comparative advantage in offering career mobility and upward progression, which many HSMWs cannot find in their home countries or other GCC nations despite having high skills that are in short supply on a global basis.

Economic opportunities

Financial gain, traditionally the primary motivator for migration to the KSA, remained a significant factor. The interviews revealed that it is often intertwined with other motivations, such as career development and lifestyle. Nonetheless, monetary reward (tax-free salaries and competitive compensation packages) still attracted HSMWs from comparatively poorer home-country backgrounds. Participant 9 explicitly recognized the disparity of KSA salaries, stating, "I won't get the same salary as I am getting here." This common view was held by migrants from lower-wage economies (including the Philippines and Egypt). Participant 1 confirmed this sentiment: "The money is key, because it's very clear that the Saudi gives us more salary than the Philippines." Interestingly, the financial benefits were seen as a means to an end, for example supporting families back home, future career opportunities, and migrant lifestyles in the short and long term. Particularly for Western migrants, the financial incentive was less about immediate gains and more about the long-term benefits of working in the KSA. Participant 13 (from the UK) stated, "It's absolutely the money ... where it's tax-free ... much more than we would get in the UK." And then contended his rate of saving was a major advantage in planning to return to the high cost of living in the UK or other Western country. The findings show a mutually reinforcing benefit of short-term good salaries and long-term increased personal market value.

Religious significance

For many Muslim migrants, the opportunity to live and work in the KSA is deeply connected to religious identity. Participant 12 stated, "For people coming from Muslim countries ... the first priority is religion. The second priority is, of course, money." The proximity to Mecca and Medina, two of the holiest cities in Islam, serves as a powerful motivator for those seeking to fulfil religious obligations while advancing their careers. Participant 8 proposed, "My first priority is religion because of Mecca and Medina," and other Muslim migrants identified the ability to perform Umrah and Hajj added a "special" spiritual dimension to their decision to migrate. Participant 14 stated, "I want to come to Saudi Arabia to perform Umrah and Hajj, and also bring my children from Egypt to perform Umrah and Hajj." This highlights the deep connection between faith and migration for Muslim HSMWs and a deeper fulfilment of religious duties whilst enjoying the country's economic and professional opportunities. Additionally, some migrants expressed a desire to preserve their religious values in a more conservative environment. Participant 6 noted, "I know some people who left Canada ... just for the sake of keeping their religious values awake in them and in their kids." The KSA's Islamic environment, where religious practices permeate daily life, provides a significant attraction for such migrants to uphold and strengthen their religious commitments at home and work, particularly those from more secular societies.

Sense of belonging and family connections

For second- and third-generation migrants, as well as those with familial ties to the KSA, a strong sense of "belonging" played a key role in their decision to remain in the country. These migrants viewed the KSA as their home, with personal connections to the country outweighing other considerations. Participants from countries like Yemen, Sudan, and Egypt demonstrated how familial history and deep-rooted ties to the KSA influenced their migration decisions. This sense of belonging creates a more emotional connection to the country, making the KSA more than just a place of employment but also "a multi-faceted home." This was particularly true for migrants who were born and raised in the KSA or who have family members living in the Kingdom who exhibited very strong personal and professional factors and a deep emotional attachment to the country and its culture.

Gender dynamics

The exploration of gender dynamics in KSA workplaces revealed both progress and persistent challenges for skilled female migrants. Interviewees acknowledged the significant changes in the status of women in the workplace. Traditional cultural values still play a major role, influencing professional behavior and expectations. For example, one interviewee highlighted the concept of "distance" between male and female coworkers, such as separate spaces for breaks and prayer, which is a cultural norm in the country and must be respected to maintain workplace harmony. Evolving societal norms are creating more inclusive environments, especially in sectors influenced by national policy, and women often face barriers to professional advancement due to stereotypes and lingering societal perceptions. Women were regarded as "less committed" to their careers, particularly if planning to have children. Some participants noted that these biases can limit opportunities for female leadership roles or hinder career progression.

There is also interview evidence of progress and a decreasing gender pay gap (and increased openness to job opportunities for women), which shows a shift toward meritocratic employment practices and gender equality in many sectors. The proactive role of HR departments was found to support positive gender dynamics and ensure fairness in recruitment and promotion practices. However, mixed findings revealed that lingering cultural norms and stereotypes continue persist for career-minded female professionals.

Nationality differences in experience

The experiences of HSMWs were wide-ranging, and differences between nationalities were detected. Interviewee 13 (British) argued that Western nationals experience preferential treatment and fewer restrictions, stating discrimination is "probably not so much for British people, though I'm sure [my Filipino partner] . . . will say that there is a lot of restrictions on Filipinos and the other nationalities. But on our side, we're looked after pretty well." Participant 8 (Indian) reflected on significant privileges perceived for Western HSMWs and claimed a "passport disparity" and elitism. They argued "basically, migrants from Western countries are highly privileged, and huge difference is based on the passport you hold" (Interviewee 8, Indian). They then stated that international pay differentials (biased toward Western nationalities) existed, which was supported by the majority of interviewees. They stated, "different passports have different positions and different pay structures and different 'exchange value' for them." They each have a different worth and value in this country (Interviewee 8, Indian). Such duality extended for HSMWs from non-Western backgrounds, and "exceptions were made for individuals from European, American, or Australian backgrounds, underlining the privilege associated with these nationalities" and "Migrants have to change their career path to match Saudi regulations . . . unless they are a European or American or Australian, these nationalities are an exception."

Arab HSMWs (with knowledge of the local culture and language) were perceived as "valuable assets" and received better opportunities, improved communication, and enhanced integration and assimilation than others. The Arab migrants benefited from improved conditions as a result of language and cultural proficiency, where "better opportunities and chances existed when you can talk, you can defend, you can debate, you can represent yourself, you can hang out at any place in a better way you can ... you know ... communicate" (Interviewee12, Pakistani).

Discussion and conclusion

The findings offer a rich understanding of the dynamic and evolving landscape for HSMWs in the KSA. The Kingdom's current reliance on skilled migrants is set within organizational dynamics that shape their experiences, and individual factors influencing migration decisions. The Kingdom's 2030 Vision and its initiatives drive economic transformation, shifting the country from a rentier model to a diversified, knowledge-based economy.

The existing literature, with a predominantly negative viewpoint of the kafala system (AlShehabi, 2021; Chidiac, 2014), has largely been drawn from studies of LSMWs labor, which offer their physical, not knowledge-based, skills to the KSA. However, the modern challenge is to engage migrants with higher-level managerial and executive skills. These sectors include shortfalls in specialized fields such as IT, healthcare, and education, while the national workforce is increasingly competent to fill roles in other traditional short-fall sectors (government education and healthcare establishments in urban areas). Thompson and Almoaibed (2021) argue that, despite state-led efforts to encourage the nationalization of the labor market, the private sector remains dominated by expatriates, with only 40 percent of private sector positions being held by Saudis. However, the experience and tacit knowledge of nationals is not, in certain sectors, at a level where nationals can lead large-scale transformational projects, and thus, the demand for migrants remains.

The existing migrant studies literature (Dito, 2015), for the specific focus on the kafala system, presents the kafeel as the key actor whose authority is unchallengeable, and upon whom the migrant worker is dependent. Such a subservient relationship, with an individual, has high risks and the potential for abuse by the kafeel. The latter is the most typical of case study research and the exploitation of the migrant within the LSMWs workforce. The findings of this study show that the power of the kafeel is not universal and, in general terms, the migrant has been granted significant benefits under the new kafala system, which has curtailed the potential for abusive use of the system by unscrupulous kafeels. In specific conditions, usually larger organizations with well-developed HRM practices and officials, the technical skills and up-to-date knowledge of HRM specialists govern the relationship with the migrant and relegate the kafeel to duties that are more administrative unless the kafeel is determined as "the organization" versus a person. When the kafeel is a corporate entity, the most natural specialist to manage such external relations is the HRM department, and this relationship (and move to an HRM-led kafala system in practice) has been perceived by migrants and experts as a superior model to the LSMWs kafala interpretation. The study finds many positives and reciprocal mutuality and trust between migrants and the HRM specialist. However, this scenario largely describes the experiences of migrants in large corporations and transformation projects. The experience of small businesses, even with HRM specialists, is more varied and less positive from the migrant's view (these settings remain the prerogative of individual kafeels).

When the practice of HR management in the KSA is reviewed, the practices equate to those of any large-scale migrant workforce economy and Western economies in particular. The literature also suggests that the relationship was one of economic trading of skills for pay, but this study finds significant disagreement with such a view (ILO, 2017; Khan and Harroff-Tavel, 2011). Instead, this study has found significant levels of marketing and reverse marketing of employers, such that employers present themselves as the "right type" of employer, and migrants are more selective in seeking the "right type" of employer. These practices were most evident in the attention to detail in the recruitment and socialization processes of HR specialists.

HR professionals are therefore playing (as a group of professionals) a critical, central role in structuring fair and supportive work environments, especially in government-owned establishments. These professionals are essential to supporting, mediating between migrants and employers, ensuring compliance with updated labor laws, and fulfilling a quasi-managerial role that reduces the need for direct kafeel oversight. The HR profession in the KSA has moved from an administrative role to one of strategic importance in the labor market, and their processes are now designed to recruit only the best available talent and to nurture it so as to maximize the economic value of migrants "from day one." The HR professionals have a dual role of both advocating for migrant employees and have done so without resorting to the coercive power used in traditional methods for LSMWs. This is an important shift in designing new organizational cultures, for sustained employee satisfaction and high productivity, and for longevity of migrant contracts in the modern inclusivity and "fair" employment in government and private sectors.

The power of the kafeels, in general, had weakened due to government initiatives aimed at standardizing the administration of migrant workers and implementing platforms to facilitate easier management of official regulations in the KSA. Most migrants appreciated the new "self-service" and transparent government systems. This shift towards transparency is further supported by the introduction of the Qiwa platform, which provides a digital, self-service interface for both employees and employers to manage contracts, amendments, and renewals. By empowering skilled migrants to handle these processes directly, Qiwa reduces dependency on kafeels for administrative tasks and promotes greater clarity and independence. This platform enhances the general move towards contracts that clearly outline workplace rights and remedial actions for migrants. This study, therefore, contradicts the dominant view in the literature, as the 'new contract' system, combined with tools like the Qiwa platform, has liberalized the kafala system to a position that is far removed from the accounts associated with LSMWs.

The KSA has also moved to greater diversity in the workplace and hosts a wide range of migrants from many nations. These migrants were expected to assimilate into working and social life with much more effectiveness. The traditional (oil extraction) accounts of migrants suggest the opposite, and huge conurbations of migrants in small communes of exclusively migrant workers (e.g., Texans and US workers). However, this study detected some positive perceptions of living amongst fellow migrants, but equally more engagement with the Saudi culture, language, and fellow workers. There was much less insularity detected amongst skilled migrants.

The study does raise some issues which have not yet been explored by other contemporary studies of the kafala system. The first is the role of the woman in the workplace and migrant women in particular. The study finds some legacy cultural behaviors that restrict and potentially cause discrimination against women, especially those who may wish to have children (economic bias). The study also finds migrants believe there is a "differential status" amongst nationalities where Westerners are considered to have preferential treatment to access the best jobs (unless the company kafeel seeks to recruit migrants that are from the same country as the management/leaders of the company). Also, migrants believed those from Arabic countries were those most likely to assimilate, engage with coworkers, and stay in the country. These migrants enjoyed the status of being in the country and gained significant pleasure and fulfilment from the religious and cultural aspects of the KSA lifestyle. However, some migrants (second and third generations of original migrants to the KSA) were in a "no man's land," where they could not hold Saudi citizenship; they were loyal and had spent more than thirty years as residents, but could not leave.

In conclusion, this chapter has addressed the significant yet underexplored experiences of HSMWs in the KSA, a critical component of the Kingdom's efforts to meet the growing demand for expertise in knowledge-based industries under Vision 2030. The findings highlight the essential role of HSMWs in bridging workforce skills gaps, particularly in knowledge-driven sectors such as technology, healthcare, and education, which are vital for Saudi Arabia's long-term sustainable growth and global competitiveness.

Future efforts to sustain the inflow of HSMWs and support their contributions to the KSA's knowledge economy must prioritize the development of inclusive policies, address workplace inequalities, and foster a culture that values the skills and well-being of this essential workforce. Ultimately, this chapter emphasizes the strategic importance of balancing national talent development with the targeted recruitment and retention of international expertise to achieve Vision 2030's ambitious goals.

Notes

1 The GCIM, in its 2005 report, highlighted that selective immigration policies focusing exclusively on high-skilled labor overlook the critical contributions of low-skilled workers in various sectors, including construction, domestic services, and other labor-intensive industries essential for economic and social stability. It emphasized that a balanced migration approach is vital for sustainable economic development.

2 The latter would have resulted in the job title in other HSMWs countries such as the UK and Germany.

3 The NETAQAT scheme was introduced in 2011 by the Ministry of Human Resources to enhance the effectiveness of "Saudization" policy so as to reduce the level of unemployment among youth in the Kingdom.

Bibliography

Adham, A. (2023). Structural demand for migrant labour: A bottom-up analysis of labour market segmentation in Saudi Arabia. *Journal of Ethnic and Migration Studies, 49*(7), 1746–67.

Afiouni, F., Ruël, H., and Schuler, R. (2014). *HRM in the Middle East: Toward a greater understanding*. Taylor & Francis.

Alghadir, A. H., Zafar, H., and Iqbal, Z. A. (2020). Experiences of overseas trained physical therapists working in Saudi Arabia: An observational study. *International Journal of Environmental Research and Public Health, 17*(10), 3406.

Almeida, S., Fernando, M., Hannif, Z., and Dharmage, S. C. (2015). Fitting the mould: The role of employer perceptions in immigrant recruitment decision-making. *The International Journal of Human Resource Management, 26*(22), 2811–32.

Alogla, H. O. (1990). *Obstacles to Saudization in the private sector of the Saudi Arabian labor force*. Michigan State University.

Alshahrani, S. T., and Morley, M. J. (2015). Accounting for variations in the patterns of mobility among conventional and self-initiated expatriates. *The International Journal of Human Resource Management, 26*(15), 1936–54.

AlShehabi, O. H. (2021). Policing labour in empire: The modern origins of the Kafala sponsorship system in the Gulf Arab States. *British Journal of Middle Eastern Studies, 48*(2), 291–310.

Cerdin, J.-L., Diné, M. A., and Brewster, C. (2014). Qualified immigrants' success: Exploring the motivation to migrate and to integrate. *Journal of International Business Studies, 45*(2), 151–68.

Chidiac, Omaya. 2014. Migrant construction and domestic workers in the Arab Gulf States: Modern-day slaves? Master of Laws thesis, Graduate Program in Law. York University Toronto, Ontario.

Crowley⊠Henry, M., O'Connor, E., and Al Ariss, A. (2018). Portrayal of skilled migrants' careers in business and management studies: A review of the literature and future research agenda. *European Management Review, 15*(3), 375–94.

Dito, M. (2015). Kafala: Foundations of migrant exclusion in GCC labour markets. *Transit states: Labour, Migration & Citizenship in the Gulf*, 79–100.

Farashah, A. D., & Blomquist, T. (2020, February). Exploring employer attitude towards migrant workers: Evidence from managers across Europe. *Evidence-based HRM: A Global Forum for Empirical Scholarship* 8(1), 18–37.

GCIM (Global Commission on International Migration). (2005). *Migration in an interconnected world: New directions for action*. GCIM.

Guo, C., and Al Ariss, A. (2015). *Human resource management of international migrants: Current theories and future research*. Taylor& Francis.

ILO (International Labor Organization). (2017). Employer⊠migrant worker relationships in the Middle East: Exploring scope for internal labour market mobility and fair migration. ILO.

Khan, A., and Harroff-Tavel, H. (2011). Reforming the Kafala: Challenges and opportunities in moving forward. *Asian and Pacific Migration Journal, 20*(3–4), 293–313.

Khraif, R. M., Salam, A. A., Nair, P., and Elsegaey, I. (2019). Migration in Saudi Arabia: Present and prospects. In S. Irudaya Rajan and Prem Saxena (eds.), *India's low-skilled migration to the Middle East: Policies, politics and challenges* (pp. 99–123). Singapore: Springer Nature.

Michaels, E., Handfield-Jones, H., and Axelrod, B. (2001). *The war for talent*. Harvard Business Press.

Rahman, M. M. (2018). Beyond labour migration: The making of migrant enterprises in Saudi Arabia. *International Sociology, 33*(1), 86–106.

Saudi Vision 2030. (2016). *Saudi Vision 2030*. Retrieved from https://www.vision2030.gov.sa/

Syed, J., and Özbilgin, M. (2009). A relational framework for international transfer of diversity management practices. *The International Journal of Human Resource Management, 20*(12), 2435–53.

Tharenou, P., and Kulik, C. T. (2020). Skilled migrants employed in developed, mature economies: From newcomers to organizational insiders. *Journal of Management*, *46*(6), 1156–81.

Thompson, M. C., and Almoaibed, H. (2021). "Good jobs and bad jobs": Employment attitudes, perceptions, and priorities in Saudi Arabia. *Dirasat*, *61*.

Zikic, J. (2015). Skilled migrants' career capital as a source of competitive advantage: Implications for strategic HRM. *The International Journal of Human Resource Management*, *26*(10), 1360–81.

5

Current Drivers and Future Prospects for Arab Migration to Saudi Arabia

Françoise De Bel-Air

Introduction

Historically, Arab populations from the Mashreq have migrated to Saudi Arabia in large numbers. Since the 1950s, the oil-induced economic and infrastructural development process attracted growing international migration flows to the Gulf region. Arabs made up most of the foreign workforce in the Kingdom from the onset (Seccombe and Lawless, 1986: 548). Today, the six Gulf Cooperation Council (GCC) countries attract the bulk of the migrants from most Mashreq Arab states: UN data last available for 2020 indicated that three-quarters of the then-recorded 3.6 million Egyptian migrants worldwide and two-thirds of the Jordanian emigrants were residing in the GCC region that year, with Saudi Arabia being their first destination.[1]

However, the drastic socio-economic reform processes ongoing since the late 2000s, which aim to diversify and decarbonize Gulf economies, seek to perform a transition from labor-intensive to internationally competitive, knowledge-based, and innovative economies, fostering high-value-added industries. This process implies attracting, as well as retaining, increasing numbers of skilled and highly skilled workers. Moreover, the overhauling of migration policies in the region and especially, the workforce nationalization policies such as the *Nitaqat* policy conducted in Saudi Arabia since 2011, aim to better control and monitor the numbers, dynamics and skills, as well as profile of work migration from Arab states to the GCC region, and especially, to Saudi Arabia, their main destination. The question of importance for Arab countries of origin, and for Gulf destination countries, is whether the context of the socio-economic transition process changes the prospects of migration to the Gulf states and to Saudi Arabia for Arab migrants, who played a decisive role in the establishment of the region's administrative and infrastructural apparatuses from the 1950s onwards.

This question is of relevance for Arab-sending countries, where a combination of socio-economic and political challenges, including food and energy crises, is exacerbating socio-economic disparities and public services destruction, thus aggravating the emigration pressure. As "Western" country destinations become increasingly difficult to reach, Gulf states offer several assets to Arab migrants. Focusing on the period 2010 to the present, the chapter examines Arab migration to Saudi Arabia. It focuses on skilled and highly skilled migrants,[2] and takes Egyptian, as well as Jordanian, nationals as examples and case studies. The chapter seeks to emphasize the extent of the migration pressure from the Mashreq Arab states, analyses its determinants (drivers), and highlights their structural nature. Migration drivers are the many factors of various natures, scales, and timeframes that interplay together at the micro, "meso," and macro levels and lead to the specific patterns of the "inception" of migration and the "perpetuation" of the movement (Massey et al., 1998). Our approach is that of political demography, "the study of the size, composition, and distribution of population in relation to both government and politics" (Weiner, 1971: 567), informed by neo-institutionalist approaches.

The chapter is based on available statistical data from origin countries and from Saudi Arabia, stemming from official National Statistical Offices (NSOs),[3] as well as from migration surveys. However, Saudi data disaggregated by migrants' citizenship are rare and basic. Available statistics do not allow for analysing migration and employment dynamics for specific nationalities, nor do they permit a quantitative evaluation of the outcomes of the reform measures on Arab migrants' prospects in the Kingdom. Therefore, we had to resort to indirect evidence and to desk research based on secondary sources such as press articles and selected research reports, to evaluate these prospects. Other sources used include policy measures and discourses pertaining to migration and to employment, as well as results of surveys conducted every year on large panels of Arab youth (Arab Barometer; Arab Youth Survey, . . .). These surveys offer a glimpse into Arab youth's perceptions of their socio-economic and political situation and, therefore, of their propensity to migrate.

The chapter first analyses recent trends and patterns of Arab migration to Saudi Arabia. Using the various sources mentioned above, it will then identify the major drivers of Egyptian and Jordanian migration to the region, from close, economics-related drivers to more remote drivers of a socio-political nature. An analysis of the drivers of immigration to Saudi Arabia for Arab professionals, and Saudi policies towards migration, employment, and socio-economic reforms, eventually concludes that prospects for future migration from Arab states to Saudi Arabia are mixed.

Profile of Arab migrants and trends of Arab migration to Saudi Arabia

Saudi Arabia did not publish any data disaggregated by migrants' nationality before 2020. That year, figures of workers in the private and public sectors by workers' country of citizenship started being disclosed annually by the Saudi Ministry of Human Resources and Social Development (MHRSD). In 2022, datasets on workers in the civil service detailed employees by country of citizenship, sex, age, detailed geographic location, education level, and more.[4] However, only 0.5 percent of all foreign workers and 1 percent of Arab workers in the country are civil servants (Table 5.1). The General Authority for Statistics (GAStat), Saudi Arabia's National Statistical Organization (NSO), also released partial results of the last census conducted in 2022 in the country, namely, the numbers of foreign residents by country of citizenship, with gender disaggregation. Nothing more is available in these datasets regarding Arab residents' and workers' socio-demographic and employment characteristics. The information collected during the census in the household questionnaire (interviewee's country of birth, parents' country of birth, residency abroad, year of entry to Saudi Arabia, and the place of residence five years ago (GAStat, n.d.: 35), which should presumably be processed for the upcoming "Migration and diversity" module, is still unpublished, as of October 2024.

Arab populations in Saudi Arabia

The Saudi census of 2022 recorded 13,382,962 foreign nationals, of whom 5,245,451 were from Arab countries.[5] Arab nationals thus composed 39 percent of all foreign residents at the time of the 2022 census. Yemenis and Egyptians largely outnumbered other Arab nationalities.

Data available on the three largest Arab nationalities (Egyptians, Sudanese, and Yemenis) highlight their imbalance in terms of gender and the predominance of men among them. While Morocco displays a mostly feminine population (62 percent women in the total population recorded during the 2022 census), Tunisia and Mashreq countries' nationals (Jordanians, Syrians, Lebanese, for instance), on the contrary, are closer to gender parity. Shares of women among them stand markedly above the average of 23.5 percent females in total foreign populations (Table 5.1).

Table 5.1 also indicates that Arab nationals made up almost a third of all foreign workers, but that half of those were employed in the government sector. This may be due to their knowledge of Arabic, and to the long-term presence and contribution of certain nationalities (Egyptians, Jordanians,

Table 5.1. Saudi Arabia: Employed and Total Non-Saudi Arab Populations, by Country of Citizenship and Sector of Employment (2022)

	Employed Arabs/ *Foreign nat.*				Total Arabs/ *Foreign nat.*	
	Gov. Sector	**% fem.**	**Private sector**	**Total employed in gov. and private sectors**	**Number**	**% fem.**
Yemen	583	13.9	840,881	**841,464**	**1,803,469**	**26.0**
Egypt	11,408	32.8	837,134	**848,542**	**1,471,382**	**19.7**
Sudan	8,562	47.2	354,988	**363,550**	**819,575**	**17.8**
Syria	1,708	13.9	140,953	**142,661**	**449,314**	**42.2**
Jordan	1,495	20.2	66,072	**67,567**	**204,249**	**44.4**
Palestine	100	24.0	32,970	**33,070**	**129,869**	**47.6**
Lebanon	45	22.2	30,245	**30,290**	**52,779**	**37.9**
Morocco	74	33.8	18,028	**18,102**	**48,796**	**62.3**
Tunisia	1,516	38.7	12,311	**13,827**	**24,818**	**42.3**
Total Arab nationals	**25,771**	**35.4**	**2,338,123**	**2,363,894**	**5,245,451**	**25.8**
Total foreign nationals	***43,180***	***47.6***	***7,744,139***	***7,787,319***	***13,382,962***	***23.5***

Sources: MHRSD, and GAStat (census 2022). For details, see: https://gulfmigration.grc.net/glmm-database/demographic-and-economic-module/?search=1&cmct=Saudi+Arabia.

and Palestinians, especially) to the building of the Saudi governmental apparatus (public education and health sectors, administration) since the 1950s. Sixty-five percent of Arab public sector employees indeed held a university degree in 2022, compared with 22.5 percent among Asian nationals in the sector, for instance.[6] Women among them were a minority (35 percent on average), except for the Sudanese. Yet, the bulk of Arab migrants worked in the private sector (Table 5.1).

Inferring migrants' skill levels from existing data

The absence of data on domestic workers, and on employment patterns and characteristics disaggregated by workers' citizenship or regional origin, forces us to infer information from the limited range of data available in Saudi statistics and to resort to secondary information sources to describe these populations.

Sponsoring family dependents in Saudi Arabia is only permitted for expatriates in specific, mostly managerial and/or highly skilled positions.[7] The relatively balanced gender structure prevailing among residents from Mashreq countries (Jordanians, Syrians, Palestinians, especially), combined

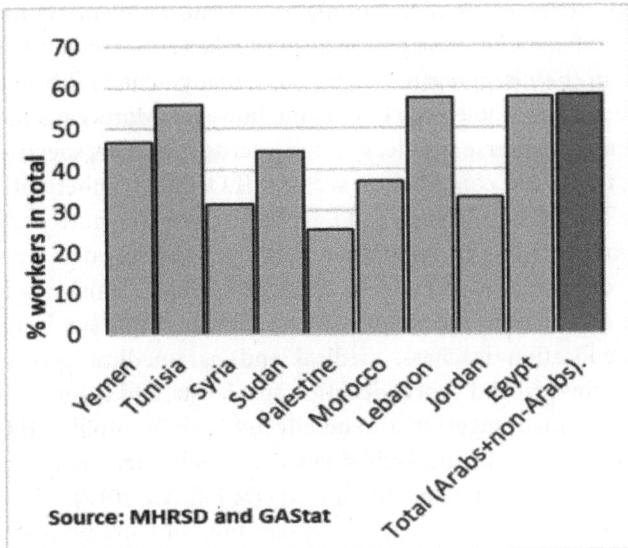

Figure 5.1. Share of workers among Arab nationals residing in Saudi Arabia, by country of citizenship (2022).

with the comparatively lower share of workers employed in the public and private sectors among them (Figure 5.1) suggest the presence of family members, which could therefore signal the high share of highly skilled workers among these nationals. However, we know that Saudi Arabia hosts many (de facto) refugee families from Syria and Yemen (Osmandzicovic, 2019).[8] Inflows of refugees from Palestine established themselves over decades and are present at all skill levels and types of occupations, including business and retail (Lysa, 2023).

Jordanian residents are also largely composed of non-workers (66 percent), which suggests a level of skills high enough on average to allow many Jordanian migrants to bring their families to the Kingdom. Field visits made in Gulf countries, as well as the study of sectoral bilateral agreements concluded between Jordan and Gulf states, indeed suggest that Jordanian expatriates in the region are often employed in the engineering, medical and pharmaceutical sectors, and in the media and information technologies, in education, and in the banking and financial sectors, for instance. A survey revealed that 85 percent of Jordanian expatriates in Gulf states were holding a university degree in 2017–2018. Ninety-five percent of Jordanians in the region originated from Jordan's urban areas (Jordan Strategy Forum, 2018). In the mid-2010s, half of working Jordanian engineers were based in Saudi Arabia and elsewhere in the Gulf region.[9]

The high share of women among Moroccan residents confirms the employment of some of these nationals in the domestic sector,[10] which does not appear in the disaggregated figures of employment in the government and private sectors (Table 5.1). In general, however, Moroccans in the Gulf states have a very diverse profile, spanning across the skills spectrum in the hospitality, trade, and construction sectors (ILO, 2022). Other nationalities, such as the Tunisians, Lebanese, and Egyptians, comprise more workers than family members. Tunisian emigration to the Gulf states developed in the framework of bilateral development cooperation, and Tunisian workers are most often seconded to the Saudi public sector, as university lecturers and secondary education teachers, medical and paramedical specialists and technicians, physical and sport education specialists, and culture and leisure practitioners, which suggests a generally high skills profile (ILO, 2023). Lebanese immigrants in the Gulf states are mostly men, as indicated, but their profile in the Gulf is generally skilled (De Bel-Air, 2017).

The gender distribution among Egyptian migrants (80 percent of men), however skewed, is not comparable to that observed among populations quasi-exclusively composed of low-wage workers, such as the Bangladeshis (92 percent males), or the Nepalis (98 percent males). The share of 57.7 percent of workers, though higher than among other Arab nationalities, indicates the presence of non-working family members among Egyptians. The ratio stands much above that observed among Asian or sub-Saharan African mostly low-skilled populations, among whom non-workers are very few. The relative male predominance suggests the presence of many low-wage male workers without families, alongside more skilled workers with families, hence the diversity in the skills profile of this large population. According to the Saudi then-Ministry of Labor, in the early 2010s, Egyptian workers were often employed in white-collar, skilled, and semi-skilled technical fields such as accountancy and marketing, for instance, in addition to agriculture and husbandry (MEMO, 2014). Results from the Household International Migration Survey (MED-HIMS) survey on Egypt migration and return migration conducted in 2013 also suggested that migration from urban areas was increasing with education, while most Egyptian migrants to Arab states (including Saudi Arabia) were coming from mainly rural Upper Egypt region, which may contribute to explaining the diversity of skill levels among Egyptian migrants (Farid, et al., 2016: 36). Statistics on work permits granted to Egyptians by destination and education level in 2018 indeed indicated that a third of Egyptian emigrants to Saudi Arabia were holding a "higher education" level (as opposed to 42 to 58 percent of Egyptians to the UAE, Bahrain, Oman and Qatar, and 4 to 22 percent respectively in Jordan and Kuwait) (CAPMAS, 2019). Unfortunately, no detailed data are available for recent, post-COVID-19 periods.

The significant share of non-active family members thus confirms the skilled and highly skilled profile of most Arab nationals.

Recent immigration trends and dynamics

Annexed Table 1 confirms the increased attractiveness of Gulf states for selected Arab nationalities: one-quarter of Lebanese, 66 percent of Jordanian migrants, and three-quarters of Egyptian emigrants were residing in the region in 2020, up from 10 percent to half of migrants from these countries in 1990. Only Yemenis have been steadily present in the GCC states in large numbers (80–85 percent since 1990). Annexed Table 2 underlines the specific attraction of Saudi Arabia to Arab migrants in the Gulf.

Saudi Arabia's official statistics of employment (Table 5.2) indicate an upward trend in the employment of Arab and other workers since the unprecedented drop in the number of foreign employees in the Kingdom in 2020, caused by the COVID-19 pandemic and subsequent economic downturn. The stocks of Arab and other foreign civil servants have been dropping, in line with policies of reserving governmental jobs to nationals since 2011, but have increased in the private sector. Numbers of Arabs went up by 12.3 percent year-on-year (2021–2022), while total foreign workers increased by 17 percent. The number of Jordanian workers registered a very modest increase (+2 percent), while that of Egyptians gained 16 percent. No data are available on the skill profile of workers by country of citizenship. However, in line with policies enacted within the realm of Saudi Vision 2030, it is likely that highly skilled among them were especially attracted to the Kingdom. Egyptian medical personnel, for instance, are currently in demand

Table 5.2: Saudi Arabia: Egyptian, Jordanian, Arab, and Total Workers Employed in the Governmental and Private Sectors (2020–2022)

	Civil service			**Private sector**		
	2020	**2021**	**2022**	**2020**	**2021**	**2022**
Egypt	13,429	12,516	11,408	715,122	721,573	837,134
Jordan	1,815	1,687	1,495	63,223	64,654	66,072
Arab countries	**29,124**	**27,860**	**25,771**	**1,991,432**	**2,081,271**	**2,338,123**
Total migrant workers	**1,278,278**	**1,254,313**	**1,209,279**	**8,285,417**	**8,516,072**	**9,937,146**

Source: Ministry of Human Resources and Social Development (MHRSD). For details, see: https://gulfmigration.grc.net/glmm-database/demographic-and-economic-module/.

in Saudi Arabia,[11] as well as engineers from Jordan.[12] Saudi Arabia is thus resuming its position as a major labor migration outlet, especially for Egyptians.

Outward migration from Egypt and Jordan: Structural issues as drivers of migration to the Gulf states

Young Arab citizens are eager to emigrate, as witnessed in every youth survey conducted over the last two decades. In 2015, 14 percent (Egypt) to 34 percent (Tunisia) of young people had expressed their intention to move abroad within the next five years (Pedersen and Tiltnes, 2017: 11–12). The trend is confirmed in the seventh wave of the Arab Barometer Survey conducted in the MENA region in 2022, which found that on average, at least a fifth of the surveyed Arab population reported considering emigration. However, in Jordan, the share of those wanting to emigrate reached nearly half (48 percent) of the surveyed population, and 63 percent of those aged 18–29 years, while Egypt ranked at the bottom of the list with only 13 percent wanting to emigrate (all interviewees) and 18 percent among the youth (Arab Barometer, 2022). The 15th edition of the Arab Youth Survey Public Views of Migration in MENA also pointed out similar findings: outside the Gulf states, 53 percent of people aged 18–24 in the Mashreq countries (North Africa including Egypt: 48 percent) expressed their intention to migrate abroad (ASDA'A BCW, 2023: 59).[13] The last wave of the Arab Barometer for 2023–2024 confirms that migration remains a significant concern for Tunisia, where 46 percent of the surveyed population was considering migration, followed by Jordan at 42 percent and Lebanon at 38 percent. In Morocco, 35 percent express similar intentions, compared to 25 percent in Palestine (Arab Barometer, 2024).[14] This attitude towards emigration, especially from Jordan, is rooted in the socio-economic development process of the two countries, itself an outcome of the political economy and history in most of the Arab region.

Assessing youth unemployment as a proximate driver of migration to the Gulf states

The top five concerns of young Arabs interviewed in 2022 by the Arab Youth Survey were: rising living costs (89 percent), unemployment (86 percent), the state of their national economy (84 percent), corruption (83 percent) and income inequality (81 percent) (ASDA'A BCW, 2023: 41). Besides conflicts, economic instability and a dearth of local jobs were the main reasons interviewees cited for considering emigration (ASDA'A BCW, 2023: 59). The section explores the characteristics of youth unemployment in the region (in Jordan and Egypt principally), and assesses whether this assumption holds true, that youth unemployment, and especially, graduates' unemployment, are direct and major drivers of emigration.

Youth and graduates' unemployment

Youth unemployment is a reality among the 15–29-year-olds in the Mashreq region.[15] While displaying the world's highest share of young adults aged 15 to 29 in total populations (26 percent), the Arab region also has the highest youth unemployment levels, estimated at 23 percent in 2019.[16] Unlike in other regions, most of these are university graduates.

However, the age groups concerned by migration to the Gulf states, and especially highly skilled migration, are older: We therefore concentrate on the age group 25–34 years, old enough to have obtained their postgraduate degrees and thus more likely than younger citizens to seek employment abroad.

Unemployment rates in the age group reached 11 percent and 22 percent of all actives in 2022, respectively, in Egypt and Jordan (Table 5.3). These levels are higher than general unemployment rates (in the population aged 15 and above), which stood between 7 percent (Egypt) and reached 18 percent of the labor force in Jordan.

Disaggregated figures suggest that females, in general and in these age groups, suffer much more from unemployment than males: 29 percent and 27 percent, respectively, in Egypt and Jordan. Young males' unemployment levels, though very high in Jordan, stand comparatively lower (Table 5.3).

Table 5.3. Egypt and Jordan: Unemployment Rates in Total Populations and Age Group 25–34 Years by Sex (2022)

	Age category	**Unemployment rates**		
		Males	**Females**	**Total**
Egypt	**25–34**	6.8	28.7	10.6
	Total (15+)	**5.1**	**18.5**	**7.3**
Jordan	**25-34**	18.3	27.0	21.7
	Total (15+)	**16.4**	**35.3**	**18.2**

Sources: Egypt: Labor Force Surveys; Jordan, Employment and Unemployment Surveys, in: ILO Statistics

Unemployment rates among young women aged 25 to 34 are four times higher than those observed among young men in Egypt.

The unemployment of university graduates has been a particular concern in the region, which produces a lot of them.[17] Young generations indeed benefited from the generalization of higher education in the region: the proportion of tertiary-educated among the 25 to 34-year-olds reached 23 percent in Egypt in 2018, and up to 27 percent in Jordan (2021 data). Young Jordanian females in the age group were even more often tertiary-educated than males (31.4 percent of women and 24 percent of men in the age category).

However, tertiary education ceased being a guarantee of employment already in the 1990s. In the region, youth in "advanced" levels of education, holding a BA and above,[18] generally display significantly higher unemployment rates than less educated ones. In Egypt, for instance, rates stood below 5 percent among the holders of a "basic" (primary, lower-secondary) education and below (males and females), as opposed to 21 percent among university graduates (in the "advanced" education category). Unemployment rates reached above 35 percent for university graduates in Jordan in 2022, as opposed to "only" 15 percent among the population holding no degree (Table 5.4). Females with "intermediate" education[19] are also largely unemployed in most countries, along with the most educated.

Youth unemployment in Arab states is also a long-term situation: the distribution of the unemployed by length of unemployment in ILO data

Table 5.4. Egypt and Jordan: Unemployment Rates in Age Group 25–34 Years by Sex and Aggregate Education Levels (2022)

		Unemployment rates (25–34 years)		
	Education (aggregate levels)	**Males**	**Females**	**Total**
Egypt	**Less than basic**	2.3	NA	2.4
	Basic	3.4	14.2	4.4
	Intermediate	5.5	24.8	7.7
	Advanced	14.4	36.1	21.4
	Not stated	NA	29.1	17.5
	Total	**6.8**	**28.7**	**10.6**
Jordan	**Less than basic**	17.6	3.0	14.8
	Basic	18.0	15.3	17.8
	Intermediate	9.4	44.7	13.0
	Advanced	29.4	44.4	35.5
	Total	**18.3**	**27.0**	**21.7**

Sources: Egypt: Labor Force Surveys; Jordan, Employment and Unemployment Surveys, in: ILO Statistics

indicated that half of unemployed young males (in age groups 15–24 and 25–34) and up to 70 percent of young females had spent more than one year searching for employment. Fifty-five percent of the unemployed Egyptian females aged 25 to 34 in 2018 had spent more than two years in continuous unemployment. The Egyptian and Jordanian Labor Market Panel Surveys of 2012 and 2010 had already underlined similar dynamics, especially concerning female Egyptians (Assaad and Krafft, 2016).

Youth unemployment in context

Unemployment rates and their variations thus depict unemployment as a long-term situation deeply scarring young Arabs' life-course, and therefore, could logically act as a proximate driver for migration. Yet, aggregated unemployment figures are based on the definition of unemployment as a share of the labor force (those registered as employed and those looking for employment), but some young Arabs are in fact employed (Egyptian males), or are outside the labor force (inactives), especially among females (Table 5.5). At 13 percent of the age group, the share of the unemployed among active males aged 25–34 years is indeed low in Egypt, if compared to the 78 percent who are employed. However, 27 percent of young, active, educated Jordanians are unemployed, a higher share, while 65 percent are employed. In both countries, advanced education even deters from employment, as the share of employed among the highly educated stands below levels found in the total male population.

Among females, by contrast, inactivity prevails, even if in both countries, advanced education grants higher activity levels: slightly higher shares of women are employed as compared with global female populations, and they are significantly more often unemployed, which means that the educated women seek employment ("only" 45 (Jordan) to 60 percent of them (Egypt) are inactive), when less educated ones may not.

This puts into perspective the issue of unemployment as the main factor of alienation for young nationals and a main driver for emigration, as suggested by young interviewees in the Arab Youth Survey. As a matter of fact, the 2010 Jordan Labor Market Panel Survey indicated that 94 percent of the surveyed expatriate Jordanians were employed before migrating, of whom 79 percent were working in the private sector (Wahba, 2012: 3). Seventy-four percent of Egyptian migrants, who are males in their vast majority as we have seen, were also employed in Egypt before they emigrated, according to the HIMS survey: 86 percent among those with no and some education; 59 percent among those holding a higher education (Farid, et al., 2016: 61). A significant share of employed among male emigrants, coupled

Table 5.5. Egypt and Jordan: Population Aged 25–34 by Sex and Relation to the Labor Market (Advanced Education Level; Total) (2022)

		In the labour force						Outside the labour force					
	Education category	Employment-to-population ratio (% employed in age group)			Unemployment-to-population ratio (% unemployed in age group)			Activity rate			Inactivity rate		
		Males	Females	Total	Males	Females	Total	Males	Females	Total	Males	Females	Total
Egypt	**Advanced**	78.1	26.2	51.3	13.1	14.8	14.0	**91.3**	**40.9**	**65.3**	**8.7**	**59.1**	**34.7**
	Total	**86.7**	**13.3**	**49.6**	**6.4**	**5.4**	**5.9**	93.1	18.7	55.5	6.9	81.3	44.5
Jordan	**Advanced**	64.7	30.8	46.7	26.9	24.6	25.7	**91.6**	**55.4**	**72.4**	**8.4**	**44.6**	**27.6**
	Total	**74.7**	**19.2**	**50.4**	**16.7**	**10.5**	**14.0**	91.4	29.7	64.4	8.6	70.3	35.6

Sources: Egypt: Labor Force Surveys; Jordan, Employment and Unemployment Surveys, in: ILO Statistics.

with large shares of inactive among young females and above-average proportion of unemployed among both thus question the attractivity of the labor market, and the quality of the jobs available in the two countries.

Economic crises, structural adjustment policies

Mashreq countries' economies indeed face difficulties in integrating their highly educated youth, mostly due to the impetus given to structural adjustment measures since the 2000s. The fall of oil revenues from the late 1980s and geopolitical divides within the region in the 1990s dried out Arab aid to non-oil-producing states. This compelled all Mashreq countries to enact socio-economic reforms and structural adjustment measures, most of them under international financing and monitoring. Public sector employment, the main outlet for young graduates in the region, suffered extensive cutbacks everywhere in the region. International treaties, bilateral and free trade agreements, and World Trade Organization (WTO) accession processes signed during the 1990s and 2000s expanded massive liberalization and deregulation policies, as the region was inscribing into the global economy. Investments were geared towards labor-intensive, low-wage and low-skilled activities in the industrial subcontracting, assembly, and textile manufacturing sectors. Structural adjustment measures did not solve economic crises in the region and aggravated socio-economic inequalities. For instance, the $12 billion loan received by Egypt from the International Monetary Fund (IMF) in 2016 required the country to implement a series of austerity measures that have pushed almost a third of the 102 million Egyptians into poverty. The war in Ukraine, which disrupted imports of wheat to the country, of which more than 80 percent comes from Russia and Ukraine, further exacerbated Egypt's economic troubles, resulting in skyrocketing prices of bread and oil, thus compounding existing stressors (Talaat, 2022).

Like in the rest of the region (UNDP/RBAS, 2016: Chapter 3), graduates' unemployment in Egypt and Jordan is, more generally, an issue of transition from school to work, whereby, "[n]ew entrants are a large percentage of the unemployed and make up an even higher proportion among the long-term unemployed." This "labor insertion phenomenon," characteristic of the region, likely signals "young inexperienced graduates' preference for formal or public sector work over lower quality employment in the private sector," especially among young females (Assaad and Krafft, 2016: 9–10), and in former "rentier economies" like Jordan. The sense of entitlement among the local youth, or "welfare state ethos" (Louër, 2008: 47) pushes highly educated citizens expecting public sector jobs to choose unemployment instead of taking on jobs available in the private sector, where the economic rationality of supply and demand proposes lower salaries than the public sector, longer hours, less or no incentive packages (paid leaves, health protection, . . .). Such conditions are also not prone to motivate discouraged inactives. One example is the export-processing special economic zones (formerly called Qualifying Industrial Zones), set up in Jordan in the aftermath of the peace negotiations with Israel in 1994. These were originally intended to provide income and employment to young rural populations, especially women. However, unattractive wages and labor conditions in the zones failed to channel local unemployed youth to semi-skilled manufacturing jobs. Foreign laborers became an increasing share of the labor force in these plants—up to 75 percent in the late 2010s.[20]

Economic reforms thus failed to provide compelling conditions for youth. Moreover, personal connections and *wasta*[21] are considered still needed to supplement qualifications and merit. In a 2013 Gallup poll, 85 percent of Jordanian youth agreed with the statement that, "knowing people in high positions is critical to getting a job" (Milton Edwards, 2018: 3). Arab Youth Surveys pinpointed *wasta* as "corrod[ing] societies, impair[ing] growth, fuel[ing] unrest and squander[ing] the potential of so many young Arabs who simply want the dignity of fair opportunity" (ASDA'A BCW, 2019: 10). Economic liberalization measures indeed failed to dismantle clientelist systems and monopolies of power, and pervasive clientelism was found still prevailing in the region today, even in countries which underwent regime changes after the uprisings of 2010–2011 (Diamond and Plattner, 2014; Elbadawi and Makdisi, 2016).

More than a lack of available jobs, economic reform policies and the type of job created, which do not meet the expectations of educated youth, added to the difficulties in accessing opportunities for those not connected to patronage networks, may thus be considered among the main drivers of youth emigration from Jordan and Egypt, and especially, that of the most educated youth, which is characterizing Jordan. "Insufficient income in Egypt" and "need to improve standard of living" were the main motivations to emigrate from Egypt to other Arab states, all skill levels included (Farid et al., 2016: 44). This confirms the hypothesis that the gap between employment-related expectations and reality acts as a major driver for the emigration of university-educated youth.

Socio-economic inequalities, emigration, and political control

Egyptian emigration gained momentum after 1971, following a phase of legal restrictions on emigration under Gamal Abdel Nasser's regime. The economy and national borders were opened to the circulation of goods and persons (*infitah*) under President Sadat. The right to migrate was enshrined in the 1971 constitution. The 1973 war and the ensuing hike in oil prices stimulated strong workforce needs in oil-producing countries; large numbers of emigrants left Egypt for Saudi Arabia and the other Gulf states, Iraq, and Libya. Gulf states' oil-based economic expansion and workforce needs also spurred the emigration of Jordanian nationals to Gulf oil-producing countries, from the 1950s onwards and especially after 1973.

The "open-door" policies to emigration had a mediating function on migration from the two countries, but Jordan's Hashemite regime was especially prone to encourage nationals' emigration from the onset of the oil-induced Gulf states' infrastructural development process. The 1948 and 1967 wars and the following political tensions pushed several waves of refugees from Palestine to the country. Nationals' emigration thus alleviated the economic pressure of demographic expansion and supplied migrants' households with remittances. Expatriates' remittances made up 25 percent of Jordan's GDP in the late 1980s, and still around 12 percent today, according to the Jordanian Central Bank. This expansion of households' revenues played a determinant role in the development of a consumption-based, non-productive economy and mode of wealth accumulation, as well as increasing the Jordanian workers' reservation wages (the minimum salary considered to take a job).

"Open-door" policies to emigration also served the political interests of the regime and supported the "pan-Arabist claims" (Schlaim, 1988) of the ruling Hashemite dynasty. Emigration compensated for the eviction of some citizens from the capital redistribution process. Among these were some of the 1948 Palestinian refugees and 1967 displaced persons who failed to incorporate into patronage and clientelism networks existing on the East Bank (Czichowski, 1990: 149). Inequality in the process of resource distribution acted as a proximate driver for the emigration from Jordan; yet, this driver operated in a selective manner, as it primarily affected Jordanians of Palestinian origin (De Bel-Air, 2012).

The open-door apparatus

Besides the search for economic revenues in encouraging migration, "open-door" policy also warded off potential dissent against the two regimes. Providing an outlet for frustrated would-be elites and attempting to keep political control, thus also acted as proximate drivers of Egypt's and Jordan's migration policies. Emigration as an outlet for educated youth, and possibly as a political safety valve, continues to be the dominant policy in the two sending states today. For example, a document issued by the Egyptian Council of Ministers, entitled

"Features of the strategic directions of the Egyptian economy during the period 2024–2030," expresses the government's intentions to "open new markets," presumably abroad, in artificial intelligence, information technology services, nursing, biotechnology, and other specializations for about one million Egyptians. The government also indicated plans to increase remittances from Egyptians working abroad by an annual rate of 10 percent from 2024 to 2030, to reach about 53 billion dollars (Al-Masry, 2024).

Over the years, Egypt has achieved high levels of institutionalization in its emigration policies, which could contribute to streamlining the emigration process, besides migrants' personal networks. The country has been running a "multi-tier emigration policy" (Tsourapas, 2018) increasingly turned towards accommodating the needs and wishes of Egyptian expatriates in Western countries, labeled "permanent emigrants," at the expense of labor migrants to the Arab region (the Gulf States and Jordan), considered "temporary" migrants. The Section of Emigration and Egyptian Expatriates' Affairs within the Ministry of Foreign Affairs seeks to strengthen the bonds between Egypt,[22] its diaspora, and expatriates' host states, enforce dialogue and assistance to expatriates, investigate bilateral agreements, and coordinate with concerned national, regional, and international organizations to exchange information and fundraise for diaspora-related projects.[23] Egypt also deploys labor counselors in each GCC country (Awad and Abdelaziz, 2017: 234). As of October 2024, the Ministry of Manpower oversees employment, labor relations, and emigration of Egyptian workers. The Section for Employment Abroad finds and advertises jobs abroad and matches registered jobseekers with opportunities, while the Ministry of Interior issues the final clearance and "permit to work abroad."

Contrary to Egypt, where the Central Agency for Public Mobilization and Statistics (CAPMAS), Egypt's official National Statistical Office, processes statistics on "temporary," "permanent" and other types of emigrants produced by the various institutions involved, Jordan has no systematic registration system for its expatriates. One possible reason for this is that Jordanian migrants are generally highly skilled, which enables some of them to secure employment abroad through their own resources. Many emigrants indeed do not rely on governmental or other institutional employment programs. Alternatively, if we consider that keeping records on expatriates means acknowledging that they are a part of the citizenry (one "counts" (i.e., matters) if one "is counted" (i.e., enumerated)[24]), the lack of data may confirm the political stakes of Jordan's "open-door" policy (eviction of potential socio-economic or political discontent), as described earlier.

Nonetheless, the Department of Expatriates of the Ministry of Foreign Affairs and Expatriates (MoFAE) maintains consular records through the consular services of Jordanian embassies. The Ministry of Labor (MoL) encourages and facilitates Jordanian labor emigration by collating job vacancies abroad. Through electronic platforms,[25] the MoL maintains an employment office and online portal, which is managed by the Employment Directorate. The Recruitment Offices Division regulates and supervises the activities of private recruitment agencies and operates under the Employment Directorate of the MoL (as of October 2024).[26] The Directorate of International Relations also coordinates with international partners to promote the employment of Jordanians abroad.[27] The recently created Labor Market Studies Unit has two departments: the Labor Market Information Department and the Surveys and Studies Department. The Ministry also appointed "labor consultants" in Jordanian embassies in the Gulf in the late 2000s, to organize the training and placement of Jordanians abroad and to defend their rights (Ministry of Labor, 2009: 24–26).

After COVID-19: Increased emigration pressure

Since the late 2010s, protests surged in countries that did not experience the Arab uprisings of 2010–2011, including Sudan, Iraq, Lebanon, Morocco, and Jordan. Beyond calling for changes in their political systems, protesters demanded a comprehensive overhaul of their economic systems as well, denouncing soaring prices, wealth disparities, elite capture of resources and rent streams, and the absence of economic justice (Arafeh, 2024). Domestic political crises have since then deepened, like in Tunisia and Lebanon; conflicts, and regional and global geopolitical tensions, durably weaken the region's economies, limiting especially local and international investments in non-Gulf Arab states. The COVID-19 pandemic, the war in Ukraine, and the ensuing debt, food, and energy crises that hit the region have further exacerbated socio-economic disparities (Arafeh and Meddeb, 2024) inherited from the socio-political conditions and neoliberal reforms described in previous sections. Moreover, despite their having triggered the Arab uprisings, structural factors such as corruption remain "a paramount challenge in the Arab Mediterranean countries [...], exerting profound influence on development while eroding trust in the public sector" as anti-corruption efforts are yet to yield significant results (Dandashly and Kourtelis, 2024). Consequently, the degradation of the purchasing power and living and working conditions, the collapse of public services, and, more generally, the decline in personal and social security in most Arab states are spectacular. The results of the last wave of the Arab Barometer Survey confirm that economic dissatisfaction is a major driver behind emigration, most strongly in Jordan (90 percent) and Tunisia (89 percent), followed by overwhelming majorities in Lebanon (72 percent) and Mauritania (69 percent). Security concerns also drove 27 percent of potential migrants in Lebanon to consider leaving, while political issues and corruption were motivating 23 percent and 24 percent of potential Lebanese migrants, respectively (Arab Barometer, 2024).

While all workers, and especially the employees of crumbling public sectors, are affected by this mix of circumstances, the highly skilled among them find opportunities of escape abroad. The case of doctors, who started emigrating from their countries in exceptionally large numbers, is emblematic. In 2021, the World Health Organization estimated that nearly 40 percent of Lebanon's doctors had emigrated,[28] and similar reports are coming out from Iraq, Morocco, Tunisia, and Jordan, for instance (Schaer and Guizani, 2023), citing low wages and poor conditions as reasons for quitting. A survey of medical personnel's motivation for emigrating to Saudi Arabia confirmed that the main reasons for healthcare migration were the social and economic problems with healthcare systems in origin countries, such as poor planning of the health workforce, low job satisfaction, political and economic instability, discrimination, and corruption (AlMansour et.al., 2023). In Egypt, especially, the ratio of doctors in the government sector to those licensed to practice the profession is 40.8 percent, revealing the scale of practitioners' emigration, which brought down the ratio of doctors to citizens to 9 for every 10,000 citizens, far below the world average of 23 per 10,000 (MEMO, 2022). In 2018, it was estimated that 60 percent of Egyptian doctors, or 69,000 of them, were working in Saudi Arabia alone (Ezz, 2024).

Drivers of inward migration to Saudi Arabia

The "push" factors to emigrate from the Middle East and North African region, and especially from Jordan and Egypt, thus play a major role as drivers for migration. This is confirmed by the prevalence of "country of origin"-related factors, which 42 percent of current emigrants to Arab states quoted as "most important motive for first migration." Current emigrants in other destinations (Europe and North America) put a higher emphasis on country of destination-related factors (Farid et al., 2016: 44). Nonetheless, Gulf states also offer specific drivers for Arab migrants.

Cultural and geographic proximity

The Gulf states' geographic proximity to Jordan and Egypt, which allowed for mobility between home and host states, predisposes Middle Eastern highly skilled workers to emigrate to the region. This was found as an important factor driving Lebanese emigrants to the Gulf region (De Bel-Air, 2017). Linguistic proximity is also an asset for migrants. Jordanian professionals, for instance, were said to produce up to 80 percent of the online Arabic content, especially from their host Gulf states (Al Ajlouni, 2023). A survey of medical personnel in Saudi Arabia also underlined the importance of the cultural and religious proximity of Gulf states, and especially Saudi Arabia, to Arab and Muslim populations: About 80 percent of the Muslim participants to the survey said that religion and the proximity of the Muslim Holy Shrines were one of the pull factors for working in Saudi Arabia (AlMansour et al., 2023). The security and stability offered by the Gulf region were also considered compelling drivers in numerous accounts and field surveys on reasons to migrate to the Gulf since the COVID-19 period. This compares to the politically unstable and economically deteriorating contexts in Arab origin countries as described earlier, but also to Western destinations perceived as increasingly unsafe for Arab Muslim families and home to anti-Muslim popular stances.

Wage differentials between origin countries and Saudi Arabia, economic growth

Wage differentials between sending and receiving countries and higher, tax-free salaries granted to professionals in the region attracted Arab migrants to the Gulf. For instance, university professors could earn more than four times their original salaries in the Gulf States in the 2000s (Alami, Bhatti, and Dumalaon, 2014). Wage differentials are indeed very high: For instance, Qatar wages, relative to Egypt, stood at 750 percent in tourism, 859 percent in transportation, 927 percent in construction (Awad and Abdel Aziz, 2017: 231). As socio-economic contexts are now deteriorating further, the average salary for a resident doctor in Egypt is only around 3,700 Egyptian pounds ($201). However, the minimum monthly salary for a doctor in Saudi Arabia is 22,000 Egyptian pounds, roughly equivalent to wages received in Northern European countries (MEMO, 2022).

More generally, the strength and steadiness of the region's economic environment, despite the global context of economic turbulence, offer a large range of employment opportunities for foreign professionals, among whom large numbers are highly skilled Arab expatriates. As confirmed by the Hays GCC salary guide 2024, 67 percent of employers in the Gulf region were planning to grow their organization's headcount during the year. Seeking to compete with the UAE, Saudi Arabia offers competitive salaries to attract highly skilled professionals to its "buoyant labor market" and emerging position as "financial hub" in the Middle East.[29]

Vision 2030, the socio-economic reform process and employment opportunities

Faced with the need to diversify and decarbonize their economies to alleviate their vulnerability to the volatility of hydrocarbon revenues, as well as to quell the emergence of structural unemployment among young citizens, Gulf states and among them, Saudi Arabia set up ambitious socio-economic development goals, which impose sustaining high economic growth levels.

The set goal of Vision 2030, Saudi Arabia's reform masterplan launched in 2016,[30] is therefore to create a knowledge-based economy in the Kingdom through investing in education, fostering innovative, high value-added industries, e.g., promoting technical innovation (such as "green" economy, development of AI research and applications, of information technologies (ICTs)), and developing new economic sectors (tourism, health, sport, entertainment . . .).

The process of transition from a labor-intensive to an internationally competitive, knowledge-based, and innovative economy, fostering high-value-added industries, includes prioritizing the attraction of more skilled and highly skilled workers. This creates an ecosystem favorable to the many unemployed, inactive, and dissatisfied employed highly skilled Arab professionals.

In this context, the current acceleration of the recruitment of medical personnel, especially from Egypt (Ezz, 2024), was discussed in this chapter. The development of sports facilities, initiatives aiming to develop a healthy lifestyle in the country, which are part of the development vision, may well offer opportunities to reinforce the recruitment of Arab specialists in the field, Tunisians, for example (ILO, 2023). The setting up of an entertainment industry, almost from scratch in Saudi Arabia, may also require the expertise of nationals from other Arab states with long experience in the arts, movie and TV film production, acting, and showbusiness activities, especially Syrians and Egyptians (Medhat, 2025).

Saudi Arabia's Labor Market Initiative, which entered into force in March 2021, claims to have canceled the "kafala" sponsorship system in the Kingdom. The measure introduces a contractual relationship between the employer and the employee. Workers can apply directly for posts in Saudi Arabia via an e-government portal, and their residency is no longer tied to a specific employer or employment status, while the work contract must be certified by the government. Exit, re-entry, and final exit is free and not conditional on the employer's consent. These measures, intending to improve job mobility, flexibility, and competition, allegedly aim to boost the productivity of the private sector, in line with international labor regulations (AlShammari,

2020). The measure may decrease the rights and career prospects gaps between employment conditions in the West and in Gulf states, and enhance the attractiveness of the Saudi labor market for highly skilled Arab workers.

Beyond employment: attracting and retaining "high-value-added" expatriates and investors

To appear even more attractive to "high potential" expatriates, Saudi Arabia opened avenues for long-term residence and even naturalization to selected expatriates. Saudi Arabia introduced in 2019 the Premium Residency Card (PRC) scheme, or "Green Card," a new type of residency without a sponsor. Permanent residency may be granted for SR800,000 (US$213,000) or a one-year renewable permit for SR100,000. Permanent Residency Card holders can travel in and out of the Kingdom without restrictions on duration. Expected to benefit wealthy individuals who have lived in Saudi Arabia for years without permanent residency or multinational companies seeking to do long-term business in the Kingdom, the new system is marketed as an important source of revenues to boost the Saudi economy and contribute to the creation of jobs, hence serving nationals' interests (Arab News, 2019). Since 2023, among the Premium Residency "products" proposed by Saudi Arabia's Premium Residency Center,[31] the Special Talent Visa caters to executives and professionals who specialize in healthcare, science, and research, and aims to attract individuals with unique skills and experiences who can contribute to knowledge and technology transfers. The Saudi Arabian Premium Residency Program targets the "gifted," investor, entrepreneur, and real estate owner categories as potential beneficiaries of long-term residency schemes (Khaleej Times, 2024). Saudi Arabia also opened the door to naturalization for distinguished scientific innovators and cultural professionals who could meet the required criteria (Reuters, 2021).

Conclusion

The chapter aimed to highlight the drivers of highly skilled emigration from Arab states to Saudi Arabia, with a focus on emigration from Egypt and Jordan, two Mashreq countries sending most of their highly skilled workers to Saudi Arabia. The prevalence of unemployment and unsatisfying employment (among males) and that of inactivity were underlined as major proximate determinants for seeking emigration. The structural background of this situation was analysed: Arab states' "open-door" policies to emigration, to alleviate political discontent due to "discriminatory clientelism" (Hertog,

2006: 120), against certain sectors of the Jordanian population in Jordan, for instance. Structural adjustment reforms in both countries failed to open avenues of employment suitable for the highly skilled professionals trained in the region's numerous tertiary education establishments. Since the wave of "Arab uprisings" of 2011, the popular protests of 2019, followed by a chain of crises (COVID-19, the Ukraine War, the debt, food, and energy crises, and regional developments of the Hamas-Israel war), have exacerbated socio-economic disparities and distrust towards local regimes. Ailing public sectors deteriorated further, along with personal security, which accentuated the emigration pressure among highly skilled professionals in all branches.

Since Mashreq countries' citizens are primarily emigrating to the Gulf, and to Saudi Arabia particularly, the context of the socio-economic reform process towards a knowledge-based economy should offer welcome avenues for Arab professionals in the Kingdom, together with the recent measures passed in the country to streamline the labor market, and attract and retain highly skilled and wealthy investors (the Premium Residency Card, especially). Arab women, whom we saw were particularly alienated from local labor markets, make up a large pool of skills to tap into. The sustained reform path and economic growth rates, which guarantee income much higher than in origin countries, is a major factor of attraction of Arab highly skilled migrants to Saudi Arabia.

However, the outcomes of the *Nitaqat* policy of "Saudization" of the workforce, launched in 2011, on Arab migrants still need to be assessed. The program seeks to reduce employers' reliance on foreign workers and better match foreign migrants' skills with employers' needs, to promote nationals' employment. However, data are unavailable, which could (1) precisely map the Arab competences by profession on the Saudi labor market, and (2) measure the effects of Saudisation measures by profession and origin country. Nonetheless, recent increases in Saudisation quotas for highly skilled professions often performed by Arab citizens, such as teaching[32] or engineering,[33] may eventually limit the prospects of migration to Saudi Arabia for some highly skilled workers in the "Professionals" and "Technicians" categories of professions,[34] more likely to be filled by Saudi citizens.

The political instability in the region may also affect migration inflows from Arab states. In the aftermath of the Arab revolts and political turmoil experienced in the Arab world since 2011, the Gulf states have enacted various measures to reverse immigration flows or limit the numbers of selected Arab nationals from countries having experienced regime changes (De Bel-Air, 2018). In the current dire situation of most Arab states, it is hoped that the Israel-Hamas and Israel-Hezbollah conflicts will not affect the employment prospects of these nationals in the Gulf region.

Notes

1 Author's calculations, based on UN data (United Nations Department of Economic and Social Affairs, Population Division. *International Migrant Stock by origin and destination* 2020).

2 Those classified in the three highest categories of occupations: the "Managers," "Specialists," and "Technicians" in the ILO ISCO-08 classification of occupations.

3 Reprocessed, for a part, by the International Labour Organisation (ILO).

4 See the processing of the datasets in GLMM database: https://gulfmigration.grc.net/saudi-arabia-workers-employed-in-the-private-sector-by-country-of-citizenship-2022/; https://gulfmigration.grc.net/saudi-arabia-workers-employed-in-the-government-sector-by-country-of-citizenship-and/ ; more tables on workers in the civil service are available here: https://gulfmigration.grc.net/glmm-database/demographic-and-economic-module/?search=1&cmct=Saudi+Arabia.

5 https://gulfmigration.grc.net/saudi-arabia-arab-population-by-country-of-citizenship-and-sex-census-2022/. Arab countries are the Arab League member countries, minus Somalia, Djibouti, and the Comoros.

6 https://gulfmigration.grc.net/saudi-arabia-workers-employed-in-the-government-sector-by-country-of-citizenship-and-education-level-2022-2/.

7 https://thevisaproject.com/experience/saudi-arabia/change-professions-for-family-visa-saudi-arabia/.

8 Saudi Arabia, along with most Arab states, does not recognize refugees' international protection status because it did not ratify the 1951 Geneva Convention relating to the status of refugees or its 1967 Protocol. However, specific nationalities, among which some Syrians, Yemenis, and Rohingyas from Burma, for instance, are currently acknowledged as refugees in Saudi Arabia and offered some protection by the state.

9 https://www.jordantimes.com/news/local/50-working-jordanian-engineers-based-gulf-region-%E2%80%94-halaseh.

10 https://www.moroccoworldnews.com/2015/11/173518/morocco-will-no-longer-validate-employment-contracts-for-maids-working-in-saudi-arabia.

11 https://masryyasaudia.com/jobs/.

12 https://www.jordannews.jo/Section-109/News/JEA-taking-steps-to-provide-jobs-for-Jordanian-engineers-in-Saudi-13072.

13 Jordan, Syria, Iraq, Lebanon, and Palestine, as well as Yemen in the Arabian Peninsula.

14 Data from Palestine were collected between September 28 and October 6, before the onset of the Israeli-Hamas war https://www.arabbarometer.org/media-news/press-release-migration-trends-in-the-middle-east-and-north-africa-revealed-in-latest-arab-barometer-survey/.

15 Unless stated otherwise, data used in this and the following sections are taken from the International Labor Organization (ILO), ILOSTAT database (https://ilostat.ilo.org/data/)

16 Among the 15–24-year-olds. The Arab region is followed by the Europe and Central Asia region with 15.5 percent of unemployed youth (ILO, ILOSTAT database). The unemployment rate is the number of persons who are unemployed as a percent of the total number of employed and unemployed persons (i.e., the labor force).
17 For instance, Jordan has 10 public universities, 16 private ones, and 51 community colleges, for a population of some 11 million (including refugees).
18 Aggregate levels of education, in ILO statistics. For the correspondence with UNESCO ISCED 11 and 97 classifications, see: https://www.ilo.org/ilostat-files/Documents/description_EDU_EN.pdf, p. 2.
19 Corresponding to upper secondary and post-secondary, non-tertiary education in other classifications.
20 Jordan Ministry of Labor, Statistical Yearbooks.
21 Intermediation, or reliance on family, friends, and other social connections to access anything from a job to political favors or business opportunities.
22 The Section was a Ministry of State (Ministry of State for Emigration and Egyptian Expatriates' Affairs (MoSEEA)) but was integrated into the MoFA in 2024.
23 https://www.emigration.gov.eg/DefaultEn/Pages/default.aspx.
24 Adapted from Bookman, 1997: 71.
25 The National Electronic Employment Services (nees.jo) was replaced by the National Employment Platform, Tashghîl (http://sajjil.gov.jo/), as of 2021.
26 http://www.mol.gov.jo/EN/Pages/Private_Employment_Offices_Directory.
27 http://www.mol.gov.jo/ebv4.0/root_storage/ar/eb_list_page.
28 https://www.emro.who.int/media/news/joint-statement-by-dr-tedros-adhanom-ghebreyesus-who-director-general-and-dr-ahmed-al-mandhari-regional-director-for-the-eastern-mediterranean-on-lebanon.html.
29 https://www.hays.ae/documents/d/global/hays-saudi-arabia-salary-guide-2023.
30 www.vision2030.gov.sa/en.
31 https://pr.gov.sa/
32 https://www.argaam.com/en/article/articledetail/id/1493196.
33 https://www.hrsd.gov.sa/sites/default/files/2024-01/n25012024.pdf.
34 Categories 2 and 3 in the ILO-ISCO 08 classification.

Bibliographic references

Al Ajlouni, E. 2023. "Over 50 percent of Arabic Content on the Internet is of Jordanian Origin," *Arab America*, May 31. https://www.arabamerica.com/over-50-of-arabic-content-is-jordanian-origin/

Alami, A., J. Bhatti, and J. Dumalaon. 2014. "Employment in the Gulf: Not Always What It Seems," *Fanar Media*, January 13. http://www.al-fanarmedia.org/2014/01/employment-in-the-gulf-not-always-what-itseems/

AlMansour, H., A. Aldossary, S. Holmes et al. 2023. "Migration of Nurses and Doctors: Pull Factors to Work in Saudi Arabia," *Hum Resour Health* 21: 25. https://doi.org/10.1186/s12960-023-00809-5

Al-Masry, M. 2024. "To Raise Dollar Inflows, the Government Aims to Employ One Million Egyptians Abroad in 6 Years," *Al-Masrawy*, 8 January, https://www.masrawy.com/news/news-banking/details/2024/1/8/2521060/-لرفع تدفقات-الدولار-الحكومة-تستهدف-تشغيل-مليون-مصري-بالخارج-في-6?fbclid=IwAR1YV-uOZZZEshQ1kCbEmRoEfo6BjpYJE-nTYTP23ib7AOTTuK8Gs3rQ_S4_aem_AYFLGgZh4i18UolUbXywQVViUGbEaO2gXUZ8TjsYVzWAodd6LFx_4gBtKtYTOuhJoYA

Alshammari, R. 2020. "Saudi Arabia's Labor Reforms Seen as Big Boost for Private Sector," *Arab News*, 4 November. https://www.arabnews.com/node/1758456/saudi-arabia

Arab Barometer –Wave VIII. 2024. *Migration in the Middle East and North Africa*, August.

Arab Barometer –Wave VII. 2022. *Public Views of Migration in MENA*, July.

Arab News. 2019. "Saudi 'Green Card' Online Platform is Open for Business," *Arab News*, 23 June. https://www.arabnews.com/node/1514921/saudi-arabia

Arafeh, N. 2024. "Economic Injustice is Anchoring Itself in the Arab World." Working paper, Malcolm H. Kerr Carnegie Middle East Center, Beirut: Carnegie Endowment for International Peace, February. https://carnegieendowment.org/posts/2024/02/economic-injustice-is-anchoring-itself-in-the-arab-world?lang=en

Arafeh, N. and H. Meddeb. 2024. "Misfortune to Marginalization: The Geopolitical Impact of Structural Economic Failings in Egypt, Tunisia, and Lebanon." Working paper, Malcolm H. Kerr Carnegie Middle East Center, Beirut: Carnegie Endowment for International Peace, January 2024. https://carnegie-production-assets.s3.amazonaws.com/static/files/Hamza_Nur_PE_FINAL1.pdf

ASDA'A BCW. 2019. *A Call for Reform. A White Paper on the findings of the 11th annual ASDA'A BCW Arab Youth Survey 2019*. ASDA'A BCW.

ASDA'A BCW. 2023. *Arab Youth Survey 2023. White Paper: Living a New Reality*, Dubai: ASDA'A BCW.

ASDA'A Burson-Marsteller. 2017. *The Middle East—A Region Divided. A White Paper on the findings of the ASDA'A Burson-Marsteller Arab Youth Survey 2017*. ASDA'A Burson-Marsteller.

Assaad, R. and C. Krafft. 2016. "Labor Market Dynamics and Youth Unemployment in the Middle East and North Africa: Evidence from Egypt, Jordan and Tunisia." Economic Research Forum Working Paper 993, April. https://erf.org.eg/publications/labor-market-dynamics-and-youth-unemployment-in-the-middle-east-and-north-africa-evidence-from-egypt-jordan-and-tunisia/

Awad, I. and N. Abdel Aziz. 2017. "Egyptian Irregular Migration in the GCC Countries." In: Ph. Fargues and N. Shah (eds.), *Skilful Survivals. Irregular Migration to the Gulf*, 225–41. Cambridge: Gulf Research Centre.

Bookman, M. 1997. *The Demographic Struggle for Power: The Political Economy of Demographic Engineering in the Modern World*. London, Portland: Frank Cass and Co.

CAPMAS. 2019. Annual Bulletin of Work Permits Issued for Egyptians to Work Abroad, Cairo: CAPMAS, https://www.capmas.gov.eg/Pages/Publications.aspx?page_id=5104&Year=23492.

Czichowski, F. 1990. *Jordanien: Internationale Migration, Wirtschaftliche Entwicklung und Soziale Stabilität (Jordanie : migrations internationales, développement économique et stabilité sociale)*, Hamburg: Deutsches Orient-Institut (Schriften des Deutschen Orient-Institut).

Dandashly, A., and C. Kourtelis. 2024. Political Corruption in the Arab Mediterranean Countries: An Innovative Typology. *Democratization* 31(8), 1844–65. https://doi.org/10.1080/13510347.2024.2343621

De Bel-Air, F. 2012. "Migration, Security and the Palestinian Question. Palestinian Refugees in Jordan and Lebanon: Granting Rights, or Pushing for Resettlement?" CARIM Research Report 2012/02, San Domenico Di Fiesole (Florence, Italy): Robert Schuman Centre for Advanced Studies (RSCAS), European University Institute (EUI). http://www.carim.org/index.php?callContent=484&callText=1737

De Bel-Air, F. 2017. "Arab Female Highly Skilled Migrants to the GCC Countries." In Z. Babar (ed.) *Arab Migrant Communities in the GCC*, 169–96. London: Hurst and Co. https://doi.org/10.1093/oso/9780190608873.003.0008

De Bel-Air, F. 2018. "'Blocked' Youth: the Politics of Migration from the SEM Countries Before and After the Arab Uprisings," *International Spectator* 53: 52–73.

Diamond, L. and M. F. Plattner (eds). 2014. *Democratization and Authoritarianism in the Arab World (A Journal of Democracy Book)*. Baltimore: Johns Hopkins University Press.

Elbadawi, I. and S. Makdisi (eds). 2016. *Democratic Transitions in the Arab World*. Cambridge: Cambridge University Press.

Ezz, M. 2024. "Health Ministry Spox on Specialized Doctors 'Loan' to Saudi Arabia: I Don't Know Anything About This Decision," *MadaMasr*, 10 March.

Farid, S., A. Nour El-Deen and R. El-Batrawy (eds). 2016. *Egypt Household International Migration Survey 2013: Volume I: Determinants and Consequences of International Migration*. Cairo, Egypt: Central Agency for Public Mobilization and Statistics.

GAStat (General Authority for Statistics). 2022. 2022 CENSUS Program Progress and Documentation (May). https://www.stats.gov.sa/documents/20117/2435133/1+VGA_templatized_20230607_1600+Census+2022_Documentation_compressed.pdf/5429a795-4a73-8ec9-04a4-b969c74ef64c?t=1769086386623

Hertog, S. 2006. "Segmented Clientelism: The Political Economy of Saudi Economic Reform Efforts." In P. Aarts and G. Nonneman (eds), *Saudi Arabia in the Balance*, 111–43. London: Hurst and Co.

ILO (International Labor Organization). 2022. *L'impact socioéconomique de la COVID-19 sur les travailleurs marocains résidant à l'étranger*. ILO.

ILO. 2023. *Etude exploratoire sur les opportunités de placement des travailleurs tunisiens dans les pays du Golfe (Arabie Saoudite, Bahreïn et Qatar)*. ILO.

Khaleej Times. 2024. "Saudi Arabia Launches New Visas to Attract Investors, Entrepreneurs," *Khaleej Times*, 11 January. https://www.khaleejtimes.com/world/gulf/saudi-arabia-launches-5-new-visas-to-attract-talents-investors-entrepreneurs.

Louër, L. 2008. "The Political Impact of Migration in Bahrain," *City & Society* 20: 32–53.

Lysa, C. 2023. "Governing Refugees in Saudi Arabia (1948–2022)," *Refugee Survey Quarterly* 42(1): 1–28. https://doi.org/10.1093/rsq/hdac027.

Massey, D., Joaquin Arango, Graeme Hugo et al. 1998. *Worlds in Motion: Understanding International Migration at the End of the Millennium*. Oxford: Clarendon Press, 1998.

Medhat, M. 2025. "Future Migration from Egypt to Saudi Arabia in a Context of Transnational Socio-Economic Transformation." In F. De Bel-Air and N. Shah (eds.), *The Future of GCC Countries: Migrants' Aspirations, Labour Reforms, and Politics*, 117–140. Singapore: Springer.

MEMO. 2014. "Egyptians Represent 40 Percent of Saudi Arabia's Total Expatriate Workforce." *Middle East Monitor*, 14 September. https://www.middleeastmonitor.com/news/africa/14187-egyptians-represent-40-per-cent-of-saudi-arabias-total-expatriate-workforce

MEMO. 2022. "Egyptian Doctors' Migration: Why Do They Resign?" *Middle East Monitor*, 22 April.

Milton Edwards, B. 2018. "Marginalized Youth: Toward an Inclusive Jordan," *Brookings Doha Center Policy Briefing*, June.

Ministry of Labor. 2009. *Strategic Plan and Executive Program (2009-2011)*. Amman: Ministry of Labor.

Osmandzikovic, E. 2019. "The Saudi Approach to Reception and Accommodation: The Case of Displaced Syrians," *Commentaries*, Riyadh: King Faysal Center for Research and Islamic Studies (KFCRIS), 22 April. https://www.kfcris.com/pdf/fe3af8ac2e531357caf7ba3fb41812fb5cc81bf7d330f.pdf

Pedersen, Jon and Age Tiltnes. 2017. "Youth in the Southern and Eastern Mediterranean: Between Informality and Precariousness." *The Middle East in London* 13(3) (April-May): 11–12.

Reuters. 2021. "Saudi Arabia Grants Citizenship to Group of "Talented" Expats," *Reuters*, 15 November. https://www.reuters.com/world/middle-east/saudi-arabia-grants-citizenship-group-talented-expats-2021-11-15/

Seccombe, I. and R. Lawless. 1986. "Foreign Worker Dependence in the Gulf, and the International Oil Companies: 1910–50," *International Migration Review* 20: 548–74.

Schaer, C. and T. Guizani. 2023. "Is Violence Driving Doctors in Middle East to Emigrate?" *Deutsche Welle*, 25 January.

Schlaim, A. 1988. *The Politics of Partition. King Abdullah, the Zionists and Palestine 1921–1951*. Oxford: Oxford University Press.

Talaat, N. 2022. "Why Are More Egyptians Taking to the Mediterranean?", *New Arab*, 5 October. https://www.newarab.com/analysis/why-are-more-egyptians-taking-mediterranean

Tsourapas, G. 2018. "Egypt: Migration and Diaspora Politics in an Emerging Transit Country," *Migration Information Source*, Washington, DC: Migration Policy Institute, August 8.

Wahba, J. 2012. "Immigration, Emigration and the Labor Market in Jordan." Economic Research Forum Working Paper 671, May. https://erf.org.eg/app/uploads/2014/08/671.pdf

Weiner, M. 1971. "Political Demography: An Inquiry into the Consequences of Population Change." In *Rapid Population Growth: Consequences and Policy Implications*, prepared by a Study Committee of the Office of the Foreign Secretary: National Academy of the Sciences. Baltimore: Johns Hopkins University Press.

United Nations Development Program Regional Bureau for Arab States (UNDP/ RBAS). 2016. *Arab Human Development Report 2016–Youth and the Prospects for Human Development in a Changing Reality*. Beirut: UNDP.

Annexed Table 1. Estimates of the distribution of Arab migrants from selected countries by aggregated region of destination (1995-2020)

		1990	1995	2000	2005	2010	2015	2020
Egypt	Australia and New Zealand	3.1	2.7	2.3	2.2	1.7	1.5	1.4
	Europe	10.2	10.3	10.2	12.1	10.2	8.9	9.1
	GCC	53.0	49.1	47.6	58.2	68.1	72.7	73.4
	North America	7.0	8.2	8.9	9.2	7.2	8.0	7.6
	Other countries and regions	26.6	29.7	31.1	18.2	12.9	9.0	8.5
	Total	**100.0**	**100.0**	**100.0**	**100.0**	**100.0**	**100.0**	**100.0**
Jordan	Australia and New Zealand	0.7	0.9	0.9	0.9	0.9	0.9	1.0
	Europe	11.0	9.6	8.5	7.7	6.0	5.4	5.9
	GCC	50.0	50.9	52.4	53.6	62.2	65.2	65.9
	North America	10.8	12.8	14.4	14.2	12.3	12.5	12.9
	Other countries and regions	27.6	25.9	23.7	23.6	18.6	15.9	14.3
	Total	**100.0**	**100.0**	**100.0**	**100.0**	**100.0**	**100.0**	**100.0**
Lebanon	Australia and New Zealand	16.1	15.0	14.1	13.9	12.8	12.3	11.8
	Europe	29.5	29.3	28.7	29.1	27.7	27.0	29.0
	GCC	14.0	13.8	13.9	16.2	20.9	24.4	25.8
	North America	27.3	29.5	31.6	30.7	29.4	27.4	25.1
	Other countries and regions	13.0	12.3	11.7	10.0	9.1	8.8	8.3
	Total	**100.0**	**100.0**	**100.0**	**100.0**	**100.0**	**100.0**	**100.0**
Sudan	Australia and New Zealand	0.2	0.4	0.5	1.5	2.1	1.1	1.0
	Europe	1.4	1.9	2.5	2.4	2.8	2.6	3.6
	GCC	43.2	34.3	32.7	26.8	40.0	32.4	34.3
	North America	1.0	2.1	3.1	3.2	4.5	3.0	3.0
	Other countries and regions	54.2	61.3	61.3	66.1	50.6	60.9	58.2
	Total	**100.0**	**100.0**	**100.0**	**100.0**	**100.0**	**100.0**	**100.0**
Syrian Arab Republic	Australia and New Zealand	0.9	1.0	1.0	1.0	0.9	0.2	0.3
	Europe	11.9	13.2	14.3	15.3	13.2	7.9	15.5
	GCC	53.6	51.7	50.5	53.7	55.5	11.5	11.0
	North America	7.6	9.0	10.2	9.3	7.9	2.1	1.7
	Other countries and regions	26.0	25.1	24.1	20.6	22.6	78.3	71.5
	Total	**100.0**	**100.0**	**100.0**	**100.0**	**100.0**	**100.0**	**100.0**
Yemen	Australia and New Zealand	0.0	0.1	0.1	0.1	0.1	0.1	0.1
	Europe	1.3	2.3	3.2	3.1	2.4	2.3	2.7
	GCC	84.2	81.7	80.3	82.1	85.8	84.2	84.8
	North America	1.2	2.7	3.9	4.6	4.3	4.4	4.6
	Other countries and regions	13.3	13.2	12.5	10.2	7.5	9.0	7.9
	Total	**100.0**	**100.0**	**100.0**	**100.0**	**100.0**	**100.0**	**100.0**

Source: **Author's calculations from UN/DESA International Migrant Stock by Origin and Destination 2020** https://www.un.org/development/desa/pd/content/international-migrant-stock

Annexed Table 2. Estimates of the distribution of Arab migrants from selected countries by GCC country of destination (1995-2020)

		1990	1995	2000	2005	2010	2015	2020
Egypt	**Bahrain**	3.1	3.2	3.1	4.0	3.8	3.2	3.6
	Kuwait	19.4	14.6	14.7	12.2	9.6	16.9	15.9
	Oman	2.7	3.8	3.5	2.6	1.7	3.0	3.3
	Qatar	0.0	0.0	0.0	4.6	7.7	7.1	6.9
	Saudi Arabia	51.1	50.0	46.3	44.2	34.3	33.7	36.3
	UAE	23.7	28.4	32.2	32.5	42.9	36.0	34.0
	Total	**100.0**	**100.0**	**100.0**	**100.0**	**100.0**	**100.0**	**100.0**
Jordan	**Bahrain**	2.2	2.3	2.4	3.3	3.4	3.0	3.3
	Kuwait	13.6	10.5	11.2	10.4	8.9	10.9	10.2
	Oman	2.9	5.1	5.4	3.5	2.0	3.7	4.1
	Qatar	7.0	7.8	7.1	6.1	7.2	7.0	6.1
	Saudi Arabia	57.6	53.7	49.2	49.7	40.6	41.8	44.8
	UAE	16.6	20.7	24.6	26.9	37.9	33.6	31.5
	Total	**100.0**	**100.0**	**100.0**	**100.0**	**100.0**	**100.0**	**100.0**
Lebanon	**Bahrain**	1.0	1.1	1.1	1.8	2.1	1.8	2.0
	Kuwait	6.4	4.9	5.3	4.5	4.0	6.2	5.7
	Oman	NA	NA	NA	NA	NA	NA	NA
	Qatar	4.3	4.6	4.1	3.3	4.0	4.5	3.8
	Saudi Arabia	80.5	79.8	77.8	75.4	65.8	66.7	69.6
	UAE	7.8	9.6	11.7	15.0	24.0	20.8	18.9
	Total	**100.0**	**100.0**	**100.0**	**100.0**	**100.0**	**100.0**	**100.0**
Sudan	**Bahrain**	1.7	1.8	1.8	2.0	2.0	1.8	1.9
	Kuwait	11.7	9.0	9.7	9.0	8.3	7.6	6.9
	Oman	1.9	3.2	3.4	2.3	1.4	2.6	2.8
	Qatar	1.3	1.3	1.1	2.6	4.5	3.1	3.2
	Saudi Arabia	70.7	68.8	65.1	67.8	61.1	64.4	66.7
	UAE	12.7	15.8	18.9	16.3	22.7	20.4	18.5
	Total	**100.0**	**100.0**	**100.0**	**100.0**	**100.0**	**100.0**	**100.0**
Syrian Arab Republic	**Bahrain**	0.5	0.6	0.6	0.6	0.7	0.6	0.6
	Kuwait	3.3	2.6	2.8	2.5	2.5	2.9	2.5
	Oman	NA	NA	NA	NA	NA	NA	NA
	Qatar	0.2	0.2	0.1	0.8	1.5	1.0	2.7
	Saudi Arabia	91.9	91.6	90.3	91.0	87.8	89.0	88.6
	UAE	4.0	5.0	6.2	5.1	7.6	6.6	5.7
	Total	**100.0**	**100.0**	**100.0**	**100.0**	**100.0**	**100.0**	**100.0**
Yemen	**Bahrain**	1.5	1.6	1.7	2.0	2.0	1.8	2.0
	Kuwait	9.5	7.4	7.8	7.0	6.3	7.1	6.4
	Oman	NA	NA	NA	NA	NA	NA	NA
	Qatar	2.7	2.9	2.5	3.0	4.5	3.8	3.2
	Saudi Arabia	74.6	73.8	70.9	72.1	64.2	66.9	69.8
	UAE	11.6	14.4	17.1	16.0	23.0	20.5	18.6
	Total	**100.0**	**100.0**	**100.0**	**100.0**	**100.0**	**100.0**	**100.0**

Source: **Author's calculations from UN/DESA International Migrant Stock by Origin and Destination 2020** https://www.un.org/development/desa/pd/content/international-migrant-stock

Part Three

Low-Skilled Migration and Economic Development in Saudi Arabia–Asia Migration Corridor

6

Brain Circulation and Mobility of Talents: Indian Skilled Migration in the United Arab Emirates and Saudi Arabia—A Comparative Perspective

Omar Bortolazzi

Introduction

India has consistently been the largest source of annual emigration to the GCC countries, with a significant portion of its emigration volume directed towards the Gulf, accelerating the importance of the India-GCC corridor to a measure that cannot be over-emphasized and continues to gain momentum over the years. Both the economic transformation and reform and socio-political atmosphere across the Gulf are partially owed to its Indian immigrant population. While there is a substantial body of literature concerning Indian laborers and low-wage workers in the UAE and Saudi Arabia (KSA), there remains a significant gap in research regarding the international movement of highly skilled professionals and the subsequent impacts on the host country.

This research aims to redirect attention away from the traditional analysis of labor mobility and instead places an emphasis on the international transfer of human talent as a vital component of economic resources and creative power across various sectors such as business, science, technology, and culture. The significant presence and distribution of the Indian community in both the UAE and KSA contribute to the growth of transnationalism. Skilled emigrants engage fully in the economy and society of their host country while maintaining strong connections with their country of origin, facilitating the rapid transfer of knowledge and fostering creativity, innovation, and entrepreneurship. At the same time, the demand for directly productive talent in the workforce is interrelated with the demand for capital, and with India still developing high levels of under employment, a migration flow will inevitably form towards the country that offers superior economic opportunities. Simultaneously, transfer states play a crucial role in the stability and functioning of the "brain circulation" system. They enhance the efficiency of cross-border investments, international trade, and facilitate GCC's post-rentier economic diversification plans.

Through a comparative empirical and theoretical perspective, I will examine how the migrant identity has evolved, mobilizing as transnational entrepreneurs or return migrants, who are uniquely positioned among the discourse of "brain drain" and "brain gain," and are increasingly influencing the policies and practices of both the Indian and GCC governments. The "brain circulation" literature introduces a novel concept distinct from the traditional "brain drain-brain gain" perspective. It highlights an international phenomenon characterized by the exchange of intellectual capital, as migrants play a crucial role in transmitting technology and tacit knowledge across borders. The same individuals who left India in search of bigger and better opportunities are reversing and transforming brain drain into "brain circulation" as they return home to work, establish partnerships, or start new companies while maintaining business and professional ties with the United Arab Emirates and KSA. In this sense, the circular movement of highly skilled migrants is benefiting both sending and receiving countries. As GCC countries continue to recognize the value of "brain circulation," policies that support and facilitate this phenomenon are likely to become increasingly important in the pursuit of global competitiveness and sustainable development.

Theoretical considerations

South to North migration

South-to-North migration, specifically within the context of skilled migration, represents a crucial dimension of global labor mobility. This phenomenon is marked by the movement of skilled individuals from developing regions in the Global South to advanced economies in the Global North. It raises significant questions regarding the political economy of migration, the dynamics of global inequality, and the role of state policies in shaping migration flows. This section contextualizes South-to-North migration within broader theoretical paradigms, emphasizing its relevance to skilled Indian migration to the Gulf Cooperation Council countries.

The phenomenon of South-to-North migration among highly skilled individuals remains a contentious subject within contemporary policy literature, which frequently emphasizes the developmental implications—or the absence thereof—for the countries of origin. The prevailing perspective suggests that migration is primarily driven by disparities in income, employment, and other opportunities across regions. While this approach appears logical, it oversimplifies the complex factors underpinning migration. Rooted in modernization theory, neoclassical migration theory interprets international migration as a response to geographic imbalances in labor supply and demand. According to this framework, wage differentials between labor-surplus, low-wage regions and labor-scarce, high-wage regions incentivize workers to migrate. While neoclassical migration theory effectively conceptualizes migration as a macro-level phenomenon, it offers limited insight into the micro-level dynamics and individual motivations of migrants. Its underlying assumption, rooted in a Panglossian optimism, presumes that all voluntary labor migration will ultimately yield positive outcomes for all parties involved. Additionally, migration to economically prosperous regions can be further examined through analytical frameworks such as the "push-pull" model, which delineates the economic, environmental, and demographic factors that drive individuals away from their places of origin (push factors) and attract them toward specific destinations (pull factors). This theory, however, can be critiqued as overly "rationalist," as it narrowly concentrates on economic decision-making, depicting migrants as isolated actors who uniformly and passively respond to external stimuli. Such an approach fails to adequately account for the phenomenon of return migration. Both the neoclassical and "push-pull" models, alongside much of the existing scholarly literature on labor migration to Gulf countries, lack sufficient consideration of human agency[1]—defined as individuals' capacity to make autonomous decisions informed by personal motivations, aspirations, and abilities. Instead, these frameworks reduce migrants to mere economic units of labor, neglecting the complexity of their lived experiences and choices.

South to South migration

A substantial body of literature analyzes the complex economic aspects of South-South migration. Lowell and Findlay (2002) consider the evolving nature of the Indian diaspora's economic contributions in host countries, emphasizing the shift from low-skilled labor to a more diverse and skilled workforce. This transformation has implications for both sending and receiving countries, as explored by Jain and Oommen (2016), who argue that the brain drain of skilled Indian professionals to South-South destinations may hinder domestic development but can simultaneously contribute to the economic growth of host nations.

Remittances, a central aspect of South-South migration, have been a subject of extensive study. Ratha and Shaw argue that Indian migrants in South-South corridors, particularly in the GCC countries, contribute significantly to remittance flows, aiding economic development in India (Ratha and Shaw 2007). However, a branch of literature also highlights the challenges associated with remittance dependency, such as the risk of economic instability when remittance flows fluctuate.

Skilled migration from India, referred to as the "brain drain" has been a subject of debate. Kuptsch and Pang (2006) argue that the movement of skilled professionals from India to other developing nations contributes to a global knowledge exchange, fostering innovation and development. Conversely, the loss of skilled workers poses challenges for India's domestic growth, prompting calls for policies that balance the benefits of skilled migration with strategies to retain and utilize talent domestically (Czaika and Parsons, 2017). The role of South-South migration in the global labor market is a key theme explored by Sasikumar and Hussain (2008), who analyze the implications of Indian migration in sectors such as information technology, construction, and healthcare in countries like the United Arab Emirates and Singapore. The authors argue that South-South migration channels provide an alternative pathway for Indian workers to access global job markets and contribute to the economic development of both India and host countries. Moreover, the economic impact of Indian migration is not limited to individual remittances. Varma (2020) emphasizes the role of Indian diaspora networks in promoting trade and investment between India and South-South host countries. These networks serve as conduits for business collaborations, facilitating economic linkages that extend beyond the realm of remittances.

The economic dimensions of South-South migration, with a focus on Indian migration, encompass a complex interplay of remittances, skilled labor mobility, and diaspora-driven economic connections. The literature underscores both the opportunities and challenges arising from these economic dynamics, providing a nuanced understanding of the broader implications for the involved nations and their development trajectories.

Nationalist vs. internationalist

The discourse surrounding the costs and consequences of talent migration originates from compelling academic debates that emerged among economists during the 1960s, characterized by a dichotomy between the "nationalist" and "internationalist" perspectives. Johnson's (1968) "internationalist" model adopts a cosmopolitan liberal stance, aligning with the views of many highly educated international migrants who regard the global movement of human capital as inherently advantageous. This perspective is grounded in Immanuel Wallerstein's world-systems theory, which conceptualizes international migration as an inevitable outcome of the expansion of capitalist markets in developing regions (Suter, 2005). The internationalist perspective emphasizes that the mobility of talent arises from the pursuit of superior economic opportunities beyond the migrant's country of origin. This movement is seen as generating significant benefits both for the individual and the global economy. By facilitating the reallocation of resources from regions of lower productivity to those with higher productivity, this process is argued to contribute to an increase in global income and overall welfare (Solimano, 2008). Johnson (1968) further contends that the externalities associated with brain drain—such as its beneficial effects on receiving countries and adverse effects on sending countries—tend to offset one another. As a result, he argues against the establishment of systematic mechanisms requiring migrants to compensate their home countries for leaving. Consequently, Johnson's perspective is frequently invoked to defend the right to emigrate from countries seeking to curtail brain drain, while being less relevant to arguments aimed at restricting immigration by states exercising their national sovereignty. Patinkin's (1968) "nationalist" model, in contrast, critiques the concept of "world welfare" as lacking practical significance and underscores the vital role of human capital in national economies. Patinkin asserts that middle-income developing countries grappling with brain drain do not endorse the notion of a "free flow of resources" when such resources comprise their highly skilled population. The discourse on "brain drain" in the 1960s was heavily shaped by the perception of a unidirectional flow of human capital from peripheral to core nations, highlighting an unequal distribution of benefits for source countries that had initially invested in the education and training of skilled individuals (Solimano, 2008). Patinkin's rejection of the notion that the "world" should be treated as a single aggregate for welfare considerations—arguing instead that global welfare is not best achieved through unrestricted resource flows—has been criticized by economists such as Johnson as embodying an illiberal and nationalistic anarchism. Unlike Johnson, however, Patinkin did not anticipate the concept of "brain circulation," which envisions a multidirectional movement of talent and the reciprocal benefits arising from new opportunities created by globalization.

"Brain drain," "brain gain," and "brain bank"

The mobility of skilled human resources, both outward and inward, profoundly influences the generation and dissemination of knowledge, national productivity levels, international competitiveness, and potentially the expansion of a middle class. Traditionally, migration has been associated with adverse effects on the source country, such as diminished entrepreneurial activity, reduced innovation and economic growth, and a depletion of human capital. However, the phenomenon of "brain drain" does not constitute the entirety of its consequences, as, over time, the broader effects can become advantageous due to the inherent dynamics within such processes. Scholars such as Beine et al. (2001), Kapur and McHale (2005), and Solimano (2008) have analyzed the beneficial impacts of migration prospects on the source country. The emerging literature on modern "brain drain" theory departs from traditional narratives emphasizing the costs associated with high-skill emigration. Instead, it highlights mechanisms that facilitate a beneficial "brain drain," including the inflow of remittances, transfer of innovative technologies and ideas, and the enhancement of goods and services, which collectively benefit both consumers and producers in the source country. Solimano (2008) argues that talent emigration diminishes the domestic supply of human capital, thereby increasing the remuneration for this factor of production. Over the medium term, this dynamic may stimulate educational development in the source country, driven by the potential for higher wages for educated migrants or through the return of human capital and associated complementary investments from wealthier to less affluent nations. This counterbalancing mechanism is encapsulated in the concept of the "brain gain effect" (Ozden and Schiff, 2006: 11).

The emigration of skilled individuals from low-income countries has a complex impact on domestic innovation. On the one hand, the departure of highly talented individuals can undermine local knowledge networks, leading to a "brain drain" effect that hinders the domestic capacity for innovation. This is particularly significant as the productivity of innovators—often clustered in urban centers—relies heavily on access to technological knowledge. Empirical findings indicate that, concerning knowledge accessibility, the localization effect, where countries benefit from retaining their highly skilled workforce, outweighs the benefits of the diaspora effect. On the other hand, there are potential benefits associated with skilled emigration, which can be framed as a "brain bank" effect (Agrawal et al., 2011). This refers to the accumulation of knowledge abroad by the emigrant innovators, which can facilitate the transfer of knowledge back to domestic inventors. The diaspora can help remaining innovators access valuable knowledge accumulated abroad, and in some cases, this knowledge access conferred by the diaspora is particularly valuable in the production of a country's most important inventions, as measured by citations received. Additionally, migration to more supportive environments can raise global innovation, and some gains may flow back to the poor country through imports of products with improved technology or lower cost, as well as through returnees who bring back enhanced skills, personal connections, and ideas for innovation. Furthermore, financial remittances and the flow of ideas and technologies from the diaspora highlight the benefits to the country of origin from international migration. While the emigration of skilled individuals can harm domestic knowledge access on average, the diaspora can provide significant benefits, particularly for high-value innovations. The optimal emigration level may depend on balancing the competing strengths of co-location and diaspora effects for accessing knowledge.

"Brain circulation"

Since the 1980s, scholarly attention has increasingly focused on the concept that international migrants can sustain multifaceted economic, social, cultural, and political connections with their countries or societies of origin, even as they integrate into the host nation. Chacko (2007) elucidates that while concerns regarding the outflow of skilled individuals persist, such emigration is progressively perceived as a strategic asset for the source country. In cases where migration follows a cyclical pattern and individuals return to their home country, their reintegration can foster significant developmental outcomes. The concept of "brain circulation" exemplifies a shift toward a "brain gain" framework, highlighting the global exchange of expertise, wherein migrants act as key conduits for the transfer of technology and implicit knowledge across international borders. Individuals who initially emigrated from India in pursuit of greater opportunities are now contributing to a transformation of the "brain drain" phenomenon into brain circulation by returning to their home country to work, forge collaborations, or establish enterprises while maintaining professional and commercial connections with the Gulf region. This cyclical mobility of highly skilled migrants generates mutual benefits for both origin and destination countries (Riemsdijk and Qingfang, 2017). This perspective aligns with Saxenian's (2001) research on social networks, which highlights how the transnational Indian community in Silicon Valley, along with its most prominent entrepreneurs, is fostering connections with India. Saxenian's case study demonstrates India's advantageous position to leverage brain circulation, facilitated through entrepreneurial networks such as The Indus Entrepreneur (TIE), an organization based in Silicon Valley—one of the world's leading hubs for information and communication technology—which has initiated the creation of chapters in major Indian cities. The increasing recognition of non-resident Indian (NRI) entrepreneurs, coupled with the global achievements of Indian companies such as Infosys and Satyam, is fostering an environment that inspires aspiring Indian entrepreneurs while simultaneously facilitating investment by NRIs in promising Indian start-ups. Consequently, the concept of "brain circulation" has also spurred the implementation of administrative programs aimed at promoting return entrepreneurship. Notably, initiatives such as "Make in India," championed by Prime Minister Narendra Modi, seek to attract foreign investment and stimulate economic growth within the country.

Empirical research has demonstrated that the benefits of "brain gain" may be overemphasized in the contemporary brain-drain literature, highlighting three key observations: (a) the extent of "brain gain" is less substantial than previously suggested, (b) the associated capital gains are comparatively modest, and (c) several adverse impacts, such as diminished human capital, reduced welfare, and slower economic growth, remain underexplored (Ozden and Schiff, 2006). Additional areas requiring investigation include the phenomenon of "brain waste," where migrants are employed in positions that do not correspond to their skill levels, and the potential trade-offs between increased investment in education and reduced public expenditure on other sectors, such as healthcare, in the countries of origin. The degree of impact derived from brain gain and brain circulation is likely influenced by migration patterns and destinations. For instance, the contributions of NRI migrants in the United Kingdom may differ in scale from those residing in the United Arab Emirates or Saudi Arabia. However, empirical evidence in this area remains limited.

Human capital and socio-economic demographic profiles of Indian migrants in the GCC countries

Indian migrants in the Gulf Cooperation Council countries represent a heterogeneous socio-demographic composition and have made substantial contributions to the region's economic development. The GCC has emerged as a central destination for expatriate labor, encompassing both semi-skilled and skilled workers, thereby attracting a significant influx of human capital from India.

The population of the GCC countries has experienced a substantial increase, growing from 4 million in 1950 to 55 million in 2017, with projections indicating continued expansion. Indian labor migrants have played a significant role in this demographic growth. The number of Indian workers in the Gulf region rose from approximately 14,000 in 1948 to 40,000 during the 1970s, reaching 8.7 million in 2017 (Rahman, 2023: 91–119). This represents a more than fivefold increase in the Indian migrant population over the past twenty-five years. Economic contributions by Indian migrants have been instrumental in advancing developmental projects across the Arab Gulf states, where demand for both skilled and unskilled foreign labor has been substantial. Skilled labor constitutes approximately 30 percent of the Indian migrant workforce in the region, while the remaining 70 percent is comprised of unskilled and semi-skilled workers. Among the Gulf nations, Saudi Arabia and the United Arab Emirates emerge as the most prominent destinations, collectively accounting for over 60 percent of the Indian migrant population in the region (Rahman, 2023: 108).

The economic conditions of Indian migrants have been shaped significantly by the immigration policies implemented by GCC countries, which have undergone periodic shifts. For example, between 1997 and 1999, these countries introduced localization policies aimed at reducing the proportion of non-native populations, which consequently impacted the influx of Indian labor migrants. Conversely, the period from 2000 to 2008 witnessed a surge in demand for semi-skilled and unskilled labor, driven by rising oil prices and increased revenue, which supported expansive infrastructure projects. During this time, an average of approximately 471,000 Indian workers annually secured contractual work permits for employment in the Gulf region (Rahman, 2023: 108).

Indian migration to the Gulf countries has been a dynamic process, influenced by economic conditions, immigration policies, and regional developments. The socio-demographic profiles of Indian migrants in the Gulf, particularly skilled workers, reflect a significant portion of the Indian diaspora that possesses specialized skills and professional qualifications. Skilled Indian professionals in the Gulf, including Saudi Arabia and the United Arab Emirates, are engaged in various sectors such as healthcare, engineering, information technology, finance, and education. They play a crucial role in the economic development of these countries, contributing to the knowledge-based economy and filling the gap in the local workforce. Over the years, the expatriate population in the Gulf countries has significantly exceeded the size of the local population. By 2010, non-nationals accounted for approximately 48 percent of the total population of 44.6 million across the six GCC states.[2] As of 2023, expatriates constitute approximately 50 percent of the total population across the six GCC countries, which include Bahrain, Kuwait, Oman, Qatar, Saudi Arabia, and the United Arab Emirates. Significant variation exists among individual member states: in 2023, for example, expatriates make up about 88 percent of the population, with Emirati citizens constituting roughly 12 percent.[3] While in Kuwait, expatriates account for approximately 68 percent of the population, with nationals making up the remaining 32 percent (Huda Ata, 2025). The GCC countries adhere to the jus sanguinis principle of citizenship, which restricts the naturalization of foreign labor. Consequently, NRIs in the Gulf region face structural inequalities compared to NRIs residing in developed nations such as the United States or Australia. These disparities include the inability to acquire permanent citizenship status, limited access to social security benefits, restrictions on property ownership, and the prohibition of full ownership rights to businesses. This dynamic has characterized the India-Gulf migration corridor as one defined by circular migration, marked by temporary residence and an inevitable return to the country of origin, which has contributed to a continual demographic flux within the GCC states. Given that emigration flows from India have tripled over the past decade, this trend, combined with the developmental conditions in the GCC countries—driven by sustained economic and social transformations, rapid urbanization, advancements in transportation and communication, and robust Indo-Gulf migration networks—indicates that the coming decade is likely to witness a further increase in emigration from India to the Gulf region. The GCC countries have introduced nationalization initiatives, such as "Saudization" in Saudi Arabia and "Emiratization" in the United Arab Emirates,[4] designed to reduce unemployment among local citizens by replacing expatriate workers with nationals. These policies have significant repercussions for skilled Indian professionals, who may encounter heightened competition and stricter labor market regulations. In response to these challenges and to promote the sustainable development of human capital, GCC countries are prioritizing improvements in education and training systems. This includes advancing the quality of primary and higher education, enhancing math and science curricula, upgrading management schools, and expanding internet accessibility in educational institutions. Furthermore, there is a concerted effort to improve the availability of specialized training programs and strengthen staff training initiatives to equip the workforce with the skills necessary to adapt to the demands of a rapidly evolving economic environment.

As far as migration is concerned, Saudi Arabia and the United Arab Emirates have positioned themselves as key destinations for population inflows, with the economic benefits of immigration largely attributed to the integration of cost-effective and highly motivated labor into their economies (Anjum, 2017). The GCC states collectively host over 6 million Indian workers across a wide range of professions, including doctors, nurses, engineers, architects, accountants, and managers, with a notable concentration in white-collar roles (Anjum, 2017). This diverse labor force plays a vital role in ensuring the efficient operation of these economies, particularly in sectors such as education, healthcare, and the development of contemporary infrastructure. Indian nurses, in particular, constitute a critical segment of the healthcare workforce, underpinning the functionality of healthcare systems in these countries. Nevertheless, these advantages are accompanied by challenges, including the potential increase in unemployment rates among younger populations and a growing dependence on foreign labor, which may pose long-term risks to the socioeconomic stability of the host nations (Kumar, 2016).

Globalization of human capital and implications for skilled international labor migration to emerging economies

Skilled migrants face a range of challenges in local labor markets, including systemic, institutional, personal, and professional obstacles (Ewers et al., 2022: 271). They are differentially incorporated into labor markets that are segmented by skill, nationality, and gender, leading to a migrant division of labor. Additionally, skilled migrants may experience insecurity due to labor nationalization programs designed to increase the proportion of citizens in key occupations and sectors, as well as the lack of protections in some countries' relatively new policies. Social and cultural differences, such as differences in social norms, freedom of expression, or religious laws, can also affect their hiring and workplace experiences. Furthermore, skilled migrants may face resentment from local citizens, especially when they receive wages far above the local market rate (Ewers et al., 2022: 272).

Skilled migrants may find that their qualifications, experience, or professional licenses are not readily recognized in the new country. This can lead to underemployment or the necessity to undergo additional certification processes, which can be costly and time-consuming. Skilled migrants can also face language and communication barriers. Even when proficient in the language of the host country, they may face difficulties with local dialects, professional jargon, or cultural nuances in communication, which can affect their employability and workplace interactions. Adapting to the social and cultural norms of the host country can be challenging. Differences in work culture, business practices, and social interactions can create additional stress and affect job performance. Skilled migrants may encounter discrimination based on their nationality, ethnicity, or accent. This can manifest in the hiring practices, promotion opportunities, and workplace dynamics, potentially limiting their career progression. Furthermore, local labor markets often operate on networks and relationships. Skilled migrants may lack the social capital and local networks necessary to access job opportunities and professional advancement.[5]

As far as the legal framework is concerned, immigration policies can be restrictive and may limit the ability of skilled migrants to work in certain sectors or change employers. Visa restrictions can also affect their long-term job security and the willingness of employers to invest in their professional development. Skilled migrants are subject to the same economic fluctuations and labor market conditions as local workers. However, they may be more vulnerable during economic downturns, as they can be considered expendable or may be targeted by labor nationalization policies.

Moreover, skilled migrants often face a phenomenon known as "credentialism," where the emphasis on formal qualifications over practical experience can lead to over-qualification and underemployment. This can result in skilled migrants accepting positions for which they are overqualified, leading to job dissatisfaction and underutilization of their skills. Establishing oneself within professional communities and associations can be more difficult for migrants, which can impact their professional identity and sense of belonging within their field.

Recent global trends such as Brexit and the COVID-19 pandemic (2020) have the potential to significantly impact the patterns and dynamics of highly skilled migration. The rise of nationalism and legislation aimed at stemming migration, as evidenced by Brexit and the policies of the Trump administration, could lead to a decline in the levels of migration overall, including highly skilled migration. These trends reflect a shift towards more nationally oriented economies and less porous borders in Western countries (Ewers et al., 2022: 279). The COVID-19 pandemic has further complicated the situation by revealing the risks associated with a highly interconnected world. Most countries have imposed restrictions on the movement of foreigners, which has disrupted the flow of international migrants, including those who are highly skilled. This has led to a reevaluation of global mobility and may result in more stringent immigration policies and health security measures that could persist even after the pandemic subsides (Ewers et al., 2022: 279).

However, these trends could also present opportunities for emerging or booming economies if they maintain relative openness, retain talent that may have otherwise left, and attract new flows of talent from other emerging economies. As traditional destinations for skilled migrants become less accessible due to tighter immigration controls, emerging economies could capitalize on this shift by positioning themselves as attractive alternatives for global talent (Ewers et al., 2022: 279).

Saudi Arabia

Countries like Saudi Arabia, the United Arab Emirates, and India have adopted various strategies to attract highly skilled migrants—each tailored to their economic and social contexts—balancing the need for skilled labor with the development of their local workforce and the engagement of their diaspora.

Saudi Arabia's main goal is to increase the employment rates of local citizens and limit medium- and low-skill migrants in the country by implementing additional monthly taxes per foreign employee on companies with higher numbers of foreign workers. The Nitaqat system outlines Saudization (nationalization) quotas for different industries, classifying companies based on their number of Saudi employees, penalizing those companies that do not achieve quotas, and setting a minimum wage for Saudi citizens working in the private sector. Despite these measures, Saudi Arabia recognizes the need for certain highly skilled foreigners, especially in key post-oil sectors and specialized occupations.

Within the context of economic diversification and Vision 2030, Saudi Arabia has been implementing various strategies to attract highly skilled migrants to diversify its economy and reduce its dependence on oil. By creating new sectors such as health, education, infrastructure, recreation, and tourism and expanding existing ones, the country is generating opportunities for highly skilled migrants in various fields. To attract top talent, Saudi Arabia offers competitive salary packages, often tax-free, to highly skilled migrants. These packages can include benefits such as housing, transportation, and health insurance, which are attractive to foreign professionals.

The country is also investing in large-scale projects like NEOM, a planned cross-border city in the Tabuk Province, which is expected to be a hub for innovation and a draw for international experts in technology, energy, and biotech. Likewise, efforts are being made to improve the work environment for expatriates, including reforms to the *kafala* sponsorship system, which historically tied workers to their employers. Changes are aimed at improving job mobility and rights for foreign workers.

Saudi Arabia has also announced plans to develop a "green card" system for foreign investors and highly qualified experts. This system would allow them to sponsor themselves, obtain permanent residency, buy property, and run businesses, which is a significant incentive for highly skilled migrants. The country is also entering into strategic partnerships and collaborations with foreign companies and institutions, which often involve the transfer of knowledge and expertise, creating opportunities for skilled professionals. By implementing these strategies, Saudi Arabia is working to create an environment that is conducive to attracting and retaining highly skilled migrants to support its long-term economic goals.

On the other side, India has focused on developing investment and business ties with its large diaspora. The government encourages overseas citizens to invest in the Indian economy, leveraging the human and social capital they have gained abroad. While there are some initiatives to attract back scientists and academics through scholarships and funded research programs, skilled overseas Indians often engage in transnational activities rather than return. However, India is seen as an attractive destination for returning diaspora due to opportunities for more professionally challenging jobs, lower labor costs, better government support for launching new products, and personal reasons such as family care.

Indian skilled workers are driven to start their own businesses in Saudi Arabia due to a combination of factors. One key motivator is the opportunity to improve their economic status. Migrants perceive entrepreneurship as a compelling alternative to wage work, offering the potential for better economic returns when compared to their home country, and the opportunity to set a role model for others, which can spur more migrants to become entrepreneurs over time. As observed by Md. Mizanur Rahman's (2017) study on Bangladesh migrant entrepreneurs in Saudi Arabia, the legal and structural constraints of the *kafala* system, which bars medium-skilled migrant entrepreneurs from owning businesses, lead migrants to seek alternative pathways to entrepreneurship. They manage to circumvent these restrictions by arranging a *kafeel* for immigration sponsorship and managing a mutually beneficial relationship with them, despite the risk of potential exploitation. The sponsorship system in Saudi Arabia presents, therefore, both a challenge and a driving force for entrepreneurship. These factors, combined with the migrants' willingness to take risks and their resourcefulness in mobilizing start-up capital from various sources, including personal savings, borrowing from friends, *kafeels*, and relatives, or other sources such as informal credit, drive Bangladeshi migrants to start their own businesses in Saudi Arabia.

Indian skilled workers and talent management in Saudi Arabia

An empirical study conducted by Navas and Vijayakumar (2015: 30–8) discusses the challenges faced by Indian migrants in talent management while working in Saudi Arabia. Their study explores determinants such as talent recognition, training and career development, compensation, promotion, capabilities of supervisors, performance assessment, evaluation process, reward scheme, and qualification. According to this study, Indian migrants in Saudi Arabia face several challenges in talent management, including adjusting to an employer-dominant atmosphere where talent management practices often favor nationals due to the nationalization process. Despite their expertise, these migrants may find themselves unable to utilize their skills and experience fully due to the responsibilities and positions available to them, which may not align with their qualifications. Additionally, salary constraints are a significant issue, as expatriates are sometimes forced to accept lower wages compared to nationals. These challenges can weaken their career development and hinder their ability to contribute effectively to their organizations.

Talent recognition and career development significantly impact the experiences of Indian migrants in Saudi Arabia. When their talents are recognized and career development opportunities are provided, it can lead to greater job satisfaction, motivation, and a sense of value within the organization. However, Indian migrants often face challenges in this regard due to a preference for national employees in the talent management processes as part of the nationalization efforts in the GCC countries. The inability to fully utilize their skills and experience can lead to a situation where Indian migrants are unable to secure positions and responsibilities commensurate with their qualifications, which in turn weakens their career development. This can result in a feeling of underutilization and a lack of professional fulfillment. Moreover, salary constraints can also affect their experiences, as expatriates may be forced to accept lower wages compared to nationals, which can further demotivate them and impact their long-term career prospects. The challenges faced by Indian migrants in Saudi Arabia, such as limited opportunities for career advancement and the potential for salary discrepancies, can hinder their ability to contribute effectively to their organizations and achieve their professional aspirations.

Among the factors that influence the professional performance and assessment of Indian skilled migrants in Saudi Arabia:

1. Nationalization policies: As previously mentioned, the nationalization process, such as Saudization, aims to increase the employment of Saudi nationals in the workforce, which can influence the performance assessment of Indian migrants. There may be a preference for promoting and retaining nationals over expatriates.
2. Cultural differences: Cultural norms and expectations can affect the evaluation process. Indian migrants may have different work styles and communication methods, which might not always align with the expectations of Saudi management practices.
3. Language barriers: Proficiency in Arabic can be a significant factor in performance assessment. Indian migrants who are not fluent in Arabic may face challenges in communication, which can impact their performance evaluations.
4. Employer dominance: The employer-dominant atmosphere in Saudi Arabia can lead to a situation where Indian migrants have limited

bargaining power and may have to conform to employer expectations without much negotiation, which can affect their performance reviews.

5. Economic factors: Salary discrepancies and economic benefits can also influence performance assessment. Indian migrants may be evaluated based on their cost-effectiveness in addition to their productivity and contribution.
6. Legal and regulatory framework: The legal status and work permits of Indian migrants can influence their job security and, consequently, their performance assessment. Those with less stable legal status may face more scrutiny and pressure to perform.
7. Professional development opportunities: Access to training and professional development can influence performance. Indian migrants with limited opportunities for growth may not be able to demonstrate their full potential.
8. Economic and market conditions: Fluctuations in the oil market and economic conditions in Saudi Arabia can influence business operations and, in turn, the performance assessment process. During economic downturns, there may be increased pressure on performance and cost-saving measures.

These factors can create a difficult environment for Indian skilled (and semi-skilled) migrants, where their performance assessment may not solely be based on their skills and work output but also on external and contextual factors.

United Arab Emirates

As countries like the United Arab Emirates move up the technology ladder, they are increasingly seeking workers with specific, certified skills. Suri and Kumar (2020) analyze the benefits and importance of skill-mapping projects, focusing on the India-UAE skill harmonization program. This pilot project for the mapping, harmonization, and accreditation of India's skill development programs with the specific job requirements in the UAE and Saudi Arabia emphasizes the need for international collaboration, efficient planning, and coordination between government ministries and organizations. The impact on workers' living conditions and remittances, as well as the potential extension of the program to other sectors and countries, is also considered.

Skill-mapping projects offer several potential benefits for both source and destination countries. For source countries, these projects can lead to the upskilling of their workforce, enabling workers to command a wage premium for their skills and move up the value chain. This can improve the living conditions of the workers and increase the remittances they send home, which can have a positive impact on the economy of the source country.

For destination countries, skill-mapping ensures that they receive workers whose skills are aligned with their specific requirements, thereby improving productivity and reducing the need for additional training. It also provides a degree of assurance regarding the quality of the incoming workforce, as the workers are certified and their skills have been verified. The integration of IT platforms for the verification of certification, as seen in the collaboration between NSDC (National Skill Development Corporation) and Takamul,[6] streamlines the recruitment process and ensures that the skills of migrant workers are recognized and meet the host country's standards. This can lead to a more regulated and efficient labor market, benefiting both employers and employees.

The India-UAE skill harmonization program aims to strengthen the India-GCC migration corridor through several initiatives, including: (a) aligning UAE and Indian occupational qualifications to ensure that Indian workers have the skills that are in demand in the UAE, thereby facilitating their mobility and employability in the region; (b) training and upskilling Indian workers and providing them with certification that is recognized by the UAE. This certification process is designed to meet the standards required by the UAE market; (c) the recognition of Indian awarding bodies by the UAE, which adds credibility to the certifications awarded to Indian workers and ensures that their skills are acknowledged and valued; (d) incentivized recruitment: The UAE has introduced financial incentives for employers to hire workers with certified skills by reducing the work permit fee for certified workers by an average of 50 percent. This creates a significant financial incentive for employers and encourages the recruitment of skilled labor; (e) the collaboration with Saudi Arabia's Ministry of Labor for a Skills Verification Program (SVP) that indicates a broader interest in the region for skill harmonization initiatives similar to the India-UAE program; (f) Expansion of Skilling Centers: The NSDC is expanding its network of skilling centers across India to certify workers for jobs in the Gulf, which will further support the migration corridor by ensuring a steady supply of skilled labor.

The India-UAE skill harmonization program aims, therefore, to create a skill-mapping and a template that could be replicated in other countries in the Gulf or beyond, potentially improving labor mobility and workforce quality in various regions.

Indian entrepreneurs have found success in a wide array of sectors in the UAE, contributing significantly to the country's economic diversification and growth. Their involvement spans across various industries (Bajeli-Datt, 2023):

1. Retail: Indian entrepreneurs have made a mark in the UAE's retail sector, with conglomerates like the Lulu Group, which operates a chain of

hypermarkets and retail companies across the Middle East, becoming household names. In addition to Lulu Group, Micky Jagtiani, chairman of Landmark Group, is another prominent Indian entrepreneur within Dubai's retail sector. Commencing his venture into the retail industry during the 1970s, Jagtiani initiated the import and export of textiles from Bahrain. Subsequently relocating to the UAE, he founded a modest store specializing in baby clothes, a venture that eventually evolved into Landmark Group.

2. Healthcare: The healthcare sector has seen substantial contributions from Indian entrepreneurs, with entities like Aster DM Healthcare establishing a strong presence in the Middle East. Founded by Dr. Azad Moopen, Aster DM Healthcare has grown into a healthcare conglomerate with a wide network of hospitals, clinics, and pharmacies. Dr. B.R. Shetty is another renowned Indian entrepreneur in the UAE due to his support of the healthcare and financial sectors. Dr. Shetty founded the UAE Exchange in 1980, and it soon became one of the largest remittances and foreign exchange companies in the world, with a presence in over thirty countries. NMC Health Care, which he founded in 1975, is a leading provider of healthcare services in the UAE and beyond.
3. Real estate and construction: The Sobha Group, founded by P.N.C. Menon, is a multinational real estate and construction group with diversified interests and investments. Indian entrepreneurs have been involved in several construction projects in the UAE. Rizwan Sajan, chairman of Danube Group, is another Indian entrepreneur in Dubai actively involved in the construction and retail industries.
4. Hospitality: Indian business leaders have ventured into the hospitality industry, managing and owning hotels, restaurants, and catering services that add to the UAE's reputation as a global tourism hub.
5. Financial service: The financial sector has also seen Indian entrepreneurs at the helm of various operations, contributing to the UAE's status as a banking and financial center.
6. Manufacturing: With a focus on diversification, Indian entrepreneurs have invested in manufacturing facilities in the UAE, contributing to the country's non-oil economy.
7. Technology and start-up: The rise of technology and start-ups has attracted Indian tech professionals and entrepreneurs to the UAE. With Dubai positioning itself as a hub for innovation, Indian entrepreneurs have been at the forefront of this transformation, founding and investing in start-ups across various tech sectors.
8. Education: Indian entrepreneurs have also made inroads into the education sector, establishing and managing schools and educational

institutions that cater to the diverse expatriate community in the UAE. Sunny Varkey is a renowned Indian entrepreneur in the UAE for his significant impact on the field of education. Serving as the chairman of GEMS Education, he has been instrumental in reshaping the educational panorama not only within the UAE but also on a global scale. GEMS Education stands as the largest provider of K–12 education globally, boasting a network of more than 250 schools across 13 countries.[7]

9. Fashion and luxury goods: The fashion industry has seen Indian designers like Ayesha Depala gain international acclaim, while entrepreneurs like Kunal Kapoor have founded luxury goods marketplaces such as The Luxury Closet, which have a global customer base.
10. Electronics retail: The electronics retail sector has prominent Indian entrepreneurs like Ashish Panjabi, who runs Jacky's Group of Companies, contributing to the UAE.

These contributions demonstrate the significant role of Indian entrepreneurs in advancing the UAE's economic development across key sectors. Their achievements highlight both their business inclination and the opportunities offered by the UAE's supportive economic policies. As the UAE continues to diversify its economy and pursue growth in non-oil industries, Indian entrepreneurs are well-positioned to further contribute to its economic progress through innovation and investment.

Conclusion

The comparative analysis of skilled Indian migration to the United Arab Emirates and Saudi Arabia demonstrates the complex dynamics of human capital mobility within the Gulf Cooperation Council region. This chapter highlights the profound socio-economic and political implications of "brain circulation" and talent mobility, illustrating how it transcends the simplistic dichotomies of "brain drain" and "brain gain." By contributing to the creation of transnational networks and enabling the transfer of knowledge, skills, and entrepreneurial capacities, Indian professionals have emerged as key agents of transformation, simultaneously benefiting their host and origin countries.

The UAE and Saudi Arabia, though divergent in their policy frameworks and developmental trajectories, share a mutual dependence on expatriate labor as an essential element of their economic diversification and growth. Indian skilled migrants play an indispensable role in advancing this agenda, contributing to vital sectors such as healthcare, technology, finance, and education. However, these contributions are mediated by systemic barriers, including nationalization policies, cultural boundaries, and limited pathways for long-term integration. These constraints not only challenge the sustainability of talent retention in the GCC but also limit the full realization of the potential embedded in transnational human capital exchanges.

This study reaffirms the necessity of viewing migration as a dynamic process shaped by the interplay of economic imperatives, governance frameworks, and individual agency. As global shifts in migration policies and labor market demands evolve, the GCC region must face the difficulties of fostering inclusivity while pursuing national interests. Targeted policy innovations, such as skill harmonization programs and initiatives to bridge socio-cultural divides, are crucial to enhancing the efficacy of migration governance and ensuring that the benefits of skilled migration are equitably distributed.

Ultimately, the phenomenon of "brain circulation" epitomizes the reciprocal enrichment of sending and host countries in a globalized economy. The GCC's strategic embrace of this model, supported by proactive reforms and transnational partnerships, will determine its long-term competitiveness and socio-economic resilience. For India, the sustained engagement of its diaspora through entrepreneurial and professional collaborations represents a transformative opportunity to harness its global human capital. The findings of this study provide a foundation for future research on the nexus between migration, governance, and development, emphasizing the imperative of crafting forward-thinking strategies to maximize the shared gains of skilled mobility.

Notes

1 Labor migration to Gulf countries tends to be seen as a structural phenomenon in which migrants appear as "stock" or "labor force." This has promoted social anthropologists like Anh Nga Longva (1997) to present the approach of human agency in international labor migration, which puts emphasis on the individual itself and calls for the investigation to why people decide to move, stay, remain abroad or return home (Suter 2005).
2 www.uaestatistics.gov.ae.
3 "United Arab Emirates." *The World Factbook*, Central Intelligence Agency, 12 October 202.
4 These policies refer to the campaigns carried out throughout the Gulf to nationalize certain areas of employment. International companies in the region have to recruit a certain percentage of employees from the local workforce. Experts predict that this percentage will increase in the future.

5 Bourdieu defined social capital as the "aggregate of the actual or potential resources which are linked to the possession of a durable network of more or less institutionalized relationships of mutual acquaintance and recognition" (Bourdieu 1986).

6 Established in 2011, Takamul represents an innovation initiative in the United Arab Emirates designed to assist inventors and foster innovation throughout the nation. With a strategic focus on propelling the UAE to become one of the world's leading innovative nations, Takamul actively promotes the entire innovation cycle. This spans from the conception of ideas to their practical implementation in commercial activities, thereby contributing to the country's economic and social development. The program extends its support to inventors across diverse categories and levels, encompassing both individuals and corporations. Since its inception, Takamul has consistently witnessed a yearly increase in the number of registered patents. Additionally, the program plays a crucial role in raising awareness about various facets of innovation, with a particular emphasis on the legal aspects safeguarding inventors' intellectual property. https://takamul.gov.ae/Site/index.html.

7 https://www.beststartupstory.com/top-10-indian-entrepreneurs-in-the-uae/#1-yusuffali-ma-%E2%80%93-managing-director-of-lulu-group-international-

Bibliography

Agrawal, A., D. Kapur, J. McHale, and A. Oettl (2011). Brain Drain or Brain Bank? The Impact of Skilled Emigration on Poor-Country Innovation. *Journal of Urban Economics*, 69(1): 43–55. https://doi.org/10.1016/j.jue.2010.06.003

Anjum, F. (2017). Indian Diaspora in GCC Countries. *International Journal of Research, Culture and Society*, 1(10): 82–8.

Bajeli-Datt, K. (2023). The Rise of Indian Entrepreneurs in the UAE. Indiaspora. https://www.indiaspora.org/features/the-rise-of-indian-entrepreneurs-in-the-uae-not-just-ambassadors-of-india-but-the-entire gulf#:~:text=%22Many%20Indian%20entrepreneurs%20and%20 start,Times%2040%20under%2040%20honor.

Beine, M., F. Docquier, and H. Rapoport (2001). Brain Drain and Economic Growth: Theory and Evidence. *Journal of Development Economics*, 64(1): 275–89. https://doi.org/10.1016/s0304-3878(00)00133-4

Bortolazzi, O., and N. Khan (2023). From "Brain Drain" to "Capital Gain": Indian Skilled Migration to the UAE. In M. M. Rahman and A. Al-Azm (eds.), *Social Change in the Gulf Region*. Gulf Studies, vol 8., 223–48. Springer: Singapore. https://doi.org/10.1007/978-981-19-7796-1_14

Bourdieu, P. (1986). "The Forms of Capital." In J. G. Richardson (ed.), *Handbook of Theory and Research for the Sociology of Education*. New York: Greenwood Press.

Chacko, E. (2007). From Brain Drain to Brain Gain: Reverse Migration to Bangalore and Hyderabad, India's Globalizing High Tech Cities. *GeoJournal*, 68(2–3): 131–40. https://doi.org/10.1007/s10708-007-9078-8

Czaika, M. and C. R. Parsons (2017). The Gravity of High-Skilled Migration Policies. *Demography*, 54(2): 603–30.

Ewers, M. C., N. Khattab, Z. Babar, and M. Madeeha (2022). Skilled Migration to Emerging Economies: The Global Competition for Talent Beyond the West. *Globalizations*, 19(2): 268–84. https://doi.org/10.1080/14747731.2021.1882816

Huda Ata. (2025). Kuwait's Population Hits 4.9 Million, with Expats Making Up More Than Two-Thirds. Gulf News, 10 May.

Jaber, A. (2024). Expats Still Make Up Two Thirds of Population as Some Communities Grow. *Kuwait Times*. Archived from the original on 25 February 2024. Retrieved 25 February 2024.

Jain, P. C., and G. Z. Oommen (2016). *South Asian Migration to Gulf Countries: History, Policies, Development*. London: Routledge.

Johnson, H. (1968). An Internationalist Model. In W. Adams (ed.), *The Brain Drain*, 69–91. New York: Palgrave Macmillan.

Kapur, D., and J. McHale (2005). The Global Migration of Talent: What Does it Mean for Developing Countries? Centre for Global Development Brief.

Kumar, N. (2016). Recent Trend and Pattern of Indian Emigration to Gulf Countries: A Diaspora Perspective. Retrieved from Princeton: http://paa2014.princeton.edu/papers/141653.

Kuptsch, C., and E. F. Pang (2006). Competing for Global Talent. Published by the International Institute for Labour Studies.

Longva, A. N. (1997). *Walls Built on Sand. Migration, Exclusion and Society in Kuwait*. New York: Routledge.

Lowell, B. L. and A. Findlay (2002), Migration of Highly Skilled Persons from Developing Countries: Impact and Policy—Synthesis Report. International Migration Papers 44. International Migration Branch, International Labor Branch, Geneva. https://www.ilo.org/wcmsp5/groups/public/---ed_protect/---protrav/---migrant/documents/publication/wcms_201706.pdf

Navas, S., and M. Vijayakumar (2015). Talent Management: An Analysis on Challenges Faced by Indian Migrants in Saudi Arabia. *Global Journal of Quantitative Science*, 2(4): 30–8.

Ozden, C., and M. Schiff (eds.). (2006). *International Migration, Remittances, and the Brain Drain*. New York: Palgrave MacMillan.

Park, K., and E. S. Ng (2022). Neither Here Nor There: Status Incongruence in Migration and Mobility in Emerging Markets. Academy of Management Proceedings, 2022(1). https://doi.org/10.5465/ambpp.2022.17190abstract

Rahman, A. (2023). Migrating Human Capital: A Case Study of Indian Migrants in the GCC Countries. In A. Mishrif, M. Karolak and C. Mirza (eds.), *Nationalization of Gulf Labor Markets*, 91–122. Singapore: Springer. https://doi.org/10.1007/978-981-19-8072-5_4

Rahman, M. M. (2017). Beyond Labour Migration: The Making of Migrant Enterprises in Saudi Arabia. *International Sociology*, 33(1): 86–106. https://doi.org/10.1177/0268580917745770

Ratha, D., and Shaw, W. (2007). South-South Migration and Remittances. World Bank Publications, Paper No. 102. © Washington, DC: World Bank. http://hdl.handle.net/10986/6733

Riemsdijk, M. V., and W. Qingfang (2017). *Rethinking International Skilled Migration*. Abingdon: Routledge.

Sasikumar, S.K., and Z. Hussain (2008). Managing International Labour Migration from India: Policies and Perspectives. International Labour Organization. https://www.ilo.org/wcmsp5/groups/public/---asia/---ro-bangkok/---sro-new_delhi/documents/publication/wcms_123412.pdf

Saxenian, A. (2001). Transnational Communities and the Evolution of Global Production Networks: The Cases of Taiwan, China, and India. *Industry and Innovation*, 9(2): 1–35. East-West Center Working Papers.

Solimano, A. (2008) (Ed.). *International Mobility of Talent; Types, Causes and Development Impact*. New York: Oxford University Press.

Suri, N., and M. Kumar (2020). Mapping Skills: A Roadmap for India and the UAE. ORF Special Report No. 112. Observer Research Foundation.

Suter, B. (2005). Labour Migration in the United Arab Emirates Field Study on Regular and Irregular Migration in Dubai. Master Thesis. IMER. Malmö University, Sweden.

Varma N.S. (2020). Indian Diaspora: Analysis of Its Advantage to the Home Country and to the World. *International Review of Business and Economics*, 4(1): 433–9.

7

Bridging Migration Challenges with Vision 2030: Exploring the Socio-Economic and Labor Conditions of Bangladeshi Migrants in Saudi Arabia

Mohammad Jalal Uddin Sikder and Selim Reza

Introduction

Saudi Arabia's Vision 2030 is a bold national reform plan that aims to diversify the economy, lessen the nation's dependency on oil, and promote the growth of new sectors and employment opportunities (Saudi Vision 2030, n.d.; Grand and Wolf, 2020; Sharma, 2022). This is essentially a long-term project that will require significant adjustments to be made to the labor force, the economy, the introduction of new technology, the adoption of best practices within manufacturing and services, the development of entirely new industries, and so forth. A key element of this goal is the creation of a highly qualified, long-lasting workforce that satisfies the global standards and encourages innovation and productivity across a variety of industries. Foreign workers in Saudi—many of whom are from Bangladesh—are essential in meeting the labor demands within industries including construction, hospitality, and domestic services, making them essential to the achievement of this goal (FairSquare, 2020; Harshan, 2024; UNB, 2024).

Against this backdrop, Bangladesh continues to be a primary supplier of labor to Saudi Arabia, which represents a key destination for thousands of Bangladeshi workers each year. The Bangladesh Bureau of Manpower, Employment and Training (BMET) reports that, on average, 804,465 Bangladeshis traveled per year between 2015 and 2024, in search of both temporary and short-term jobs. More than 80 percent of these migrants went to the Middle East, with Saudi Arabia being the most popular destination. In 2024, Saudi Arabia accounted for almost 62 percent of the 628,564 Bangladeshi workers who left the country (BMET, 2026). Over the years, the Bangladeshi economy has been hugely supported and vastly strengthened by the large remittance inflows resulting from this migration, which have been essential to maintaining economic stability. Since 1991, this remittance income has steadily increased, reaching US$21.92 billion in 2023, US$26.89 billion in 2024, and US$32.8 billion in 2025 (BMET, 2026). Interestingly, remittances from Saudi Arabia alone generated over US$5.08 billion in 2025 (Bangladesh Bank, 2026).

Even though remittance flows make a considerable economic impact, Bangladeshi migrant workers in Saudi Arabia nevertheless face multiple challenges, related to issues such as the recruitment procedures, visa provisions, workplace and living conditions, and social integration. These elements affect the migrants' financial and personal outcomes as well as their larger economic contribution to Saudi Arabia, especially in light of Vision 2030. The goal of this paper is to fill important knowledge gaps and analyze in detail the factors that influence migration from Bangladesh to Saudi Arabia, and to expose the goals and socioeconomic circumstances that motivate people to hunt for opportunities overseas. It assesses the recruitment procedures, costs, and visa arrangements, as well as the migrants' daily working life and housing conditions, that influence their path. Based on primary data, the paper will explore how the circumstances encountered by migrants from Bangladesh correspond with—or deviate from—the ethical labor standards and economic inclusiveness that Saudi Vision 2030 aims to achieve.

This paper consists of nine sections. The goal of the study is presented in section one. The conceptual framework and literature review, which provides significant research and theoretical foundations, are examined in section two. The methodology section is examined in section three. The socioeconomic background of Bangladeshi migrant workers is explored in section four. The factors and pathways of migration are highlighted in section five. The workplace settings in section six. Section seven critically examines their living circumstances and health. Section eight evaluates migrants' social interactions and workplace dynamics. The discussion section interprets the significant findings from the preceding sections. Lastly, the final section's conclusion and policy recommendations provide helpful ideas for enhancing migrant workers' experiences and achieving Saudi Vision 2030s goals.

Conceptual framework and literature review

The conceptual framework of this paper is based on two theories: Evans's bounded agency (2002) and De Haas's Aspirations-Capabilities (2010) frameworks, which locates the experiences of Bangladeshi migrant workers in Saudi Arabia within the wider objectives of Saudi Vision 2030. Karen

Evans (2002: 512–13) employed the notion of "bounded agency" to examine how young adults manage structural influences and exercise individual agency when experiencing changes in their educational, professional, and personal lives. The ability of young people to make decisions and take action, however, is a significant determinant of their life path and means of subsistence. In the case of migrant workers, this idea emphasizes how the socioeconomic obstacles that this group encounters in both their home and host countries influence both their choices and personal goals. Limited social mobility, a reliance on informal recruitment methods, and restricted access to skilled occupations are some of the structural barriers faced by Bangladeshi migrants. Despite the difficulties that those with this category of visa face, these limitations influence migrants' agency and their decision to seek work overseas, frequently under free or work visa arrangements.

In addition to "bounded agency" theory, this paper also employs De Haas's Aspirations-Capabilities framework (2010), which enhances the knowledge presented here. This framework presumes that migration is motivated by both "aspirations" and the resources available for attaining them. It integrates individual aspirations and capabilities within broader structural settings. Migrants' goals frequently include raising their family's standard of living, sending money home, and earning a steady income. With the help of this framework, we can comprehend how the economic contributions of migrants meet their objectives and how policy gaps may be preventing them from achieving their goals in the Saudi labor market. Employing these two frameworks will produce an analysis that is considerate of both individual agency and systemic obstacles, shedding light on the connections between the experiences of Bangladeshi migrants and the wider objectives of Saudi Vision 2030.

Literature review

Migration from Bangladesh to Saudi Arabia has historically been driven by economic hardship, a lack of domestic jobs, and the prospect of earning a higher income overseas (Rahman, 2011; Shahi et al., 2021; Bossavie, 2023). According to studies on South Asian migration, family remittances are a major motivator, and economic necessity frequently prevails over concerns about possible risks (Martin, 2014; Rajan, 2023). In Bangladesh, migrant remittances from Saudi Arabia play a major role in the economy. Rahman (2018) and Gardner (2010) highlighted how remittances can promote local economic development in addition to increasing household income. Nonetheless, Morad et al. (2022) note that, for many workers, the financial advantages of migration are diminished by the high migration costs and restricted access to labor rights.

In particular, migrants on free visas frequently report paying more to renew their work permit and find a job through unofficial channels, which can lessen the total effect of remittances. The International Labor Organization (ILO; 2014), the International Organization for Migration (IOM; 2020), and Remesh et al. (2020) also show that high migration costs and unofficial recruitment channels increase vulnerability. Given that different types of visas involve varying recruitment processes, costs, and working conditions that influence migrants' experiences considerably.

The kafala system, which binds workers to specific employers and frequently restricts their movement and autonomy, impacts labor conditions in Saudi Arabia, especially for South Asian migrants (Alsharif, 2022; Kurdi and Elyas, 2022; Al-Saud, 2023). Despite substantial regulatory reform, research continues to document asymmetric outcomes for some low-wage workers — particularly in domestic work and construction — pointing to areas where enforcement and protection mechanisms require further strengthening.(Aref, 2021: 133; Rashid, 2022: 75; Truluck, 2023: 157). The social dynamics and workplace hierarchy that exist in Saudi Arabia are regularly influenced by nationality and visa status; South Asian migrants are typically subjected to prejudice and occupy lower-status positions (Sinha, 2021; Hammer and Adham, 2023; Babar, 2024). Thiollet (2022) found that workers on free visas had lower security, because they lacked access to official benefits like vacation and sick leave. People on free visas, who must find their own jobs, are usually more susceptible to exploitation and frequently complain of having a poor relationship with their employers, especially in industries where the workers are categorized by country. Although migrants' rights have attracted more attention as a result of Vision 2030, critics argue that their implementation remains uneven and that workers on free visas frequently enjoy less protection than those on work visas (Hammer and Adham, 2022; Adham, 2023).

These challenges make Saudi Vision 2030s objectives to develop an inclusive and sustainable workforce all the more crucial. Vision 2030 seeks to solve some of these structural difficulties by improving the integration of foreign workers and diversifying the economy (Moshashai et al., 2020). However, Faudot (2019) points out that certain adjustments will be necessary in order to meet Vision 2030s goals because industries like construction and domestic services continue to rely heavily on foreign labor. In order to connect labor practices with the objectives of Vision 2030, Grand and Wolff (2020) stress that regulatory measures that increase the protection for low-wage workers—particularly those in vulnerable positions due to their visa status—are vital. The necessity for more equal procedures is also emphasized by scholars such as De Bel-Air (2015) and Thiollet (2022), who point out the inadequacies within the labor laws that currently impact the welfare of low-wage workers.

While existing studies have emphasized the obstacles to labor migration and the work conditions for South Asians in Saudi Arabia, less focus has been placed on the unique experiences of Bangladeshi migrants on various types of visas, particularly in light of Saudi Vision 2030. To fill these gaps, this study examines the migration routes, work conditions, and socioeconomic backgrounds of those on both work and free visas.

Methodology

In order to investigate the experiences of Bangladeshi migrants in Saudi Arabia, this study employs a mixed-methods approach, integrating quantitative and qualitative techniques. A total of sixty migrants, equally split between those on work visas and those on free visas, took part in the study. A minimum of two years of work experience was a prerequisite for selection, and the duration of their migration ranged from two to fifteen years, with an average of approximately 5.68 years.

The fieldwork, which included both in-person and remote (online) interviews, took place between February and August 2024. Interviews were conducted in the Saudi Arabian cities of Madinah, Riyadh, Makkah, and Jeddah. The research team also conducted interviews with migrants who were on holiday in Bangladesh, in order to supplement this data. According to data from the BMET and their high migration rates, four districts—Munshiganj, Comilla, Narshingdi, and Tangail—were chosen for these interviews. To develop a more comprehensive understanding of the problems affecting Bangladeshi migrants in Saudi Arabia, this study also interviewed academics, migrant workers, and members of civil society organizations (CSOs).

All of the research activities were conducted in accordance with the ethical standards laid down by the University Review Board/Ethics Review Committee, which also provided guidance and approval regarding the interviews, confidentiality, participant permission, and data processing. The findings were all revealed through the use of thematic analysis to detect and analyze patterns in the data.

Who are the Bangladeshi migrants?

The socioeconomic and demographic makeup of Bangladeshi migrants in Saudi Arabia offers significant signposts to the factors that influence their migration choices. With 42 percent of them being aged 18–25 and 33 percent being aged 26–35 prior to their migration, this group of migrants is generally young, as Table 7.1 shows. Once the younger migrants have adjusted to the demands imposed by working in Saudi, these age distributions change slightly. The fact that 75 percent of migrants are currently married despite 67 percent of them having been single prior to leaving Bangladesh is noteworthy because it reflects the changes in family dynamics that frequently accompany prolonged migration. Additionally, the migrants frequently come from larger households—58 percent of them support one to three people, while 17 percent support more than six—underscoring the wide-ranging family networks that frequently depend on remittance income.

As Table 7.2 shows, 50 percent of the migrants have no formal education, and 40 percent have only completed basic schooling, indicating limitations in

Table 7.1 Demographic Profile of the Migrants

Variable	Pre-migration status	Number of respondents	Percentage (%)	Current status	Number of respondents	Percentage (%)
Age	18–25	25	42	18–25	20	32
	26–35	20	33	26–35	30	50
	36–45	10	15	36–45	5	9
	46+	5	10	46+	5	9
Total		**60**	**100**		**60**	**100**
Marital Status	Unmarried	40	67	Unmarried	15	25
	Married	20	33	Married	45	75
Total		**60**	**100**		**60**	**100**
Number of Household Members				1–3	35	58
				4–6	15	25
				More than 6	10	17
Total					**60**	**100**

Table 7.2 Pre-Migration Educational Background

Educational level	Number of respondents	Percentage (%)
No formal education	30	50
Primary School	24	40
Secondary School	05	8
Above Higher Secondary	01	2
Total	**60**	**100**

Table 7.3 Total Family Income

Variable	Pre-migration status	Number of respondents	Percentage (%)	Current status	Number of respondents	Percentage (%)
Number of income earners'	1 income earner	14	23	1 income earner	20	33
	2 income earners	12	20	2 income earners	7	12
	3 or more income earners	4	7	3 or more income earners	3	5
Total		**60**	**100**		**60**	**100**
Total family income (BDT/Month)	Less than 20,000 BDT	26		Less than 20,000 BDT		
	21,000–40,000 BDT	17		21,000–40,000BDT	19	
	41,000–60,000 BDT	9		41,000–60,000 BDT	17	
	61,000–80,000 BDT	5		61,000–80,000 BDT	12	
	81,000–1,00,000 BDT	2		81,000–1,00,000 BDT	7	
	More than 1,00,001	1		More than 1,00,001	3	
Total		**60**	**100**		**60**	**100**

their formal schooling. The fact that so few of them have completed secondary school or higher education means that they tend to have lower-paid jobs. However, many of the workers reported that they had left these low-paid, unstable occupations in search of better opportunities abroad since they did not enjoy their previous jobs. Albeit comparable in nature, these migrants found Saudi Arabian manual labor more enticing because of the possibility of higher wages and improved economic prospects.

Furthermore, after moving to Saudi Arabia, 25 percent of the migrants were able to obtain technical skills through on-the-job training in fields like driving, machine operation, welding, and plumbing. None of them had obtained any official accreditation for these skills, however, which restricted their upward mobility and access to the job market. Although they had gained invaluable real-world experience, their inability to obtain certification meant that they remained categorized as unskilled workers, which further limited their ability to grow in their career and find better employment.

Table 7.3 displays the family income trends before and after migration, thus providing insights into the financial motivations driving migration. Twenty-three percent of Bangladeshi homes formerly had just one wage earner; this changed after migration, as the other family members now shoulder additional financial responsibilities. The majority of the migrants had generated only a small monthly family income prior to migrating, with 26 percent making less than 20,000 BDT (629 SAR)[1] per month. Their earnings, however, had slightly improved recently, with 28 percent now earning 41,000–60,000 BDT (1288–1886 SAR). While this financial trajectory illustrates the role that remittances play in maintaining economic stability, it also shows that migration provides many families with gradual rather than revolutionary financial benefits.

Drivers and pathways of migration

The main reasons why Bangladeshis migrate to Saudi Arabia are shown in Table 7.4. Economic considerations predominate; according to 25 percent of the respondents, one of the main causes of migration is money problems. The necessity to provide for their family through remittances (18 percent) and the prospect of better wages (15 percent) highlight how financial factors impact the migration decision for many. Furthermore, the physically taxing nature of agricultural labor (10 percent) and lack of local job opportunities (10 percent) encourage people to seek openings overseas. Moreover, 8 percent of the reasons for migrating were related to environmental concerns, such as natural calamities like flooding and riverbank erosion, suggesting

Table 7.4 Principal Reasons for Migration

Reasons for migration	**Number of respondents**	**Percentage (%)**
Economic hardship	15	25
Higher wages in Saudi Arabia	9	15
Support family via remittances	11	18
No work in Bangladesh	6	10
No benefits working in agriculture/hard work in agriculture	6	10
Natural disasters (e.g., flood and riverbank erosion)	5	8
For a better living	3	5
The lack of agricultural land	1	2
Business loss in Bangladesh	1	2
Political violence	1	2
No return to education in Bangladesh	1	2
A fascination about working overseas	1	2
Total	**60**	**100**

that migration can also be a survival tactic. The lack of return on education in Bangladesh was mentioned by another respondent, who held a diploma. He mentioned that, even though his brother, who was also a migrant, had paid for his education, he was unable to find employment in Bangladesh that paid him enough to live on. Some educated people may believe that their qualifications are not valued by the local job market, which is reflected in this sentiment.

The sources of knowledge on migration are listed in Table 7.5, which shows that intermediaries and personal networks are crucial for migrants. For the 37 percent of those with work visas, their main source of information was family members overseas whereas, for the 30 percent of participants with free visas, middlemen or *dalals* were essential, thus underscoring the importance of their type of visa. This also shows that those with work visas may access more official channels of information because of their overseas family ties. In Bangladesh, local networks, like family and neighbors, provide information to approximately 23 percent and 8 percent of the migrants, respectively, although they are less important than the middlemen and international contacts.

The processing of visas is handled by intermediaries, as Table 7.6 demonstrates, especially in the case of free visas. In contrast to 37 percent of the work visa holders, who use recruiting firms, 50 percent of those with free visas rely on *dalals*. Migration becomes more expensive, and migrants are more susceptible to exploitation as a result of this dependence on external

Table 7.5 Sources of Migration Information

Source of information	Free visa holder		Work visa holder		Total Respondents	Total Percentage (%)
	Total respondents	Percentage (%)	Total respondents	Percentage (%)		
Family members in Bangladesh	8	27	6	20	14	23.33
Family members abroad	7	23	11	37	18	30
Friends/Neighbors in Bangladesh	3	10	2	7	5	8.33
Friends/Neighbors abroad	3	10	0		3	5
Middlemen/Dalal/ Intermediaries	9	30	11	37	20	33.33
Total	**30**	**100**	**30**	**100**	**60**	**100**

intermediaries. Only a small percentage of people receive assistance with obtaining a visa from their immediate family and wider relatives, suggesting that Bangladesh's migration system offers little institutional support.

Lastly, Table 7.7 shows the migration costs related to the different types of visas, which vary widely. The average cost for those with a free visa is slightly higher, at 448,000 BDT (14,080 SAR), whilst those with a work visa normally pay 434,333 BDT (13,650 SAR). While free visas can cost up to 850,000 BDT (26,720 SAR), work visas start at a minimum of 160,000 BDT (5,030 SAR). This broad range reflects the additional costs related to using unofficial methods as well as the frequently unregulated nature of migration for those with free visas.

The range of costs for those with free visas, however, was wider, ranging from 120,000 BDT to 850,000 BDT. Due to the fewer regulations and decreased market demand, some migrants who left decades ago were able to keep their initial costs low. On the other hand, more recent migration costs significantly more. To obtain a visa during a period when Saudi visas for Bangladeshis were temporarily restricted during 2016–2017, one respondent, who was forced to migrate immediately owing to political risks, paid an

Table 7.6 The Official/Individual Who Handled the Visa Processing

Who processed the visa?	Free visa holder (total respondents)	Work visa holder (total respondents)	Total
Families	4 (13%)	3 (10%)	7 (12%)
Relatives	3 (10%)	4 (13%)	7 (12%)
Friends		3 (10%)	3 (5%)
Recruitment agencies	8 (27%)	11 (37%)	19 (32%)
Dalals/intermediaries/ middlemen	15 (50%)	9 (30%)	24 (40%)
Total	**30 (100%)**	**30 (100%)**	**60 (100%)**

Table 7.7 Migration Cost by Visa Types (Visa, Recruitment, and Related Costs)

Cost of migration	Free visa holder	Work visa holder	Combined (both visa type)
Minimum	120,000 BDT / 3,772 SAR	160,000 BDT/ 5,030 SAR	120,00 BDT/ 3,772 SAR
Maximum	850,000 BDT / 26,720 SAR	805,000 BDT/ 25,300 SAR	850,000 BDT/ 26,720 SAR
Average	448,000 BDT 14,080 SAR	434,333 BDT/ 13,650 SAR	441,167 BDT/ 13,870 SAR

extraordinary 1,200,000 BDT (37,723 SAR). This hefty charge indicates how access restrictions and political susceptibility can increase the costs. Another free visa holder also related how, even after making all of the stipulated payments, his *dalal* insisted on receiving an extra 1,70,000 BDT (SAR 5344) upon his arrival, claiming that his *Kafeel* had incurred further costs. Under such circumstances, migrants are exposed to unforeseen demands that frequently feel like a "trap," leaving them financially vulnerable. Although all visa categories attract significant migration expenses, the holders of free visas are more vulnerable to financial risk and uncertainty, since they must rely on middlemen and lack access to employer-sponsored benefits. This discrepancy highlights how the initial migration costs can rise considerably, impacting migrants' long-term prospects and financial security in Saudi Arabia.

The majority of migrants who paid their migration costs in cash did not receive a receipt, accounting for 80 percent of those with work visas and 87 percent of those with free visas. Seven percent of those with free visas and 10 percent of those with work visas paid by check only, whereas 7 percent of those holding each type of visa paid using both cash and checks. There was a higher likelihood that migrants who paid by check would have an official receipt, as confirmation of their payment. For individuals who paid mostly in cash, on the other hand, the lack of a receipt significantly hampered their ability to pursue legal action in the event of fraud or payment disputes. The results highlight the structural problems within Bangladesh's migration system, where the high migration costs and unofficial recruitment channels increase migrants' vulnerabilities, particularly for those seeking less-established visa options.

Work conditions and labor rights

The labor rights and work conditions of Bangladeshi migrant workers in Saudi Arabia show a diverse environment that is influenced by the type of visa, with major ramifications for access to benefits, work hours, and income stability. The employer categories are broken down per visa category in Table 7.8. Private or government-run companies typically provide more structured work environments, and about 17 percent of migrants with free visas and 23 percent of those with work visas are employed by these types of companies. Employer-sponsored perks, like housing and healthcare, are more frequently offered to work visa holders, and the employees of these companies report steadier incomes and more regular job assignments. Free visa holders, on the other hand, who work for comparable companies, must

Table 7.8 Employment and Employer Type by Visa Category

Who did/do you work for?	Free visa holder (total respondents)	Work visa holder (total respondents)	Total
Private or govt. company	5 (17%)	7 (23%)	12 (20%)
Kafeel	7 (23%)	4 (13%)	11 (18%)
Bangladeshi/Saudi businessman/entrepreneur	8 (27%)	11(37%)	19 (32%)
Labor supplier company	10 (33%)	8 (27%)	18 (30%)
Total	**30 (100%)**	**30 (100%)**	**60 (100%)**

frequently purchase their own Iqama (residency permit) renewal, which can result in substantial annual expenses.

About 13 percent of those on work visas and 23 percent of those on free visas are employed by individual sponsors, or Kafeel, who are crucial to the administration of their residency permits (Iqamas). Due to this dependency, those with free visas are solely responsible for obtaining and renewing their Iqamas on an annual basis, frequently at additional cost, imposed by the Kafeel. Our field notes emphasize that different Kafeels treat free visa holders differently; some offer prompt Iqama renewals at fixed prices, while others cause delays or demand exorbitant payments based on arbitrary calculations. Unlike the more conventional, employer-managed Iqama procedures that work visa holders tend to encounter, free visa holders face a substantial financial burden due to their reliance on Kafeel for their Iqama renewals.

Free visa holders are more likely to work for Saudi or Bangladeshi business owners; 37 percent of work visa holders and 27 percent of free visa holders are employed by small enterprises or entrepreneurs. While small firms present opportunities, they are frequently more informal in character. However, 33 percent of migrants with free visas and 27 percent of those with work visas are employed by labor supplier companies, who mostly serve as middlemen rather than direct employers. These companies outsource work to other companies and are frequently run by non-Saudis, such as Indians, Pakistanis, or Bangladeshis. Migrant workers, particularly those employed in the labor supply companies, report unpredictable workdays and timetables, and a dearth of benefits. Despite early assurances, these companies typically provide fewer rights, thus depriving workers of sick days and annual leave. These companies often employ migrants who report working only 10–12 days a month, which restricts their income and drives them to look for more stable work elsewhere. Work visa holders are frequently pushed by this circumstance to change to a free visa so that they can seek more work opportunities independently. Although this change gives workers more flexibility at work, it also comes at a financial cost, because they must pay for their own Iqama renewals, which can amount to 12,000 SAR annually.

The majority of free visa holders (77 percent) work a typical eight-hour day, although many works longer days of up to nine or twelve hours, depending on the demands of their employers (Table 7.9). A significant percentage (30 percent) of the work visa holders report working 9–10 hours daily, with 47 percent reporting an eight-hour working day. This range highlights how the work visa holders' jobs are structured, but demanding. Despite the fact that the majority of workers report working six days a week, 70 percent of those with free visas and 87 percent of those with work visas corroborate this arrangement. However, 30 percent of those with free visas work seven days a week, which reflects their need to maximize their revenue in order to pay off their debts and cover their personal needs.

Due to their freedom to choose their job, those on free visas often receive somewhat higher pay, although their incomes vary according to the kind of visa (Table 7.10). Both categories' average monthly salary is approximately 51,500 BDT (1619 SAR), although some workers earn more than 80,000 BDT (2515 SAR). While free visa holders may earn more, their net income is

Table 7.9 Working Hours and Daily Tasks by Visa Types

Work hours per day	Free visa holder	Work visa holder	Total
Less than 8 hours			
8 hours	23 (77%)	14 (47%)	37 (62%)
9-10 hours	3 (10%)	9 (30%)	12 (20%)
11-12 hours	3 (10%)	6 (20%)	9 (15%)
Above 13 hours	1 (3%)	1 (3%)	2 (3%)
Total	**30**	**30**	**60**
Total days in a week			
6 days	21 ((70%)	26 (87%)	47 (78%)
7 days	9 (30%)	4 (13%)	13 (22%)
Total	**30**	**30**	**60**
Breaks (per day)	Free visa	Work Visa	Total
No break	1 (3%)	5 (17%)	6 (10%)
1 break	26 (87%)	19 (63%)	45 (75%)
2 breaks	3 (10%)	6 (20%)	9 (15%)
Total	**30**	**30**	**60**

Table 7.10 Wages by Visa Type (BDT/SAT per . . . . . .)

Wages	Free visa holder	Work visa holder	Combined (both visa type)
Minimum	30,026 BDT / 943.09 SAT	32,724 BDT / 1027.89 SAR	30,026 BDT / 943.09 SAT
Maximum	89,000 BDT / 2797.80 SAR	89,525 BDT / 2814.71 SAR	89,525 BDT / 2814.71 SAR
Average	51,246 BDT /1611.27 SAR	51,589 BDT / 1621.21 SAR	51,481 BDT / 1616.24 SAR

impacted by the extra expenses they must pay for necessities like housing, healthcare, and visa renewals. Compared to work visa holders, who report payment delays only 17 percent of the time, free visa holders report them 60 percent of the time. Due to these delays, which frequently exceed ten days—some free visa holders must wait up to thirty days—it becomes more difficult for them to pay their bills on time and send money home. As a result of the stability of the official work visa arrangements, the work visa holders, on the other hand, report a more consistent source of income, with fewer instances of late payments.

The experiences of both the free and work visa holders are further distinguished by the availability of corporate benefits, such as sick leave, vacations, and bonuses. In general, those on work visas enjoy greater access to these benefits; 93 percent of them can take sick leave, compared to 60 percent of those with free visas. Sick leave for work visa holders frequently necessitates completing medical paperwork, and is easier for those employed by reputable organizations to obtain. Work visa holders also benefit from vacations; 73 percent report having annual vacations, compared to 57 percent of those on free visas, who frequently need to save up and take longer leave. Compared to 63 percent of those on work visas, just 40 percent of those on free visas report receiving bonuses, usually during Eid. Although these bonuses are frequently unpredictable, especially for the migrants employed by the supply chain organizations, they help to offset Saudi Arabia's high cost of living.

Significant challenges arise due to delayed payments, particularly for those on free visas, since 60 percent of them report delayed pay checks, compared to 17 percent of those on work visas. These delays sometimes cause financial difficulties, such as problems managing their daily expenses and sending money home. Delayed payments also cause tension and anxiety, which may impact the migrants' mental and financial health. The serious consequences of these late payments highlight the huge vulnerability of those on free visas, as their salaries are less dependable compared to those on official work visas.

Living conditions and health

The majority of migrant workers, regardless of their type of visa, share rooms. Employer-provided housing is the norm, with 93 percent of both the work visa and free visa holders receiving this, which highlights how hugely these migrants depend on their employers for their basic necessities. However, 3 percent of those on free visas reside in rental housing, showing that a tiny percentage must find lodgings for themselves, which increases their financial burden. In terms of shared living arrangements, 13 percent of those on free visas and 20 percent of those on work visas live with more than five other people, whilst 80 percent and 50 percent, respectively, share rooms with three to five other people. This high living density may make the situation difficult and claustrophobic, affecting the migrants' comfort and personal space.

Ten percent of those on work visas and 30 percent of those on free visas also depend on employer-provided meals. Some of the free visa holders, however, claimed that the employer's food allowance or direct provisions were insufficient, requiring them to supplement their needs out of their own pocket. There is inconsistent employer support for migrants' basic nutritional needs, as evidenced by the fact that 67 percent of those on work visas and 47 percent of those on free visas pay for all of their own food. This further indicates an uneven approach to food provision as, depending on the type of job or business, 23 percent of those on both free and work visas reported a mixed arrangement, whereby only certain meals were provided by their employer, and they were required to fund the remaining meals themselves.

The disparity between those on work and free visas was further demonstrated by their access to healthcare services. Employer-sponsored healthcare is available to 70 percent of those on work visas and 47 percent of those on free visas, suggesting a sizable disparity in healthcare coverage, whereby free visa holders are disadvantaged. Although public healthcare facilities are available, these might inadequately address the health requirements of 30 percent of those on free visas and 17 percent of those on work visas because of a lack of funding or communication difficulties. Significantly, 37 percent of those on free visas stated that their company did not provide them with any healthcare, so they had to pay for private medical care themselves, which caused them financial hardship.

The findings clearly show how the migrant workers' living environments depend on which type of visa they are on, with those on work visas typically enjoying better access to housing, medical treatment, and meals. This discrepancy highlights the wider, systemic issues that free visa holders face, as their less regulated work arrangements may result in uneven access to necessary services, which might lower their general standard of living while in the host country.

Social interactions and workplace dynamics

Having analyzed the social interactions and workplace dynamics that Bangladeshi migrant workers encounter while in Saudi Arabia, significant differences were found. Their relationships with their coworkers and supervisors differed greatly, with the workers often commenting that how they were treated by their bosses varied depending on the type of job and the organizational structure of the company. About 60 percent of those on a work visa stated that their superiors treated them in either a supportive or neutral manner, whereas 40 percent of those on a free visa stated that their supervisors treated them in a somewhat disrespectful or negligent manner. This discrepancy may be due to the fact that work visa holders, who are legally bound to a single employer, enjoy a more stable position than free visa holders, who change occupations regularly.

There is also a great deal of variation in terms of workplace hierarchy. According to 70 percent of the work visa holders, their workplace operates according to a strict, controlled hierarchy. Comparatively, approximately half of those on free visas stated that they have more freedom but less control over their workplace, frequently as a result of their less organized jobs. Since the free visa holders frequently operate outside the official job frameworks, this liberty is usually accompanied by a lack of consistent support. About 30 percent of those on free visas reported experiencing prejudice because of their nationality or visa status, compared to 15 percent of those on work visas. Because their status is seen as less stable, those on free visas frequently express feeling marginalized. Furthermore, around 40 percent of the respondents in both visa categories mentioned that nationality appears to affect their treatment, with workers from particular nations—like India—frequently receiving preferential treatment, possibly as a result of embassy influence or long-standing cultural links with Saudi Arabia.

Overall, the integration, job satisfaction, and stability of Bangladeshi migrants in the workplace are impacted by social interactions and workplace dynamics that are influenced by both their visa status and also wider sociocultural factors. Many feel that these factors not only shape their daily lives but also reinforce a sense of social hierarchy among migrant workers.

Main discussion

The experiences of Bangladeshi migrant workers in Saudi Arabia are highlighted in this study, paying particular attention to occasions when socioeconomic factors, migration paths, and working conditions interact with Saudi Vision 2030s goals. The primary motive to migrate among Bangladeshi workers is a desire for higher earning, a steady income, and financial security for their families. However, migrants face a heavy financial burden due to the high costs of migrating. The findings show that many workers also report spending significantly more than the government's requirements. These expenses affect the workers' financial security when they arrive in their destination. Therefore, economic necessity forces workers into a position of bounded agency, where financial susceptibility frequently results in them facing limited choices in their host country.

In order to balance these financial demands, free visa holders tend to work longer hours and/or on the weekends, which highlights the significance of fair wage laws and labor regulations. Although free visa holders have the freedom to select their employers, the data shows that they also face substantial financial and administrative costs, such as variable working hours and expensive Iqama renewals. Work visa holders, on the other hand, are typically employed in more organized settings, particularly in larger organizations that offer reliable job benefits and Iqama sponsorship. Workers employed by supply companies, however, experience volatility, suggesting that the level of job security and uniformity across the different visa categories might be improved.

Each form of visa attracts different labor rights, such as overtime, paid vacations, and sick leave. While individuals on free visas and those who are employed by smaller or supply chain organizations experience less consistency, work visa holders—especially those who are employed by well-established companies—generally claim to enjoy better access to these advantages. Since many workers' expectations of equitable treatment and steady pay are frequently unmet, these observations are in line with the aspirations-capabilities framework.

The significance of unified workplace policies is further demonstrated by the social interactions and workplace dynamics, and coworker and supervisor relationships, as well as the noted disparities in treatment according to different workers' nationality or type of visa. The hierarchical organizational arrangements, which frequently assign Bangladeshi workers to lower-level roles with little autonomy, serve to entrench these discrepancies further. This also highlights areas where encouraging inclusive policies might successfully increase worker satisfaction and output.

Conclusion and policy recommendations

The variegated experiences of Bangladeshi migrant workers in Saudi Arabia were examined in this study. According to the present study, migrants on free visas face higher financial burdens and experience huge uncertainty about retaining their legal status, although they do enjoy greater freedom regarding their career options. On the other hand, those on work visas encounter more regimented work settings, frequently accompanied by employer-sponsored benefits, although their ability to change jobs is restricted, and they occasionally face unfair labor practices in supply chain organizations. These relationships highlight how the migratory experience is shaped by the complex interplay between vulnerability and economic opportunity.

Policy recommendations and future directions

The findings presented in this paper call for reforms in the following areas:

> Streamlining migration costs: By establishing uniform fees and licensing procedures for recruiting agencies, the governments of Saudi Arabia and Bangladesh might collaborate to control the migration expenses, enabling workers to remit their earnings more efficiently and guaranteeing that migration is a financially sound option.
>
> Increasing access to worker benefits: Simplified regulations for larger number of workers might be guaranteed basic benefits like sick leave, paid vacations, and overtime compensation by strengthening the protections for all visa types, including those on free visas.
>
> Programs for skill development and certification: Saudi Arabia might offer training and certification options that would enable migrants to acquire job-specific skills, to boost their career prospects and complement the skill-building emphasis of Vision 2030.
>
> Enhancing fair treatment and workplace inclusion: Establishing workplace regulations and implement culturally inclusive policies that encourage equitable treatment for people of all nationalities and lessen discrimination would help to create a more productive workplace.

By prioritizing these policy areas, Saudi Arabia might improve the working conditions for migrant workers and build a more equitable, sustainable workforce, as outlined in Saudi Vision 2030. Coordination with Bangladesh, as required, may strengthen these objectives. Together, these countries may establish safe, effective migration routes, that support both Bangladesh's development aims and also Saudi Arabia's economic ambitions by standardizing the work standards, enhancing access to fundamental rights, and putting in place transparent recruitment procedures.

Notes

1 Saudi Ryal (SAR) equal to 31.81 Bangladeshi Taka (BDT). Available from: https://www.xe.com/currencyconverter/convert/?Amount=1&From=SAR&To=BDT.

Bibliography

Adham, A. (2023). Structural demand for migrant labour: A bottom-up analysis of labour market segmentation in Saudi Arabia. *Journal of Ethnic and Migration Studies*, *49*(7), 1746–67.

Al-Saud, M. A. (2023). *Transforming the Kafala in Saudi Arabia: Turning weaknesses into opportunities* (Doctoral dissertation, Cranfield University). Retrieved from https://dspace.lib.cranfield.ac.uk/server/api/core/bitstreams/320b009a-9b21-4a7f-8af8-e4a29e48f32f/content

Alsharif, F. (2022). Undocumented migrants in Saudi Arabia: COVID-19 and amnesty reforms. *International Migration*, *60*(1), 188–204.

Aref, A. (2021). Social inclusion and exclusion in GCC labour policy transformations: Evidence from Qatar and Saudi Arabia. *Journal of Politics and Law*, *4*(2), 124–42.

Babar, Z. (2024). The buying of freedom: Migrant workers and the "Azad" Visa in the Persian Gulf. *International Migration*. Retrieved from https://doi.org/10.1111/imig.13240

Bangladesh Bank. (2026). Monthly economic trends February 2026. Dhaka: Bangladesh Central Bank. Retrieved from https://www.bb.org.bd/en/index.php/publication/publictn/3/10

BMET. (2026). Overseas employment and remittances (Country wise - Yearly) from 1976–2025. Dhaka: Bureau of Manpower Employment and Training (BMET), Government of the People's Republic of Bangladesh. Retrieved from https://bmet.gov.bd/pages/static-pages/6922de24933eb65569e1887f

Bossavie, L. (2023). *Low-skilled temporary migration policies: The case of Bangladesh*. Background paper to the World Development Report 2023: Migrants, Refugees, and Societies. World Bank. Retrieved from https://thedocs.worldbank.org/en/doc/3ab0cffdc2e4621f8b5a70a0410213d5-0050062023/original/Bangladesh-case-study-FORMATTED.pdf

De Bel-Air, F. (2015). The socio-political background and stakes of "Saudizing" the workforce in Saudi Arabia: The Nitaqat policy. Retrieved from https://cadmus.eui.eu/handle/1814/34857

De Haas, H. (2010). Migration and development: A theoretical perspective. *International Migration Review*, *44*(1), 227–64.

Elyas, T., and I. Kurdi (2022). Representations of Kafala Sponsorship System in Western Newspapers: A Critical Discourse Analysis. *Global Media Journal*, *20*(49). Retrieved from https://www.proquest.com/openview/0417eca6f0f9d9aba7b5ed256339b07c/1?pq-origsite=gscholar&cbl=29638

Evans, K. (2002). Taking control of their lives? The youth, citizenship and social change project. *European Educational Research Journal*, *1*(1), 497–521.

FairSquare. (2020, October). Migrant labor in Saudi Arabia: A FairSquare policy brief (No. 1). FairSquare Projects. Retrieved from https://fairsq.org/wp-content/uploads/2020/11/FS-Policy-Brief

Faudot, A. (2019). Saudi Arabia and the rentier regime trap: A critical assessment of the plan Vision 2030. *Resources Policy*, *62*, 94–101.

Gardner, A. M. (2010). *City of strangers: Gulf migration and the Indian community in Bahrain*. Cornell University Press. Retrieved from https://doi.org/10.26530/OAPEN_627411

Grand, S., and K. Wolff (2020). *Assessing Saudi Vision 2030: A 2020 review*. Atlantic Council, Washington, DC, 1–80. Retrieved from https://www.atlanticcouncil.org/wp-content/uploads/2020/06/Assessing-Saudi-Vision-2030-A-2020-review.pdf

Hammer, A., and A. Adham (2022). Mobility power, state, and the 'Sponsored Labour Regime' in Saudi Capitalism. *Work, Employment and Society*, *37*(6). Retrieved from https://doi.org/10.1177/09500170221080373

Hammer, A., and A. Adham (2023). Mobility power, state, and the 'sponsored labor regime' in Saudi capitalism. *Work, Employment and Society*, *37*(6), 1497–1516.

Harshan, A. (2024). Expatriates as key contributors to Saudi Arabia's Vision 2030 transformation. Global Business Outlook. Retrieved October 28, 2024, from https://globalbusinessoutlook.com/economy/expatriates-key-contributors-saudi-arabias-vision-transformation/

ILO (International Labor Organization) (2014). *The Cost: Causes of and potential redress for high recruitment and migration costs in Bangladesh*. Dhaka: ILO. Retrieved from https://probashi.portal.gov.bd/sites/default/files/files/probashi.portal.gov.bd/publications/0af3257a_31f1_4989_b303_d3ab0ae7374b/The%20Cost%20Report.pdf

IOM (International Organization for Migration) (2020). *Mapping of labour migration recruitment practices in Bangladesh*. Dhaka: IOM. Retrieved from https://bangladesh.iom.int/sites/g/files/tmzbdl1006/files/documents/report-mapping-of-recruitment-practices-in-bangladesh_iom_jan-2020.pdf

Martin, P. (2014). Lower migration costs to raise migration's benefits. *New Diversities*, *16*(2), 12. Retrieved from https://newdiversities.mmg.mpg.de/wp-content/uploads/2015/01/2014_16-02_02_Martin.pdf

Morad, M., A. A. Rabby, D. Sacchetto, and N. Haque (2022). Shattered dreams and the return home: Bangladeshi migrant workers in the Gulf Cooperation

Council countries during COVID-19. *Two Homelands, 56*. Retrieved from https://doi.org/10.3986/dd.2022.2.02

Moshashai, D., A. M. Leber, and J. D. Savage (2020). Saudi Arabia plans for its economic future: Vision 2030, the National Transformation Plan, and Saudi fiscal reform. *British Journal of Middle Eastern Studies, 47*(3), 381–401.

Rahman, M. M. (2011). Emigration and the family economy: Bangladeshi labor migration to Saudi Arabia. *Asian and Pacific Migration Journal, 20*(3–4), 389–411.

Rahman, M. M. (2018). Beyond labor migration: The making of migrant enterprises in Saudi Arabia. *International Sociology, 33*(1), 86–106.

Rajan, S. I. (2023). Migration in South Asia: Old and New Mobilities. In S. I. Rajan (ed.), *Migration in South Asia* (pp. 3–16). Cham: Springer.

Rashid, M. M. (2022). The political economy of the Kafala abolishment in Saudi Arabia. *International Studies: Interdisciplinary Political and Cultural Journal (IS), 29*(1), 69–83.

Remesh, B. P., A. R. Dutta, and M. Mani (2020). Migration in South Asia: Poverty and Vulnerability. Kathmandu: *South Asia Alliance for Poverty Eradication (SAAPE)*. Retrieved from https://saape.org/wp-content/uploads/2023/12/Migration-in-South-Asia-Report-2020.pdf

Saudi Vision 2030. (n.d.). Vision 2030: Story of Transformation. Retrieved from https://www.vision2030.gov.sa/media/qnxn3igg/vision-2030_story-of-transformation.pdf

Shahi, R., K. Karim, M.J.U. Sikder, and V. Bansal (2021). Shattered Dreams: Bangladeshi Migrant Workers during a Global Pandemic. *Journal of Modern Slavery, 5*(2). Retrieved from https://slavefreetoday.org/journal_of_modern_slavery/v6i2a05_ShatteredDreamsBangladeshiMigrantWorkerduringGlobalPandemic.pdf

Sharma, A. (2022). *Change Management in Societal Transformation: The Case of Saudi Arabia's 'Vision 2030.'* ORF Special Report No. 194. Observer Research Foundation. Retrieved from https://www.orfonline.org/public/uploads/posts/pdf/20230421001625.pdf

Sinha, M. (2021). Treatment of Migrant Workers in the Middle East: Modern-Day Slavery? *ANU Undergraduate Research Journal, 11*(1), 144–54.

Thiollet, H. (2022). Illiberal Migration Governance in the Arab Gulf. In J. Hollifield & N. Foley (eds.), *Understanding Global Migration* (pp. 50–80). California: Stanford University Press. Retrieved from https://sciencespo.hal.science/hal-03522786

Truluck, E. (2023). Using Islam to protect the rights of migrant workers: Bringing Kafala into Sharia compliance in Saudi Arabia. *UCLA Journal of Islamic and Near Eastern Law, 20*. Retrieved from https://escholarship.org/uc/item/1ht6n3qz

UNB (2024, October 28). Keen to recruit more workers from Bangladesh: Saudi envoy. The Daily Star. Retrieved from https://www.thedailystar.net/news/bangladesh/diplomacy/news/keen-recruit-more-workers-bangladesh-saudi-envoy-3738396

8

Most Favored Destination for Pakistani Migrants, Saudi Arabia: Trends, Patterns and Issues

Nasra M. Shah and Memoona Qazi

Introduction

Pakistan and the Kingdom of Saudi Arabia (KSA) have had a strong relationship for many decades. Just four years after its independence, Pakistan signed a Treaty of Friendship with the KSA in 1951, laying down the foundation of mutual cooperation and assistance (Consulate General, 2021). At a public level, the KSA is revered as the custodian of Islam due to the location of the two holiest sites. Thousands of Pakistanis regularly visit Makkah and Madinah for pilgrimage. At a diplomatic level, many high-level visits have been made by leaders of each country, the last one to Pakistan by the Crown Prince Muhammad Bin Salman in February 2019, when memoranda of understanding worth twenty billion dollars were signed (Afzal, 2019). Fairly frequent visits to the KSA are made by high-ranking political and military leaders from Pakistan. The KSA has been a generous sponsor of many educational and health facilities in Pakistan, and landmarks such as the King Faisal mosque in Islamabad and the city of Faisalabad have been named after some of them. The KSA is the largest source of remittances received by Pakistan. According to the State Bank of Pakistan website, in fiscal year 2024, about US$30.3 billion were remitted to Pakistan; 7.4 billion (24 percent) from the KSA (https://www.sbp.org.pk/ecodata/index2.asp). Pakistan has assisted the KSA in terms of strengthening its military and security capabilities, as well as selling arms to it. Pakistan is the only Muslim country in the region with nuclear capability that could bolster the region's as well as the KSA's security (Younus, 2022; Reidel, 2008). Furthermore, Pakistan has been able to fulfill some of the KSA's labor force shortages through a steady flow of migrant workers.

Over the years, the KSA has also exerted cultural and religious influence on Pakistan, especially through the establishment of the madrassa educational system, funded largely by private Saudi donors. The madrassa system is based on a more austere interpretation of Islam influenced by the Wahhabi thought, compared with Pakistan's more relaxed indigenous practices. It is believed by some that such influences may have led to the trend towards political and religious extremism and violence in Pakistan (Weinbaum and Khurram, 2014). In a historical context, Saudi-Pakistan ties deepened further during the Afghan war against the Soviet Union in the 1980s and the growth of the Afghan "Mujahideen" (civil warriors), later known as "Taliban," who took up arms against the Afghan occupation. The mujahideen were provided support and military training by Pakistan with funding from Saudi Arabia. Both Pakistan and Saudi Arabia became close allies of the USA during that time (Shams, 2012). With the ample supply of arms, a militant culture took root, and an indigenous group of militants organized themselves as Tehreek-Taliban, Pakistan (TTP), with the collaboration of the Afghan Taliban. The TTP is banned in Pakistan, but the country has been suffering from terrorist activities for many years, until the present, with the TTP masterminding some of these activities.

Beyond the cultural influences exerted by the madrassa education, Pakistani migrants who work in the KSA have also been instrumental in generating social remittances that define certain aspects of everyday life, such as the appropriate roles of women and their modes of dress. This was most evidently seen in the 1980s when General Zia ul Haq, heavily influenced by the Saudi Wahabi version of Islam, introduced new sets of laws known as Islamization laws and the Hudood Ordinance aimed at segregating the workplaces and defining the role of women in society. Scholars have situated these reforms within the broader regional religious-conservative currents of the period, including their influence on dress and conduct codes for public-sector employees in Pakistan, particularly women. Female employees were forced to wear a head scarf or cover their heads in workplaces; for instance, female anchors on state television and female teachers and students in schools were policed to conform to this dress code (Ali and Syed, 2018). The effect of this Saudization of the Pakistani culture, as some scholars put it, continues to date as Pakistan has witnessed a rise in the orthodox Wahabi-influenced practices among both men and women in the society over the years. A visible demonstration of such practices is the greater prevalence of the Saudi-style *abaya* (long gown covering the whole body, and sometimes the face) and *hijab* (head covering) (Hoodbhoy, 2009; Ali and Syed, 2018).

Within this broad overview of the longstanding association between Pakistan and the KSA, this paper focuses on the contribution made by Pakistani migrants to take up jobs in a variety of sectors, ranging from high-skilled doctors and engineers to low-skilled workers and general helpers. The paper is organized as follows. After describing the legislative structure and data sources, we discuss the trends and patterns of migration from 1971 to the present in terms of the volume, occupational distribution, and place of origin within Pakistan. We then address four major issues related to Pakistani migration to the KSA, focusing on (i) the high cost of recruitment; (ii) the continued low level of migrant skills and efforts at upskilling; (iii) irregular migration; and (iv) exceptionally high rates of incarceration and executions of Pakistani migrants in the KSA. The final section presents the main conclusions.

Legislative structure and data sources

Overseas migration from Pakistan, especially to the Gulf countries, increased rapidly in the early 1970s owing to the ambitious development goals of those countries and the need for foreign workers to achieve them. In Pakistan, the Bureau of Emigration and Overseas Employment (BEOE) was established in response to the increasing volume of migration from Pakistan to the Gulf countries. An Emigration Ordinance was passed in 1979 to regulate and organize labor migration outflows. The emigration rules established under the above ordinance have undergone periodic updates, as described in a recent document published by the BEOE (2023). The BEOE supervises the work of migrant protectorates that were established to scrutinize the demand for overseas workers. There are nine protectorates in various parts of the country that organize and approve the migration of workers. These protectorates also provide pre-departure training.

In order to cater to heightened demand for Pakistani workers, a cadre of overseas employment promoters (OEPs) was established. The work of OEPs is supervised and organized by a Ministry, currently designated as the Ministry of Overseas Pakistanis and Human Resource Development (MOPHRD). The Ministry provides a license to the OEPs for facilitating the outflow of migrant workers, and has laid out specific rules for the amount to be charged and other matters related to migrant welfare. Currently there are 2,752 OEPs holding valid licenses in Pakistan. However, it is well known that the work of the licensed agents is supported by a vast network of agents belonging to communities from which they can recruit migrant workers by charging an additional fee than allowed by the government. Cases of fraudulent engagement and misinformation provided to potential migrants are known to be frequent, as discussed in a later section.

Data on migrant workers is sent on a regular basis by each protectorate to the BEOE research unit in Islamabad, which publishes tabulations on its website, updated every month. Information is published on the occupational distribution, skill level of migrant, district and province of origin, and protectorate that arranged the move. No data are routinely published according to age, gender, or wages. Also, the country does not have a system for documenting return migrants.

All Pakistani workers who leave the country on a work visa are required to register with the BEOE. Those workers, who may have left on a visit visa and find a job in the KSA, or another country, are not required to register with the BEOE. Similarly, those who move to another country on an immigrant visa are not required to register with the BEOE. In the case of the KSA, it is safe to presume that almost all workers would be registered with BEOE since most of them would need a work permit processed in Pakistan to take up employment in the KSA. Some workers who earn at least 4,000 Saudi riyals (about US$1,065) per month are allowed to bring their family members with them. Data on the number of people who are accompanied by their family members is not collected by the BEOE.

Data for this paper were provided by the BEOE upon request by the authors. The published data are not disaggregated by host country in terms of migrant characteristics, and special tabulations for migrants to the KSA were therefore run.

Trends and patterns of migration from Pakistan to the KSA

The total number of Pakistanis working and living in the KSA was estimated as 2.3 million in June 2021 (Shah et al., 2022). The 2022 Census of the KSA reported the number of the Pakistani population as 1.8 million, third-largest after India and Bangladesh (De Bel-Air, 2023). A majority of the migrants to the KSA are males, only some of whom are accompanied by their families.

Since 1971, when data on yearly overseas labor migration have been systematically collected and published, a cumulative total of 13.85 million workers left Pakistan after registering with the BEOE through various protectorate offices. Between 1971 and 2010, 51 percent of all workers headed for the KSA (Figure 8.1). For most years between 2011 and 2023, migrants to the KSA accounted for about half or more of the total outflows. Worker outflows from Pakistan declined markedly during the COVID-19 years, 2020–2021. However, the KSA remained the largest recipient, accounting for 61 percent in 2020. Major exceptions were in 2017 and 2018, when less than 30 percent went to the KSA, and this negatively impacted the overall outflow from Pakistan. According to an analysis by the World Bank (2018) the sudden decline in migration outflow from Pakistan reflects a combination of

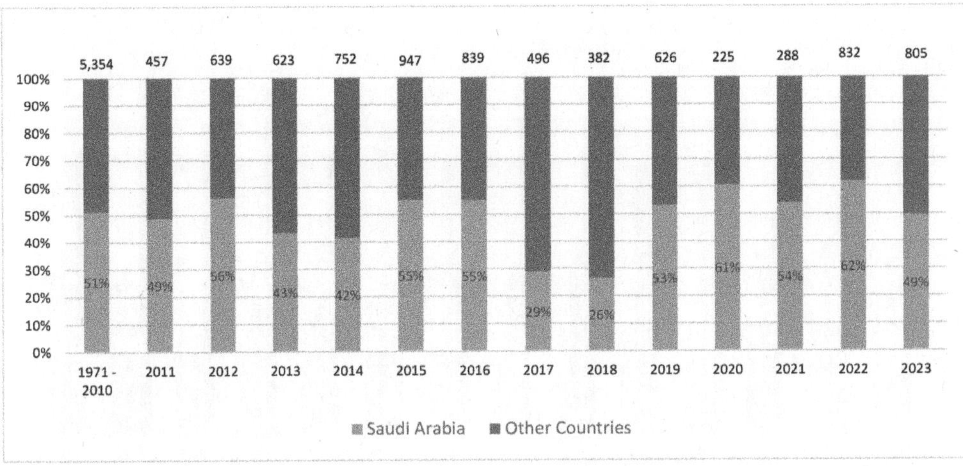

Figure 8.1. Percentage of Pakistani migrant outflows to the KSA among all migrants, 1971–2023 (thousands). Source: BEOE database, various years.

factors wholly out of Pakistan's control, including a fall in oil prices, a shift in Saudi labor policies favoring nationals over immigrants, the imposition of higher fees on migrants bringing dependents into Saudi Arabia, and increased competition from other labor migrants. Furthermore, the fact that Pakistani migrants are mostly concentrated in occupations where labor is replaceable without specialized skills, such as laborers and drivers, means that they are largely exposed to competition with other low-skilled migrants. The downward trend experienced in 2017–2018, however, reversed in 2018 when a total of 626,000 migrants left the country, 53 percent to the KSA. The predominance of the KSA in labor outflows from Pakistan has persisted since 2019.

In addition to the KSA, the United Arab Emirates (UAE) is the other most popular destination for Pakistanis. Since 2011, these two countries have attracted about three-fourths or more of all Pakistani workers in most years (Figure 8.2). However, Pakistani migration to the UAE declined substantially in 2021, when only about 10 percent went to that country, but the lost ground seems to have recovered recently. In 2023, almost half of all labor migrants went to the KSA, 26.7 percent to the UAE, and the remaining 22.3 percent to the rest of the world, including other Gulf countries. Pakistan has been seeking diversification of destinations beyond the Gulf countries and has launched several programs to achieve this.

During the pre-COVID year, 2019, about 60 percent of all migrant workers from Pakistan to the KSA were skilled, while 39 percent were

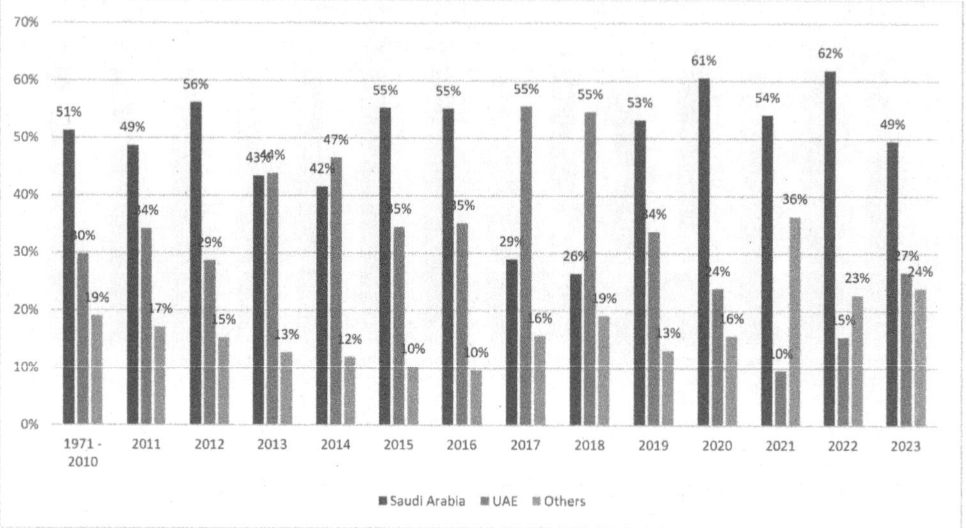

Figure 8.2. Centrality of the KSA and the UAE as a destination for Pakistani labor migrants, 1971–2023. Source: BEOE database, various years.

unskilled or semi-skilled, and less than 1 percent were highly skilled/qualified, as shown in Table 8.1. The percentage of skilled workers shows a decline over the last five years from about 60 percent in 2019 to 40 percent in 2023. At the same time, the percentage of unskilled workers increased from about 36 percent in 2019 to 53 percent in 2023. A further disaggregation by specific occupations indicates that the decline in skilled workers seems to have been caused largely by the reduction in outflow of drivers, from 53 percent in 2019 to only 34 percent in 2023 (Table 8.2). The decline in demand for drivers may be related to the fact that women in the KSA were allowed to drive starting in 2018, while they were forbidden to do so earlier (BBC News, 2018). Thus, a majority of Pakistani workers are currently employed in the KSA as unskilled workers, and a small minority are highly skilled, contrary to the KSA's goals and vision for encouraging the growth of highly skilled workers in the future (Saudi Vision 2030). The persisting demand for unskilled workers is probably related to the recent upsurge in infrastructure projects such as NEOM, a 1.5 trillion-dollar multipurpose urban area in Tabuk, Saudi Arabia. This project was launched in 2017 by Crown Prince Mohammad Bin Salman and has generated a large number of jobs, including 140,000 construction workers (Bell, 2024).

Pakistani migrants to the KSA are drawn from all provinces of the country (Table 8.3). A majority (53 percent in 2023) of all migrants belong to Punjab,

Table 8.1. Skill Level of Pakistani Migrants Employed in KSA, 2019–2023 (Percentages)

Skill Level	Pre COVID-19	COVID-19		Post COVID-19	
	2019	**2020**	**2021**	**2022**	**2023***
Highly Qualified	0.6	0.6	1.0	0.6	1.2
Highly Skilled	0.1	0.0	0.1	0.1	0.1
Skilled	59.7	54.9	52.8	44.1	40.1
Semi-Skilled	3.7	3.2	3.4	6.3	5.9
Un-Skilled	35.9	41.2	42.7	48.9	52.7
Total numbers	332,449	136,459	155,541	514,602	424,696

Source: BEOE database, various years.

Notes: Highly qualified includes doctors, dentists, engineers, teachers, accountants, and managers. Highly skilled includes nurses, foremen/supervisors, technicians, operators, surveyors, computer programmers/analysts, designers, pharmacists, riggers, draftsmen, photographers, and artists.

Skilled includes welders, secretaries/stenographers, storekeepers, clerks/typists, masons, carpenters, electricians, plumbers, steel fixers, painter mechanics, cable jointers, drivers, tailors, fitters, dentists, goldsmiths, blacksmiths, and salesmen. Semi-skilled includes cooks and waiters/bearers.Unskilled includes agriculturists, laborers, and farmers.

*2023 data till November

Table 8.2. Top Three Occupations of Pakistani Labor Migrants in KSA, 2019–2023 (Percentages)

Occupation	Pre COVID-19	COVID-19		Post COVID-19	
	2019	**2020**	**2021**	**2022**	**2023***
Driver	53	49	47	35	34
Labor / Helper	31	37	39	41	39
Gen. Worker	4	4	3	7	13
Others	12	11	11	16	14
Total numbers	332,449	136,459	155,541	514,602	424,696

Source: BEOE database, various years

*2023 data till November

consistent with the largest number of people who reside in this province. The province of Khyber Pakhtunkhwa (KPK) has been sending a larger percentage of workers to the KSA relative to their proportional share of the population. However, a downward trend from KPK seems to have occurred during the post-COVID years, 2022 and 2023. Outflows from Sindh and Balochistan are lower than the proportion of population residing in these provinces, as observed for the country as a whole (Shah et al., 2020).

When viewed as a percentage of the total male labor force in Pakistan, about 0.28 percent migrated to the KSA in 2021. A larger percentage of the labor force emigrated to the KSA in 2023 (0.77 percent) compared with 2021 (0.28 percent). Marked provincial differences were present. The outflows from the province of KPK were much larger (0.72 percent) compared to 0.26 percent from Punjab and only 0.04 percent from Baluchistan (Table 8.4). In 2023, about 1.74 percent of the male labor force emigrated from KPK,

Table 8.3. Percentage Distribution of Pakistani Migrants in the KSA by Province of Origin, 2019–2023

Province	Pre COVID-19	COVID-19		Post COVID-19	
	2019	2020	2021	2022	2023*
Azad Jammu and Kashmir	3.4	3.3	3.5	3.6	3.7
Baluchistan	0.5	0.8	0.7	0.9	0.6
Gilgit Baltistan	0.1	0.1	0.2	0.1	0.2
Islamabad	0.4	0.4	0.4	0.4	0.5
Khyber Pakhtunkhwa	40.5	40.2	38.4	36.6	31.7
Punjab	47.8	49.3	50.4	51.0	52.7
Sindh	7.4	6.0	6.5	7.4	8.3

Source: BEOE database, various years.

*2023 data till November.

Table 8.4. Male Labor Force Population and Overseas Registered Migrants to the KSA by Province

Province/ Area	Male labor force (LFS 2020–2021)	Emigrants to KSA (2021)	Emigrants to KSA in 2021 as percentage of male labor force (%)	Emigrants to KSA (2023)*	Emigrants to KSA in 2023 as percentage of male labor force (%)	Percentage point differential between 2021 and 2023 (%)
Pakistan	54,920,000	155,541	0.28	424,696	0.77	0.49
Khyber Pakhtunkhwa	8,270,000	59,696	0.72	144,272	1.74	1.02
Punjab	30,250,000	78,368	0.26	223,785	0.74	0.48
Sindh	13,270,000	10,088	0.08	35,243	0.27	0.19
Balochistan	3,120,000	1,121	0.04	2,643	0.08	0.04

Source: Pakistan Labor Force Survey, 2020–2021; BEOE, various years.

*2023 data till November.

compared to 0.74 percent from Punjab. Several factors may account for the differences in outflows from various provinces, a major one being the role of social networks that encourage persons from the same origin to migrate. KPK seems to have established very strong networks that foster chain migration, whereby the previous migrants provide information as well as financial and social support to future migrants.

Major issues in Pakistan-KSA migration

High recruitment costs

If the existing laws were to be followed under the 'employer payment' model, the employer in the KSA would be responsible for paying the cost of the migrant's move to the host country, with the exception of any processing and other fees that are legally charged in Pakistan. The employer would also provide a job for which he/she is sponsoring the migrant worker. Major exceptions to the above "ideal" situation are present in reality. The structure that governs the employment of foreign workers in the KSA, and other Gulf countries requires that each migrant worker have a sponsor or *kafeel* who is responsible for ensuring the legal entry, stay, and departure of that worker. Furthermore, the *kafeel* must be the employer of the foreign worker. Violations of the above rules are rampant, however. Work visas are sold by the potential *Kafeel* (or agents on his/her behalf) to bring in workers on the understanding that they are allowed to find a job and work for another employer, which puts the migrant in an irregular status. Such work visas, known as "free" or "azad" visas, are sold through various intermediaries located in the host as well as home countries. The cost of buying the visa is borne by the migrant worker.

In a comprehensive survey on the costs paid by Pakistani workers to go to the KSA and the UAE, conducted as part of the World Bank's KNOMAD surveys, it was reported that the average cost for moving to the KSA and the UAE was US$3,493.8 and US$1,818.4, respectively. The study used snowball sampling of low-skilled migrants who had worked in the two countries or were currently employed there. Of the total cost paid by the worker, the informal visa fee accounted for 81 percent in the KSA and 77 percent in the UAE (ILO, 2016; Amjad et al., 2017). About 67 percent of the migrant workers had borrowed the money to finance their move. The KNOMAD cost survey also showed that over 85 percent of migrants who borrowed to migrate obtained a loan from their social network, either through a friend or a relative. For migrants who took a loan from a money lender or a bank, the median annual interest rate they reported was about 35 percent. These high up-front costs likely create substantial barriers to migration, reducing opportunities to migrate for workers from poorer households. This in turn significantly limits the options of utilizing overseas employment for poverty reduction (World Bank, 2018). The high cost of recruitment is rooted in the existence of a 'visa market' in Pakistan that is of course linked to the availability of work visas that can be bought from a Saudi sponsor.

Intermediaries in both countries play a central role in arranging the work visa. The two main types of intermediaries consist of friends/family members or recruitment agents and sub-agents. Among the agents, some are licensed and regulated by the Pakistan government, designated as overseas employment promoters (OEPs), as mentioned earlier, while many work informally as sub-agents/brokers. The ILO (International Labor Organization) survey found that friends and relatives were the source of the work visa for 52 percent of the Saudi migrants, while agents and sub-agents accounted for the rest. The survey also reported that the cost of recruitment was similar in both cases. Intermediaries, especially unlicensed informal brokers in the home as well as host countries, have been blamed by some analysts as the source of incorrect information about wages, working, and living conditions in the host country. Based on interviews with Pakistani returnee migrants and potential migrants in Islamabad, Babar (2022) reported that some of the respondents had been duped by the recruitment agents, arriving in the Gulf only to find that they had paid far too much money for their visa, the jobs promised to them did not exist, or the recruiters through which they had obtained the job had suddenly vanished and could not be contacted for any support. Others found on arrival in the Gulf country that their job description and nature of work were totally different from what they had been promised, and they often faced delayed payment of wages.

A few studies have looked at the challenges faced by OEPs and unlicensed emigration promoters who facilitate labor migration from Pakistan to the KSA. Interviews with thirteen OEPs in Pakistan led Babar (2020) to conclude that unscrupulous companies and sub-agents in Pakistan extracted huge profits from potential migrants. She also reported that there was a lack of support from both the home and host countries to address core issues that minimized the migrants' success. Furthermore, the OEPs stationed in Pakistan were unable to mediate on behalf of migrants who faced any difficulty in the KSA. A study by the ILO (2020) about the role of informal intermediaries reported that the OEPs depended massively on finding potential migrants through such intermediaries since they were trusted by community members. The addition of this layer of mediation, however, increased the cost of migration since the sub-agent charged a certain amount for his services, and in some cases indulged in fraudulent practices.

The MOPHRD is trying to reduce dependence on intermediaries by publishing overseas jobs on its website. Furthermore, an online complaint management system has been established to address the grievances of emigrants to ensure ethical recruitment practices. A specific effort to reduce migrant vulnerability is the institution of the Foreign Service Agreement by the Protectorate of migrants. This agreement documents the type of occupation, skill level, name and country of employer, salary, employment promoter's details, as well as the total recruitment cost paid by the prospective migrant (www.beoe.gov.pk). The objective of including the recruitment cost on this form is to discourage the practice of overcharging by the intermediaries. An affidavit written in Urdu is also signed by the worker to ensure that he/she fully understand the terms of employment and have not been subjected to fraud or misinformation (Shah et al., 2022).

Low skill level of migrants

As described in a preceding section, a majority of the migrants from Pakistan to the KSA are unskilled and low skilled, and their relative proportion has increased during the last five years. The low skill level of Pakistani migrants is related to the generally low level of literacy and education in the country. About 37 percent of Pakistan's population aged 10+ was illiterate in 2020–2021. A wide gender discrepancy was present, with about 27 percent of the males and 48 percent of the females being illiterate. Even among the literate persons, the level of education was quite low. Only about 28 percent of males and 20 percent of females had attained an education beyond the tenth grade, and only 6.6 percent of males and 5.5 percent of females had attained a college degree or higher (PBS, 2022). When viewed in terms of the total labor force of 71.8 million in 2020–21, 38 percent were illiterate, and 9 percent had attained a college degree or higher education. The latest Census shows that an alarming percentage of children were out of school in 2023. Of the seventy-one million children aged 5–16, 25 million (36 percent) were out of school; with 28 percent never going to school and 7 percent dropping out (PBS, 2024). The above situation indicates that Pakistan's population continues to suffer from illiteracy and low education level, and may be left behind other countries to compete for the higher level of skills now required in the KSA and other Gulf countries.

Pakistan has been trying to upgrade the skill level of Pakistani workers and provide Pakistani migrants with skill verification certificates. In December 2021, Pakistan signed an agreement through the National Vocational and Technical Training Commission (NAVTTC) with the "TAKAMOL" of the Saudi Ministry of Human Resources and Social

Development to provide skill verification certificates to the Pakistani migrant workers. The aim of this agreement is to oversee and verify the workers' skills in order to ensure a longer market engagement in the KSA. With the onset of the Skill Verification Program, Pakistani workers will no longer require a sponsor and will be able to directly attain contracts from Saudi companies (Pro Pakistani, 2022). More than 23,000 Pakistani workers have found employment through this joint initiative.

The Pakistani government has a wide-ranging policy to enhance skills for employability of all entrants to the labor force through diversification of skills, competency-based training, and recognition of prior learning. The country has a broad network of agencies that aim to provide technical and vocational training of various types and durations. The primary focus of these programs is to provide applied training, primarily at the semi-skilled and mid-skilled levels, to fulfill the needs of the industry within Pakistan as well as enhance overseas migration. The government has also established five Centers of Excellence for technical and vocational training with the assistance of the European Union and the German Organization for International Cooperation. Since 2006, about 600,000 Pakistani workers have been provided vocational and technical training by NAVTTC, a majority in conventional trades. Some training courses are also provided for women in occupations such as beauty salon workers, cooking, and hospitality services. At the higher skilled level, about 65,000 have been trained in hi-end trades such as electrical engineering, and mobile application development, and 85,000 in hi-tech trades, such as advanced Python programming and application, artificial intelligence, and robotics, etc.

Irregular migrants

A Pakistani migrant to the KSA may acquire an irregular status in several ways. He/she may enter the country illegally, but this is generally rare. Overstaying a valid visa is probably the most common reason for an irregular status. Several thousand Pakistanis visit the two holy sites in Makkah and Medina every year; some of them overstay their legal duration of visa. The second major reason for irregular status is employment by someone other than the *kafeel*, since such employment is against KSA rules and regulations.

As judged from the number of persons who regularize their status or depart during amnesties declared by the KSA, the volume of irregular migrants in the country is massive (De Bel-Air, 2014; Shah, 2014). While disaggregated data by nationality is not available, it was estimated by De Bel-Air (2014) that during the six-month period from April 3 to November 3, 2013, an estimated 4.7 million foreign workers corrected their status, and another 1 million were either expelled from the country or left voluntarily by availing the amnesty. Thus, very large numbers of foreign workers in Saudi Arabia were affected by the amnesty, either through regularization of status or departure/expulsion. Despite the corrections of status and departure of irregular workers, many workers did not avail the amnesty and continued to reside in the KSA in an irregular status. Among Pakistanis living in Jeddah in an irregular status in 2008–2009, 92 percent did not plan to leave if an amnesty were declared (Al-Sharif, 2021).

Deportations of Pakistanis from various countries seem to be increasing, with the KSA being the largest one. Data from the concerned authorities indicate that the total number of deportees increased from 89,207 in 2015 to 123,093 in 2017. Deportees from the KSA accounted for 76 percent of all deportees in 2017, numbering 93,736 (Shah et al., 2020). The Pakistani government recognized the problems faced by Pakistani workers during the six-month amnesty in 2013, which it felt was part of the Saudization drive to regulate the labor market and maximize Saudi nationals' participation in the workforce. The government was making concerted efforts to prevent the negative impacts of Saudi policies on Pakistanis in the KSA (GoP, 2013). Recent data on the deportations of Pakistanis from the KSA are not available to us.

Exceptionally high rate of incarceration and executions

Pakistanis are reported to face exceptionally high rates of imprisonment and executions in the KSA, especially if found with drugs in their possession. Some Pakistani nationals fall prey to migrant traffickers and are used as drug carriers. Once apprehended, the migrants are left to the mercy of a foreign criminal justice system without translators or legal assistance. It was estimated that of the 11,000 Pakistanis in foreign prisons in 2014, the largest number (3,309) were in Saudi jails, some on death row (Malik, 2017). A report was recently presented by the Pakistan Foreign Affairs Ministry to the National Assembly about Pakistanis imprisoned abroad. It was noted that more than 12,000 Pakistanis were incarcerated abroad, with 3,100 in the KSA. A large percentage of those in Saudi jails were accused or convicted of drug smuggling (Tribune, July 21, 2023).

Saudi Arabia executes more Pakistanis than any other foreign nationality annually, nearly all for heroin smuggling, including twenty in 2014, twenty-two in 2015, seven in 2016, and seventeen in 2017 (HRW, 2018). An analysis of the reasons for the exceptionally high rate of executions of Pakistanis in the KSA was carried out by Hoyle et al. (2023). They suggested that drug laws and penal policies of the KSA result in susceptibility to capital punishment. In addition, networks of drug traffickers in Pakistan further enhance the vulnerability of migrants who are used as 'mules' to carry drugs without knowledge of the risks they undertake.

Following the announcement of broader judicial reforms in recent years, observers have monitored trends in the application of capital punishment in Saudi Arabia, including in cases involving foreign nationals. It has been noted by a human rights NGO, Reprieve, that the practice of awarding the death penalty has not declined. From 2010 to 2021, 490 foreign nationals were executed in the KSA; of these, the highest number was that of Pakistanis, 164. Moini (2023) raises concerns about transparency and due-process safeguards in the application of capital punishment to foreign nationals. Human Rights lawyers and advocates within Pakistan have been urging the Pakistan government to end its tolerance towards the abuses faced by its citizens in prisons all over the world (Malik, 2017; Rizvi, 2018).

Human Rights Watch (2018), in a study of Pakistani returnees previously detained in Saudi Arabia, documented interviewee accounts of difficulties with legal representation, prolonged pretrial detention, pressure to sign confessions, and inadequate translation services. The violations included long periods of detention without charge or trial, no legal assistance, pressure to sign confessions and accept predetermined prison sentences to avoid prolonged arbitrary detention, and ineffective or pernicious translation services for defendants.

In addition to drug-related crimes, apprehension of Pakistani migrants who were headed to the KSA for begging purposes has recently been reported by Pakistani authorities (Pro Pakistani, 2023). In October 2023, a group of sixteen people, including men, women, and children traveling on umrah pilgrimage visas, was apprehended and offloaded from a flight in Multan. The sixteen people were heading to the KSA for begging purposes. The Ministry of Overseas Pakistanis and Human Resource Development has reported to the Senate Committee on Overseas Pakistanis that a significant proportion of beggars are trafficked abroad through illegal channels. Furthermore, a staggering 90 percent of beggars apprehended in foreign countries belong to Pakistan (Dawn, September 24, 2023). The Ministry recently reported to the same Committee that several Gulf countries have complained to the government about the misbehavior of overseas Pakistanis. The UAE and Saudi Arabia don't want Pakistani workers and have asked Pakistan to give its citizens lessons in "proper behavior." The KSA has complained about the organized gangs of beggars traveling to that country as pilgrims (Ali, 2024).

In addition to arrests and executions, work-related injuries and illnesses pose serious hazards to Pakistani workers. The ILO survey of migrants to the KSA and the UAE found that about half of the migrant workers had been ill or injured during their stay abroad. Only about one-fourth of them had been compensated during this period, and such compensation was subject entirely to the employer's discretion (World Bank, 2018).

Conclusion

The KSA is one of the most important destinations for Pakistani migrants. Of the 13.85 million workers since 1971, 51 percent have headed to the KSA. During the COVID-19 pandemic, the KSA remained a major destination despite the overall decline in annual outflows. A large percentage of Pakistani migrants belong to unskilled and semi-skilled categories. Drivers have comprised the largest occupational category in the past, but their percentage among all Pakistani migrants has declined in the last two years. This trend may be attributable to the fact that Saudi women are now allowed to drive and may be fulfilling some of the driving needs of the household.

The vision of the KSA is to attract and retain qualified and skilled talent from across the world to contribute to the country's economic development and attract foreign investment (Saudi Vision, 2030). The profile of Pakistani migrants in the KSA suggests that there is a general mismatch between the KSA's development vision and the type of migrants that Pakistan is able to provide in terms of satisfying this vision in the future. The continued outflow of Pakistani unskilled and semi-skilled workers to the KSA suggests, however, that some of the infrastructure development plans of the KSA may absorb Pakistani workers at least in the short term. Pakistan's efforts at upskilling its workforce must be sped up for economic development at home as well competing with the overseas demand for workers.

The lack of protection and support for Pakistani workers, evidenced by the large number of incarcerations and executions in the KSA, is a cause of concern. Many of the arrests and executions are related to drug offenses. The Pakistani government should make greater efforts at stemming the outflow of drugs, often through innocent victims used by traffickers. The government in the KSA must also take another look at its judicial processes that subject such victims to capital punishment. Appropriate legal and consular support should be made available, along with language interpreters, to ensure a fair chance of defense for those apprehended. The seemingly increasing incidence of travel by Pakistanis for begging in the KSA is also a cause for concern, especially since the host country has complained about the matter and may increase travel restrictions for pilgrimage as well as employment.

The primacy of the KSA in migration from Pakistan is likely to continue in the future. A closer monitoring of the host country's demand for workers and the potential supply of workers must ensure that both parties can devise mechanisms to benefit each other maximally. Skill certification of Pakistani workers will be an important element of the continued absorption of future migrants. The appropriate protection and welfare of the migrant must, of course, remain central to the entire process.

Bibliography

Afzal, M. (2019). "Saudi Arabia's hold on Pakistan." Policy Brief, Brookings. https://www.brookings.edu/articles/saudi-arabias-hold-on-pakistan/

Ali, F., and Syed, J. (2018). "'Good Muslim women' at work: An Islamic and postcolonial perspective on ethnic privilege." *Journal of Management & Organization*, 24(5), 679–97.

Alsharif, F. (2021). "Undocumented migrants in Saudi Arabia: COVID⊠19 and amnesty reforms." *International Migration*, 60(1), 188–204.

Ali, K. (2024). "Gulf employers not hiring Pakistanis due to 'deplorable standard'." Dawn News, July 31. https://www.dawn.com/news/1849093

Amjad, R., G. M. Arif, and N. Iqbal (2017). "The cost of migration from Pakistan to Saudi Arabia and the UAE." *The Pakistani Diaspora: Corridors of Opportunity and Uncertainty*, Lahore School of Economics, 137–50.

Babar, Z. (2020). "Purveyors of dreams: labour recruiters in the Pakistan to Saudi Arabia migration corridor." *Migration and Development*, 10(1), 68–85.

Babar, Z. (2022). "Two bad places at once: Pakistani labour migrants and the transnational recruitment industry to the Gulf." In C. A. Ennis and N. Blarel (eds.), *The South Asia to Gulf Migration Governance Complex* (pp. 103–24). Bristol University Press.

BBC News. (2018). "Saudi Arabia's ban on women driving officially ends." BBC News, June 24. https://www.bbc.com/news/world-middle-east-44576795

Bell, J. (2024). "Saudi Arabia's NEOM: New video shows rapid progress at mega project, workers doubled." Al Arabiya News, May 23. https://english.alarabiya.net/News/saudi-arabia/2024/05/23/saudi-arabia-s-neom-new-video-shows-rapid-progress-at-mega-project-workers-doubled

BEOE (Bureau of Emigration and Overseas Employment) (2023). *Emigration Rules, 1979 Updated 2023*. Bureau of Emigration and Overseas Employment, Government of Pakistan. https://beoe.gov.pk/legal-framework

Consulate General of Pakistan. (2021) "Pakistan-Saudi Arabia Relations." Consulate General of Pakistan, Jeddah, March 22. https://parepjeddah.org/pakistan-ksa-relations/

Dawn. (2023). "'90pc of beggars' arrested abroad are of Pakistani origin, Senate body told." Dawn News, September 27. https://www.dawn.com/news/1778152

De Bel-Air, F. (2014). *Demography, Migration and Labour Market in Saudi*

Arabia. Explanatory Note EN - No. 1/2014. Gulf Labour Markets and Migration (GLMM).

De Bel-Air, F. (2023). "Major Innovations in the Saudi Census 2022." Policy Brief No. 3/2023, Gulf Labour Markets and Migration (GLMM). https://www.gulfmigration.grc.net

GoP. (Government of Pakistan) (2013). "Problems being faced by Pakistani Workers in Saudi Arabia." Ministry of Foreign Affairs, Government of Pakistan https://mofa.gov.pk/problems-being-faced-by-pakistani-workers-in-saudi-arabia

Hoodbhoy, P. (2009). "The Saudization of Pakistan." Newsline.com. https://eacpe.org/content/uploads/2017/05/Saudization-of-Pakistan-updated.pdf

Hoyle, C., J. Hutton, and L. Harry (2023). "A disproportionate risk of being executed: Why Pakistani migrants are vulnerable to capital punishment in Saudi Arabia." *British Journal of Criminology*, 63(6), 1423–40.

HRW. (2018). "'Caught in a web.' Treatment of Pakistanis in the Saudi criminal justice system." Human Rights Watch Report with Justice Project Pakistan, March. https://www.hrw.org/sites/default/files/report_pdf/saudiarabia0318_web.pdf

ILO (International Labor Organization) (2016). *The Cost of Migration: What Low-Skilled Migrant Workers from Pakistan Pay to Work in Saudi Arabia and the United Arab Emirates*. International Labor Organization.

ILO (International Labor Organization) (2020). *Recruitment Agency Business Practices and the Role of Intermediaries in the Foreign Employment Industry in Pakistan*. International Labour Organization. https://www.ilo.org/wcmsp5/groups/public/---ed_protect/---protrav/---migrant/documents/publication/wcms_756251.pdf

Malik, Z. Z. (2017). "Pakistani citizens, including children, on death row in Saudi Arabia and Iran." Dawn News, December 26. https://www.dawn.com/news/1378783

Moini, Q. A. (2023). "No end to executions in Saudi Arabia, report shows." Dawn News., February 2. https://www.dawn.com/news/1734877#:~:text=The%20report%20says%20that%20there,use%20against%20foreigners%20and%20women

PBS (Pakistani Bureau of Statistic). (2022). *Labor Force Survey* 2020–2021. Pakistan Bureau of Statistics. https://www.pbs.gov.pk/labour-force-publications

PBS (Pakistani Bureau of Statistic) (2024). *7th Population and Housing Census 2023: Key Findings Report*. Pakistan Bureau of Statistics. https://www.pbs.gov.pk/sites/default/files/population/2023/Key_Findings_Report.pdf

Pro Pakistani (2022). "Saudi Arabia officially launches verification program for skilled workers in Pakistan." Pro Pakistani, November 2. https://propakistani.pk/2022/11/02/saudi-arabia-officially-launches-verification-program-for-skilled-workers-in-pakistan/

Pro Pakistani (2023). "FIA arrests 16 beggars travelling to Saudi Arabia from

Multan." Pro Pakistani, October 1. https://propakistani.pk/2023/10/01/fia-arrests-16-beggars-travelling-to-saudi-arabia-from-multan/

Reidel, B. (2008). "Saudi Arabia: Nervously watching Pakistan." Brookings, January 28. https://www.brookings.edu/articles/saudi-arabia-nervously-watching-pakistan/

Rizvi, Y. (2018). "The time to demand Saudi Arabia to treat Pakistani workers properly is now." Dawn News, October 1. https://www.dawn.com/news/1436145

Saudi Vision 2030 (n.d). https://www.vision2030.gov.sa/en/

SBP (State Bank of Pakistan) (n.d). *Economic Data—Country-wise Workers' Remittances*. https://www.sbp.org.pk/ecodata/index2.asp

Shah, N. M. (2014). "Recent amnesty programmes for irregular migrants in Kuwait and Saudi Arabia: some successes and failures." Migration Policy Centre, Gulf Labour Markets and Migration, Explanatory Note, 09/2014. https://hdl.handle.net/1814/34577

Shah, N. M., R. Amjad A. Shahzad, and M. Hameed (2020). *Pakistan Migration Report 2020*. Centre on International Migration, Remittances and Diaspora, (CIMRAD), Lahore School of Economics.

Shah, N. M., A. Shahzad, and S. Quddus (2022). *Pakistan Migration Report 2022*. Centre on International Migration, Remittances and Diaspora, (CIMRAD), Lahore School of Economics.

Shams, S. (2012). "Islamic extremism." DW News, August 24. https://amp.dw.com/en/the-wahabi-republic-of-pakistan/a-16191055

Tribune (2023). "Over 12,000 Pakistanis in jails abroad, NA told." Express Tribune, July 21. https://tribune.com.pk/story/2427237/over-12000-pakistanis-in-jails-abroad-na-told

Weinbaum, M. G., and A. B. Khurram (2014). "Pakistan and Saudi Arabia: Deference, dependence, and deterrence." *Middle East Journal*, 68(2), 211–28.

World Bank Group (2018). "A migrant's journey for better opportunities: The case of Pakistan." World Bank Group. http://documents.worldbank.org/curated/en/540841530861637430/A-migrant-s-journey-for- better-opportunities-the-case-of-Pakistan

Younus, U. (2022). "Pakistan can resolve Saudi Arabia's growing security concerns." Atlantic Council, July 1. https://www.atlanticcouncil.org/blogs/southasiasource/pakistan-can-resolve-saudi-arabias-growing-security-concerns/

Part Four

Emerging Trends and Development on the Saudi Migration–Development Nexus: Labor Market Transformation

9

Energy Diversification and a Shifting Labor Market in Saudi Arabia: Green Jobs and Education Potential in the Development of a Clean Hydrogen Sector

Cian Mulligan and Sebastian Sons

Introduction

In times of comprehensive efforts to diversify its oil-reliant economy (Bianco and Sons, 2021), the Kingdom of Saudi Arabia is undergoing a process of energy transition that aims to develop a "green economy" (Abdelraouf and Luomi, 2016) in order to generate additional revenues from non-fossil fuels, create jobs and develop a national educational system in alternative energy sectors (Akhonbay, 2019). As global demand for fossil resources is expected to decline in the upcoming decades and the interest in green energy is growing, Saudi Arabia aims to position itself as a regional champion in alternative energy production and to fulfill the international obligations of climate agreements (Badawi, 2022). In the framework of Saudi Arabia's modernization and diversification agenda Vision 2030, the Kingdom is pushing its efforts to adapt to climate change and shifting global energy needs in order to consolidate its status as a "global investment powerhouse" (Havrlant and Darandary, 2021) and a know-how society (Nurunnabi, 2017) in which energy transition is an integral pillar (Zumbraegel, 2022). In concrete terms, Saudi Arabia aims to increase its share of renewables to 50 percent of the domestic electricity mix by 2030 and is pursuing net zero emissions by 2060 (BBC, 2021). As a consequence, numerous initiatives and programs such as the Saudi Green Initiative, the Middle East Green Initiative, the Circular Carbon Economy National Program, the National Renewable Energy Program, and the Saudi Energy Efficiency Program have been introduced to promote mitigation measures to climate change and energy transition.

In particular, Saudi Arabia seeks to develop capacities to export clean hydrogen (and derivatives) to global markets (Braun et al., 2023). In doing so, green energy diversification is promoted (Sim, 2022), and national jobs in the hydrogen industry are expected to be created. However, Saudi Arabia still faces challenges to achieve such goals: an inefficient but improving labor market structure and national educational system that needs refocusing in order to include hydrogen education into the respective curricula. In light of such obstacles, the need for the recruitment of expatriate workers in the hydrogen industry still features prominently in Saudi Arabia's labor market transformation. Despite the fact that nationalization ('Saudization') of the labor market in energy-related sectors such as the hydrogen industry remains a key priority, the demand for non-Saudi talent will continue to remain high, which will have implications for the growth of the hydrogen sector.

Against this backdrop, this chapter provides an analysis of the current development in Saudi Arabia's labor market, outlining the special character of Saudi/non-Saudi occupational preferences and the potential to create jobs in the renewable energy sector. Here, we focus on hydrogen as it provides a new potential for job creation. With insights from empirical case studies, the further elaborates on current initiatives and trends in the Saudi educational system to promote green jobs for nationals and non-nationals with a particular focus on hydrogen. The also sheds light on remaining challenges to promote local talent and human development and provides insights into the needs of short- to mid-term recruitment of foreign labor in the hydrogen sector.

Structure of the Saudi labor market: Transformative shifts in times of "Saudization"

The characteristics of Saudi Arabia's labor market structure will seem unusual to those familiar with employment in other high-income countries, but for those with knowledge of other countries in the Arab Gulf and of the labor market impact of large endowments of extractive resources, this uniqueness fades to local peculiarities. Like its oil-rich Gulf neighbors, such as Bahrain, Qatar, Kuwait, and Oman, until recently, employment in Saudi Arabia has been a tale of two labor markets: one for Saudi nationals that offered high-paying wages in the public sector, and another offering low-wage jobs, often in services and construction, to less-skilled expatriate workers in a weak private sector.

While Saudi Arabian authorities had frequently dabbled with labor market nationalization policies (or Saudization) in previous decades, from the early 2010s, the tool became an integral part of Saudi employment policy. In 2011, the Nitaqat system formalized quotas in the private sector by industry and company size (Koyame-Marsh, 2016). Minimum Saudization rates for specific industries were mandated, leading to penalties and rewards depending on company performance, and the necessity to consider Saudization in hiring policies was imprinted on every company in the country. While the policy undoubtedly convinced the private sector that Saudization was there to stay, the effect of Nitaqat is nuanced. Simply implementing mandatory Saudization quotas did not suddenly change the quality of jobs on offer in the private sector, and various ways of overcoming the regulations became prominent (Hertog, 2018). More empirically, Peck (2017) found that the policy discouraged firms from expanding past the minimum threshold that would activate Nitaqat obligations, as this would require hiring more higher-wage Saudis.

Towards the end of the 2010s and in line with Vision 2030, authorities focused on a more targeted approach to Saudization, and in addition to Nitaqat began designating certain areas as reserved occupations for Saudi nationals. This policy, reflecting the skills mismatch between the generally low-skill jobs available in the private sector and the skill levels of highly educated Saudi workers, began to ringfence occupations more closely aligned to Saudi skills and interests. Initially targeted at specific retail positions,[1] this targeted Saudization now dictates blanket Saudization in areas such as pharmacy work, consultancy professions, or aviation.[2]

At the same time as these sweeping changes to employment in the Saudi private sector, softer reforms were also implemented that attempted to bring working conditions more in line with those in the highly sought-after public sector. Minimum wages for Saudi workers were introduced in this period, along with strict rules on vacation allowances, work hours, and statutory time off for national holidays (Saudi Gazette, 2021).

As the private sector also undergoes substantial reforms, conditions also improved for expatriate workers as a result of the increased Saudi presence. Many of the new regulations—such as time off for vacation and holidays—also applied to non-Saudi workers, as well as improvements in the working environment. However, increased Saudization ultimately aims to limit the job opportunities for these foreign workers. Policies such as expat levies, introduced at that time, sought to incur penalties for maintaining stocks of expatriate workers. These levies also applied to the families of the workers, making domestic life for expatriate families less affordable and leading to the repatriation of the family and often ultimately the main breadwinner. All of these policies aimed to increase the cost to employers of hiring expatriate workers and therefore erode the employer preference for cheap foreign labor.

Overall, expatriate workers are faring much better in the country, especially since the abolition of the Kafala system in 2021. The abolition granted freedom of labor mobility to foreign workers for the first time (Alsharif, 2021), meaning employers did not have so much control over their expatriate workers, and therefore, a main benefit of preferring foreign workers was removed.

All these reforms have transformed the Saudi labor market over the past decade. While at the start of the 2010s, it was rare to see even a Saudi man working in retail, by 2019, Saudi women were seen working in malls all over the country. Between 2018 and 2022, female labor force participation doubled to 33 percent (Mati and Rehman, 2022). The number of women already exceeded the number of men attending colleges and universities in 2015 (Alsharif 2019), and in 2023, almost 40 percent of all SME are run by females. As a result, the increased participation rate of women in the workforce has already exceeded the 2030 target.[3] By 2023, 47 percent of Saudi nationals worked in the private sector, compared to 29 percent in 2018 (GAStat, 2023).

Despite such efforts, the labor market remains segmented, and the old system of public/private sector split between Saudi and non-Saudi workers has been replaced by a new segmentation within the private sector—one for Saudi nationals in an attempt to replicate public sector employment within a new improved private sector, and one for expatriates that is very similar to the previous iteration, albeit supercharged with Vision 2030 and giga-project investment.

At a basic level, a Saudi worker is very different from an average expatriate worker in the country, which can be seen using demographic data from the labor force survey. 47 percent of Saudi workers are under the age of 35, compared to just 24 percent of expatriate workers. Expatriate workers are overwhelmingly men (82 percent), while the integration of Saudi women into the labor force now means women account for almost 40 percent of Saudi workers.

Saudi workers are younger, more gender-balanced, and also more educated than their expatriate counterparts. In Q2 2023, almost 43 percent of all Saudi workers held a university degree, compared to 25 percent of non-Saudi employees. Further, 58 percent of Saudi nationals worked in the most high-skilled and well-paid occupations of the ISCO-08 classification (Table 9.1). Saudi and expatriate workers work in different sectors and occupations, as portrayed in Figures 9.1 and 9.2. While Saudi nationals still tend to prefer public administration (mostly in public sector jobs), education and retail trade, expatriate workers are mostly employed in households, retail trade, construction, and manufacturing.

Table 9.1: Descriptive Statistics of Saudi and Expatriate Workers, Q2 2023

	Saudi	**Expatriate**
Age	25–34 (34%)	35–44 (40%)
Possession of a Third Level Degree (%)	43%	25%
Most likely Economic Activity (ISIC4)	Public Administration	Domestic Work
Most likely occupation (ISCO08)	Skilled (57%)	Less-skilled (68%)
Sector	Public (52%)	Private (70%)
Wage (SAR)	9,924	4,662
Hours worked	41	48

Source: Author's calculations based on GAStat

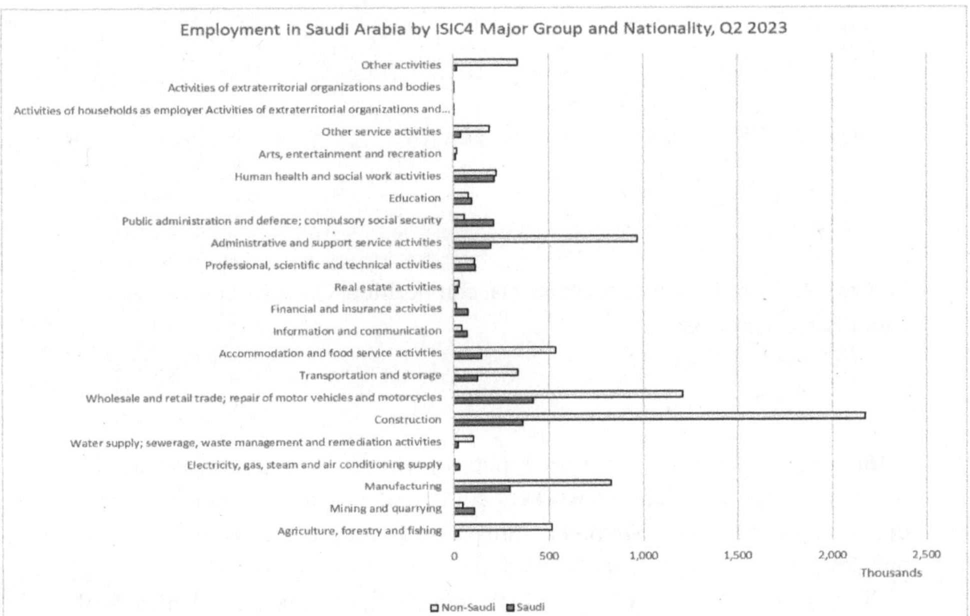

Figure 9.1. Comparison of sectoral employment, Q2 2023. Source: Saudi Labor Force Survey, GAStat.

All these differences translate to very different labor market outcomes for Saudi and non-Saudi workers. There is a significant Saudi wage premium when comparing Saudi and non-Saudi wages, and this premium exists at every level of education (Figure 9.3). Further, in this most recent labor force survey, Saudi workers worked an average of forty-one hours per week

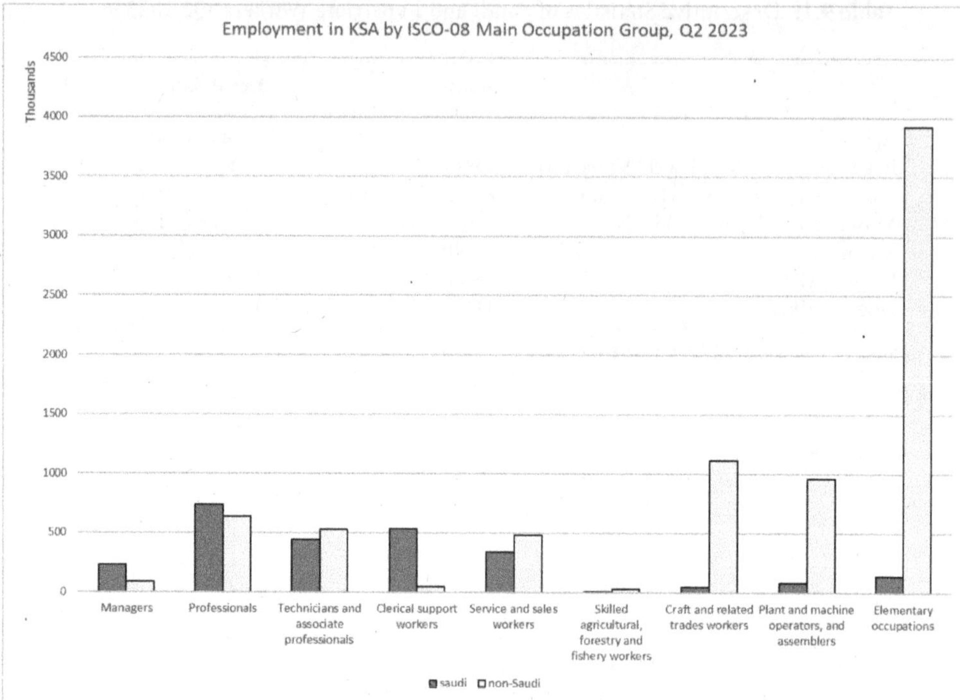

Figure 9.2. Comparison of occupational composition, Q2 2023. Source: Saudi Labor Force Survey, GAStat.

compared to forty-eight hours for expatriates. Difficult to ignore also are the sheer numbers of expatriate workers compared to Saudi nationals: In this period, out of a total employment count of 15.45 million, the Saudi share was only 25 percent.

This section has seen how recent reforms have overturned historical labor market segmentation in Saudi Arabia, where the segmented labor market, divided between nationals who work in high-paying public sector jobs, complemented by lower-skilled, low-paid expatriate labor in the private sector, has been systematically replaced in the preceding decade by policies aimed at integrating the Kingdom's growing population into the private sector. The private sector now boasts working conditions that are on a path to converge with public sector positions. The following section looks at how this historical structure still has an effect, through the lens of a high-potential new industry in the country—employment in clean hydrogen.

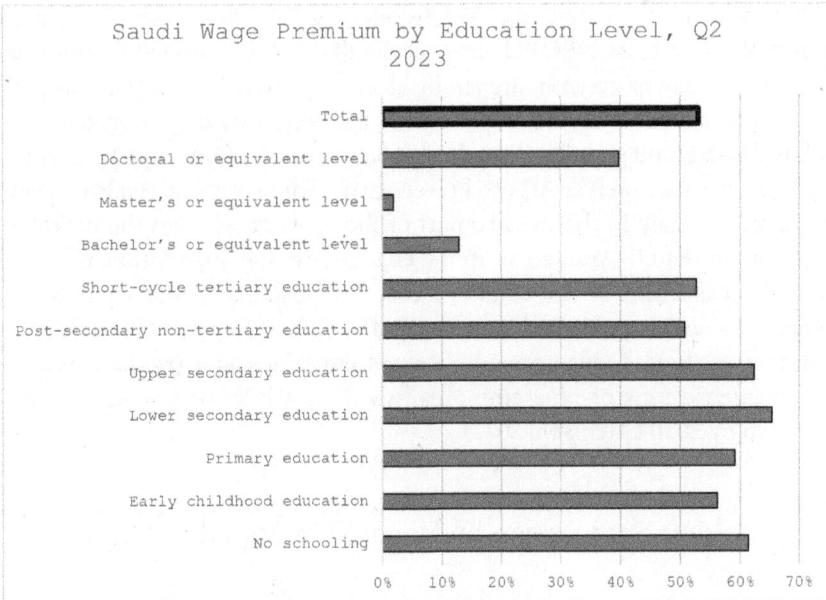

Figure 9.3. Saudi wage premium by education level, Q2 2023. Source: Author's calculations based on GAStat. Note: The Saudi wage premium is calculated as the difference between the Saudi and expat average wages divided by the Saudi wage.

Energy diversification: Developing a national hydrogen industry

In recent years, Saudi Arabia and other Gulf states started to invest heavily in the hydrogen industry, aiming at promoting non-oil energy diversification, attracting new external investments, empowering and educating new talents in the green industry and along the respective supply chains, and transforming and reforming the educational system (Ansari, 2022). Based on large gas resources for blue hydrogen and abundant solar radiation and wind speeds for green hydrogen, combined with outstanding expertise as a global energy leader, Saudi Arabia has the potential to establish itself as the world's biggest hydrogen producer. In promoting the hydrogen industry, the Kingdom aims to increase resilience and energy security, both as an export commodity and for domestic use (Koch, 2022). To achieve this mid- and long-term goal, the development of a hydrogen industry is prioritized by the Kingdom's energy diversification efforts. In particular, it is estimated to produce about four million tons of hydrogen by 2030 (Reuters, 2021). Saudi Arabia's mega project, the smart city NEOM located at the Red Sea, is expected to produce 650 tons per day of green hydrogen by electrolysis and 1.2 million tons per year of green ammonia, making it one of the largest hydrogen production facilities being built globally (Kingdom of Saudi Arabia, 2021). Institutionally, energy companies such as ACWA Power are in charge of the green hydrogen production mainly in the western part of the country, whereas the national oil company Saudi Aramco is more engaged in the installation of blue hydrogen capacities in the country's east. For instance, Saudi Arabia's oil company Aramco published its first Sustainability Report in June 2022, outlining goals to reduce greenhouse gas emissions and produce eleven million metric tons of blue ammonia, which is a relevant carrier of blue hydrogen by 2030 (Atchison, 2022).

Employment in clean hydrogen: Untapped potential

Recently, green job creation inside the Kingdom has emerged as a hot topic in terms of its ambitions to develop a comprehensive hydrogen industry. However, again, the employment potential of clean hydrogen varies on a number of factors, the most important of which is the final use of the product itself. Many countries have plans for a "hydrogen economy" where hydrogen will be used domestically to fuel homes, industry, and public and private transportation. A recalibration of a country's energy mix around a new clean fuel undoubtedly will have a great effect on employment. Notwithstanding, Saudi Arabia's plans seem to focus on becoming a global leader in the export of clean hydrogen. Little has been announced on the Kingdom's plans for the domestic use of hydrogen, which generates a blind spot for the plans of (Saudi and non-Saudi) job creation in the hydrogen industry. Therefore, our analysis of the employment potential of hydrogen in Saudi Arabia focuses on production. In particular, we investigate the employment potential of renewable energy (used to make green hydrogen), electrolyzers, and carbon capture capabilities (covering blue hydrogen).

Renewable energy

In general, much attention is given in Saudi Arabia to the employment potential of its renewables push, focusing not only on hydrogen but also on the solar and wind industry. Analysis of the actual employment needs of renewable energy generation, however, paints a different picture. Based on

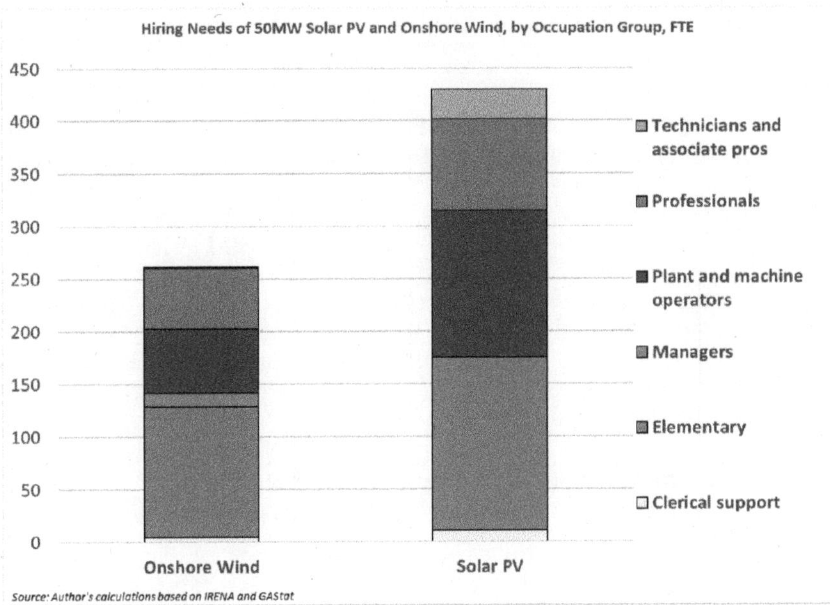

Figure 9.4. Occupational needs of solar PV and onshore wind, full time equivalence (FTE).

data from the International Renewable Energy Association (IRENA), Mulligan (2023b) found that many of the jobs on offer throughout the value chains of both solar PV and onshore wind were in elementary and machine operator occupations (Figure 9.4). Using nationality shares of employment in these occupational groups, Figure 9.5 implies that much of the employment in both solar PV and onshore wind would naturally go to expatriate workers. These ISCO-08 major groups are generally less-skilled and, on average, low paid. This analysis does not consider the implementation of Saudization mandates on the renewables sector, however, these jobs do not seem to be a skills match for highly educated Saudi workers, and if Saudized, the introduction of Saudi minimum wages (see Figure 9.3) to the sector may affect price points and undermine the profitability of renewable energy production in the country—targeted to be the cheapest in the world.

Electrolyzers

The production of hydrogen using the process of electrolysis is still untested at a large scale, and therefore, estimates of employment are less reliable.

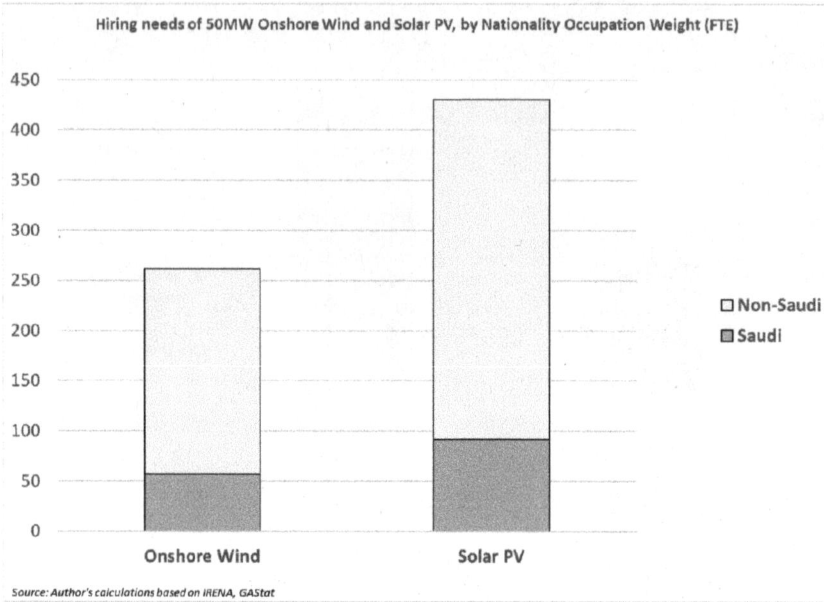

Figure 9.5. Nationality weighted occupational needs of solar PV and onshore wind (FTE).

However, Rhodium (2023) published a market study of occupational and employment needs for a 100MW facility that can be compared to the previous analysis on renewable energy. It is found that workforce needs are similarly front-loaded in the construction phase of the electrolyzer plants, with only a limited number of permanent ongoing positions necessary for the everyday running of the plant. While there is potential for further employment in the supply chain, the short-term nature of the bulk of the employment limits the potential for building a viable industry around the plant, particularly if the site is in a remote location.

Regarding distinct occupational needs, the major requirement for the construction phase is for metal workers and assemblers, as well as legal workers and engineers. While the metal workers and assembler jobs sound more in line with less-skilled jobs for expatriate workers, the legal and engineering occupations may be a good fit for Saudi workers. However, some of the technical jobs are highly specialized, with highly skilled migrant labor needed to fill skills gaps. In the operations and maintenance phase of ongoing employment, many of the occupational needs are for less-skilled workers, such as for installation and repairs.

Carbon capture

Included within the umbrella of clean hydrogen is hydrogen created with traditional energy sources, albeit with the added step of carbon capture that mitigates emissions, which also has employment implications. Carbon capture employment analysis described by Rhodium (2023) is not directly comparable to the renewable energy and electrolyzer segments above, as the unit of analysis is on kilotons of carbon captured per year rather than on the output capacity of the plants described previously. This reflects the possibility that carbon capture technology may be an add-on to an existing hydrogen facility, and therefore, the capacity depends on this factor. An additional element of this is that the carbon capture project may be a retrofit and, therefore, is more labor-intensive than a new build, resulting in robust employment figures for this initial period. As in the case with the other projects, ongoing operation and maintenance employment is at a much lower level.

The occupational needs for carbon capture are more construction-focused due to the assumption of the retrofit process, and metal workers and assemblers are also important on a similar scale to the electrolyzer plant above. Machinery installers, maintenance and repairers dominate the expected ongoing jobs in operations and maintenance, which again seems more suited to expatriate workers rather than Saudi nationals.

Developing a national hydrogen education: In need of local talent empowerment

While expectations are high for clean hydrogen as a driver of employment, Saudi Arabia has not published a comprehensive strategy for its domestic hydrogen industry as yet, and thus, the concrete potential for green jobs in the hydrogen industry is difficult to estimate. The same holds true for the demand for Saudi nationals and non-nationals in the hydrogen sector. As already outlined, the production of electrolyzers still requires metal workers and assembler jobs on a less-skilled level, as well as high-skilled expatriates in the handling of proton exchange membranes (PEM). As the carbon capture sector is labor-intensive in construction, expatriate workers are also in greater demand than nationals.

Against this backdrop, the hydrogen job market could constitute a significant dualism regarding the employment opportunities for Saudi nationals and non-nationals. As Saudization will remain a top priority in

Saudi Arabia's labor market reforms, a strategic interest in developing jobs for nationals will remain high. However, in order to meet the demands of the hydrogen job market, a tailor-made institutional setup in hydrogen education is needed to create a national workforce comprising a pool of Saudi talent in the hydrogen industry. So far, however, only a limited number of educational institutions and initiatives focus on capacity development, training, and education in hydrogen despite the fact that educational reforms have been introduced in recent years to improve effectiveness, efficiency, international competitiveness, and compatibility with labor market demands. Vision 2030's Human Capability Development Program (HCDP) does not explicitly mention hydrogen as a cornerstone of educational reforms, but provides the general framework for a more comprehensive approach to harmonize nationwide efforts in hydrogen education. However, based on the growing economic demand, the hydrogen industry could attract a growing number of Saudi graduates in different disciplines. In this regard, HCDP outlines specific goals to reform the educational system, aiming at empowering Saudi nationals in competing globally in terms of skills and values. In the HCDP outline, renewable energy and engineering are specifically mentioned among the four main fields of knowledge on which the educational reforms aim to focus. Upskilling and supporting innovation and entrepreneurship culture have been defined as key pillars of Saudi Arabia's educational reforms to prepare the young generation for the future local and global labor market. In doing so, the government wants to overcome traditional shortages in the educational system that was traditionally dominated mainly by religious studies, engineering, and education but was lacking training in natural sciences, technology, mathematics, foreign languages, arts, and vocational skills. The strategy thus explicitly outlines remaining challenges as "traditional and non-renewable educational methods and curriculum continue to be used in the Kingdom's educational system" (Vision 2030) and defines the system as non-flexible and compulsory. Hence, nationalization efforts and educational reforms aim to promote so-called good jobs that are influencing the way in which work affects family life, social integration, and health and are influenced by contextual social factors such as socioeconomic and/or educational background, class, and gender (Almoaibed and Thompson, 2023). By taking this definition by Almoaibed and Thompson (2021) into consideration, "good jobs" provide basic needs, the ability to save, and the opportunity to lead a productive and healthy life. Against this backdrop, educational reforms in Saudi Arabia also intend to prepare the youth for "better jobs tomorrow" (Almoaibed and Thompson, 2023) that not only aim to generate income but also incorporate values such as environmentalism or sustainability. As such, specific parts of the young, well-educated Saudi population become more aware of environmental issues, green sustainability, and "global youth activism" (Cloughton, 2021)—similar to other Gulf societies, such as in the UAE (Alzeer and Rosmer, 2023). They engage in educational, philanthropic, and cultural initiatives to promote environmental awareness (Derbal, 2014, 2022) and are involved in transnational exchange formats that are addressing joint regional climate action (Winkel and Sons, 2023). For example, the Saudi Youth for Sustainability (SYS) was established by students from King Abdullah University of Science and Technology (KAUST). It is a youth-led national organization that aims to connect young leaders and drive positive changes toward a sustainable future. Another example is the "Environmental Development Association" (*Faseel*), which is a non-profit organization registered by a ministerial decree at the Saudi Ministry of Labor and Social Development.

In times of growing business opportunities in green jobs and more awareness of a young Saudi generation in energy diversification from a socio-economic and social perspective, hydrogen education provides an opportunity for Saudi young nationals to find a job opportunity and, at the same time, better engage in environmental action (see more on this concept in Arnold et al., 2009 and Benkenstein et al., 2020).[4] This will include renewables (mainly solar and wind), electrolysis systems producing hydrogen, in addition to innovative demand-side processes that enhance energy efficiency. Human capital in transport, storage, services, maintenance, or management is needed in specific sectors such as the manufacturing of non-complex PV components, wind energy components, and electrolyzers. Furthermore, the hydrogen economy requires substantial infrastructure development, initial R&D (Bachhaus et al., 2021), transmission, and transportation, technology development and support, operation services, and maintenance (Rodríguez, 2023).

Despite growing demand and interest, the Saudi educational system still finds itself in an early stage when it comes to hydrogen education. So far, only a limited number of educational institutions (universities, research centers, and energy companies) are offering comprehensive educational programs and training courses in hydrogen engineering.

Tertiary education

- The most outstanding example is the **King Saud University (KSU),** which has developed a Master of Science in Renewable Energy, including its three specialization tracks: (1) solar energy technology, (2) wind energy technology, and (3) hydrogen energy technology. Out of twenty-four courses, four are dedicated to hydrogen.

- Furthermore, the **Hydrogen Energy Group** at KSU's Sustainable Energy Technologies Center (SETC) aims to design first-generation prototype devices, which can generate hydrogen from catalytic water splitting based on solar energy and focuses on hydrogen production, storage, and utilization (KSU, 2023a). SETC also provides Graduate Studies & Training courses and cooperates with local and international partners such as KACARE, KACST, Électricité de France (EDF), the German national aeronautics and space research center (DLR), Tokyo University from Japan, and the Massachusetts Institute of Technology (MIT), to only mention a few (KSU 2023b).
- The **King Fahd University of Petroleum and Minerals (KFUPM)** has launched its interdisciplinary research center for hydrogen and energy storage (IRC-HES) in May 2021, which aims to explore multiple promising fields in applied sciences with a special focus on the production of blue and green hydrogen, hydrogen separation and storage, and hydrogen utilization. The center has also inaugurated the Carbon Capture and Conversion program, which focuses on sorbents for CO2 capture, oxy-fuel combustion for cost-effective CO2 capture, electrochemical CO2 conversion, and thermo-catalytic CO2 conversion. It further aims to establish industrial partnerships with relevant companies and national entities, promote innovation and entrepreneurship, and develop teaching graduate programs in the field of hydrogen and energy storage (KFUPM Interdisciplinary Research Center for Hydrogen and Energy Storage, n.d.).
- The **KAUST Solar Center (KSC)** serves as a platform for experts in materials science, chemistry, and physics to explore innovative solutions for the harvesting and conversion of solar energy (i.e., the KAUST Research Centers (n.d.)). No detailed information on hydrogen-specific R&D is available, but KSC offers excellent potential to include such components in its research portfolio.
- The Center of Research Excellence in Renewable Energy and Power Systems (CREPS) at **King Abdulaziz University (KAU)** provides consultation and solutions to utilities, companies, and governmental bodies in the field of renewable energy and electrical power systems, as well as the necessary training for technicians, engineers, and researchers.
- Saudi Polytechnic Institute for Renewable Energy (SPIRE) is a vocational training center operated under license from the Technical and Vocational Training Corporation (TVTC) in the al-Jawf region, which offers post-secondary education to train locals for technical employment in the nearby Sikaka solar PV plant and Damwmat al-Jandal wind farm.

Technical and vocational education and training (TVET)

Despite such initiatives in tertiary education, challenges to develop a nationwide comprehensive hydrogen education system remain high: First, analysis of education requirements for employment in hydrogen production indicates that technical and vocational training is more valuable than tertiary education, such as university degree programs. While skills outlooks often focus on relevant degree programs, much more important in this case is relevant and practical training in vocational programs. This poses problems for Saudi Arabia in the localization of jobs in clean hydrogen, as Technical and Vocational Education and Training (TVET) in the country is still in development.

Saudi Arabia's TVET system has recently been centralized in the newly formed Technical and Vocational Training Corporation (TVTC). The TVTC is a well-funded and modern institution, fully backed by Saudi Vision 2030 and accompanying Human Capability Development Fund. However, it does face significant barriers, despite achieving government targets of 26 percent of high school graduates enrolled in TVET courses in 2022. Chief amongst these barriers are cultural attitudes and preferences for academic degrees from Saudi youth, which means many will not even consider a technical or vocational course as an option when making career decisions. As with many norms in modern Saudi Arabia, these beliefs are changing (Almoaibed, 2020), and TVET courses are introduced to students early on in high school in order to introduce these as options in the career choice. However, it remains to be seen whether the country can produce enough adequately trained technicians to justify potentially heightened Saudization mandates. Even in countries with traditionally robust uptake in TVET courses, such as Germany and the Netherlands—both also with major clean hydrogen strategies—have foreseen skills shortages in the technician roles for employment in the hydrogen economy.

So far, TVET courses in hydrogen are mainly conceptualized and organized by private companies and service providers cooperating with state-owned entities such as Saudi Aramco, NEOM, and ACWA Power that have developed internal centers of excellence to train and empower their own staff in hydrogen topics. Those companies established training centers and facilities, and also developed their own curricula in different areas related to energy production, including hydrogen.[5] The motivations behind such educational efforts to promote hydrogen are business-oriented, as job creation is the top priority. For instance, ACWA Power provides diploma programs for water and energy technicians and discusses plans to include hydrogen in such initiatives. As outlined by ACWA Power representatives, those efforts aim to overcome the urban-rural divide and educate experts across the country. So far, the academic programs are mainly concentrated in urban centers, which neglect other parts of the population.[6] External consultants are giving free training for employees to develop their own institutional knowledge. Here, hydrogen has become a new topic of interest. The SABIC Research and Innovation Center engages in petrochemicals education and could thus provide a future platform for hydrogen education. For instance, programs such as NUSANED are promoting localization efforts and SME's. In addition, SABIC has launched the Saudi HR Think Tank (SHRTT) in 2018 in partnership with the Ministry of Human Resources and Social Development to support capacity development in the Kingdom (SABIC). Other SABIC initiatives include scholarship programs for chemical engineering, industrial engineering, and mechanical engineering, and investment in MADAC Academy to train students in educational issues such as environmental and climate action (SABIC, 2022). In general, those programs could also incorporate hydrogen training courses into their future portfolio. Such initiatives aim to educate Saudi and non-Saudi hydrogen experts along the total supply chain, seeking to create additional direct and indirect jobs in the petrochemical and chemical industry, mobility, mining, or further industries such as steel, cement, food and beverage, or agriculture. Saudi universities could thus become "green laboratories" in the field of hydrogen education (Koch 2018).

However, challenges to specialized education in the field remain high: First, coordinated efforts to harmonize curricula and programs are lacking, and training-for-trainers (T&T) courses are still not in place properly. Secondly, experts in environmental education are still needed as the local human capital and the educational institutions do not meet the high expectations of the Saudi energy transition yet. So far, the main focus of such activities and programs is on hydrogen engineering, whereas an interdisciplinary approach including other disciplines such as social sciences is lacking. Thirdly, environmental education does not seem to be a priority in the academic hydrogen programs.[7] A comprehensive national clean hydrogen strategy is still needed, and the landscape of hydrogen education providers is fragmented, and coordination needs improving.[8] Fourthly, cross-institutional and multi-disciplinary cooperation networks are limited between companies and universities, and know-how transfer depends mainly on individuals. Finally, local expertise needs more promotion and empowerment to realize localization efforts, as external consultants are oftentimes highly involved in the development of training schemes.[9]

Recruiting expatriates in the hydrogen sector

As the analysis of the current situation of hydrogen education has indicated, the short- and mid-term availability of local talents trained and empowered in the Saudi system remains limited. As demand might grow in the upcoming years, Saudi Arabia will continue its efforts to establish a comprehensive educational landscape in the hydrogen sector based on the needs of the market, the interconnectedness of the relevant stakeholders, such as universities, energy companies' training centers, TVET, and the private sector. So far, however, the hydrogen educational structure lacks the capabilities to meet the growing demand. Against this backdrop, it seems likely that at least in the early years of developing the clean hydrogen industry in Saudi Arabia, migrant labor in these technical positions will be needed. Based on international data, most jobs in the development phase of hydrogen projects are mainly for semi- and non-skilled migrant laborers rather than for Saudi nationals (IRENA, 2022). In fact, job creation during the operation stage is less than a tenth of the early years during the construction of the project (Gielen et al., 2023). Most of the jobs are linked to hydrogen application, transport, or storage, and not production, which also needs to be taken into consideration. Additionally, R&D jobs needed in the inauguration phase of the hydrogen economy are likely to be replaced with a growing number of low-skilled jobs in the construction and operation of green hydrogen production plants and the required infrastructure for hydrogen.[10]

On the high-skilled level, demand could be met with recruitment from Europe, Asia, and the United States to overcome an existing shortage in educational and technical national experts in different areas of the hydrogen industry, ranging from training and technological maintenance to production and services. Here, the existing agreements with international partners could assist in establishing comprehensive recruitment schemes in collaboration with European academic and research institutions, universities, companies, and governmental institutions. Saudi and European partners could jointly engage in upskilling or reskilling of the existing workforce, initiate academic exchange formats and summer schools in hydrogen education, or develop scholarship programs. Such collaboration could further intensify the Saudi efforts in climate diplomacy and international green agenda-setting (Al-Saidi et al., 2019). EU educational and vocational initiatives, such as Erasmus+ and Erasmus Mundus, could also focus on participants from Saudi Arabia.[11] As outlined in the REPowerEU decarbonization strategy and the Joint Communication "Strategic partnership with the Gulf," the EU considers energy and education as relevant pillars to enhance cooperation with the GCC. As Saudi Arabia aims to position itself as an early mover in the hydrogen industry and considers Europe as an important off-taker market, joint efforts in hydrogen education could help boost future partnerships and create people-to-people networks on a commercial, academic, and political level. In this regard, hydrogen education could promote youth and female empowerment, which is a top priority for both Saudi Arabia and the EU. Further, Saudi Arabia could benefit from higher-skilled green employment, such as in sustainability leadership, green finance, and other professional and scientific occupations that will be in-demand due to the energy transition and associated climate change mitigation policies. In terms of hydrogen education, the long-term experiences in the oil, petrochemicals, and mining sectors provide Saudi Arabia with the requested knowledge and infrastructure to enhance learning mechanisms for hydrogen-related education as part of the "good jobs" narrative on an academic, vocational training, and community-based level. Against this backdrop, new academic and corporate programs for education, accreditation, and vocational training, upskilling or reskilling of the existing workforce, including on-the-job trainings need to be developed. As compatibility exists between the oil and hydrogen industries, requirements to start developing an educational system from scratch are low, and there is potential to tailor these trainings to unique Saudi circumstances.

Conclusion

The article has shown that hydrogen constitutes a relevant pillar for Saudi Arabia's energy transition and provides interesting potential for job creation for both Saudi and non-Saudi workers. Vision 2030 and its accompanying giga projects—of which Saudi's ambitious energy transition plans are inarguably a part of—are set to produce a high number of job opportunities, and it is understandable that a great many of these high-quality and high-paying jobs are potentially earmarked for Saudi nationals. In times of such Saudization efforts, the government has focused on regulations and initiatives to promote the Saudi share in the labor market. It is therefore possible that the Saudi authorities could ringfence jobs in hydrogen energy production and in-demand occupations resulting from the energy transition with strict Saudization mandates to ensure that the benefits of the green economy are reaped by Saudi citizens.

However, expectations need to be managed properly. Labor market interventions such as Saudization are not without consequence. We have seen in this chapter that Saudi nationals are paid more on average than expatriate workers at every level of education, and therefore increasing Saudi shares in green industries and occupations implies a higher wage bill for employers in the Saudi green economy. So far, only a limited number of educational institutions and governmental programs are focusing on a comprehensive hydrogen educational system. Hence, the mid-term need for a high-skill workforce and expert recruitment from abroad remains high and could support Saudi stakeholders to engage more in hydrogen education. Furthermore, the enduring effects of the traditional Saudi labor market structure persist in occupational preferences for Saudis and expatriate workers and directly affect labor market outcomes in the specific case of employment in the hydrogen economy. In particular, the current occupational distribution of expatriate workers towards less-skilled jobs and the lack of Saudi uptake in vocational technical occupations make migrant workers well-placed to benefit from the employment potential of investment in hydrogen energy in Saudi Arabia.

Notes

1 While retail positions are not specifically a match for high-skilled workers, the integration of Saudi workers in frontline customer-facing positions helped normalize the idea of Saudis working in all levels of the private sector and served as a visible symbol of the presence of women in the labor force.

2 See Mulligan (2023a) for a history of these mandates.

3 In 2024, the Vision 2030 target was increased to 40 percent (Narayanan, 2024).

4 Interview with Saudi energy expert, Riyadh, May 24, 2023.

5 Interview with Saudi energy expert, Riyadh, May 24, 2023.

6 Interview with ACWA Power representative, Riyadh, May 25, 2023.

7 Interview with Saudi educational expert, Riyadh, May 25, 2023.

8 Interview with ACWA Power representative, Riyadh, May 25, 2023.

9 Interview with international expert on the Saudi educational and training system, Riyadh, May 24, 2023.

10 On a regional level, the potential for hydrogen-related job creation in the member states of the Gulf Cooperation Council (GCC) is estimated at 40,000–80,000 for 2030, and 400,000–900,000 for 2050 (Roland Berger Middle East W.L.L and Dii Desert Energy, n.d.). As the Kingdom has announced the most ambitious hydrogen plans in the GCC, it seems likely that a majority of those jobs could be created in the Saudi hydrogen industry in light of ongoing localization and nationalization efforts.

11 These programs sponsor EU citizens to gain cultural and professional experience in other countries.

Bibliography

Abdelraouf, M., and M. Luomi (2016). *The green economy in the Gulf*. London: Palgrave.

Akhonbay, H. (2019). *The economics of renewable energy in the Gulf.* London: Routledge.

Al-Saidi, M., E. Zaidan, and S. Hammad (2019). Participation modes and diplomacy of Gulf Cooperation Council (GCC) countries towards the global sustainability agenda, *Development in Practic*, 29(5): 545–58.

Almoaibed, H. (June 2020). Elevating the status of technical and vocational education and training in Saudi Arabia: The need for enhancing stakeholder engagement and student motivation. King Faisal Center for Research and Islamic Studies, https://www.kfcris.com/pdf/48b85a1bcdacf8b10e6ef72cbce37b4c5eeb05fa3df45.pdf

Almoaibed, H., and M. Thompson (2023). Better jobs tomorrow: The appeal and increasing relevance of alternative credentials in Saudi Arabia. King Faisal Center for Research and Islamic Studies, https://www.kfcris.com/en/view/post/407.

Almoaibed, H., and M. Thompson (2021). "Good jobs and bad jobs": Employment attitudes, perceptions, and priorities in Saudi Arabia. King Faisal Center for Research and Islamic Studies, https://www.kfcris.com/en/view/post/350.

Alsharif, F. (2021), Kafala sponsorship reforms in Saudi Arabia: Converging toward international labor standards. King Faisal Center for Research and Islamic Studies, https://www.kfcris.com/en/view/post/332.

Alsharif, F. (2019). Empowering women: Educational programs and reforms in a diversified Saudi economy. King Faisal Center for Research and Islamic Studies, https://www.kfcris.com/en/view/post/239.

Alzeer, G., and T. Rosmer (23023). Greening the desert: Emirati youth's perceptions of green branding. In Wippel, S. (ed.), *Branding the Middle East*, Berlin/Bosten: De Gruyter: 383–402.

Ansari, D. (2022). The hydrogen ambitions of the gulf States. *SWP Comment* 44 (July), 4, https://www.swp-berlin.org/publications/products/comments/2022C44_HydrogenAmbitiones_GulfStates_WEB.pdf.

Arnold, H. E., F. G. Cohen, and A. Warner (2009). Youth and environmental action: Perspectives of young environmental leaders on their formative influences. *Journal of Environmental Education*, 40(3): 27–36.

Atchison, J. (2022). Aramco targets 11 million tonnes of low-carbon ammonia production by 2030. Ammonia Energy. https://www.ammoniaenergy.org/articles/aramco-targets-11-million-tonnes-of-low-carbon-ammonia-production-by-2030/.

Bachhaus, A., C. Jongsma, C. Leguijt, and E. van den Toorn (2021). Jobs from investment in green hydrogen. Update and extension. CE Delft, https://cedelft.eu/wp-content/uploads/sites/2/2021/04/CE_Delft_200427_Jobs_from_investment_in_green_hydrogen_Def.pdf.

Badawi, F. (2022). Saudi Arabia energy transition. King Fahd University of Petroleum and Minerals. https://www.researchgate.net/publication/366633917_Saudi_Arabia_Energy_Transition.

BBC (2021). Saudi Arabia commits to net zero emissions by 2060. BBC News. https://www.bbc.com/news/world-middle-east-58955584.

Benkenstein, A., R. Chevallier, D. Kosciulek, D. Lebea, and K. Worth (2020). Youth climate action and the role of government. South African Institute of International Affairs. https://www.jstor.org/stable/resrep29503.

Bianco, C., and S. Sons (2021). Domestic economic plans and visions in the GCC and opportunities for cooperation with Europe. In S. Colombo, and A. Abdul Ghafar (eds.), *The European Union and the Gulf Cooperation Council. Towards a New Path*, London: Palgrave Macmillan, 79–104.

Braun, J. F., F. Frischmuth, N. Gerhardt, M. Pfennig, R. Schmitz M. Wietschel, B. Carlier, Réveillère, A., G. Warluzel, and D. Wesoly (2023). Clean hydrogen deployment in the Europe-MENA region from 2030 to 2050. Fraunhofer Institute. https://www.cines.fraunhofer.de/content/dam/zv/cines/dokumente/Fraunhofer_CINES_Clean_Hydrogen_Deployment.pdf.

Cloughton, I. (2021). Global youth activism on climate change. *Social Work & Policy Studies: Social Justice, Practice and Theory*, 4(1). https://openjournals.library.sydney.edu.au/SWPS/article/view/14960.

Derbal, N. (2014). Domestic, religious, civic? notes on institutionalized charity in jeddah, Saudi Arabia. In R. Lacey and J. Benthall (eds.), *Gulf charities today. Arab Islamic philanthropy in the "age of terror" and beyond*, 145–67. Berlin: Gerlach Press.

Derbal, N. (2022). *Charity in Saudi Arabia. Civil society under authoritarianism.* Cambridge: Cambridge University Press.

GAStat (General Authority for Statistics) (2023). Saudi Labor Force Survey. https://www.stats.gov.sa

Gielen, D., S. Lopez Rocha, and P. Lathwal (2023). Make Hydrogen in developing nations: Share prosperity while meeting our climate goals. *Energy Post*, January 26. https://energypost.eu/make-hydrogen-in-developing-nations-share-prosperity-while-meeting-our-climate-goals/.

Havrlant, D., and A. Darandary (2021). Economic diversification under Saudi Vision 2030: Sectoral changes aiming at sustainable growth. KAPSARC, https://www.kapsarc.org/research/publications/economic-diversification-under-saudi-vision-2030/.

Hertog, S. (2018). Can we Saudize the labor market without damaging the private sector? *King Faisal Center for Research and Islamic Studies, Special Report*, 1–18.

IRENA (International Renewable Energy Agency) (2022). Renewable energy and jobs. Annual review 2022. https://www.irena.org/-/media/Files/IRENA/Agency/Publication/2022/Sep/IRENA_Renewable_energy_and_jobs_2022.pdf.

KAUST Research Centers (n.d.). Homepage. https://www.kaust.edu.sa/en/research/.

KFUPM Interdisciplinary Research Center for Hydrogen and Energy Storage (n.d.). Homepage. https://ri.kfupm.edu.sa/irc-hes.

KSU (King Saud University) (2023a). Hydrogen energy. https://set.ksu.edu.sa/en/hydrogen-energy.

KSU (King Saud University) (2023b). About SET. Moving towards a green environment. https://set.ksu.edu.sa/en/about-set.

Kingdom of Saudi Arabia (2021). Updated first nationally determined contribution. https://unfccc.int/sites/default/files/resource/202203111154---KSA%20NDC%202021.pdf.

Koch, N. (2018). Green laboratories: University campuses as sustainability "exemplars" in the Arabian peninsula. *Society & Natural Resources* 31(5), 525–40.

Koch, N. (2022). Gulf hydrogen horizons: Why are Gulf oil and gas producers so keen on hydrogen? *Geographies of the Arabian Peninsula* (November). https://doi.org/ 10.48481/iass.2022.044.

Koyame-Marsh, R. O. (2016). Saudization and the Nitaqat Programs: Overview and Performance. *Journal of Accounting* 6(2): 36–48. http://www.jafepapers.com/uploads/2016/September/2016_10_25_3. Rita.pdf

Mati, A., and S. Rehman (2022). Saudi Arabia to grow at fastest pace in a decade, international monetary fund. https://www.imf.org/en/news/articles/2022/08/09/cf-saudi-arabia-to-grow-at-fastest-pace.

Mulligan, C. (2023a). Consult within: Analyzing the recent decision to localize consultancy professions in Saudi Arabia. *Instant Insight.* King Abdullah Petroleum Studies and Research Center (KAPSARC).

Mulligan, C. (2023b). Employment potential of renewable energy in Saudi Arabia: A value chain analysis. King Abdullah Petroleum Studies and Research Center (KAPSARC), https://doi.org/10.30573/KS--2023-DP15

Narayanan, N. (2024). Saudi Arabia targeting 40% female workforce participation by 2030: Al-Jadaan. *Arab News.* https://www.arabnews.com/node/2577394/business-economy.

Nurunnabi, M. (2017). Transformation from an oil-based economy to a knowledge-based economy in Saudi Arabia: The direction of Saudi Vision 2030. *Journal of the Knowledge Economy* 8: 536–64.

Peck, J. R. (2017). Can hiring quotas work? The effect of the Nitaqat program on the Saudi private sector. *American Economic Journal: Economic Policy,* 9(2): 316–47. https://doi.org/10.1257/pol.20150271

Reuters (2021). Saudi Arabia wants to be top supplier of hydrogen—energy minister. *Reuters,* October 24. https://www.reuters.com/business/energy/saudi-arabia-wants-be-top-supplier-hydrogen-energy-minister-2021-10-24/.

Rhodium (2023). Clean hydroegen workforce development: Opportunities by occupation. https://rhg.com/research/clean-hydrogen-workforce-development/

Rodríguez, P. (2023), Betting on green hydrogen to fulfil employment growth. https://cicenergigune.com/en/blog/green-hydrogen-employment-growth.

Roland Berger Middle East W.L.L and Dii Desert Energy (n.d.). The potential for green hydrogen in the GCC region. https://www.menaenergymeet.com/wp-content/uploads/the-potential-for-green-hydrogen-in-the-gcc-region.pdf.

SABIC (2022). Sustainable growth for a better world. Sustainability report 2022. SABIC. https://www.sabic.com/en/Images/SABIC_Sustainability_Report_2022_EN_tcm1010-40888.pdf.

Saudi Gazette (2021). Minimum monthly wage of Saudis for Nitaqat program raised to SR4,000. *Saudi Gazette*, November 18. https://saudigazette.com.sa/article/600456/SAUDI-ARABIA/Minimum-monthly-wage-of-Saudis-for-Nitaqat-program-raised-to-SR4000.

Sim, L. (2022). Renewable power policies in the Arab Gulf states. Middle East Institute. https://www.mei.edu/publications/renewable-power-policies-arab-gulf-state.

Vision 2030 (n. d.). Human Capability Development Program 2021–2025. https://www.vision2030.gov.sa/media/pgid4z3t/2021-2025-human-capability-development-program-delivery-plan-en.pdf.

Winkel, S., and S. Sons (2023). The "climate-energy-health nexus." an entry-point for environmental cooperation in West Asia and the Arabian peninsula. *Brief 24*, CARPO, https://carpo-bonn.org/wp-content/uploads/2023/11/carpo_brief_24_23-11-23_EN_final.pdf.

Zumbraegel, T. (2022). *Political power and environmental sustainability*. London: Palgrave Macmillan.

10

International Student Migration and Economic Diversification in Saudi Arabia

Md Mizanur Rahman and Sharique Umar

Introduction

The Kingdom of Saudi Arabia has embarked on a journey of economic transformation with an ambitious plan to diversify its economy away from oil. The diversification and sustainability plan, a linchpin of Saudi Arabia's Vision 2030, seeks to mitigate the risks associated with oil-centric economies and develop innovation, entrepreneurship, and knowledge-based industries. In line with this vision, the country has prioritized education and research as the main pillars of its economic diversification strategy. Realizing the potential of a sustainable educational sector, Saudi Vision 2030 emphasizes the need to improve the standard of education, enhance the research and innovation capacities of Saudi universities, and attract and retain the "finest Saudi and foreign mind" (Vision 2030, n.d.: 37). In 2023, the country allocated 17 percent of its budget, equalling US$50.4 billion, to educational and research infrastructure, providing scholarships to Saudi and international students, and building new institutions focused on the skill development of local students.[1] The government's investments in education, research, and development have solidified the country's standing on the global academic stage, with many Saudi universities, such as King Abdulaziz University and King Saud University, ranking among the best in the region. In addition, among the country's more than sixty universities, thirty-three were placed in the Q.S. Arab region's university ranking.[2] By prioritizing education and research as key pillars of its economic diversification strategy, Saudi Arabia is laying the groundwork for a sustainable economy and positioning itself as a hub for academic excellence and innovation in the region.

It is worth mentioning that a crucial aspect of this diversification initiative hinges on international student mobility. In tandem with the development in the education sector, Saudi Arabia has witnessed a considerable increase in international students, with more than 64,000 international students enrolled in tertiary educational institutions, constituting 4 percent of total tertiary enrolment.[3] International students contribute to a vibrant academic environment and foster cross-cultural exchange by bringing distinct perspectives and skills to local universities. The presence of international students enhances Saudi universities' global reputation and competitiveness, and allows them to position themselves as hubs for cultural exchanges and academic collaborations. This exposure to international perspectives creates a rich learning environment and promotes innovation and cross-cultural understanding among students and faculties. Moreover, international students contribute to the local economy by bringing in various skill sets and knowledge, further supporting the country's economic growth and development.

In addition, the outbound student mobility of international students also plays an important role in Saudi's economic diversification program. Making up one of the largest international student bodies, Saudi students who pursue education abroad gain insights, experiences, and expertise that they bring back to contribute to the Kingdom's development. The exposure of these students to global educational environments enriches the academic ecosystem of the country, which feeds into innovation, entrepreneurship, and knowledge-based industries, essential for the success of the diversification program.

The impact of international student mobility on the Kingdom's development is substantial, yet the existing literature on this subject is limited. Existing studies predominantly concentrate on outbound student mobility, primarily emphasizing the challenges Saudi students face while studying abroad (Aldosari and Mekheimer, 2013; Alsabatin, 2015; Alsaif, 2014; Alsahafi and Shin, 2019; Almotery, 2009; Binsahl et al., 2015; Unruh and Obeidat, 2015; Alhazmi and Nyland, 2013; Young and Snead, 2017). Others shed light on the experiences of returnees upon returning to their home country (Alkubaidi and Alzhrani, 2020; Alqefari, 2016; Alsulami, 2021a). The majority of these studies mostly focus on female students, examining their experiences both abroad and upon their return. There is a noticeable lack of research on inbound student mobility, which creates an obstacle to understanding the full scope of international student flows in the region. Questions arise regarding the impact of diversification initiatives on attracting international students, the demographic composition of international students in Saudi Arabia, and the challenges they encounter while studying in the country. Exploring the role of government policies, cultural exchange programs, and the integration of international students into the local academic community could provide a much-needed understanding of how international student mobility is related to the Kingdom's diversification program.

To address some of these gaps, this paper uses both secondary and primary data, which were gathered by in-person visits to Saudi Arabia as well as formal and informal conversations with international students in the country. Secondary data were gathered through document analysis of annual reports from the Ministry of Education, universities, and other non-governmental agencies. These data provide an overview of the factors influencing student mobility. By combining data from multiple sources, this study aims to offer a holistic perspective on international student mobility in Saudi Arabia and contribute insights to the existing literature.

The paper is structured into seven sections. The first section gives a concise overview of the theoretical foundations of international student mobility. The section will explain macro and micro-level factors that dictate the flow of student mobility globally. The next section briefly details the research methodology. The third section shifts focus to the trend in international student mobility to Saudi Arabia. In particular, we break down the current figures and demographics of students. In the fourth section, we examine factors that influence the flow of international students. We primarily analyze the country's pull factors and student motivations. Our analysis is enriched by accounts of students with whom we interacted in person and online. One of the things that makes international student mobility to GCC (Gulf Cooperation Council) countries distinct is the abundance of scholarships for international students. Thus, in the sixth section, we look at scholarships and other financial opportunities students have in the country. Furthermore, given that one of the objectives of this paper is to analyze the link between the ongoing economic diversification and international students in Saudi Arabia, it is paramount to investigate what policies are in place to benefit from the diverse range of skills international students bring with them. Hence, we dedicated the seventh section to examine section examines the country's visa policies concerning international students. Primarily, we were interested in studying avenues available for international students to transition to the job market after completing their education. The last section, before the conclusion, sheds light on the challenges international students face while in the country.

Conceptualizing student mobility

To fully capture the essence of international student mobility in the context of Saudi Arabia's economic diversification, it is essential to contextualize this study within the realm of relevant theoretical frameworks. We discuss traditional migration theories, brain drain versus brain gain debates, and cultural exchange models to provide an analytical foundation for the study. Traditional neoclassical economic theories offer a foundational framework for understanding labor migration, which can be applied to international student mobility (De Haas, 2010; Findlay, 2011; Geiger and Pécoud, 2013; Massey et al., 1993; Skeldon, 2012; Zelinsky, 1971). Theories on migration have highlighted two critical forces that shape the movement of international students: push factors and pull factors (Lee, 1966; Massey et al., 1993). Push factors emerge from obstacles or limitations in the home country, such as restricted access to resources or opportunities, prompting individuals to look elsewhere. Pull factors, on the other hand, are linked to the appeal of better prospects abroad, such as economic opportunities or advancements in specific fields. For instance, Saudi Arabia's ongoing economic diversification efforts present a clear pull factor due to growth in areas like education, research, and development, which attract international students. Meanwhile, the desire to gain international exposure, access unique academic perspectives, or pursue studies in specialized fields unavailable in their home countries creates push factors motivating students to seek opportunities elsewhere (King, 2002).

Besides traditional migration theories, scholars have analyzed international student mobility through the lens of migration transition theory, which explains the role of the economic and social development of countries in shaping the patterns of migration (Weber and Van Mol, 2023; Zelinsky, 1971). Weber and Van Mol (2023) suggest that the number of outgoing international students initially increases as the economy of the sending country develops; however, after a certain period, the outbound mobility decreases. From a macro-level analysis, this mobility pattern can be explained through the neoclassical economic theory, which suggests that migration of individuals from origin countries to the host countries creates equilibrium in the wage differentials of origin and host countries. Consequently, the outward flow of labor migration from the sending country decreases as the need to migrate ceases (Massey et al., 1993).

While migration transition theory focuses on the capacity to migrate, it also sheds light on the aspiration to migrate (De Haas et al., 2021). From an economic standpoint, the aspiration of an individual to migrate is closely tied to the home country's development. When economically disadvantaged nations experience growth and subsequently get embedded in the global economy, the desire and capacity to migrate among the citizens tends to rise. Capacity to migrate refers to the social and financial resources needed to overcome obstacles to migration, which individuals and households tend to gain as societies develop through the accumulation of capital, better education, and improved communication and transportation. These improvements make migration more feasible for a larger part of the population (Carling, 2002). Additionally, the aspirations of citizens to seek education and career prospects abroad also increase due to economic progress, which brings awareness of opportunities existing in other countries. International student mobility also concurs with this pattern as increased information and global connectedness provide more information about universities, scholarships, and future career opportunities.

However, scholars caution against overemphasizing the primacy of economic factors in shaping aspirations and decisions to migrate. They emphasize the role of subjectivity, emotions, and personal ambitions, treating migration as a product of individual agency. The decision to pursue education abroad is not solely based on economic calculation but involves individual aspirations, personal desires, and the cultural aspects of studying in a foreign environment. (Carling and Collins, 2018; Huang and Ren, 2023; Wu and Hou, 2023). Thus, factors such as desires for cultural experiences, academic growth, expansion of social networks, accumulation of mobility, and cultural capital come into play (Brooks and Waters, 2010; Bourdieu, 1986; Collins et al., 2014; King et al., 2016; Moriarty et al., 2015; Nam and Jiang, 2023).

Understanding the reasons behind students' decisions to move is crucial, but equally important is investigating the factors influencing their choice of study destination. According to traditional neo-economic migration perspectives, the flow of students is influenced by the developmental disparities between host and home countries. Research suggests that students seeking economic prospects are often attracted to countries offering easy access to the job market and a clear path to citizenship (Brezis and Soueri, 2011; Borozan and Bojanic, 2015; Findlay et al., 2017). However, studies exploring the personal aspects of student mobility reveal that social and cultural considerations also play a significant role. For example, Umar and Rahman (2023) note that many international students choose some GCC countries as their study destination due to religious ties, cultural similarities to their home countries, perceived safety, and available scholarships.

Research methods

Studying international student mobility in the Gulf region is a challenging task, primarily due to insufficient available public data. While some GCC states publish statistics about international students in their annual education reports, others do not. Furthermore, Saudi Arabia's practice of not differentiating between children of migrants enrolled in tertiary educational institutions and international students who come to the region for study purposes makes it difficult to draw a clear picture of international student mobility in the country. In addition, there are no clear guidelines on the study-to-job transition process in the region. Considering the dearth of research on the topic and the paucity of macro-level data, including surveys and government statistics, this study takes an exploratory approach to mapping out international student mobility in Saudi Arabia.

This study primarily uses data from the UNESCO Institute for Statistics (UIS), in addition to government-published data, due to its consistency in covering the last two decades comprehensively. The data available on ministry websites lacked uniformity, with varying years of availability, hindering a coherent analysis. Furthermore, solely relying on official data would have provided an incomplete overview of international student demographics. Additional insights beyond statistical data, such as major public and private university websites across the country, were thoroughly examined. Furthermore, to gain further clarity on various aspects of student management, such as visa regulations, scholarships, accommodation, and study-to-job transfer policies, we contacted public universities in Saudi Arabia through email communication. A wealth of information on admission procedures, immigration policies, scholarships, accommodation, spouse sponsorship policies, and other relevant information was provided by public and private universities. Most university websites delineate information for international students, facilitating the retrieval of facts and figures.

In this exploratory study, we also draw upon field trips to Saudi Arabia, where we interacted with international students in the country. These interactions provided important first-hand insights into the experiences and challenges international students face in navigating foreign countries' education systems and social environments. Through these encounters, we gained a deeper understanding of the factors influencing student mobility and the impact of migration policies on educational opportunities in the Gulf region. Although we have used direct quotes from students' testimonies, we have changed the names due to privacy issues.

International student mobility in the Gulf

The pattern of international student mobility in Saudi Arabia is closely linked to the socio-economic development of the country. Considerable investments in the education sector have enhanced the infrastructure and quality of educational institutions and also catalyzed an increase in the number of incoming international students over the past decade. This surge

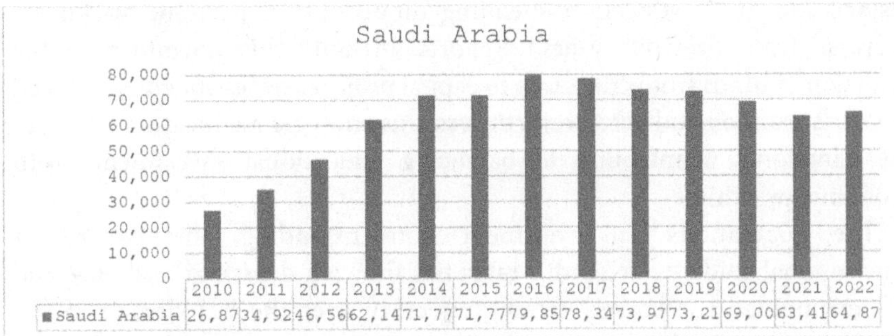

Figure 10.1. Inbound internationally mobile students in Saudi Arabia. Source: UNESCO Institute for Statistics. http://data.uis.unesco.org/#

is evident in the rise from approximately 26,871 international students in the early 2010s to a staggering 64,874 in 2022, marking a growth of over 200 percent (Figure 10.1).

This growth is a sign of the efficacy of Saudi Arabia's educational offerings and also the nation's expanding role as a global academic hub. A prime catalyst driving this trend is substantial financial allocations in the education sector. In 2015, the country's spending surpassed the average expenditure of member countries in the Organisation for Economic Co-operation and Development (OECD).[4] From 2016 to 2023, the government consistently allocated an average of around 20 percent of total government expenditure to education (Table 10.1).

However, recent years have witnessed fluctuations in education spending, with a discernible decline observed after the COVID-19 pandemic. For

Table 10.1. Government Expenditure on Education

	Saudi Arabia Education Spending	
Year	**Spending (% of GDP)**	**Annual Change (%)**
2023	17.00	-2.40
2022	19.40	0.61
2021	18.79	-0.27
2020	19.06	-0.01
2019	19.07	-0.29
2018	19.36	-2.90
2017	22.26	-2.69
2016	24.95	5.69

Note. Data from Macrotrends (https://www.macrotrends.net/global-metrics/countries/SAU/saudi-arabia/education-spending)

instance, in 2023, education spending dipped to 17 percent, marking a decrease from previous years.[5] Reports attribute this downturn to the diversion of funds from education to capital projects, necessitated by reduced revenues from oil and gas.[6] Nevertheless, this strategic reallocation points to the Kingdom's adaptability in balancing educational investments with economic priorities.

The fluctuations in investment notwithstanding, the pattern of international students in Saudi Arabia has shown a degree of resilience and has maintained a relatively steady trajectory over the last decade. While there was a noticeable surge in the numbers until 2016, subsequent years have seen a marginal decline. This begs scrutiny into the underlying factors driving this trend. Research indicates that neighboring countries, primarily the United Arab Emirates (UAE) and Qatar, have emerged as formidable competitors in diverting international student mobility. Umar and Rahman (2023) highlight that these nations have increased their educational offerings by augmenting funding in the sector and establishing educational enclaves, such as the Qatar Foundation in Qatar and Dubai Knowledge Park in Dubai. These enclaves host international university branches of top US universities. These efforts have enhanced the quality of education and have also positioned these countries as desirable destinations for international students seeking degrees from US university branches. The comparative advantage offered by the UAE and Qatar in terms of educational infrastructure, innovative pedagogical approaches, and cultural amenities presents a real challenge to Saudi Arabia.

The trend in international student mobility within the region is further illuminated when examining the demographic composition of Saudi Arabia's international student body. It includes students from various regions; the predominant source of international students is neighboring Arab and African countries, such as Yemen, Lebanon, Jordan, Egypt, Palestine, Sudan, Morocco, and Algeria (Table 10.2). These nations contribute to the

Table 10.2. International Students in Saudi Arabia by Region of Origin

Region	2016	2017	2018	2019	2020	2021
Arab States	42,372	41,615	39,453	48,872	44,101	37,053
Central and Eastern Europe	2,099	2,073	1,969	951	1,042	877
Central Asia	1,444	1,434	1,243	582	642	636
East Asia and Pacific	5,798	5,717	5,382	4,151	4,280	4,881
North America	1,258	1,219	1,126	650	652	518

Note. Data from UNESCO Institute for Statistics, http://data.uis.unesco.org/

composition of the international student body in Saudi Arabia, with the number of international students from these regions reaching a peak of 48,872 in 2019. The structure of the student body alludes to the importance of regional relationships and cultural affinities in attracting students to the country. In addition to students from neighboring countries, there is also a smaller but notable presence of students from Europe and America in the student demographic in Saudi Arabia. Although not the dominant contributor, students from Europe and America contribute to a broader cultural exchange within the academic environment, fostering a more globally interconnected learning experience. In the last couple of years, there has been a slight decline in the number of international students in the country. We found that the decrease aligns with the general downward trend observed in global student mobility due to the COVID-19 pandemic. The pandemic has had a severe impact on international student mobility, with travel restrictions, border closures, and health concerns affecting the ability of students to study abroad.

Saudi Arabia's pull factors and motivations of international students

Our research aimed to understand why students choose Saudi universities over other destinations, and we identified four key reasons. The first reason is the availability of scholarships funded by the Saudi government. These scholarships often cover tuition and housing and even provide a monthly stipend, making education affordable and accessible for many students. Second, the cost of living in Saudi Arabia is relatively low compared to other countries, which allows students from middle- or low-income families to study abroad without placing a heavy financial burden on themselves or their families. Third, Saudi Arabia's geographic location plays a big role, especially for students from nearby countries. For many, it is not only closer to home but also a more stable option compared to some neighboring countries that face political or economic instability. Lastly, the cultural and religious importance of Saudi Arabia, being home to Islam's two holiest cities, attracts many Muslim students who see studying there as both an academic and spiritual opportunity. In the forthcoming paragraphs, we will expound on each motivational factor while providing international students' perspectives.

First, Saudi Arabia has been foremost in initiating several scholarship programs. The Saudi government's provision of fully and partially funded scholarships is a significant facilitator of international student mobility. By offering financial support, Saudi Arabia aims to enhance accessibility to its universities for students from across the globe. This allows the country to create an environment of international collaboration and cultural exchange. Recent studies show the benefits provided to international students, such as university-sponsored accommodation, monthly stipends, annual tickets to their home countries, and coverage of medical expenses (Alsulami, 2021b; Umar and Rahman, 2023). Scholarship packages create a welcoming environment for international students and position Saudi Arabia as an attractive destination for academic pursuits. For instance, a PhD student from Bangladesh at King Fahd University of Petroleum and Minerals explained, "The scholarship program is the reason I am here. It covers all my costs and provides a stipend, which has allowed me to focus entirely on my research. Back in Bangladesh, opportunities like this are rare, and the facilities available here are far beyond what I could access at home." Similarly, a student from Pakistan who is also a PhD candidate in engineering in Riyadh mentioned that the scholarship covered his tuition and accommodation expenses and provided him with an annual ticket back home. Since his admission in 2021, he visited his family every year. He added, "For students like me, who come from middle-income families, such programs are a lifeline. The funding covers everything I need, including books and research-related expenses."

The second most important factor that draws international students to Saudi Arabia is Islam. The Kingdom has strategically used its image as a hub for Islamic education by leveraging its significance as the birthplace of Prophet Mohammad and its status as the home to the two holiest cities in Islam: Mecca and Madinah. While Al Azhar University in Egypt retains its reputation as one of the premier Islamic institutions globally, the Kingdom has emerged as an attractive destination for Muslim international students pursuing degrees in fields related to Islamic studies. Popular institutions, such as the Islamic University of Madinah, King Abdulaziz University, and Ummul Qura University, are key in attracting students seeking to deepen their knowledge in Islamic studies (Umar and Rahman, 2023). The academic pull of these and many other institutions in the country lies in the presence of esteemed scholars in the country and graduates who have become famous imams, preachers, and scholars of religion.

Most students we had conversations with told us that studying in Saudi Arabia offers a rare combination of academic learning and spiritual fulfillment. Ahmed, a master's student from Nigeria, shared his thoughts: "Being able to study Islamic jurisprudence while living so close to the *Kaaba* has been an incredible experience. It's not just about gaining knowledge but about living my faith every day in a place that deeply connects with my identity." This sense of connection and immersion makes Saudi universities a compelling choice for students from across the Muslim world. The opportunity to pursue advanced Islamic education while being near Islam's holiest sites is a draw that no other country can match.

The religious appeal of Saudi Arabia is so strong that it attracts students from regions far beyond the Middle East and South Asia. During our visit to the Islamic University of Madinah, we met several students from Latin American countries who had traveled thousands of miles to study Islamic sciences. For many of them, the journey was deeply personal. A graduate of Madinah University, Yusuf, who hails from Mexico, converted to Islam in his late teens and had always been curious about learning more about his newfound faith. For him, the decision to study in Saudi Arabia was clear. "There's no better place to learn about Islam than its birthplace," he told us. Studying at Madinah was not just about gaining knowledge but about experiencing life in a deeply Islamic environment that he could not find in Mexico. He described how walking in the Prophet's city every day felt like being part of something larger than himself, a connection to the roots of his faith. Similarly, we met Sajid, a preacher from the United States who came to Saudi Arabia to deepen his understanding of Islamic theology. As someone who had been actively teaching Islam in his community, he believed that formal education from a place as prominent as Saudi Arabia would lend both authenticity and depth to his work back home. He expressed gratitude for the scholarships provided by the Kingdom, which allowed him to pursue his studies without financial burdens.

For most students, studying in Saudi Arabia is about embracing a once-in-a-lifetime opportunity to live and learn in a place that holds unparalleled significance in the Muslim world. Many graduates from these institutions go on to become leaders and scholars in their home countries, carrying Saudi values with them. This unique blend of academic and cultural outreach highlights the centrality of religion to Saudi Arabia's approach to attracting international students. However, it must be noted that Saudi Arabia's strong image as a Muslim country makes it less appealing to students who are non-Muslims.

Another factor that draws students to Saudi Arabia is its relatively low cost of living compared to other major study destinations. Housing, transportation, and daily expenses are more affordable than in countries such as the United States, the United Kingdom, or even some of Saudi Arabia's regional neighbors like Qatar and the UAE. As per the recent trends, Saudi Arabia's average cost of living is $1,194 per month, which is around 50 percent lower than that of Qatar's ($1,807 per month) and the UAE's ($1,904 per month).[78] For many students, this financial accessibility eases the burden on both them and their families, making it a practical choice for higher education. A major advantage for international students in Saudi Arabia is the provision of on-campus accommodation by most universities. This arrangement eliminates additional commuting costs and creates a sense of community for students living together on campus. Many international students shared that these accommodations are not only conveniently located but also free or heavily subsidized. Additionally, those who choose to live off-campus often find Saudi cities to be relatively affordable compared to neighboring cities like Doha, Dubai, or Abu Dhabi, where housing and general living expenses are notoriously high. One student from Yemen explained, "Even when I decided to live off-campus for a while, I found that I could easily afford food, transport, and shopping without feeling a financial strain. This would not have been possible in Qatar or the UAE." Moreover, the affordability extends beyond housing. Students frequently cited how eating out at restaurants, purchasing groceries, or engaging in leisure activities was cheaper in Saudi Arabia than in most Gulf countries or Western destinations.

The country's low cost of living also means that students' stipends, provided as part of many scholarship programs, go much further. While in Qatar or the UAE, scholarship stipends may cover basic needs due to higher costs, students in Saudi Arabia often have leftover funds for savings or additional expenses. However, the affordability of Saudi Arabia does come with trade-offs. While the lower cost of living is an advantage, some students said that social and recreational activities in smaller Saudi cities were limited compared to vibrant cities like Dubai or Doha. Additionally, the diversity of academic programs in Saudi universities, particularly in fields beyond Islamic studies or STEM, can be more limited than what is offered in these neighboring countries, which can potentially narrow its appeal to students with broader academic interests.

Another key reason international students see Saudi Arabia as an ideal place to study is the linguistic, cultural, and geographic proximity for students from neighboring Arab countries and the Indian subcontinent. Many international students living in Saudi Arabia come from war-torn nations like Iraq and Yemen. These countries once had robust educational systems, but decades of conflict have devastated their infrastructure and made them unsuitable for higher education. Saudi Arabia has emerged as a natural alternative for students from these regions with its stable institutions and shared linguistic and cultural ties. The familiarity with Arabic as a medium of instruction in many universities and the cultural similarities ease the transition for students who might otherwise struggle in more foreign academic environments. For instance, a student from Iraq mentioned, "I wanted a place where I could study in peace, and being in Saudi Arabia felt like home. My uncle already works here, so it made the decision easier." Similarly, many Yemeni students seek refuge in Saudi universities not only for their academic programs but also for the support systems they find through extended family connections living in the Kingdom. The presence of relatives provides an additional layer of comfort and stability for students far from their home countries.

The appeal extends beyond Arab students. Students from the Indian subcontinent, particularly from countries like Bangladesh, Pakistan, and India, prefer Saudi Arabia because of its proximity, cultural familiarity, and conservative social values. Saud, a student from Bangladesh, remarked, "Living here feels like a continuation of my life back home. The food, the community, even the way people greet you, it's all so familiar." For students from the subcontinent, these cultural overlaps help them integrate into Saudi society, making it easier to focus on their studies without feeling alienated or isolated.

Scholarship and facilities

In our conversations with students, we discovered that almost every international student studying in Saudi Arabia receives some form of scholarship. This financial support has proven to be a key factor in making Saudi Arabia a competitive destination for higher education. Unlike traditional education hubs such as the UK, the United States, Germany, and Australia, where international students often face financial challenges (Akanwa, 2015; Calder et al., 2016; Sherry et al., 2010; Wilson et al., 2023), Saudi Arabia's scholarship programs alleviate much of the financial strain. This accessibility opens the doors for students from lower-income backgrounds and showcases the Kingdom's strategy to attract a cohort of talented individuals from around the globe.

The scholarship opportunities in Saudi Arabia can be grouped into three main categories: government-funded programs, university-specific scholarships, and support from non-governmental organizations (Figure 10.2). Saudi scholarships generally offer comprehensive financial coverage, including full tuition fees, on-campus accommodation, monthly stipends, and annual travel allowances.[9]

These arrangements help students cover personal expenses and ensure they can focus entirely on their studies without additional financial stress. For instance, the King Salman International Scholarship Program stands out as a government-funded initiative that supports undergraduate, graduate, and doctoral students from various countries. In 2023, Saudi Arabia

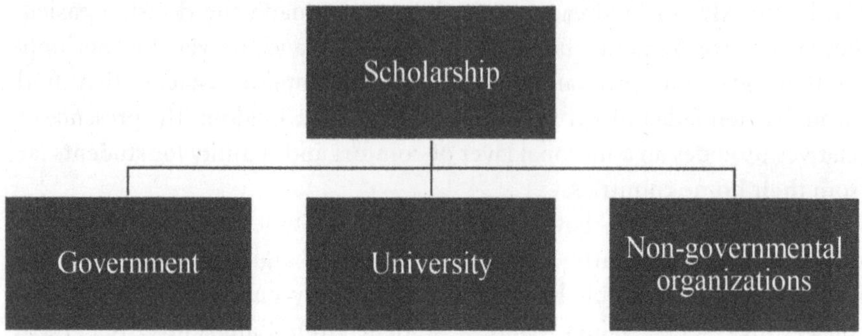

Figure 10.2. Classification of available scholarships in Saudi Arabia.

announced the "Study in the Kingdom of Saudi Arabia" initiative, part of Saudi Arabia's Vision 2030.[10] It offers numerous benefits to international students, including access to a range of educational opportunities and scholarships, providing full to partial funding. The initiative is open to students enrolled in bachelor's, master's, and PhD programs and offers courses in a variety of fields, including economics, business management, educational specialties, law, politics, media, religion, linguistics, agriculture, computer science, and engineering. Apart from scholarships, the initiative makes it easier for international students to apply through the "Study in Saudi Arabia" platform. This platform offers a wide range of educational opportunities, from short courses to long academic programs. While Saudi universities already have scholarships and educational programs, the launch of this new initiative points to a more concerted effort to showcase the country as a rising hub of education.

At the university level, institutions like King Abdullah University of Science and Technology (KAUST) and King Fahd University of Petroleum and Minerals (KFUPM) offer fully funded scholarships that cater to master's, PhD, and MBA students. These programs often include allowances for living expenses, making it easier for students to manage their day-to-day lives. KAUST, in particular, has gained a reputation for its generous funding packages, which have helped it attract students from over a hundred nationalities, building a truly international academic community. However, we found that monthly stipends vary from institution to institution. For example, a Bangladeshi student at King Abdulaziz University in Jeddah said that he and his colleagues receive around 1980 Saudi Riyals (SR), while some students in Medina universities and a university in Abha said they receive 890 SR only. Although we were unable to verify the reasons, it is most likely that a university like King Abdulaziz University (KAU) in Jeddah is among Saudi Arabia's top-tier institutions, which often benefit from larger budgets and stronger financial backing. As a flagship university, KAU likely has access to extra funding from both the government and external sources, such as endowments or research grants, which allows it to offer higher stipends. On the other hand, universities in comparatively smaller cities like Jizan or Abha might operate with more limited budgets, which could explain the lower stipends. Moreover, these institutions differ in their financial allocation priorities. For instance, universities such as KAU focus on attracting international students and building global reputations; hence, investing more in stipends is part of a larger strategy to make their programs more appealing. However, other middle-tier universities may prioritize other areas, such as expanding local access to education, rather than competing for international prestige.

Beyond government and institutional scholarships, non-governmental organizations also offer generous funding to international students. The Islamic Development Bank (IsDB) Scholarship Program is one such initiative, targeting students from its fifty-six member countries and providing support for bachelor's, master's, and doctoral studies. Similarly, the Islamic World Educational, Scientific, and Cultural Organization (ICESCO) scholarships focus on undergraduate programs for students from fifty-three member states.[11] These scholarships are particularly helpful for students from developing regions, where access to quality higher education remains limited. Abdulrahman, a student from Ethiopia pursuing a master's degree in Sharia in Abha, shared his experience: "Without the scholarship, pursuing higher education abroad would have been impossible. It's not just financial support; it's a chance to grow academically and professionally in ways I never imagined. The funding covers everything, from my tuition to my living expenses. I concentrate on my studies and not worry about how to make ends meet."

Admission, visa policies, and labor market integration

One of the defining features of Saudi Arabia's approach to international student mobility is its streamlined student visa process. Unlike countries such as the United States or many Western European nations, where students often need to follow through multiple procedures and financial burdens for visa applications (Grimm, 2019; Gopal, 2016; Urias and Camp Yeakey, 2009), Saudi universities handle much of the process. Once admitted, the university applies for the study visa on behalf of the student, which simplifies the process and reduces the costs. Afterwards, students need only visit the nearest Saudi embassy to have their visas stamped on their passports. This university approach, similar to the process in other GCC countries, eliminates many bureaucratic hurdles and ensures that students can focus on their education without worrying about visa complications. While studying in Saudi Arabia, international students are placed under the sponsorship of their respective universities, which is consistent with the country's sponsorship system for expatriates.

Some universities in Saudi Arabia allow married students to bring their spouses and offer accommodation to support their stay. However, this process is neither straightforward nor uniform across institutions. Family visas are not issued to new students upon admission. Instead, students must first arrive in the country and then formally request their universities to issue visas for their families. Even then, the type of visa granted varies widely. In some cases, universities provide only temporary visit visas valid for a few months, while others sponsor residence permits for families. Policies regarding family accommodations also differ. For instance, some universities reserve this option exclusively for graduate students enrolled in MA or PhD programs, allowing them to live with their families in university-provided housing. Conversely, in other institutions, even undergraduate students may be permitted to bring their families, though this is often determined on a case-by-case basis.

Despite these provisions, many students have expressed concerns about university housing, particularly regarding the lack of space and long waiting times for family accommodations. This has led some to seek housing alternatives outside the university. It can be said that there is no standardized policy for family visas or accommodations, and the existing system varies depending on universities and individual circumstances.

One of the imperatives of our research was to understand the policy concerning the study to job transition of international students. We sought to identify the opportunities available to students after they complete their education. In many traditional education hubs, and even in some GCC countries such as Qatar, international students are allowed to extend their visas temporarily to seek employment. In some Western countries, such as Canada, Australia, Ireland, the UK, and the United States, international students can stay for a defined period to look for jobs and transition from student to work visas. For example, Canada's Post-Graduation Work Permit (PGWP) enables international students to work for up to three years.[12] Similarly, Qatar provides graduates from its Education City universities with a one-year visa extension to support job hunting. These policies enhance the attractiveness of these countries as study destinations and enable them to retain highly skilled talent (Moltaji, 2019).

However, in our research, we found that study to job transition process in Saudi Arabia is not clearly defined. We received conflicting information regarding whether an international student can extend their student visa or transfer their sponsorship after graduating from a Saudi university. A student from Bangladesh, who was also a student community leader at KAU, mentioned that international students have the option to transfer their residency from the university to an employer if they secure a job offer. However, a few other students we interacted with told us that this was not an option for a student. Upon being asked if international students can transfer sponsorship, a Nigerian student who studied in Riyadh replied, "I am not sure of the process of transferring my visa because it's very rare to see someone getting a job after graduation. The process is not clear to me." To get clarity on the issue, we also contacted several university admission offices. Through our email correspondence with King Saud University's international student office, we learned that they do not offer a visa transfer facility to international students. In response to our email query regarding the process, they wrote, "The student is not entitled to transfer his sponsorship. According to the regulations and instructions, he must complete his transactions, issue the final exit visa, and leave within three months from the date of graduation." We did not receive responses from other universities to verify whether similar policies apply nationwide.

Based on the conflicting responses we received from students and institutions, it appears that there is a gap in the national policy framework concerning international students. While Saudi Vision 2030 emphasizes attracting international talent, our findings suggest that there is no formalized study-to-job transition policy. This may be influenced by Saudi Arabia's preference for hiring locals under Saudization policies, which prioritize employment opportunities for Saudi nationals. This becomes particularly pertinent in the context of the high youth unemployment rate observed in Saudi Arabia compared to other regional counterparts. The ongoing nationalization of the job market raises questions about whether skilled international graduates can realistically transition into the workforce. Another challenge is the bureaucratic complexity of transferring sponsorship. Even in cases where graduates secure job offers, they may face logistical barriers, such as obtaining a non-objection certificate (NOC) from their sponsoring university. These obstacles create an environment where transitioning from student to worker is not only unclear but also practically challenging. The absence of empirical studies on the success rates of such transitions further exacerbates the issue, leaving policymakers without the necessary data to assess the impact of these policies on workforce integration.

Challenges for international students

When international students first arrive in Saudi Arabia, many are met with excitement and hope, but these feelings can quickly give way to challenges that are not always anticipated. One of the first hurdles they encounter is the language barrier. For many, the lack of Arabic proficiency becomes an immediate obstacle. Everyday tasks, such as asking for directions, ordering food, or understanding official documents, can feel overwhelming. Unlike in places like the UAE or Qatar, where English often acts as a second language in public spaces, Saudi Arabia relies heavily on Arabic in daily life. This creates a sense of disconnection, as students find themselves unable to fully engage with their surroundings (Almutairi, 2020). Some describe this experience as being "invisible" in a new country, where their inability to communicate can leave them feeling marginalized (Al-Mohsen and Al-Sawi, 2015; Alasmari, 2023).

The cultural adjustment also poses a huge challenge. Students arriving from countries with different social norms often struggle to navigate the Kingdom's deeply rooted traditions. Gender-segregated spaces, specific dress codes, and expectations around public behavior can feel unfamiliar, if not restrictive. The process of learning and adapting to these norms is not always smooth, and for many, it adds to the sense of cultural shock. One student recalled his first week in Saudi Arabia as being "full of questions" about what was appropriate and what was not, a process that left him hesitant to participate fully in his new environment. Academically, the transition can also be demanding. The teaching methods and evaluation systems in Saudi universities sometimes differ significantly from what international students are used to. For instance, students accustomed to interactive or research-based learning may find the more traditional lecture-focused approach challenging. This adjustment, combined with the language barrier, can make navigating their academic journey feel like a solitary struggle.

The challenges extend beyond campus life. For many international students, the inability to work legally in Saudi Arabia presents a major difficulty. Unlike countries where part-time work is readily available to international students, Saudi labor laws and sponsorship requirements make finding jobs nearly impossible. This creates financial strain, especially for students who must manage unexpected expenses like transportation, medical bills, or additional living costs. The inability to earn or gain work experience also limits their exposure to professional environments, leaving some feeling stagnant during their time abroad.

Over time, these challenges can take a toll on students' well-being. The stress of adapting to a new culture, managing academic pressures, and dealing with financial uncertainty often leads to feelings of isolation and homesickness. However, the stigma surrounding mental health, combined with limited access to culturally sensitive support services (Alattar et al., 2021; Alluhaibi and Awadalla, 2022), leaves many students struggling in silence (Al-Mohsen and Al-Sawi, 2015). One international student described the experience as "lonely, not because people are unkind, but because I couldn't find a way to truly connect."

Conclusion

The intersection of the economic diversification plan and international student mobility is a compelling area of study that existing studies on international student mobility have not yet comprehensively captured. To achieve Saudi Vision 2030, the Kingdom has increased investment in the education sector and has fostered a hospitable environment for both local and international students through the provision of opportunities for academic and professional advancement. Saudi Arabia's comprehensive support system for international students, from scholarships to inclusive visa policies for families, shows that the nation is committed to nurturing a thriving academic community. While Saudi Arabia has made significant strides in supporting international students, the lack of a standardized post-study visa policy and a dearth of research on its effectiveness present challenges. Addressing these issues would provide international students clarity and assurance regarding their future steps and contribute to a more seamless transition from academia to the job market. Furthermore, the challenges faced due to linguistic barriers highlight the need for proactive measures, such as language support programs and cultural assimilation initiatives, to facilitate a more inclusive and supportive environment for international students in Saudi Arabia. Addressing these challenges can enhance the overall experience of international students and contribute to the successful integration of diverse skills within the Saudi academic landscape.

There are several avenues for future research in this direction. Investigating the impact of government scholarship initiatives on educational outcomes and workforce participation can help us understand the effectiveness of public policies in shaping human capital development. Besides that, comparative studies across GCC countries can offer a broader perspective on factors influencing international student mobility and strategies for attracting and retaining talent, fostering regional collaboration, and knowledge sharing.

Notes

1 GCC Education Industry August 02, 2023. Alpen Capital. Accessed December 10, 2023, from https://alpencapital.com/research/2023/gcc-education-02-aug-23.pdf.

2 QS. (2022). Q.S. Arab Region University Rankings 2022. https://www.topuniversities.com/university-rankings/arab-region-university-rankings/2023

3 UNESCO, UIS. Accessed on December 20, 2023, from http://data.uis.unesco.org/#; Saudi Arabia: Inequality in Education and Outcomes. OECD iLibrary. Accessed on December 20, 2023, from https://www.oecd-ilibrary.org/sites/3f8e39f5-en/index.html?itemId=/content/component/3f8e39f5-en.

4 Education in Saudi Arabia. OECD Library. Accessed March 29, 2024, from https://www.oecd-ilibrary.org/sites/76df15a2-en/1/3/1/index.html?_csp_=52c9984cac4fdeba56b32f54ff82555e&itemContentType=book&itemIGO=oecd&itemId=%2Fcontent%2Fpublication%2F76df15a2-en.

5 Macrotrends. Accessed March 27, 2024, from https://www.macrotrends.net/global-metrics/countries/SAU/saudi-arabia/education-spending.

6 GCC Education Industry August 02, 2023. Alpen Capital. Accessed December 10, 2023, from https://alpencapital.com/research/2023/gcc-education-02-aug-23.pdf.

7 Qatar vs Saudi Arabia - Cost of Living Comparison. (2024). LivingCost.org. Accessed October 16, 2024, from https://livingcost.org/cost/qatar/saudi-arabia.

8 Qatar vs United Arab Emirates - Cost of Living Comparison. (2024). LivingCost.org. Accessed October 16, 2024, from https://livingcost.org/cost/qatar/united-arab-emirates.

9 Saudi Arabian Government Scholarships for International Students. Oya Opportunities. Accessed October 26, 2024, from https://oyaop.com/opportunity/scholarships-and-fellowships/saudi-arabian-government-scholarships-for-international-students/

10 "Study in the Kingdom of Saudi Arabia". Statements. The Embassy of the Kingdom of Saudi Arabia. Accessed December 14, 2023, from https://www.saudiembassy.net/statements/study-kingdom-saudi-arabia.

11 200 scholarships in Saudi universities for outstanding students from ICESCO Member States. 2024. ICESCO. Accessed August 18, 2024, from https://icesco.org/en/2024/07/19/200-scholarships-in-saudi-universities-for-outstanding-students-from-icesco-member-states/

12 Help Center. Government of Canada. Accessed July 28, 2024, from https://ircc.canada.ca/english/helpcentre/answer.asp?qnum=509&top=15

Bibliography

Akanwa, E. E. (2015). International students in Western developed countries: History, challenges, and prospects. *Journal of International Students*, *5*(3), 271–84.

Alasmari, A. A. (2023). Challenges and social adaptation of international students in Saudi Arabia. *Heliyon*, *9*(5), e16283. https://doi.org/10.1016/j.heliyon.2023.e16283.

Alattar, Nada, Anne Felton, and Theodore Stickley. (2021). "Mental health and stigma in Saudi Arabia: a scoping review." *Mental Health Review Journal*, *26*(2), 180–96.

Aldosari, H., and M. Mekheimer (2019). Exploring the role of acculturation in Saudi scholars abroad: An introspective study. *Umm Al-Qura University Journal of Languages and Literature*, *22*(1), 11–54.

Alhazmi, A., and B. Nyland (2013). The Saudi Arabian international student experience: From a gender-segregated society to studying in a mixed-gender environment. Compare: A *Journal of Comparative and International Education*, *43*(3), 346–65.

Alkubaidi, M., and N. Alzhrani (2020). "We are back": Reverse culture shock among Saudi scholars after doctoral study abroad. *Sage Open*, *10*(4).

Alluhaibi, B. A., and A. W. Awadalla (2022). Attitudes and stigma toward seeking psychological help among Saudi Adults. *BMC Psychology*, *10*(1), 216.

Al-Mohsen, M., and M. Al-Sawi (2015). Alienation among expatriate scholarship students at Qassim University: A demonstration and ways to confront it. *Journal of Arabic Sciences and Humanities*, *8*, 2071–15.

Almotery, A. (2009). Saudi students' expectations, motivations, and experiences at the University of Wisconsin–La Crosse. Master's thesis, University of Wisconsin–La Crosse. MINDS@UW: University of Wisconsin Digital Repository. https://minds.wisconsin.edu/handle/1793/45118

Al Murshidi, G. (2014). Participation challenges of Emirati and Saudi students at US universities. *International Journal of Research Studies in Language Learning*, *3*(5), 33–52.

Almutairi, Y. M. N. (2020). International students' experiences at a Saudi university and academic leaders' perceptions regarding them. *Societies*, *10*(3), 70.

Alqefari, S. I. (2016). Difficulties of Saudi Arabian female students studying English abroad. *Arab World English Journal*, *6*(4), 231–44.

Alsabatin, H. Y. (2015). Experiences of Saudi students attending a U.S. university: A qualitative study. Doctoral dissertation, Wichita State University. SOAR: Shocker Open Access Repository. https://soar.wichita.edu/items/8169cb08-9ca4-42b1-b1a1-5b358ff117eb

Alsahafi, N., and S. C. Shin (2019). Factors affecting the academic and cultural adjustment of Saudi international students in Australian universities. *Journal of International Students*, *7*(1), 53–72.

Alsaif, O. A. (2014). Saudi Arabian students' opinions about co-education while studying abroad. *Journal of Emerging Trends in Educational Research and Policy Studies*, *5*(5), 614–20.

Alsulami, N. D. (2021a). Challenges of the re-entry experiences of returning Saudi international students after studying abroad. *Journal of Comparative & International Higher Education*, *13*(4), 101–17.

Alsulami, N. D. (2021b). International students in crisis times: Exploring the experiences of international students studying in Saudi Arabia during the COVID-19 pandemic. *Pegem Journal of Education and Instruction, 11*(4), 254–64.

Binsahl, H., S. Chang, and R. Bosua (2015). Identity and belonging: Saudi female international students and their use of social networking sites. *Crossings: Journal of Migration & Culture, 6*(1), 81–102.

Borozan, D., and I. B. Bojanic (2015). Migration motives of university students: An empirical research. *International Migration, 53*(1), 66–82.

Bourdieu, P. (1986). The forms of capital. In J. E. Richardson (Ed.), *Handbook of theory and research for the sociology of education* (pp. 241–58). Greenwood.

Brezis, E., and A. Soueri (2011). Why do Students Migrate? Where do they migrate to? Working Paper 25, AlmaLaurea Inter-University Consortium.

Brooks, R., and J. Waters (2010). Social networks and educational mobility: The experiences of UK students. *Globalisation, Societies and Education, 8*(1), 143–57. https:// doi.org/10.1080/14767720903574132

Calder, M. J., S. Richter, Y. Mao, K. Kovacs Burns, R. S. Mogale, and M. Danko (2016). International students attending Canadian universities: Their experiences with housing, finances, and other issues. *Canadian Journal of Higher Education, 46*(2), 92–110.

Carling, J. (2002). Migration in the age of involuntary immobility: Theoretical reflections and Cape Verdean experiences. *Journal of Ethnic and Migration Studies, 28*, 5–42. https://doi.org/10.1080/13691830120103912

Carling, J., and F. Collins (2018). Aspiration, desire and drivers of migration. *Journal of Ethnic and Migration Studies, 44*(6), 909–26.

Collins, F. L., R. Sidhu, N. Lewis, and B. S. Yeoh (2014). Mobility and desire: International students and Asian regionalism in aspirational Singapore. *Discourse: Studies in the Cultural Politics of Education, 35*(5), 661–76.

De Haas, H. (2010). Migration and development: A theoretical perspective. *International Migration Review, 44*, 227–64. https://doi.org/10.1111/j.1747-7379.2009.00804.x

De Haas, H. (2021). A theory of migration: the aspirations-capabilities framework. *Comparative Migration Studies, 9*(1), 8. https://doi.org/10.1186/s40878-020-00210-4

Findlay, A. M. (2011). An assessment of supply and demand⊠side theorizations of international student mobility. *International Migration, 49*(2), 162–90.

Findlay, A., L. Prazeres, D. McCollum, and H. Packwood (2017). "It was always the plan": International study as "learning to migrate." *Area, 49*(2), 192–99.

Geiger, M., and A. Pécoud (2013). Migration, development and the "migration and development nexus." *Population, Space and Place, 19*(4), 369–74.

Gopal, A. (2016). Visa and immigration trends: A comparative examination of international student mobility in Canada, Australia, the United Kingdom, and the United States. *Strategic Enrollment Management Quarterly, 4*(3), 130–41.

Grimm (2019). Studying to stay: Understanding graduate visa policy content and context in the United States and Australia. *International Migration*, *57*(5), 235–51.

Huang, W., and J. Ren (2023). Migration aspiration and desire of international students: Chinese international students under strain amid geopolitical tension and the COVID- 19 pandemic. *Transitions: Journal of Transient Migration*. https://doi.org/10.1386/ tjtm_00049_1

King, R. (2002). Towards a new map of European migration. *International Journal of Population Geography*, *8*(2), 89–106.

King, R., A. Lulle, L. Morosanu, and A. Williams (2016). International youth mobility and life transitions in Europe: Questions, definitions, typologies and theoretical approaches. Working Paper 86. Sussex Centre for Migration Research. https:// core.ac.uk/download/pdf/42579147.pdf

Lee, E. S. (1966). A Theory of Migration. *Demography*, *3*(1), 47–57.

Massey, D. S., J. Arango, G. Hugo, A. Kouaouci, A. Pellegrino, and J. E. Taylor (1993). Theories of international migration: A review and appraisal. *Population and Development Review*, *19*(3), 431–66.

Moltaji, G. (2019). A sociological review of the post graduate work permit program as a pathway to permanent residency for international students in Canada. Doctoral dissertation, Université d'Ottawa/University of Ottawa.

Moriarty, E., J. Wickham, S. Daly, and A. Bobek (2015). Graduate emigration from Ireland: Navigating new pathways in familiar places. *Irish Journal of Sociology*, *23*(2), 71–92.

Nam, B., and X. Jiang (2023). Aspiration for cosmopolitan capital and ambiguous loss: Chinese exchange students' experiences in US higher education institutions during the COVID-19 pandemic. *Asia Pacific Journal of Education*, *43*(4), 1256–71.

Sherry, M., P. Thomas, and W. H. Chui (2010). International students: A vulnerable student population. *Higher Education*, *60*, 33–46.

Skeldon, R. (2012). Migration transitions revisited: Their continued relevance for the development of migration theory. *Population, Space and Place*, *18*, 154–166. https://doi.org/10.1002/psp.667

Umar, S., and M. M. Rahman (2023). International Student Migration to the GCC States: A Comparative Study. *Migration and Development*, *12*(1), 111–40.

Unruh, S., and B. F. Obeidat (2015). Adjusting to learning in the US: Saudi students speak out. *Journal of Higher Education Theory and Practice*, *15*(4), 45.

Urias, D., and C. Camp Yeakey (2009). Analysis of the US student visa system: Misperceptions, barriers, and consequences. *Journal of Studies in International Education*, *13*(1), 72–109.

Van Mol, C. (2014). *Intra-European student mobility in international higher education circuits: Europe on the move*. Palgrave Macmillan.

Vision 2030, Kingdom of Saudi Arabia (n.d.). Overview. https://www.vision2030.gov.sa/media/cofh1nmf/vision-2030-overview.pdf

Weber, T., and C. Van Mol (2023). The student migration transition: an empirical investigation into the nexus between development and international student migration. *Comparative Migration Studies, 11*(1), 5. https://doi.org/10.1186/s40878-023-00329-0

Wilson, S., C. Hastings, A. Morris, G. Ramia, and E. Mitchell (2023). International students on the edge: The precarious impacts of financial stress. *Journal of Sociology, 59*(4), 952–74.

Wu, D. B., and S. Hou (2023). International student mobility as "aspiration on the go": Stories from African students at a Chinese university. *Higher Education, 85*(4), 759–73.

Young, B. N., and D. Snead (2017). Saudi Arabian International Graduate Students' Lived Experiences at a US University. *Journal of Learning in Higher Education, 13*(2), 39–44.

Zelinsky, W. (1971). The hypothesis of the mobility transition. *Geographical Review, 61*, 219. https://doi.org/10.2307/213996

11

Labor Migration and Saudi Secondary Labor Market Sustainability: Economic Diversification and Sustainable Development

AKM Ahsan Ullah

Introduction

Saudi Arabia's economic landscape has always been dominated by the oil sector, which has led to a labor market that is heavily dependent on foreign labor, especially in secondary sectors such as construction and services. This dependence poses a challenge to sustainable development and economic diversification. In response, the Saudi government has introduced measures such as Saudization, which aims to increase the employment of Saudi nationals in the private sector. The Nitaqat program, introduced in 2011, classifies companies based on their compliance with nationalization quotas and creates incentives for companies to hire more Saudi nationals (Alshanbri et al., 2015). However, the effectiveness of these measures in reducing dependence on foreign labor and promoting a sustainable secondary labor market remains controversial.

The Kingdom's Vision 2030 initiative emphasizes the need for economic diversification and sustainable development. A critical component of this vision is the transformation of the labor market to reduce dependence on foreign workers and increase the participation of Saudi nationals. Studies suggest that while the nationalization policy has led to an increase in employment among Saudis, it has also brought challenges for private sector companies, including increased labor costs and potential productivity losses (Peck, 2017). A balance between the goals of economic diversification, sustainable development, and labor market reforms is essential for Saudi Arabia's long-term economic stability and growth.

The Saudi Arabian labor market has a dualistic structure characterized by a primary sector that offers benefits such as competitive wages, structured career progression, and a skilled workforce predominantly employed by Saudi nationals. In contrast, the secondary sector comprises low-skilled positions with limited opportunities for advancement that rely heavily on migrant labor from regions such as Africa, South Asia, and Southeast Asia (Bergman, 2022). These workers often face social and economic challenges, including lower wages and limited mobility in the labor market (De Bel-Air, 2018). Understanding the dynamics between these sectors is crucial to understanding the complexity of employment in the Kingdom. This paper aims to shed light on the crucial role of migrant workers in sustaining the secondary labor market and explore strategies to align this workforce with the goals of Saudi Vision 2030, which aims to diversify the economy and reduce dependence on oil revenues (Saudi Vision 2030, 2016).

The primary labor market in Saudi Arabia is characterized by several key features that make it an attractive sector for workers seeking stability and upward mobility (Marx and Picot, 2020). Jobs in the sector tend to offer competitive pay, reflecting the importance of a skilled and specialized workforce. Bureaucratic rules and regulations govern labor relations and provide a structured framework for employees and employers. The primary market is characterized by the presence of a career ladder that allows individuals to move up through promotions and skills development (Clarke, 2008). One notable aspect is autonomy, which gives employees a sense of control over their tasks and decision-making processes.

In contrast, the secondary labor market in Saudi Arabia has clear characteristics that distinguish it from the primary sector. This market mainly offers low-skilled jobs that often require only low qualifications. Jobs in the secondary market are generally associated with lower wages, reflecting the nature of the tasks and the skill level required (Harvard Kennedy School, 2021; World Bank, 2015). The secondary sector is characterized by the lack of a clear career ladder, which limits opportunities for advancement. Autonomy at work is generally lower in the secondary market as workers often perform routine tasks under closer supervision (Brandi et al., 2023).

The differences between the primary and secondary labor markets extend not only to the characteristics of the individual sectors. One of the biggest differences lies in the wage scales, where the primary market offers much higher wages compared to the secondary market (Rubery, 1978). Advancement opportunities, which are essential for career and professional growth, are more common in the primary sector and provide workers with a structured path to advancement. In the secondary market, however, such opportunities often do not exist, so careers tend to stagnate. Work autonomy, a key factor for job satisfaction, is more pronounced in the primary labor market. Skilled workers in this sector often enjoy greater independence in decision-making and the execution of tasks. In contrast, labor structures in the secondary market tend to be more restrictive and limit the autonomy of workers with less skilled and routine-oriented tasks.

This study critically examines the role of labor migration in sustaining the secondary labor market in Saudi Arabia in the context of economic diversification and sustainable development. It highlights the importance of migrant workers, particularly from Africa, South Asia, and Southeast Asia, as an indispensable component of the Kingdom's labor market, supporting sectors that are often overlooked in policy frameworks. The study aims to assess the interaction between labor migration and the Kingdom's Vision 2030 goals, particularly in the transition to a diversified and sustainable economy. The main argument is that labor migrants are central to the functioning of the secondary labor market and that the alignment of migration policies with nationalization efforts and sustainable development goals is crucial for promoting long-term economic resilience. This research aims to provide actionable insights for integrating labor migration into economic transformation strategies while addressing the social and economic inequalities faced by migrant workers.

Migrant workers in the secondary labor market

In Saudi Arabia, the labor market is characterized by a dual structure that includes a primary sector with high-skilled, well-paid jobs, predominantly held by Saudi nationals, and a secondary sector with low-skilled, low-paid jobs, mainly held by migrant workers from Africa, South Asia, and Southeast Asia (De Bel-Air, 2018). This secondary labor market includes industries such as construction, domestic work, and the service sector, where employment conditions are often associated with limited job security, minimal benefits, and limited opportunities for advancement (International Labor Organization, 2021). Migrant workers in this sector often face problems such as inadequate legal protection, exploitative practices, and social marginalization (Human Rights Watch, 2008). The reliance on migrant labor in the secondary sector is an important aspect of Saudi Arabia's economic framework, which presents both opportunities and challenges related to the country's economic diversification and sustainable development goals (Saudi Vision 2030, 2016).

The secondary labor market in Saudi Arabia is a melting pot of diverse migrant workers, mainly from Africa, South Asia, and Southeast Asia. This multicultural workforce forms the backbone of industries requiring low-skilled labor and contributes significantly to the Kingdom's economic development (Ullah, 2017). The demographic composition reflects a variety of cultures, languages, and backgrounds, creating a dynamic and heterogeneous labor environment. According to data (World Bank, 2022), South Asian countries, including India, Pakistan, and Bangladesh, account for a significant proportion of labor migrants in the secondary market. African nations and Southeast Asian countries such as the Philippines and Indonesia also play a crucial role (Ullah, 2010). This diverse mix not only highlights the globalization of the workforce but also brings a wealth of experience and skills to the Saudi workforce.

Migrant workers in the Saudi Arabian secondary labor market face a number of social and economic challenges that are common to all nationalities. Socially, they often face language barriers and cultural adjustment difficulties, which can lead to social isolation. Many workers in this sector live in employer-provided housing complexes that are physically distant from urban residential areas, which can limit their social integration with the host community (Al-Kahtani, 2015). Economically, these workers typically receive low wages and have limited opportunities for career advancement, often due to restrictive labor policies and the nature of their employment sectors (Hertog, 2012). These conditions are compounded by limited access to social services, further marginalizing migrant workers within the Kingdom's socio-economic framework (Al-Dosary and Rahman, 2005). The nature of jobs in the secondary market often involves manual labor in the construction, manufacturing, and service sectors, resulting in physically demanding working conditions (Badri, 2012). Despite the hardships, these migrant workers play an indispensable role in supporting the Saudi economy and remit a significant portion of their earnings to their home countries.

Since the mid-1970s, Saudi Arabia has experienced a significant influx of migrant workers, particularly in the secondary labor market, highlighting a structural dependence on foreign labor. Sectors such as construction, domestic services, and retail are highly dependent on the flexibility and cost efficiencies offered by migrant labor (Kinninmont, 2017). This dependency is not just a temporary measure, but a systemic feature that is deeply embedded in the Kingdom's economic framework (Hertog, 2012). Saudi Vision 2030 recognizes the essential role of the secondary labor market in sustaining economic growth and aims to diversify the economy while reducing unemployment among Saudi nationals (Saudi Vision 2030, 2016). However, nationalization efforts such as the Nitaqat program face the challenge of fully replacing foreign workers due to the complexity of certain industries and the existing skills gap among the local workforce (Al-Dosary and Rahman, 2005).

The structural demand for migrant labor remains, highlighting the need for pragmatic policies that acknowledge this reality and harness it for the benefit of economic diversification and labor market sustainability in Saudi Arabia. The composition, shared experiences and structural demand for foreign labor in the secondary market underscore the indispensable role of migrant workers in the Saudi Arabian labor landscape (World Bank, 2022). A deep understanding of these dynamics is critical to formulating policies that not only address the challenges faced by migrant workers but also harness their potential to contribute meaningfully to the realization of Saudi Vision 2030.

A major challenge for migrant workers in the secondary labor market in Saudi Arabia is the absence of trade unions. While the primary sector benefits from their bargaining power, the secondary market functions without this important support structure. Migrant workers, most of whom are in low-skilled jobs, are in a precarious position due to the lack of collective bargaining power. The absence of trade unions denies migrant workers a platform to collectively voice their concerns, leaving them with little opportunity to fight back against injustices in the workplace (McCormack et al., 2015). Without the ability to negotiate for better working conditions, fair wages, and better benefits, migrant workers are often exploited and treated unequally in the secondary market.

The impact of the absence of trade unions goes beyond the immediate challenges faced by migrant workers. Workers' rights, which are an essential part of any thriving labor market, are compromised by the absence of collective bargaining mechanisms. Migrant workers are particularly vulnerable to exploitative practices such as long working hours, inadequate living conditions, and insufficient legal protection (Ullah, 2010; 2017). The lack of collective bargaining exacerbates the power imbalance between employers and migrant workers and makes it difficult for the latter to demand fair wages or better working conditions. This not only affects the welfare of individual workers but also hinders the overall development of a sustainable and equitable labor market.

Low wages are a pervasive problem for migrant workers in the Saudi Arabian secondary market. Many of these workers come to the Kingdom in search of better economic opportunities, only to find themselves trapped in jobs that offer meager remuneration (Auwal, 2010). The economic challenges arise from the significant gap between the cost of living and the wages of migrant workers. The economic difficulties are exacerbated by factors such as withholding of wages, delayed payments, and inadequate legal remedies. These problems not only affect workers' financial well-being but also hinder their ability to send remittances to their home countries, which are an important source of income for many families in the countries of origin (Mak et al., 2021).

Migrant workers often find themselves in dead-end jobs with limited opportunities for advancement. The secondary labor market usually offers jobs with little to no opportunities for skills development or upward mobility (Damelang et al., 2021). Migrant workers, despite their qualifications and aspirations, are faced with a glass ceiling that restricts their career progression. This lack of advancement opportunities not only inhibits individual potential but also contributes to a cycle of dependence on low-skilled jobs. Without opportunities to improve skills and career progression, it can be difficult for migrant workers to break free from the constraints of the secondary market, perpetuating a system that does not contribute to long-term economic sustainability.

Nationalization drive

Saudi Arabia has long struggled with the theoretical and empirical challenges associated with nationalizations initiatives aimed at replacing foreign workers with Saudi nationals in the labor market. The main objective of such initiatives is to reduce unemployment among Saudi nationals, increase the skill level of the labor force and promote economic self-sufficiency (Fakeeh, 2009). However, the complexity of implementing these strategies is becoming increasingly apparent.

Theoretical challenges arise from the inherent differences between the characteristics of the primary and secondary labor markets. The primary market, which is characterized by higher wages, opportunities for advancement and skilled positions, attracts a different pool of applicants than the secondary market, which relies heavily on low-skilled foreign workers (Fakeeh, 2009). Jobs in the secondary market are often manual or routine tasks that may not match the desires or qualifications of the Saudi labor force. This mismatch in skills and preferences poses a major theoretical challenge when it comes to achieving a seamless transition from foreign to domestic labor in the secondary market.

Empirically, the extent of foreign labor's contribution to the Saudi economy is a formidable obstacle. Migrant labor, particularly from Africa, South Asia, and Southeast Asia, plays a central role in sustaining the secondary market (Ramady, 2010). Their sheer numbers and the diverse skills they bring with them make them an integral part of industries ranging from construction to services. An abrupt displacement of this foreign labor force without simultaneous efforts to train and integrate Saudi nationals for these roles could lead to disruption in critical sectors of the economy (Bremmer, 2004). The challenges associated with nationalization efforts have not gone unnoticed in Saudi political circles. Government officials and policymakers acknowledge the importance of addressing the constraints associated with trying to replace foreign labor with local labor, especially in the secondary labor market. This realization is based on a realistic assessment of the structural demand for foreign labor that has become deeply entrenched over the decades (Madhi and Barrientos, 2003).

The Vision 2030 initiative led by Crown Prince Mohammed bin Salman recognizes the need for a nationalization approach. While the Vision places emphasis on developing a skilled and competitive Saudi workforce, it also recognizes the indispensable role that foreign labor plays in supporting economic activity (Madhi and Barrientos, 2003). Policy makers are aware of the fact that a sudden and large-scale replacement of foreign labor could have negative consequences for economic stability and growth.

Recognizing this, the Saudi authorities have introduced programs and policies aimed at balancing the interests of both local and expatriate workers (Al-Asfour and Khan, 2014). Skills development initiatives, vocational training programs and efforts to improve the employability of Saudi nationals in the secondary market reflect a strategic approach to overcoming the limitations of nationalizations efforts (Looney, 2004). The theoretical and empirical challenges of replacing foreign workers with Saudi nationals in the secondary labor market are recognized in Saudi policy circles (Koyame-Marsh, 2016). The pragmatic approach requires careful consideration to ensure that the objectives of economic diversification and labor market sustainability are pursued without jeopardizing the stability and productivity of critical sectors that are heavily dependent on foreign workers (Hertog, 2014).

The implementation of the Saudization policy, which aims to increase the employment of Saudi nationals, has sparked considerable debate about its impact on migrant workers and the sustainability of the secondary labor market. Critics argue that this policy could disrupt sectors that rely heavily on foreign labor, leading to labor shortages and increased operating costs. For example, the construction and hospitality industries, which are highly dependent on foreign labor, could face problems maintaining productivity and quality of service if they are forced to replace experienced foreign workers with less experienced local workers (Hertog, 2014). In addition, the abrupt decrease in the number of migrant workers could have a negative impact on the economy as they contribute significantly to various sectors (Al-Asfour and Khan, 2014).

For comparison, other Middle Eastern countries have implemented similar nationalizations strategies with varying results. The United Arab Emirates (UAE) has focused its Emiratization policy on integrating nationals into the private sector. However, the UAE has faced the challenge of balancing the employment of nationals with the need to maintain industries that rely on skilled migrant labor (Randeree, 2012). Similarly, Oman's Oman Initiative aims to reduce dependence on foreign labor by promoting local employment. Despite these efforts, certain sectors continue to rely on foreign labor due to skill shortages in the local workforce (Zerovec and Bontenbal, 2011). These cases illustrate the complexity of implementing nationalization measures without jeopardizing economic stability and development.

Gaps in secondary labor market sustainability

The Saudi economy has changed significantly, particularly in its efforts to move away from oil dependence. In 2022, revenues from oil exports reached a remarkable $325 billion due to high oil prices as a result of geopolitical tensions, including the war in Ukraine. However, oil's share of total exports declined from 84 percent in 2012–2013 to 74 percent in 2022, reflecting Saudi Arabia's ongoing diversification efforts (see Figure 11.1). This transition underlines the growing importance of sectors such as petrochemicals and

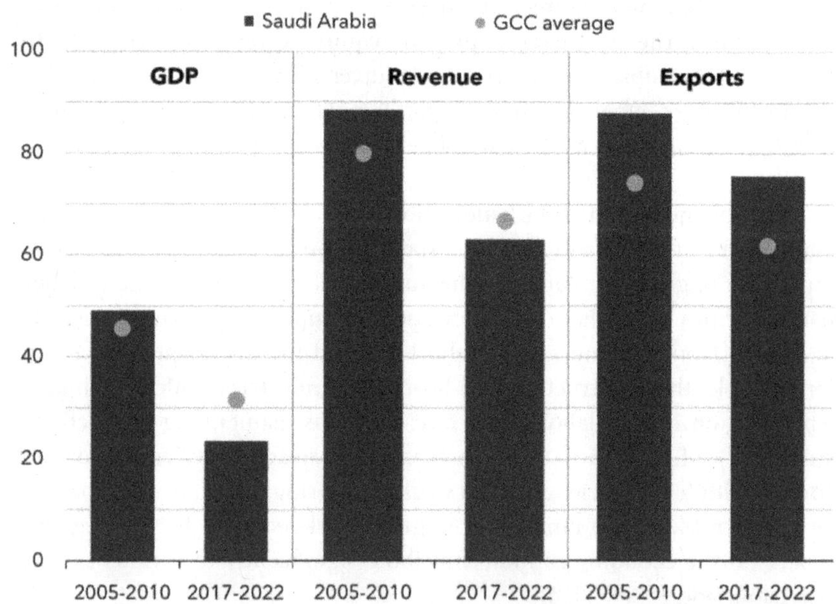

Figure 11.1. Changing composition of Saudi Arabia's exports, showing the gradual decline in oil's share and the rise of non-oil sectors. Source: Rehman and Mati, 2023.

tourism, whose share of exports increased from 9 percent and 2 percent, respectively, in 2012–2013 to 12 percent and 5 percent in 2022. The promotion of these sectors is in line with Vision 2030, a strategic framework that aims to reduce dependence on oil, promote private sector growth, and maintain the secondary labor market (Vision 2030, 2022).

Private sector growth and contributions to the non-oil economy underscore the critical role of labor market policies, including Saudization, in shaping labor market dynamics. The private sector's share of GDP rose to 39 percent in nominal terms by 2022, and the non-oil sector contributed 56 percent to GDP, up from 52 percent a decade earlier. While these changes indicate progress, sectors such as tourism, hospitality, and construction remain heavily reliant on migrant labor due to the limited availability of skilled Saudi workers. Reconciling Saudization efforts with the need for foreign expertise remains a challenge. Critics argue that replacing experienced migrant workers with less experienced locals in key sectors jeopardizes productivity and sustainability, especially in the secondary labor market (Hertog, 2014; Al-Asfour and Khan, 2014).

A comparative look shows that other countries in the Middle East are facing similar challenges. The United Arab Emirates' Emiratization policy has boosted employment in the country, but has struggled to reduce dependence on foreign labor in labor-intensive sectors. Oman's Omanization initiative was also met with resistance from companies citing a lack of local labor (Randeree, 2012; Zerovec and Bontenbal, 2011). These cases suggest that while nationalization policies aim to increase local labor participation, their success depends on complementary investments in education, vocational training, and sector-specific skills development. It is crucial for Saudi Arabia to find this balance in order to achieve economic diversification and sustainability in the labor market.

Saudi Vision 2030 is a transformative concept that sets the course for the development of a dynamic and diversified economy in Saudi Arabia. Launched in 2016 by Crown Prince Mohammed bin Salman, this ambitious vision aims to move Saudi Arabia away from its traditional dependence on oil revenues and promote a sustainable and globally competitive nation. The vision strives for a vibrant society characterized by a high quality of life, social cohesion, and cultural enrichment. Initiatives under this pillar include improving leisure and cultural offerings, promoting social engagement, and investing in education and health. At its core, Vision 2030 is based on three fundamental pillars: a vibrant society, a thriving economy, and an ambitious nation.

The economic pillar aims to reduce dependence on oil revenues by promoting a diverse and sustainable economy (Crystal, 1990). Key objectives include the privatization of state-owned enterprises, the promotion of the private sector, and the attraction of foreign investment. Strategic partnerships and the development of key sectors such as tourism, entertainment, and technology play a central role in achieving economic dynamism. Vision 2030 envisions Saudi Arabia as an ambitious nation that actively contributes to global progress. This includes strengthening the Kingdom's international reputation, promoting innovation and entrepreneurship, and fostering a culture of excellence and achievement.

Reducing dependence on oil: Economic diversification is a cornerstone of Vision 2030, which aims to reduce the Kingdom's heavy dependence on oil revenues. By developing non-oil sectors, the aim is to create a more resilient and adaptable economy that is able to withstand global economic fluctuations. Saudi Arabia's economy is undergoing a transformation as it implements reforms to reduce dependence on oil, diversify revenue streams, and improve competitiveness. This year marks an important turning point as it is the halfway point of Saudi Arabia's ambitious Vision 2030 (Rehman and Mati, 2023).

Innovation and knowledge-based industries

Vision 2030 places a strong emphasis on the promotion of innovation and knowledge-based industries. By investing in research and development, promoting entrepreneurship and utilizing technology, Saudi Arabia aims to position itself as a hub for innovation in the region. The sustainability of the secondary labor market is closely linked to the development of a skilled and competitive national workforce. Vision 2030 prioritizes education and training to equip Saudi nationals with the necessary skills for meaningful participation in various sectors, including those sectors that traditionally rely on foreign labor (Aldossari, 2020).

Promoting foreign direct investment (FDI): In order to drive economic growth and diversification, Vision 2030 actively promotes foreign direct investment. By creating a business-friendly environment, removing bureaucratic hurdles, and offering incentives, the vision aims to attract international investors who will contribute to the Kingdom's economic transformation (Derendinger and Frank, 2023).

Rationalizing the flow of migrant workers: While Vision 2030 focuses primarily on strengthening the Saudi workforce, it also acknowledges the existing and ongoing contribution of foreign workers, particularly in the secondary labor market (Hasanov et al., 2021; Lamia, 2020). The vision recognizes the need to streamline the inflow of migrant workers to ensure that their integration supports, rather than hinders, the broader goals of economic diversification and labor market sustainability. Vision 2030 recognizes the structural demand for foreign workers in certain sectors. Rather than viewing foreign labor as a temporary solution, the vision aims to strategically integrate them and ensure that their role aligns with broader economic goals.

Integration and inclusivity: The initiatives under Vision 2030 aim to promote a more inclusive society in which both Saudi nationals and migrant workers contribute synergistically to economic growth. Efforts to improve living conditions, labor rights, and social inclusion underscore the Vision's commitment to building a diverse and harmonious workforce. Saudi Vision 2030 represents a paradigm shift for the Kingdom, steering it towards a future characterized by economic resilience, social vibrancy, and global competitiveness (Bradley and Scheck, 2020). By understanding the key pillars and objectives and recognizing the central role of economic diversification, the vision lays the foundation for bridging the gap in secondary labor market sustainability. Through a balanced approach that values both domestic and foreign contributions, Vision 2030 aims to create a holistic and resilient economy that will stand the test of time.

The case of Bangladeshi labor migration

Addressing the challenges posed by the secondary labor market requires a pragmatic recognition of the structural demand for foreign labor in Saudi Arabia. The steady growth of the migrant population, particularly from Africa, South Asia, and Southeast Asia, underscores the essential role that this labor force plays in sustaining various sectors (Bel-Air, 2018). This structural demand is due to the unique skills, work ethic, and adaptability that foreign labor brings to industries such as construction, hospitality, and services.

Recognizing this structural demand requires a shift in perspective from viewing migrant workers as a temporary solution to recognizing them as a long-term and integral part of the Saudi workforce. Policy makers need to recognize the economic contribution, diversity, and flexibility that foreign workers bring to the labor market. By recognizing this need, efforts can be directed towards the optimal integration of migrant workers as part of the Saudi Vision 2030.

Aligning migrant labor flows with the overarching goals of Saudi Vision 2030 is crucial for sustainable economic development. Rather than viewing migrant labor as a stopgap measure, there is an opportunity to leverage their presence to support and enhance the goals of the vision. This alignment can be achieved through various strategic initiatives. Investing in skills training programs that improve the skills of migrant workers is in line with Saudi Vision 2030, which aims to create a highly skilled and competitive workforce. By offering training in areas that complement the needs of the secondary labor market, such as construction techniques, service industry skills, and language skills, migrant workers can contribute more effectively to the Saudi economy (Alanazi and Benlaria, 2023).

With their diverse skill sets, migrant workers can play a critical role in supporting Saudi Arabia's economic diversification initiatives. The strategic placement of foreign labor in sectors earmarked for growth and expansion can contribute to a more resilient and adaptable economy (Asfahani et al., 2023). Aligning migration flows with the target sectors identified in Vision 2030 ensures that foreign labor becomes an integral part of the broader economic vision. To ensure harmonious integration of migrant workers, social policies should be geared towards promoting inclusion (Ullah, 2022). Recognizing the contributions of foreign workers and promoting cultural exchange can create a more cohesive and collaborative work environment (Montiel et al., 2021). Such initiatives are in line with the broader societal goals of Vision 2030, which promotes a diverse and cosmopolitan Saudi society.

Bangladeshi migrant workers have been an important part of the Saudi secondary labor market for decades (Ullah, 2010). They are mainly employed in the construction, hospitality, and low-skilled service sectors and make up a significant proportion of the foreign labor force. The motivation of Bangladeshi workers to seek employment in Saudi Arabia is often driven by economic factors as they seek better opportunities and remittances to support their families back home (Rahman, 2012). Bangladeshi migrant workers in Saudi Arabia face challenges such as language barriers, cultural differences, and sometimes exploitation. However, their contribution to the Saudi economy is immense (Chy et al., 2023; Sha, H., and Bhuiyan, 2022). They play an important role in construction projects, contribute to the growth of the hospitality industry and play a crucial role in maintaining the operations of various industries.

The remittances that these workers send to Bangladesh contribute significantly to the country's economy and illustrate the interconnectedness of labor migration and economic development. Despite the challenges they face, Bangladeshi migrant workers demonstrate resilience and commitment, highlighting the potential for positive outcomes through strategic interventions (Chy et al., 2023). The Bangladeshi case study offers valuable insights that can be applied to the broader context of labor migration in

Saudi Arabia. Understanding the particular challenges faced by this group sheds light on the necessary adjustments to policy and support systems. Language training, cultural integration, and combating exploitation are crucial factors in improving the overall well-being and productivity of migrant workers. The case study shows the importance of recognizing and utilizing the unique skills of these workers. By aligning its policies with the needs and contributions of specific migrant groups, Saudi Arabia can develop more targeted and effective strategies to integrate migrant workers into the secondary market, promoting sustainable economic growth in line with Saudi Vision 2030.

Conclusion and policy considerations

The sustainable integration of migrant workers into the Saudi Arabian secondary labor market, which is in line with the goals of Saudi Vision 2030, requires a multi-faceted approach. Addressing the challenges and promoting a harmonious working environment for both migrant and local workers require strategic policies that prioritize integration, cooperation, and the protection of workers' rights. Effective integration strategies are essential to bridge the gap between migrant workers and the local community. Initiatives should focus on promoting cultural understanding, fostering integration, and creating platforms for social interaction. Workplaces can be encouraged to implement diversity training programs to ensure that both Saudi nationals and migrant workers appreciate and respect each other's cultural differences. Social events, language courses, and community engagement programs can contribute to a more cohesive working environment.

Supporting migrant workers through skills development initiatives strengthens their contribution to the Saudi economy while providing them with tools for personal and professional development. Training programs should be tailored to the needs of the secondary labor market and provide migrant workers with skills that meet industry requirements. Collaboration with vocational training institutions and private companies can facilitate targeted skills development that enables migrant workers to better adapt to changing job requirements and promote mobility within the workforce.

A collaborative approach between Saudi Arabia and the countries sending migrant workers is crucial for the smooth functioning of the secondary labor market. Bilateral agreements should be made to facilitate the ethical recruitment of labor and ensure transparency and fairness in the recruitment process. Regular dialogue between governments can address issues such as the protection of workers' rights, simplified migration procedures, and dispute resolution mechanisms. A cooperative framework should emphasize the creation of a win-win situation for all parties involved. Saudi companies benefit from the skills and labor of migrant workers, while sending countries benefit from remittances and opportunities for their workers. Policies should ensure that the contributions of migrant workers are recognized and fairly compensated to foster a sense of mutual benefit. This approach promotes a positive image of Saudi Arabia as an ethical employer and enhances its standing on the world stage.

The representation of workers in decision-making processes is an essential factor in addressing concerns and fostering a sense of agency among both domestic and migrant workers. Establishing channels for effective communication, such as grievance mechanisms and workers' councils, gives workers the opportunity to voice their opinions and find solutions to workplace challenges. This inclusive approach increases job satisfaction and contributes to a more harmonious working environment.

The protection of labor rights is a cornerstone of fostering equitable and sustainable labor market practices. This includes the rigorous enforcement of fair wages and the assurance of safe and dignified working conditions for all employees, regardless of nationality. Establishing stringent regulatory frameworks is imperative to curtail exploitative practices, ensuring that all workers receive equitable remuneration for their contributions. Regular inspections and audits are essential mechanisms for monitoring adherence to labor standards, safeguarding a work environment characterized by fairness, safety, and inclusivity. Such policy interventions are not merely ethical imperatives but also pivotal to cultivating a balanced and sustainable labor market in Saudi Arabia. By emphasizing integration, collaboration, and the robust protection of workers' rights, the Kingdom can effectively harness the diverse expertise of its migrant workforce. This approach would foster a collaborative environment where both local and foreign workers can contribute synergistically toward realizing the objectives of Saudi Vision 2030.

Addressing the challenges and leveraging the opportunities within the secondary labor market, particularly from the perspective of migrant workers, is vital to achieving the transformative goals of Saudi Vision 2030. Recognizing the enduring structural demand for foreign labor, while simultaneously integrating migrant workers into the broader Saudi workforce, constitutes a critical step toward building a resilient and diversified economy. Drawing on the case study of Bangladeshi migrant workers, this research provides valuable insights that extend beyond a single demographic group. It underscores the necessity of inclusive, well-crafted policies that acknowledge the indispensable role of migrant labor in the secondary market. Such strategies will not only support Saudi Arabia's economic ambitions but also enhance the socio-economic well-being of its diverse workforce.

Bibliography

Alanazi, Adel Saber, and Houcine Benlaria. (2023). Bridging higher education outcomes and labor market needs: A study of Jouf University graduates in the context of Vision 2030. *Social Sciences* 12(6), 360. https://doi.org/10.3390/socsci12060360

Al-Asfour, A., and Khan, S. A. (2014). Workforce localization in the Kingdom of Saudi Arabia: Issues and challenges. *Human Resource Development International*, 17(2), 243–53. https://doi.org/10.1080/13678868.2013.836783

Al-Dosary, A. S., and Rahman, S. M. (2005). Saudization (localization)—A critical review. *Human Resource Development International*, 8(4), 495–502.

Aldossari, A. S. (2020). Vision 2030 and reducing the stigma of vocational and technical training among Saudi Arabian students. *Empirical Res Voc Ed Train* 12(3). https://doi.org/10.1186/s40461-020-00089-6

Al-Kahtani, S. N. (2015). The impact of social isolation on the mental health of labor migrants in Saudi Arabia. *Journal of International Migration and Integration*, 16(3), 593–608.

Alshanbri, N., M. M. A. Khalfan, T. Maqsood, and A. Keane (2015). Saudization in construction-related companies in Saudi Arabia: A case study. *Australasian Journal of Construction Economics and Building*, 15(2), 1–15.

Asfahani, Ahmed M., Ghadeer Alsobahi, and Dina Abdullah Dahlan. (2023). Navigating the Saudi gig economy: The role of human resource practices in enhancing job satisfaction and career sustainability. *Sustainability* 15(23), 16406. https://doi.org/10.3390/su152316406

Auwal, M. A. (2010). Ending the exploitation of migrant workers in the Gulf. *The Fletcher Forum of World Affairs*, 34(2), 87–108. http://www.jstor.org/stable/45289506

Badri, Amira Yousif Babiker (2012). Social network among migrants in Saudia Arabia: Opportunities and implications. Third Gulf Research meeting. 11–14 July 2012. Cambridge University, Cambridge.

Bergman, M. E. (2022). Labour market policies and support for populist radical right parties: the role of nostalgic producerism, occupational risk, and feedback effects. *European Political Science Review*. 14(4), 520–43. https://doi.org/10.1017/S175577392200025X

Bradley, Hope, and Justin Scheck. (2020). *Blood and Oil: Mohammed Bin Salman's Ruthless Quest for Global Power*. Hachette.

Brandi, U., J. De Norre, T. Roosalu, M. Raudsepp, and A. Khadatovich (2023). Working and learning in the retail sector: A cross-country comparative view. In: J. Holford, P. Boyadjieva, S. Clancy, G. Hefler, and I. Studená (eds.), *Lifelong Learning, Young Adults and the Challenges of Disadvantage in Europe*.

Palgrave Studies in Adult Education and Lifelong Learning. Cham: Palgrave Macmillan. https://doi.org/10.1007/978-3-031-14109-6_11

Bremmer, I. (2004). The Saudi paradox. *World Policy Journal*, 21(3), 23–30. http://www.jstor.org/stable/40210233

Chy, M. T., Md. K. Uddin, and H. U. Ahmmed (2023). Forced returnee Bangladeshi female migrant domestic workers and their social reintegration experiences. *Current Sociology*, 71(1), 133–151. https://doi.org/10.1177/00113921211048533

Clarke, M. (2008). Understanding and managing employability in changing career contexts. *Journal of European Industrial Training*, 32(4), 258–84. https://doi.org/10.1108/03090590810871379

Crystal, Jill. 1990. *Oil and Politics in the Gulf*. Cambridge: Cambridge University Press.

Damelang, A., S. Ebensperger and F. Stumpf (2021). Immigrants' labour market disadvantages across Western Europe: The role of composition and context. *International Migration & Integration*, 22, 1525–50. https://doi.org/10.1007/s12134-021-00823-3

De Bel-Air, F. (2018). Demography, migration, and the labour market in Saudi Arabia. Gulf labour markets, migration and population. Gulf Labour Markets, Migration, and Population Programme. https://gulfmigration.grc.net/media/pubs/exno/GLMM_EN_2018_05.pdf

Derendinger Madison and Frank Brian. (2023). Visions of diversity: The Kingdom of Saudi Arabia's Vision 2030 and its efforts to build a diversified economy. Working Paper Series, International Trade & Economic Diplomacy. California: Middlebury Institute of International Studies.

Fakeeh, Manal Soliman (2009). Saudization as a solution for unemployment the case of Jeddah western region. Thesis. Submitted in fulfillment of the requirements for the degree of Doctorate in Business Administration. University of Glasgow Business School.

Harvard Kennedy School. (2021). The Labor Market in Saudi Arabia: Background, Areas of Progress, and Insights for the Future. Harvard: HKS.

Hasanov, Fakhri J., I. Jeyhun Mikayilov, Muhammad Javid, Moayad Al-Rasasi, Frederick Joutz, and Mohammed B. Alabdullah. (2021). Sectoral employment analysis for Saudi Arabia. *Applied Economics* 53(45), 5267–80. https://doi.org/10.1080/00036846.2021.1922590.

Hertog, S. (2012). A Comparative assessment of labor market nationalization policies in the GCC. In Hertog, S. (Ed.), *National Employment, Migration and Education in the GCC*, 65–106. Berlin: Gerlach Press.

Hertog, S. (2014). Arab Gulf states: An assessment of nationalization policies. In R. Baldwin (Ed.), *Adapting to Labor Market Change*, 58–72). Oxford: Oxford University Press.

Human Rights Watch (2008). "As if I am not human": Abuses against Asian domestic workers in Saudi Arabia. Human Rights Watch. https://www.hrw.org/report/2008/07/08/if-i-am-not-human/abuses-against-asian-domestic-workers-saudi-arabia

International Labor Organization (2021). Labor market trends and policy responses in the GCC: The case of Saudi Arabia. International Labor Organization. https://www.ilo.org/beirut/publications/WCMS_821727/lang--en/index.htm

Kinninmont, Jane. (2017). *Vision 2030 and Saudi Arabia's Social Contract Austerity and Transformation*. London: The Royal Institute of International Affairs, Chatham House.

Koyame-Marsh, R. O. (2016). Saudization and the Nitaqat programs: Overview and performance. *Journal of Economics and Sustainable Development*, 7(6), 46–56.

Lamia. Jamel. (2020). The relation between tourism and economic growth: a case of Saudi Arabia as an emerging tourism destination. *Virtual Economics*, 3(4), 29–47.

Looney, R. E. (2004). Saudization and sound economic reforms: Are the two compatible? *Strategic Insights*, 3(2), 1–15.

Madhi Salah T. and Barrientos Armando. (2003). Saudisation and Employment in Saudi Arabia. *Career Development International*, 8(2), 70–7. https://doi.org/10.1108/13620430310465471

Mak, J., C Zimmerman, and B. Roberts (2021). "I had tears in my eyes but I just left without looking back." A qualitative study of migration-related stressors amongst Nepali male labor migrants. *Journal of Migration Health*, 25(4),100042. https://doi.org/ 10.1016/j.jmh.2021.100042.

Marx, P., and G. Picot, (2020). Three approaches to labor-market vulnerability and political preferences. *Political Science Research and Methods*, 8(2): 356–61.

McCormack, Samantha, Jacqueline Joudo Larsen, and Hana Abul Husn (2015). The other migrant crisis: Protecting migrant workers against exploitation in the Middle East and North Africa. A Policy Research Report. Geneva: Inernational Organization for Migration.

Montiel, I., A. Cuervo-Cazurra, J. Park et al. (2021). Implementing the United Nations' Sustainable Development Goals in international business. *Journal of International Business Studies* 52, 999–1030. https://doi.org/10.1057/s41267-021-00445-y

Peck, J. (2017). Neoliberal Saudi Arabia: Making up the new national worker. *Antipode*, 49(4), 1035–57.

Rahman, Md Mizanur (2012). Bangladeshi labour migration to the Gulf states: Patterns of recruitment and processes. *Canadian Journal of Development Studies* 33(2), 214–30. https://doi.org/10.1080/02255189.2012.689612

Ramady, Mohamed A. (2010). *The Saudi Arabian Economy: Policies, Achievements, and Challenges*. Netherlands: Springer.

Randeree, K. (2012). Workforce nationalization in the Gulf Cooperation Council states. Center for International and Regional Studies, Georgetown University School of Foreign Service in Qatar. https://doi.org/10.2139/ssrn.2382440

Rehman, Sidra, and Amine Mati. (2023). Saudi Arabia's economy grows as it diversifies. International Monetary Fund. https://www.imf.org/en/News/Articles/2023/09/28/cf-saudi-arabias-economy-grows-as-it-diversifies

Rubery, J. (1978). Structured labor markets, worker organisation and low pay. *Cambridge Journal of Economics*, 2(1), 17–36. http://www.jstor.org/stable/23596684

Saudi Vision 2030 (2016). Kingdom of Saudi Arabia. Homepage. https://www.vision2030.gov.sa/

Sha, H., and M. R. A. Bhuiyan (2022). "Amar beton khub e kom": The role of commercial recruitment intermediaries in reinforcing gendered and racialised inequalities. *Zanj: The Journal of Critical Global South Studies*, 5(1/2), 164–92. https://www.jstor.org/stable/48676312

Ullah, AKM Ahsan. (2010). (First edition). *Rationalizing Migration Decisions: Labor Migrants in South and South-East Asia*. Aldershot: Ashgate.

Ullah, AKM Ahsan. (2017). Irregular Migration from Bangladesh to the Gulf: Is combatting it a governance challenge? In Philippe Fargues and Nasra M. Shah (Eds.), *Irregular Migration to The Gulf: The Role of Legislation, Policies and Practices*, 377–401. Cambridge: Cambridge University Press.

Ullah, AKM Ahsan. (2022). The culture of migration in Southeast Asia: Acculturation, Enculturation or Deculturation? *Journal for Cultural Research*, 26(2), 184–99. https://doi.org/10.1080/14797585.2022.2097881

Vision 2030 (2022). Saudi Vision 2030: The Kingdom's transformation strategy. Vision 2030 Official Website. https://www.vision2030.gov.sa

World Bank (2015). Data on Government Expenditure on Education, Trends in International Mathematics and Science Study (TIMSS) 2015, and Labor Force Survey Q4 2018. General Authority for Statistics. World Bank.

World Bank (2022). Migration and Remittances Data. World Bank. https://www.worldbank.org/en/topic/migration/overview#:~:text=In%202022%2C%20remittance%20flows%20to,the%20total%20of%20development%20aid.

Zerovec, M., and M. Bontenbal (2011). Labor nationalization policies in Oman: Implications for Omani and migrant women workers. *Asian and Pacific Migration Journal*, 20(3–4), 365–87. https://doi.org/10.1177/011719681102000304

12

Foreign Property Ownership in the Gulf: A Comparative Study of South Asian Migrants in the Kingdom of Saudi Arabia, the United Arab Emirates and Qatar

Lakshmi Venugopal Menon

In the Gulf Cooperation Council (GCC) states (which consist of Bahrain, Kuwait, Oman, Qatar, the Kingdom of Saudi Arabia, and the United Arab Emirates (UAE)), foreign property ownership is a complex and dynamic subject that involves a combination of legal, historical, and economic factors. Each of the GCC states has its own unique policies and regulations regarding foreign property ownership, which reflect its unique social and economic context. Historically, the reliance on oil and gas revenues has been characteristic of the Gulf region. Although these rentier incomes led to rapid economic development and urbanization, this dependence also made these states highly susceptible to the different fluctuations in global energy markets. To offset the negative impact of such fluctuations and dependence on the hydrocarbon incomes, many GCC states have diversified their economies by investing in different sectors such as tourism, finance, real estate, culture, and education (Siriopoulos, et al. 2021).

In 2021, the Kingdom of Saudi Arabia (KSA) issued a directive allowing foreigners and legal residents of the Kingdom to purchase a single property, albeit with certain conditions. The previous year, the state of Qatar established the Office for Non-Qatari Real Estate Ownership, marking the peak in interest and formal transactions that occurred in the light of FIFA 2022, despite a law allowing non-Qataris to purchase real estate in Qatar being in place since 2004. In 2006, the UAE first spelt out the designated areas where non-UAE nationals could own property (Al Tamimi & Co., 2017). This research aims to comparatively study foreign property ownership trends amongst South Asian migrants residing in the KSA, the UAE, and Qatar.

Discussing the plausibility of a greater level of integration due to foreign property ownership, this paper would explore the foreign property ownership trends through a survey investigating the interest, opportunities, considerations, and concerns in such investments, on a sample including middle-class, upper-middle-class, and affluent class South Asians who work, have worked, own businesses or investment, and/or reside in the KSA, the UAE, and/or Qatar. The South Asians, particularly Indians, are a substantial force with respect to foreign property ownership in the GCC states. For instance, approximately 20 percent of Dubai's offshore real estate[1] (which amounts to at least $146 billion in foreign wealth) is owned by investors from India, followed by UK citizens (10 percent) (Alstadsaeter et al., 2022).

The survey has a sample size of 137 participants who are South Asians (predominantly Indians and some Pakistanis) and who are currently or have previously lived in the states of Qatar, the KSA, and/or the UAE. The participants belonged to different age groups (8 or 5.8 percent of which belonged to the 18–25 age group, 62 or 45.3 percent of which belonged to the 26–40 age group, 47 or 34.3 percent of which belonged to the 41–55 age group, and 20 or 14.6 percent of which belonged to the above 56 age group). The numbers show that the vast majority, 45.3 percent, belonged to the 26–40 age category, which shows the working group of the sample, which is in its early and mid-career level. With respect to gender, the sample is largely balanced with an almost equal representation of males (65 individuals or 47.4 percent) and females (71 individuals or 51.8 percent); one of the participants chose the "prefer to not say" option. With respect to occupation, 27 or 19.9 percent of the respondents belong to the education sector (are students or working in the education sector); 48 or 35.3 percent of the respondents belong to the corporate sector; and the vast majority of the respondents, 61 or 44.9 percent of the respondents are doing business in the respective countries. With respect to nationality, the vast majority of the respondents, 128 or 93.4 percent, are Indians, and the remaining 9 or 6.5 percent are Pakistanis.

Of the respondents, 74 or 54 percent are presently living in Qatar, 41 or 29.9 percent are presently living in the UAE, 4 or 2.9 percent are presently living in Saudi Arabia, and the remaining respondents are presently living in their home countries such as India, or have moved on to other countries such as Oman, Germany, the United States, and Canada.

Although this paper focuses on the foreign property ownership policies in Qatar, the UAE, and the KSA, the paper would commence through a comprehensive appraisal of the foreign property ownership policies in the different GCC states. For this purpose, as there are few peer-reviewed publications on foreign property ownership in the GCC states, this paper also relies on government policies, government announcements, online articles, and recent news sources.

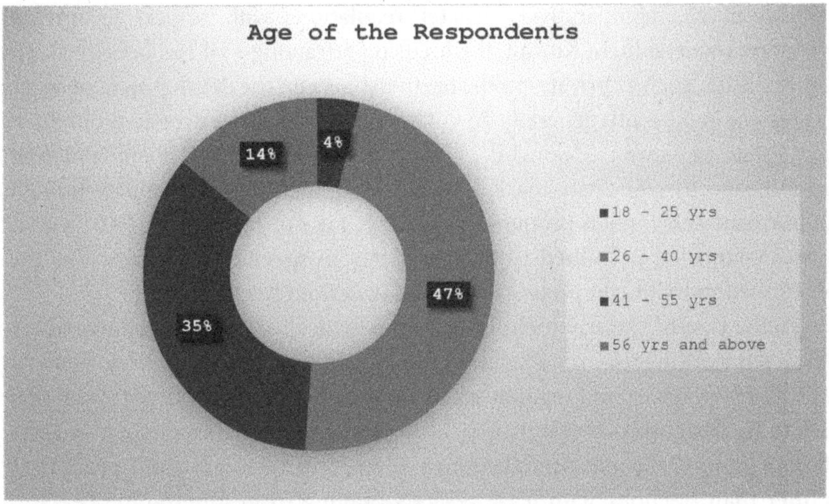

Figure 12.1. Age at which the respondents moved to Qatar, KSA, or UAE.

Foreign property ownership in the GCC states

Foreign property ownership has evolved in the GCC region with the growing aspirations of the states and efforts for economic diversification. Many efforts have been made to attract foreign direct investment (FDI) in these countries, among which foreign property ownership has also featured (Hussein, 2009; Azzam and Rettab, 2011).

FDI plays a crucial role in building a sustainable and diversified knowledge-based economy in the UAE (Mina, 2014). When discussing foreign property ownership, a regional focal point for foreign investment in real estate has been the UAE, particularly Abu Dhabi and Dubai (as seen in Figures 12.1–12.4); both of these emirates have established freehold zones such as the Business Bay area, Dubai Marina, and Palm Jumeirah, wherein non-UAE nationals can own property. In these designated zones, foreigners can own both commercial and residential properties on a freehold basis. This provides the property owners with ownership rights similar to those enjoyed by UAE nationals. However, between the emirates, regulations may vary, and certain restrictions may apply in terms of property locations and types. In Bahrain, the government has adopted various steps to encourage foreign investment, one of which is allowing non-Bahrainis to own real estate in designated zones.[2] The Bahraini government has also initiated measures to streamline and systematize the property registration process for foreign property owners and interested investors.

Kuwait has comparatively stricter regulations with respect to foreign property ownership. In Kuwait, the focus on attracting FDI has been through other means, such as private-public partnerships and the development of other sectors. Non-Kuwaitis generally do not have the permission to own or purchase real estate in Kuwait. Meanwhile, Oman has gradually been liberalizing and opening up its real estate market, by adopting measures to facilitate foreign investment and foreign property ownership. Like in some other GCC states, non-Omanis are permitted to own property in specific areas known as the integrated tourism complexes (ITCs) and in certain freehold zones.

In the case of Qatar, which is one of the focuses of this paper, the country has been working towards attracting foreign investment and thus has evolved and developed laws and regulations to allow non-Qatari residents to own real estate in designated areas, primarily in the regions of Lusail City and the Pearl Qatar.[3] Typically, foreigners are allowed to own leasehold properties rather than freehold, with lease periods ranging from ninety-nine years to shorter durations. In the KSA, the other focus of this paper, the country has introduced various initiatives, like the introduction of "White Land Tax" on underdeveloped and undeveloped foreign-owned urban land, to open up its real estate market to foreign investors and attract them.[4]

While most GCC states are working on foreign property ownership in their respective states, there are many challenges and considerations faced by these states and the interested investors. As foreign property ownership is subject to change in the Gulf states, investors must constantly update themselves regarding the evolving policies and laws that may impact their property rights. These investors are also encouraged to look into the sectors other than real estate, such as technology, tourism, and renewable energy; sectors that are being developed due to economic diversification efforts by the Gulf states (Hussein, 2009). The distinction between freehold and leasehold ownership is also crucial for foreign investors. The different GCC states offer different types of contracts for different durations. A major consideration that interested investors have is the fact that often foreign property investors are limited to previously designated specific areas for property ownership, which are part of the broader urbanization plans and economic development. Apart from the economic aspect, cultural and social considerations also play a significant role.

Figure 12.2. Challenges and considerations in foreign property ownership faced by GCC states

For foreign investors, understanding social dynamics and the local culture is essential. Cultural norms could potentially influence property management and use, and thus, foreign investors must be mindful of the social and cultural expectations of the community before making the purchase.

Foreign property ownership in the Kingdom of Saudi Arabia, and Alignment with the Saudi Vision 2030

In recent years, as the KSA has sought economic diversification and foreign investment, the foreign property ownership in the country has undergone major changes. While the country has been known for its conservative approach to foreign property ownership, with the announcement of the Saudi Vision 2030,[5] notable policy shifts and initiatives to open up the real estate market to potential foreign investors have been visible. With the Vision 2030, the government recognized the need for foreign investment and took steps to open up and liberalize certain sectors, such as real estate.

Traditionally, the Kingdom restricted foreign property ownership in order to preserve its cultural and social identity. Non-nationals were limited to leaseholds, which were for a long-term basis, and with ownership rights primarily only with Saudi citizens. However, recently, many reforms and initiatives have facilitated and supported foreign property ownership in the KSA:

- *Opening Up of the Real Estate Market*: Through Vision 2030, the government has identified the real estate sector as a key sector for attracting foreign capital and made efforts to gradually open up the market through the introduction of designated areas for foreign property ownership and other measures (Newsroom, 2023).
- *The White Land Tax*: This tax was a significant measure that was introduced by the KSA to encourage the development of unused urban land. The White Land tax, which promotes real estate development and reduces land speculation, is imposed on non-Saudi-owned undeveloped land. The tax aims to incentivize owners to develop these unused urban lands or risk facing financial penalties for the lack thereof (Zakaria et al., 2019).
- *Tourism and Entertainment Sectors*: Vision 2030 strongly emphasizes the development of the entertainment and tourism sectors, which led to the designation of certain areas for tourism projects and foreign property ownership and the subsequent property development. This includes projects such as NEOM, a futuristic city which is planned for the northwestern part of Saudi Arabia, and the Red Sea project, which is a luxury tourism destination (Farag, 2018).

- *Residential Real Estate*: Although there exist restrictions on foreign residential real estate ownership, certain areas have been designated as open for foreign investment with specific regulations varying based on the nature and location of the real estate.
- *Financing of Real Estate for Non-Residents*: The government of the KSA has taken various steps to ease the financing for real estate purchases for non-residents. The financing of real estate for non-residents is a crucial development for non-Saudi investors and acts as a major attraction for international interest in the real estate market (Sands of Wealth, 2024).

Foreign property ownership by South Asian migrants in Saudi Arabia can be a significant contributor to realizing the *Saudi Vision 2030*, as it is in alignment with the Vision's broader objectives of economic diversification, investment growth, urban development, infrastructure modernization, and strengthening the private sector, which would lead to socioeconomic inclusion, community stability, knowledge and skills transfer, and broadening of revenue systems. Diversifying the economy through foreign investments is a priority highlighted by *Saudi Vision 2030*.

Migrants from South Asia make up a significant portion of Saudi Arabia's workforce (not just blue-collar workers but also white-collar workers) and represent a largely untapped investor base for the KSA's property market. By easing property ownership rules for non-Saudis and providing the benefits of property ownership, the Kingdom could draw investments from long-term South Asian expatriates, who may buy property for investment or residence purposes. An increase in property investments will help boost real estate-related sectors such as construction, finance, and retail, which will further create economic ripple effects, aligning with the Vision's focus on broad-based economic growth. Under Vision 2030, the KSA's urbanization goals include developing smart cities, which entails expanding infrastructure and creating more urban areas with greater livability. Urban development could attract skilled expatriates, foster vibrant, economically active neighborhoods, and support the KSA's goals for environmental sustainability and higher standards of living.

Vision 2030 aims to bolster the private sector, increase the share of the private sector's GDP, and generate more private sector employment for Saudi nationals. Encouraging South Asian expatriates to own property could increase demand for real estate services, legal consultations, and financial services, enhancing the private sector's role and job creation potential. Encouraging property ownership among foreign residents also promotes socioeconomic inclusion and fosters stronger community bonds and increases residents' long-term commitment to the country's stability and prosperity. Vision 2030 emphasizes improving the quality of life, and property ownership offers migrants a stake in that vision by creating more stable and cohesive communities, improving the overall quality of living. Many South Asian migrants hold advanced knowledge in the education, construction, healthcare, technology, and finance sectors. Property investment will encourage active contribution, knowledge transfer, and skill-sharing from South Asian migrants, thus helping the vision's goal of developing a more skilled workforce. Saudi Vision 2030 also aims to diversify revenue streams for the government. Additional avenues for revenue generation through property taxes, registration fees, and other real estate-related charges come with foreign property ownership, which can also lead to increased spending on related services, which further boosts economic activity and generates additional tax revenue.

The evolution of foreign property ownership in the state of Saudi Arabia, as mentioned above, started with the Saudi Vision 2030, which was announced in 2016. The key milestones can be seen in Table 12.1 (Scott et al., 2018).

Table 12.1. Key Milestones in KSA's Foreign Property Ownership

Year	Key Milestone
April 2016	**Vision 2030 Announcement**: A comprehensive plan to transform and diversify the KSA's economy by attracting foreign investment and developing non-hydrocarbon sectors, like tourism, real estate, and entertainment
June 2016	**National Transformation Program (NTP)**: This program, which outlined specific initiatives and targets, was launched as part of Vision 2030. It focused on opening up and liberalizing different sectors, including real estate, to foreign investment (Government of Saudi Arabia, 2020).
2017	**White Land Tax Introduction**: This tax aims at encouraging the development of unused urban land and targets the non-Saudi-owned undeveloped urban lands with a goal to incentivize their development or face financial penalties for failing to do so.
2018	**Easing of Real Estate Ownership for Foreign Institutions**: The KSA allowed foreign institutions to own Saudi real estate to attract institutional investment as a part of the broader effort to diversify real estate funding sources.
2019	**Amendments to Mortgage Laws**: In order to facilitate access to financing for interested non-resident property investors, this addressed a major barrier that was faced by international investors (Clifford Chance, 2012).
2019	**Opening Tourism to Foreign Investors** launching tourism-related projects, such as NEON and the Red Sea Project, and areas for foreign investors, encouraging investment in tourism infrastructure development (Asharq Al Awsat, 2024).
2020	**FDI Law Amendments**: to attract international investors and businesses.
2021	**Amendments to Property Ownership Rules**: which signal further steps in opening up the real estate market and make KSA a more attractive market for foreign and local investors (Abboud and Jobaili, 2023).

Foreign property ownership in Qatar

Traditionally, non-Qataris were not allowed to own land in Qatar. However, in the early 2000s, recognizing the importance of foreign investment in various sectors (including the real estate sector) for economic diversification, the state of Qatar introduced various measures to open up the real estate market to international investors.

In recent years, foreign property ownership in Qatar has notably developed and evolved. Like the other five GCC states, Qatar has also been pursuing the diversification of its economy and has been bringing about new policies to attract foreign investment and diversify the Qatari economy. National foreign property ownership regulations have evolved to encourage international investors. Below is an overview of the key aspects and current status of foreign property ownership in Qatar:

- Foreign Ownership Real Estate Zones: Like in Saudi Arabia, Qatar has also designated specific zones, such as the Pearl Qatar and Lusail City, where non-Qataris can own real estate.
- Freehold vs. Leasehold: In the leasehold areas, foreigners can typically own properties on a leasehold basis for upto ninety-nine years. The leasehold areas include Msheireb (Area 13), Fereej Abdelaziz (14), Doha Al Jadeed (15), New Al Ghanim (16), Al Refaa and Old Al Hitmi (17), Aslata (18), Fereej Bin Mahmoud (22), Fereej Bin Mahmoud (23), Rawdat Al Khail (24), Mansoura (25), Fereej Bin Dirham (25), Najma (26), Umm Ghuwailina (27), Al Khulaifat (28), Al Sadd (38), Al Mirqab Al Jadeed (39), Fereej Al Nasr (39), and Doha International Airport area (48). The freehold ownership areas are WestBay (66), The Pearl Qatar (66), Al Khor Resort (74), Rawdat Al Jahaniyah (investment area), Al Qassar (administrative area 60), Al Dafna (administrative area 61), Onaiza (administrative area 63), Al Wasail (69), Al Khraij (69), and Jabal Theyleeb (69) (Qproperties, n.d.).
- The development of the Pearl Qatar and Lusail City has played important roles in the evolution of foreign property ownership in Qatar. It is a prominent example of a development where foreign ownership is permitted in Qatar. The artificial island, called the Pearl Qatar, features luxury retail, commercial, and residential spaces. Non-Qataris are permitted to own residential units and retail spaces in the pre-designated precincts of the Pearl Qatar (Wali, 2022).
- Permanent Residency through Real Estate Investment: In 2020, the Qatari government announced the permanent residency program, which they called the Qatar Permanent Residency Permit, to increase Qatar's appeal as a destination for long-term foreign investment. Individuals

who invest in properties worth one million USD or above are eligible to apply for permanent residency (Saakin, n.d.).

- Strategic Real Estate Projects: The Qatari government has been systematically and actively investing in large-scale real estate projects, which attract foreign investors and enhance Qatar's infrastructure.[6]

Table 12.2 shows the timeline of the key milestones in Qatari foreign property ownership over the years.

Foreign property ownership in Qatar also aligns with the Qatar National Vision 2030, as it aids economic diversification, urban development, and social development (Government Communications Office, Qatar, n.d.).

Foreign property ownership in the United Arab Emirates

In the early 2000s, the UAE made significant steps toward economic diversification, emphasizing market liberalism and economic openness (Hvidt, 2011). The UAE became a pioneer among the GCC states in terms of allowing foreign property ownership. The country has since seen several milestones in foreign property ownership and has been widely successful in attracting foreign investors and stimulating economic growth. Foreign property ownership opportunities in the UAE also align with UAE Vision 2021 and Centennial 2071, as it leads to economic competitiveness, sustainable development, modernization, and social and cultural integration (Telecommunications and Digital Government Regulatory Authority (TDRA), n.d.; see Images 12.1–12.4).

Table 12.2. Qatar Foreign Property Ownership—Key Milestones

Year	Key Milestones
Early 2000s	Initial Steps: Qatar commenced considering ways to attract foreign investment, including allowing foreign property ownership in designated areas as part of the country's broader efforts to diversify the economy.
Early 2000s	The Pearl Qatar Development
Early 2010s	Lusail City Project
2019	Foreign Investment Law (Hawa, 2020)
	Amendments to Property Ownership Rules: marking a notable step in liberalizing and opening up the real estate market. It made the market more attractive for local and international investors.
2020	Permanent Residency Program
2023	Continued Expansion of Foreign Ownership Opportunities—New areas added

Image 12.1. Foreign investors have plenty of freehold areas in Dubai to choose from for apartments, villas, townhouses and residential plots (Bayut, 2024).

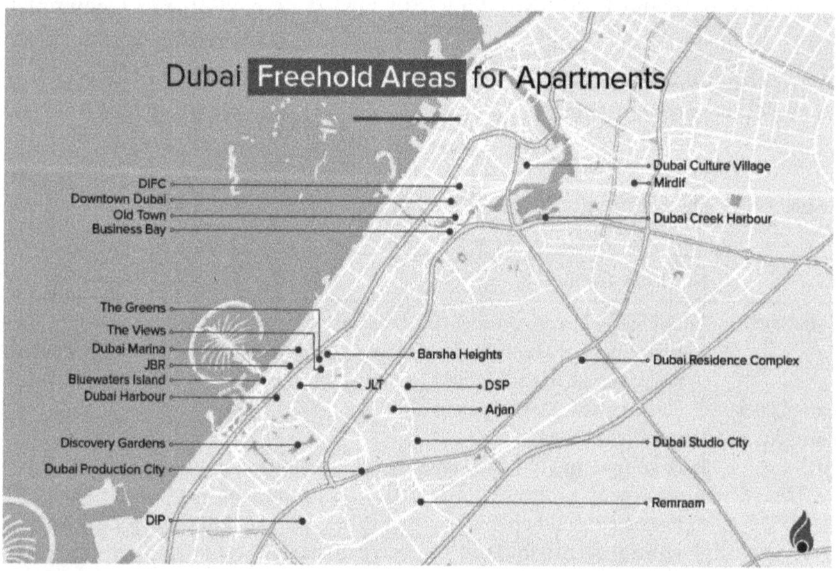

Image 12.2. Dubai Freehold areas for Apartments (Property blog, n.d.).

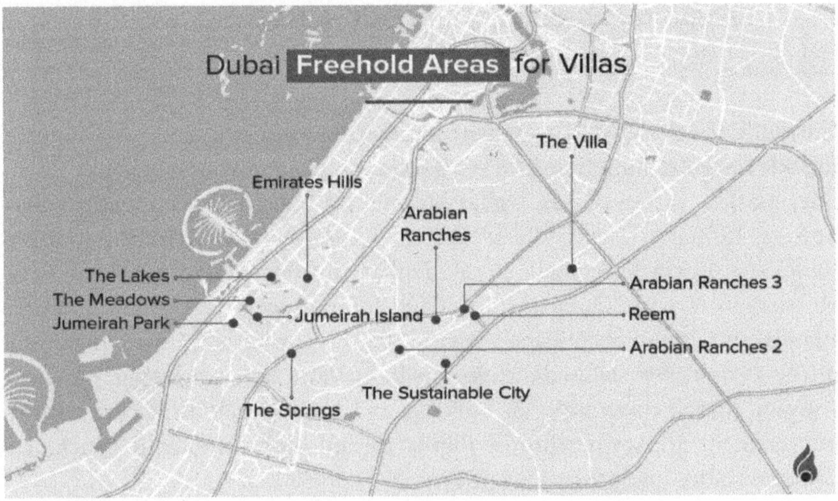

Image 12.3. Dubai freehold areas for Villas (Property blog, n.d.).

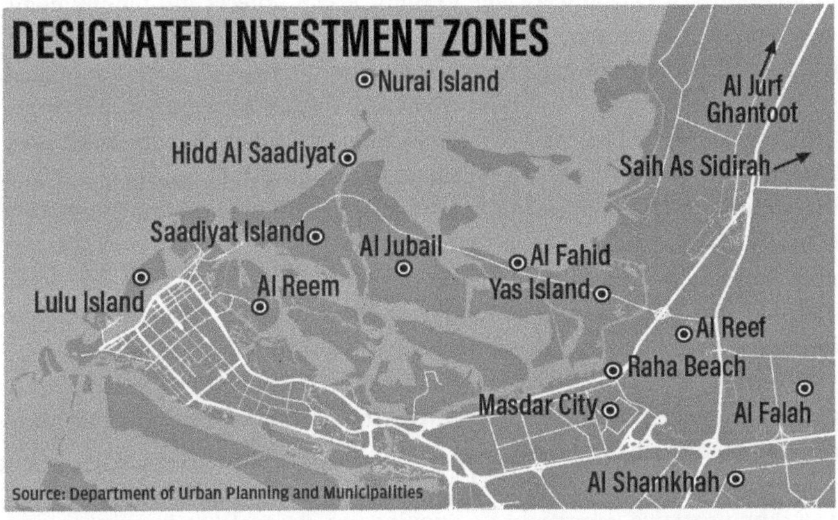

Image 12.4. Designated Investment Zones in Abu Dhabi (Property Shop Investment, 2019).

Freehold ownership in pre-designated areas, like in the KSA and Qatar

Currently, the designated areas where non-UAE nationals can own property include the Palm Jumeirah, The World Islands, Downtown Dubai, Old Town, Burj Khalifa, Business Bay, Dubai Marina, Emirates Hills, Jumeirah Lakes Towers, Jumeirah Beach Residence (JBR), Discovery Gardens, Arabian Ranches, Midriff (specified plots), Dubai Investment Park, Falcon City, Dubai Sports City, Dubai Motor City, International City, and Jumeirah Islands and Jumeirah Village (Bayut, 2023).[7] The Strata Law, which was introduced in 2006, defined the responsibilities and rights of property owners within a shared community or building and gave a legal framework for the management and ownership of jointly owned properties, which included condominiums and apartments (STA Law Firm, 2023).

In 2019, the UAE introduced a policy that made investing in the UAE's real estate market a major attraction for expatriates—offering long-term residency visas for entrepreneurs, investors, and skilled professionals. Property investors who were able to fulfil certain criteria and requirements were eligible for extended residency, which provided greater stability for those interested in investing in real estate. The Golden Visa program offered eligible investors with long-term residency, which became an additional incentive to the UAE's economic development and economic diversification. Further, the granting of citizenship to select investors made real estate investments in Dubai much more attractive to some international investors (Osmandzikovic, 2023). However, such a potential citizenship for investors policy would have long-term implications for residents, investors, and locals. The UAE has also taken steps to allow international investors to complete business ownership, wherein previously only local partnerships were allowed, which could also impact their tendency to invest in real estate. Laws were amended to facilitate international ownership in different sectors, including the real estate sector (Addleshaw Goddard, 2021).

The various above-mentioned milestones together represent the UAE's arguably proactive approach to opening up its real estate market and liberalizing the UAE's property ownership laws in order to create a business-friendly environment and encourage FDIs in the UAE's real estate sector.

Demographics of participants

Of the total participants, 25 or 19 percent moved under the age of 5; 5 or 4 percent moved between the ages of 5–11; 5 or 4 percent moved between the

Table 12.3. UAE Foreign Property Ownership—Key Milestones

Years	Key Milestone
Pre-2000s	Limited Foreign Ownership: Historically, non-UAE nationals were not allowed to own real estate directly.[8]
2002	Dubai Allowed Freehold Ownership in Pre-designated areas[9]
2005	Expansion of Freehold Ownership Across the UAE: Other emirates, such as Sharjah and Abu Dhabi, began allowing freehold ownership for non-citizens in designated areas.
2006	Introduction of Strata Law.
2009	Property Ownership by Foreign Companies broadened the scope of foreign investment in the real estate sector.
2013	Residency for Property Investors: The Residency Visa for property investors provided additional incentives for investing in the UAE.
2019	Long-Term Visas and Amendments to Business Ownership Policies: to enhance the overall investment climate in the UAE. Introduction of "Golden Visa."
2020	Amendments to Property Ownership Laws: Amended Federal Law No. 19 of 2018 to attract foreign investment, enhance competitiveness, and stimulate economic growth (Uncourt, 2021).
2021	Potential Citizenship for Investors10: The new amendment aims to "attract talents that contribute to their (the UAE's) development journey" (GetGoldenVisa, 2023).

ages of 12–20; the vast majority 88 or 65 percent moved between the ages of 20–35; and 12 or 9 percent moved after the age of 35. The majority of the respondents, 95 or 69.3 percent, did not study in Qatar/ UAE/ Saudi Arabia, while the remaining 42 or 30.7 percent studied in these countries.

Of the respondents, 54 or 40.3 percent moved to Qatar/ the UAE/the KSA for work, 46 or 34.3 percent moved to Qatar/the UAE/the KSA because their spouse was working in the respective country, and 27 or 21.2 percent moved because their parents moved to the respective country for work. 69 or 55.2 percent of the respondents are currently still living in Qatar, 37 or 29.6 percent are still living in the UAE, and 2 or 1.6 percent of the respondents are still living in Saudi Arabia. The remaining respondents have either returned to their home countries of India and Pakistan, or have moved or migrated to other countries such as Oman, Germany, Canada, and the UK.

Cultural adjustments and adaptations also become an important consideration in foreign property investments by South Asian migrants as they are faced with the need to adapt or adjust to the new culture, societal norms, and legal systems. Thus, their immediate concerns would be settling into the novel environment, adjusting to their new normal, understanding the new local customs, and, in some cases, building a sense of community or connecting with their diasporas in the local environment. Investments would also be focused on gaining stability, with their focus being on renting an accommodation or purchasing a property as a primary residence rather than as a real estate investment. Due to the need for cultural adjustments, most South Asians still prefer living in their home countries after retirement. For them, owning a house in their home country could provide a sense of permanence and stability in their adopted country, which is most often the home country. Fifty-three of the respondents said that they preferred investing in property in their own home countries. The final and perhaps one of the most crucial considerations is that of remittances. This is a financial commitment that impacts their ability to consider property investment in the host country or elsewhere. Interestingly, only six respondents from the survey cited remittances as a discouraging factor for making property investments in Qatar, the KSA, and/or the UAE.[11]

Increased financial stability and prospects for career growth could also contribute to the interest they show towards property investments. If they feel that property investment would benefit them in the long term for their career and life, they would be more likely to invest in property in the host country. If the migrants belong to families that are running businesses in the host country, then the permanency of their businesses may also push them towards investing in property. Interestingly, the majority of the respondents answered that they do see a future for themselves in the respective countries of their residence. For the question "If you are or were currently living in Qatar/the UAE/Saudi Arabia, do you see a long-term future for you in the country?",[12] 78 or 57.4 percent of the respondents answered "Yes," 17 or 12.5 percent answered "No," 32 or 23.5 percent answered "Maybe," and 9 respondents preferred to specify that they no longer live in these countries and do not see any future for themselves in these countries. For the question "If you are or were currently living in the UAE/Saudi Arabia/Qatar, do you wish to continue living in the same country until you retire?", 88 or 65.7 percent of the respondents answered "Yes," 13 or 9.7 percent answered "No," 24 or 17.9 percent answered "Maybe," and 9 respondents preferred to specify that they no longer live in these countries and do not see any future for themselves in these countries (as observed in Figure 12.4). A long-term or farsighted perspective could make them have a greater interest in investing in property as a means of building wealth and securing assets over time.

The findings show that while the vast majority, 117 or 86 percent, of the respondents haven't made any property investments in the states of Qatar, the UAE, and/or Saudi Arabia, 19 or 14 percent of the respondents have already invested in real estate in these countries. Meanwhile, the large majority of 64 or 47.1 percent of the respondents expressed strong interest in purchasing property in the UAE/Saudi Arabia/Qatar, 35 or 25.7 percent

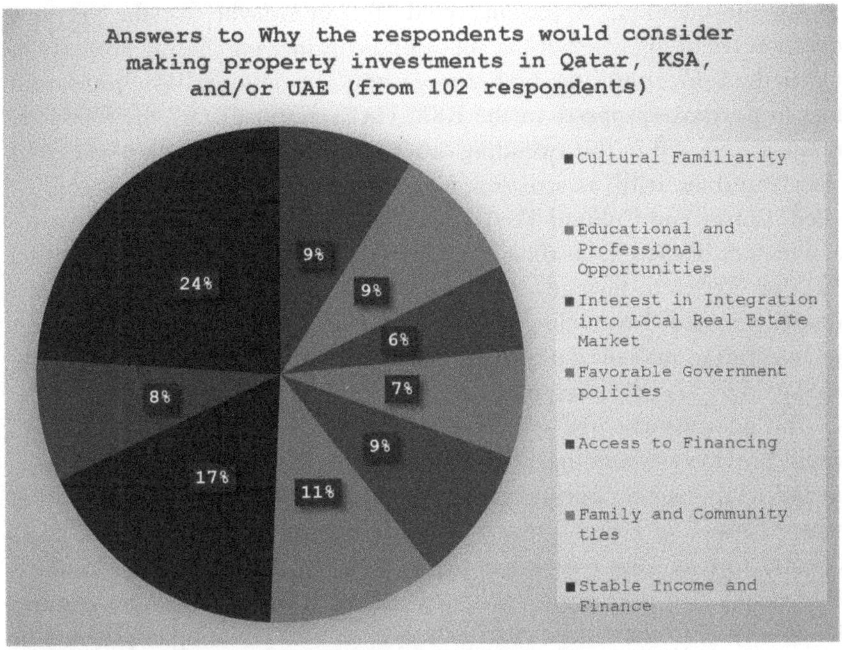

Figure 12.3. Why respondents/participants would consider making property investments in Qatar, KSA, and/or UAE (from 102 respondents).

respondents said they may consider it, and 37 or 27.2 percent respondents said they would not consider purchasing property in the UAE, Saudi Arabia, and/or Qatar due to various discouraging factors as have been mentioned in other responses.

Differences in circumstances, economic factors, personal goals, and the realities of each individual or family also play crucial roles in shaping attitudes towards investments in a foreign country and property ownership. Moreover, the overall economic climate and government policies of the host country would also determine the available opportunities and impact the migrants' decision making. Understanding the benefits of property ownership in the host country,[13] realizing the vast amounts being spent in the country as house rents with zero returns or investment benefits, migrants may become motivated to invest in property in the host country that they call home. Naturally, the existence of favorable government policies and incentives will also determine whether the migrants will invest in property. Nevertheless, one must understand that each person is influenced by a different combination of economic and personal circumstances, goals, cultural considerations, and their specific upbringings and experiences in the host country.

For the question, "If you answered "Yes" or "Maybe" for the previous question regarding whether the you would consider purchasing property in Qatar, the KSA, and/or the UAE, choose from the options, "Why you would like to purchase property in the KSA, UAE, and/or Qatar," the following reasons appeared in the ascending order of most selected reason—51 cited "Safety and Security" as a reason, 37 cited "Stable Income" as a reason, 24 cited "Family and Cultural Ties" as a reason, 19 cited "Cultural Familiarity" as a reason, 19 cited "Educational and Professional opportunities" as a reason, 19 cited "Access to finance" as a reason, 17 cited "access to healthcare" as a reason, 15 cited "Favorable government policies," and twelve cited "Interest in Integrating into the Local Real Estate Market." This question was only answered by 121 of the respondents.

This question also had an "Other" option through which the respondents could provide answers that were not included in the listed options. These included "Investment purposes" by two respondents; "It is my home ... it is where I grew up"; "high growth economy"; "quality of living"; and "good country to live." One respondent explicitly wrote, "would prefer a country that would give permanent residency." Safety, stable income, and cultural familiarity which have been cited as key reasons for investing in property in the KSA, the UAE, and Qatar, align with the "pull factors" put forth by Lee (1966, as cited in D'Alessandro and Basu, 2015), which include those linked to the place of destination such as economic and job opportunities, safety, and professional growth.

Table 12.4 shows some of the responses by those respondents who have already purchased property in the states of the UAE, Qatar, and/or Saudi Arabia. Twenty of the respondents have already invested in property in one, two, or all of these countries. While only one of these respondents, who has already purchased property in the UAE, Qatar, and/or Saudi Arabia, is doing a corporate job, sixteen of them are doing business, and only three are in the education sector. Ten of them are females, while the remaining ten are males.

Interestingly, with no influence or encouragement from the survey or the questions asked by the researcher, a migrant in the UAE who has already purchased property in the country, provided a crucial and strong reason when asked why he/she would invest in these countries—the respondent said, "It's my home—It's where I grew up" (a statement that shows how the respondent identifies the host country as 'home' compared to their actual home country). The fact that such a response was provided by a third-generation migrant who was also born in the host country is strong evidence for the role of migrant generations in influencing property investment decisions of South Asian migrants in the UAE, the KSA, and Qatar.[14]

Table 12.4. Respondents Who Have Already Purchased Property in Host Countries

Host Country (Current or Previous Residence)	Nationality	Gender	Occupation of Person/ Family	Long-Term Future	Continue Living in The Country	Encouraging Factors for Property Investment In The Host Country	Discouraging Factors For Property Investment In The Host Country
Qatar	India	Female	Business	yes	yes	Family and Community Ties	Unfavorable government policies Lack of job security
Qatar	Indian	Female	Business	yes	yes		
UAE and Qatar	Indian	Male	Business	yes	yes	Cultural Familiarity	Unfavorable government policies
UAE	Indian	Female	Corporate Job	yes	yes	Access to Financing Stable Income and Financial Literacy Safety and Security	Unfavorable government policies
Qatar	Indian	Male	Business	yes	yes	Family and Community Ties	
Qatar and UAE	Indian	Male	Business	yes	yes	Cultural Familiarity Educational and Professional Opportunities in the Long-term Perspective Interest in Integration into Local Real Estate Market Access to Financing Stable Income and Financial Literacy Healthcare Safety and Security	Unfavorable government policies Lack of job security Cultural unfamiliarity Remittances You prefer investing in property in your own country (home country).
Qatar	Indian	Male	Business	yes	yes	favorable Government Policies and Incentives Access to Financing Stable Income and Financial Literacy	Unfavorable government policies
Qatar and UAE	Indian	Male	Business	yes	yes	Family and Community Ties Safety and Security Stable Income and Financial Literacy	Unfavorable government policies Cultural unfamiliarity

(*Continued*)

Table 12.4. (Continued)

Host Country (Current or Previous Residence)	Nationality	Gender	Occupation of Person/ Family	Long-Term Future	Continue Living in The Country	Encouraging Factors for Property Investment In The Host Country	Discouraging Factors For Property Investment In The Host Country
Qatar	Indian	Female	Business	yes	yes	Family and Community Ties	remittances
Qatar	Indian	Male	Business	yes	maybe	Safety and Security	Unfavorable government policies
Qatar	Pakistani	Female	Education	yes	yes	Family and Community Ties Safety and Security Stable Income and Financial Literacy Healthcare	Unfavorable government policies Lack of job security
Qatar	Indian	Male	Business	maybe	yes	Educational and Professional Opportunities in the Long-term Perspective	
Qatar	Indian	Male	Education	yes	yes	Stable Income and Financial Literacy	Lack of job security
UAE	Indian	Male	Business	yes	maybe	Educational and Professional Opportunities in the Long-term Perspective Interest in Integration into Local Real Estate Market favorable Government Policies and Incentives Safety and Security Access to Financing Family and Community Ties Stable Income and Financial Literacy	Unfavorable government policies Lack of job security Cultural unfamiliarity Remittances You prefer investing in property in your own country (home country).

UAE	Indian	Female	Business	yes	yes	Stable Income and Financial Literacy	
UAE	Indian	Female	Business	yes	yes	Stable Income and Financial Literacy	"For a bright future"
UAE (Born in UAE)	Indian	Female	Business	yes	yes	favorable Government Policies and Incentives Family and Community Ties Safety and Security "It's my home- it's where I grew up"	Unfavorable government policies Lack of job security
Qatar (Born in Qatar)	Indian	Female	Business	maybe	yes	Interest in Integration into Local Real Estate Market	Unfavorable government policies
Qatar	Indian	Female	Education	yes	yes	Stable Income and Financial Literacy Safety and Security	Unfavorable government policies Lack of job security You prefer investing in property in your own country (home country).
Qatar	Indian	Male	Business	yes	no		You prefer investing in property in your own country (home country).

Of the respondents who had already purchased property in the studied GCC countries, eleven still cited "unfavorable governmental policies" as a discouraging factor for property investment in the respective host countries. Six of the respondents who cited this reason are currently or were previously living in the state of Qatar; two in the UAE; and three in the states of Qatar and the UAE; thus, making Qatar's total count nine and UAE's five.

A combination of the Real Estate Market theory and Planned Behavior theory provides a comprehensive framework to analyze the motivations and barriers that shape South Asian migrants' property ownership and investment decisions in the UAE, the KSA, and Qatar. These theories together aid an integrated understanding of economic, social, and individual decision-making processes. Challenges highlighted in this research, such as unfavorable policies, regulatory uncertainty, and leasehold arrangements that exist in the KSA, the UAE, and Qatar, make the Real Estate Market theory relevant to this research. Real Estate Market theory or theoretical foundations of real estate market behavior looks at how real estate investment decisions of South Asians in the host countries are influenced by demand, supply, government regulations, and external factors such as economic stability (Trinh, 2022). This works in tandem with the Planned Behavior theory, which says that migrants' property investments are influenced by the migrants' attitudes, subjective norms, and perceived behavioral control (Ajzen, 1991). The factors such as stable income, job security, favorable government policies, and cultural and familial ties which were identified as positive influences on investment intentions, while uncertainty and unfavorable policies which were identified as negative influences which would deter migrants' property investment decisions, makes the planned behavior theory relevant in this particular research.

Challenges to foreign property ownership in the GCC states

The hindrances and obstacles to foreign property ownership in the GCC states vary across the states, but can also be arguably similar. The legal restrictions that have been imposed by many GCC states historically on foreign property ownership are an obvious obstacle to this. Some of these countries have more recently designated specific areas, sometimes under specific conditions, and limited the available choices for foreign investors. However, many investors remain wary of making real estate investments in the GCC states. The leasehold arrangement structure does not grant the same level of control as freehold ownership does. National security concerns also

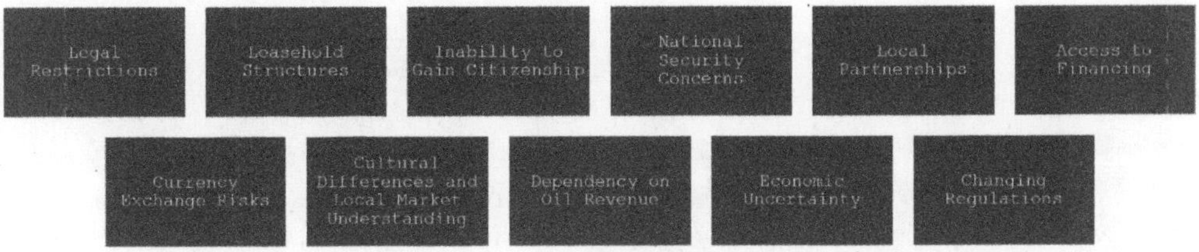

Figure 12.4. The collective list of factors affecting or influencing foreign property investment decisions of South Asian migrants residing in the KSA, Qatar, and the UAE.

play an important role in the designation of areas where foreign property ownership can be permitted. Governments would be cautious regarding strategic or vital locations and would not allow foreigners to own properties in and around such locations (Figure 12.5).

Previously, the need for local partnerships was also a hindrance to foreign property investments, as it could lead to complexities and disputes between the parties. The change in this policy and the allowance of complete ownership by foreign investors have significantly increased the attractiveness of investing in the GCC market. The constantly changing regulatory and legal frameworks also impact foreign property ownership. The dependency on oil revenues, the resultant economic uncertainty, and currency exchange risks (fluctuations in currency exchange rates will impact returns on foreign investments) are further hindrances that discourage international investors from investing in GCC states. Real Estate Market theory of real estate market behavior explains how investment decisions of South Asians in the UAE, the KSA, and Qatar are influenced by such features of the real estate market and factors that affect the real estate market.

Along with the above, cultural differences, need for local market understanding, lack of easy access to financing (specific lending criteria, and lack of ability to gain citizenship are factors that discourage international investors (Figure 12.6). It must be noted that different GCC countries have different laws and regulations and levels of liberalization with respect to foreign property ownership, and thus, investors interested in purchasing properties in the different GCC states may be faced with different challenges and hurdles in their pursuit to invest in real estate in the GCC region. Prospective investors must conduct thorough research and seek professional advice in order to navigate through the various complexities of the GCC's real estate market and must also constantly stay updated regarding the laws, regulations, rights, and responsibilities associated with foreign property ownership in these states, considering the dynamic nature of the real estate

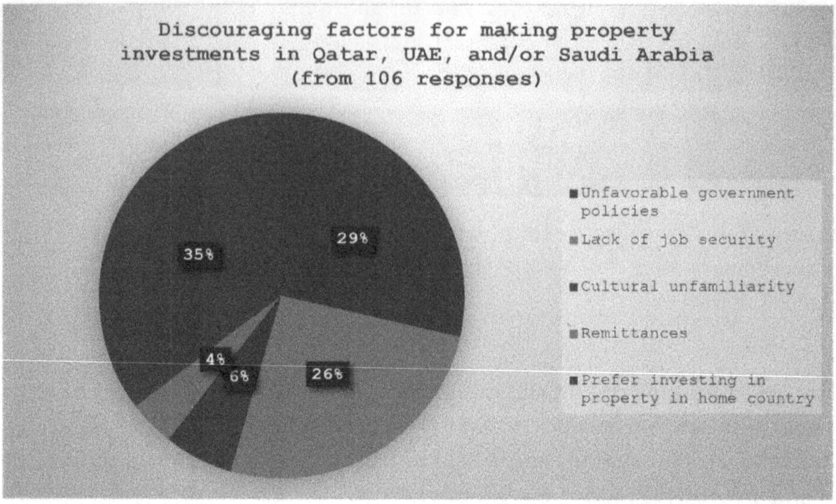

Figure 12.5. Discouraging factors for making property investments in Qatar, the UAE, and/or Saudi Arabia (from 106 responses).

sector and related policies in the GCC states. Many of these concerns are equally applicable to investors buying real estate in their own native countries; however, in the GCC states, the foreign property ownership landscape is fast-changing and more sensitive to the international oil prices, calling for greater attention from those interested in investing.

The question "Which factors would discourage you from making property investments in your host country (Qatar, UAE, and/or Saudi Arabia)?" received responses from 116 participants. The vast majority, 52 or 44.8 percent, stated that they preferred investing in property in their own country; 42 or 36.2 percent cited "unfavorable government policies" as the reason; 38 or 32.8 percent cited "Lack of job security" as the reason; 9 or 7.8 percent cited "cultural unfamiliarity" as the reason; and 6 or 5.2 percent cited "Remittances" as the reason. Through the other option, some other reasons were also provided by the respondents—"for a bright future" with a tone of sarcasm; "uncertainty about maintaining residential status"; "unfavorable return on investment"; "No chance for citizenship" by two respondents; "Exorbitant prices"; "Prefer investing in other countries"; and "uncertain expatriate property rights."

Conclusion

In the GCC, while some states have embraced foreign property ownership in their pursuit of economic diversification, others have been more cautious in their approaches and have focused on alternative diversification methods. With the further modifications and developments that foreign property ownership regulations will undergo in the GCC states, the real estate sectors would eventually evolve and present new opportunities and challenges for the investors who are seeking a foothold in this geo-strategic region. The respective approaches to foreign property ownership of Saudi Arabia, the UAE, and Qatar have evolved significantly in recent years, driven by their respective national visions and diversification plans. However, it is crucial for interested investors to conduct comprehensive market research, obtain legal advice, and stay well-informed regarding regulatory developments in order to make good decisions in the dynamic landscape of the GCC real estate sector, as when investing elsewhere.

Despite the various government initiatives, potential investors and buyers face certain challenges when it comes to foreign property ownership in Saudi Arabia and Qatar: the restrictive and selective geographic access that requires the interested investors to understand the strategic importance of the designated locations for international investment; the regulatory uncertainty that is an added source of tension as the investors must stay updated regarding the regulations in order to make informed investment decisions; the investors require awareness regarding cultural considerations and the local customs and traditions which may influence the properties' usage; and finally, the persisting economic dependency of the Saudi or the Qatari economy on rentier incomes despite the economic diversification efforts which makes the country's economy highly sensitive to global factors which impact oil prices and the overall economic stability, subsequently affecting the real estate market.

Most survey participants (93.4 percent) were Indians, with 6.5 percent Pakistanis, and the 26–40 age group represented the largest demographic (45.3 percent), primarily consisting of mid-career professionals. The study found that the majority of surveyed migrants (86 percent) have not invested in GCC property, though 47 percent expressed interest. Business owners (44.9 percent) were most likely to consider property investment, compared to those in the corporate or education sectors. The most cited reason for interest in investment in the states of Qatar, UAE, and/or Saudi Arabia was "Safety and Security," and the most cited discouraging factor was "prefer investing in own country (home country)." Stable income and family ties were other key motivators for property investment, while unfavorable policies and a preference for investing in their home countries were major deterrents. Cultural familiarity and access to healthcare and education emerged as secondary pull factors influencing decisions. Regulatory uncertainty, cultural unfamiliarity, economic instability, high remittance obligations, lack of job security, and a stronger inclination to invest in their home countries also hinder investment in the host country.

Notes

1 In Dubai, the terms onshore and offshore real estate typically relate to legal, regulatory, and ownership frameworks rather than physical location. Onshore real estate refers to properties located within Dubai's mainland or freehold areas regulated by the Dubai Land Department (DLD). In designated areas, freehold properties allow foreign investors to own property completely without restrictions. Offshore real estate refers to properties owned or held through offshore companies registered in jurisdictions like the Jebel Ali Free Zone (JAFZA) or Ras Al Khaimah International Corporate Centre (RAK ICC), etc.

While onshore properties are typically for personal use, rental income, or straightforward investment purposes and have transactions that are more transparent and directly tied to the Dubai real estate market, offshore ownership structures are used for commercial purposes or for high-net-worth individuals seeking confidentiality, and may involve trusts or holding companies for cross-border investments.

Offshore properties also provide potential tax benefits, privacy advantages, and can simplify estate planning and inheritance transfers, compared to onshore properties.

2 The designated zones in Bahrain include Amwaj Islands, Juffair, Seef, and Riffa.

3 The designated areas for foreign property ownership in Qatar have recently been expanded to include more zones.

4 Although the goal to encourage real estate development exists, many regulations are subject to change, and foreign property ownership is restricted to areas that are deemed to be of strategic importance.

5 The Saudi Vision 2030 announced in 2016 by the Crown Prince Mohammed bin Salman is an ambitious plan which aims at transforming the Saudi economy and steering it away from complete dependency on oil and hydrocarbon sectors.

6 The Msheireb Downtown Doha is one such project that offers foreign investment opportunities and focuses on sustainable urban planning.

7 It must also be noted that foreign ownership rights tend to vary depending on the location of the property or the specific emirate. While some designated areas fall under freehold ownership, other areas have restrictions.

8 The maximum that was allowed was the leasing of properties or land for a limited period of time.

9 Dubai pioneered in the region in allowing freehold property ownership in specific and designated areas. A policy aimed at attracting international investment and the growth of the real estate sector.

10 The UAE cabinet, executive councils, and local courts will be authorities to nominate candidates who are eligible for UAE citizenship.

11 Migrants have to send remittances back to their immediate or extended family residing in the home country. The remittances could be a sizeable

amount, which could deter or delay property investment in the host country, and further persuade them to make property investments in their home country. This could be a part of the family support as their families back in the home country would be able to live in the newly acquired property, which could be an added factor economically and perhaps, culturally and socially too.

12 Migrants who live in a host country for a longer duration naturally show greater attachment towards the particular host country and will be more inclined towards investing in the host country than individuals who live for shorter durations.

13 Such an understanding of the pros and cons of making property investments in the host country could also come from the experiences of individuals from the same community who have previously made real estate investments in the particular GCC country.

14 This topic will be explored in a consecutive research paper, which will explore the dimensions of identity and sense of belongingness amongst South Asian migrants in making foreign property ownership decisions.

Bibliography

Abboud, J., and G. E. Jobaili (2023). *Foreign Ownership of Real Estate in Saudi Arabia: The Freehold Boom*. BSA Law, LLP. https://bsalaw.com/insight/foreign-ownership-of-real-estate-in-saudi-arabia-the-freehold-boom/

Addleshaw Goddard. (2021). *Changes to Foreign Ownership Laws in the UAE*. https://www.addleshawgoddard.com/en/news/2021/changes-to-foreign-ownership-laws-in-the-uae2/

Ajzen, I. (1991, December). The theory of planned behavior. *Organizational Behavior and Human Decision Processes, 50*(2), 179–211.

Al Tamimi & Co. (2017). *Who can own Real Estate in Dubai and Where?: Part 2 of Know Your Rights for Real Estate Investors in Dubai Guide Who can own Real Estate in Dubai and Where?: Part 2 of Know Your Rights for Real Estate Inv*. Tamimi & Co. https://www.tamimi.com/law-update-articles/can-real-estate-dubai-part-2-know-rights-real-estate-investors-dubai-guide/

Alstadsaeter, A., B. Planterose, G. Zucman, and A. Økland (2022). Who Owns Offshore Real Estate? Evidence from Dubai. EU Tax Observatory: Working Paper 1.

Asharq Al Awsat. (2024). *Saudi Arabia Opens Doors to Int'l Investment on 'World Tourism Day'*. Asharq Al-Awsat, , January 23. https://english.aawsat.com/business/4572661-saudi-arabia-opens-doors-int'l-investment-'world-tourism-day'

Azzam, A., and B. Rettab (2011). Are restrictions on foreign ownership counter-productive? Evidence from Dubai, United Arab Emirates. *International Journal of Economic Policy in Emerging Economies, 4*(1), 1–19.

Bayut. (2023). *The complete list of freehold areas in Dubai*. Bayut, December 11. https://www.bayut.com/mybayut/complete-list-freehold-areas-dubai/

Bayut (2024). *The complete list of freehold areas in Dubai*. Bayut, October 21. https://www.bayut.com/mybayut/complete-list-freehold-areas-dubai/

Clifford Chance. (2012). *Saudi Arabian mortgage, finance and court reform*. Clifford Chance, September. https://www.cliffordchance.com/content/dam/cliffordchance/briefings/2012/09/saudi-arabian-mortgage-finance-and-court-reform.pdf

D'Alessandro, S., and P. Basu (2015). Push-pull factors in migration to regional areas: A service marketing perspective and research agenda. *Rethinking the region and regionalism in Australasia Subtitle of host publication: Challenges and opportunities for the 21st Century* (pp. 1–9). East Sussex: Regional Studies Association.

Farag, A. A. (2018). The Story of NEOM City: Opportunities and Challenges. In S. Attia, Z. Shafik, and A. Ibrahim (Eds.), *New Cities and Community Extensions in Egypt and the Middle East: Visions and Challenges* (pp. 35–49). Springer Link.

GetGoldenVisa. (2023, May 4). *UAE Golden Visa Ultimate Guide: UAE Citizenship by Investment*. GetGolden Visa. https://getgoldenvisa.com/uae-citizenship-by-investment-or-talent

Government Communications Office, Qatar. (n.d.). *Qatar National Vision 2030*. Government Communications Office, Qatar. https://www.gco.gov.qa/en/about-qatar/national-vision2030/

Government of Saudi Arabia. (2020). *Saudi Vision 2030*. https://www.vision2030.gov.sa/en/vision-2030/vrp/national-transformation-program/

Hawa, F. (2020). Qatar and prospects of foreign investment from a developing legal perspective. *Arab Law Quarterly*, *35*(4), 488–500.

Hussein, M. A. (2009). Impacts of foreign direct investment on economic growth in the Gulf Cooperation Council (GCC) Countries. *International Review of Business Research Papers*, *5*(3), 362–76.

Hvidt, M. (2011). Economic and institutional reforms in the Arab Gulf countries. *The Middle East Journal*, *65*(1), 85–102.

Menon, L. V., and T. B. James (2023). The Impediments for Second-generation Migrants to Enter Higher Education in the Gulf Cooperation Council Countries. In Z. R. Babar, K. Matsukawa, and A. Watanabe (Eds.), *Transnational Generations in the Arab Gulf States and Beyond* (pp. 57–75). Springer Nature.

Mina, W. (2014). United Arab Emirates FDI Outlook. *The World Economy*, *37*(12), 1716–30.

Newsroom. (2023). *2030 in Saudi Arabia's Push for 100% Foreign Ownership*. Newsroom, November 27. https://www.azimuth-gulf.com/2030-in-saudi-arabias-push-for-100-foreign-ownership/

Osmandzikovic, E. (2023). The Golden Visa: Anatomy of making a long-term home in the UAE. *Migration and Diversity*, *2*, 183–205.

Property blog. (n.d.). *Freehold Property Areas in Dubai*. Property blog. https://www.dubizzle.com/blog/property/freehold-property-areas-dubai/

Property Shop Investment. (2019). *Freehold investments in Abu Dhabi*. Property Shop Investment, April 25. https://blog.psinv.net/freehold-investments-in-abu-dhabi/

Qproperties. (n.d.). *Areas Foreigners Can Own Properties in Qatar*. QProperties. https://qproperties.qa/areas-foreigners-can-own-properties-in-qatar/

Saakin. (n.d.). *List of Areas in Qatar Where Foreigners Can Own Properties*. Saakin. https://www.saakin.qa/blog/list-of-areas-in-qatar-where-foreigners-can-own-properties

Sands of Wealth. (2024). *Buying property in Saudi Arabia as a foreigner: a full guide*. Sands of Wealth, January 7. https://sandsofwealth.com/blogs/news/saudi-arabia-real-estate-foreigner

Scott, J., M. K. Baksh, and M. Negm (2018). *Law Firm / Insights / Law Update / May 2018 / Overview of Saudi Real Estate Laws and Practice Overview of Saudi Real Estate Laws and Practice*. Tamimi & Co. https://www.tamimi.com/law-update-articles/overview-of-saudi-real-estate-laws-and-practice/

Siriopoulos, C., A. Tsagkanos, A. Svingou, and E. Daskalopoulos (2021). Foreign direct investment in GCC countries: The essential influence of governance and the adoption of IFRS. *Journal of Risk Financial Management, 14*(6), 264–5.

STA Law Firm. (2023). *Overview: Abu Dhabi's Strata Law and its Implications*. STA Law Firm, October 4. https://www.stalawfirm.com/en/blogs/view/abu-dhabis-strata-law-and-its-implications.html#:~:text=The%20strata%20law%20means%20the,the%20part%20of%20the%20property.

Telecommunications and Digital Government Regulatory Authority (TDRA). (n.d.). *UAE Centennial 2071*. Telecommunications and Digital Government Regulatory Authority (TDRA). https://u.ae/en/about-the-uae/strategies-initiatives-and-awards/strategies-plans-and-visions/innovation-and-future-shaping/uae-centennial-2071

Trinh, T. H. (2022). Theoretical foundations of real estate market behavior. *Cogent Business & Management, 9*(1), 1–18.

Uncourt, C. (2021). *8 Ct. Uncourt 23 (2021) Abu Dhabi: Legislative Amendments to Freehold Ownership Laws*. HEIN Online. https://heinonline.org/HOL/LandingPage?handle=hein.journals/counco8&div=9&id=&page=

Wali, R. (2022, May). *What makes properties for sale in Lusail desirable to global investors in 2022?* The Pearl Gates. https://www.thepearlgates.com/about/case-studies-and-insights/what-makes-properties-for-sale-in-lusail-desirable-to-global-investors-in-2022/

Zakaria, N., Ali, Z., and M. Z. Awang (2019). White land tax: Evidence in the Kingdom of Saudi Arabia. *Journal of Accounting and Auditing: Research & Practice*, 1–12.

Epilogue

Fahad Alsharif

This edited book offers a thoughtful and in-depth look into labor migration in Saudi Arabia and the rest of the Gulf region. We want to capture the exciting changes that are happening and give a critical and human-centered view of labor migration. To achieve this, we worked with renowned scholars, researchers, and practitioners, many of whom have first-hand experience in the Gulf. These chapters have moved beyond numbers and policy analysis to tell interesting stories and make hopeful predictions about the future.

The book starts by talking about the lengthy history of migration in the area, showing how people moved about in interesting ways long before the spectacular oil boom of 1938 (Figure C.1). This early crucial setting shows that migration has been a part of Gulf countries for quite a long time, and that it is closely linked to trade, pilgrimage, tribal ties, and the effects of colonization. As Saudi Arabia's political economy changed throughout the years, so did its migration policies and patterns in interesting ways. The transition from a subsistence economy to a petroleum-driven developmental state has created new opportunities for attracting workers, who had a positive impact on the Kingdom's demographics, labor market, and identity.

As Vision 2030 reshapes the country's priorities, it's especially thrilling to witness the careful revaluation of the social compact between the state, citizens, and expatriates (Figure C.2). As more people discuss economic diversity, Saudization (localizing the labor force), and sustainable development,

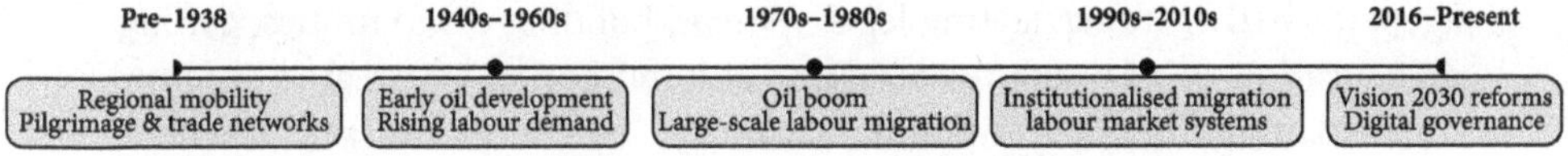

Figure C.1. Historical Evolution of Labor Migration in Saudi Arabia. Conceptual timeline illustrating key phases in the development of labor migration to Saudi Arabia, from early regional mobility and pilgrimagerelated movements to largescale labor migration associated with oilled development and contemporary economic transformation. Source: Author's conceptual illustration based on the migration literature.

Figure C.2. Migration and Economic Transformation under Vision 2030. Three-layer conceptual framework illustrating how migration governance reform, labour market restructuring, and economic diversification interact within Saudi Arabia's Vision 2030 development strategy. Source: Author's conceptual framework.

migration has become a pressing issue in the country. This volume confidently accepts these tensions and welcomes them, showing the exciting possibilities of reconciling national employment goals with economic competitiveness and the gratifying path of protecting workers' rights while pushing for big changes.

One of the main ideas reiterated in this book is that migrant workers are more than just economic contributors: they must also be active participants in politics. They deserve appreciation and a good policy response for their agency, whether it's navigating legal systems, building communities, getting an education, or adapting to social and cultural norms. It's great to see how different migrants are: domestic workers, engineers, nurses, teachers, construction workers, and students all face different problems and bring different skills to the table. The real-world data and analytical insights in this book show that there is a great chance for a more open, evidence-based system for managing migration. Saudi Arabia has a great opportunity to lead the region by establishing a migration model that is effective and grounded in the region's realities and best practices from around the world.

This book makes a case for a new commitment to a collaboration between different stakeholders, including ministries, for a more comprehensive and transparent management of the issues raised by migration. The changes that Saudi Arabia is making to its labor laws, residency rules, and worker rights are forward-looking and necessary. But as various chapters have pointed out, there is still room for improvement in how the rules are put into action and enforced. Making policy goals match up with what people really experience is an exciting chance that will influence migration governance for the next ten years. Researchers in academia and think tanks need to be able to get good data on migration in the Gulf now more than ever. The Kingdom has made good progress by making more statistics and reports available. If the authorities keep investing in independent research, working with institutions, and long-term studies, the future looks bright. Scholars have a great chance to look more closely at how gender, class, nationality, religion, and legal status all work together to make migrants' lives better.

Current problems and bright future ahead

We know that this book, albeit long, only gives a little flavor of the many stories that make up Saudi Arabia's migration history. Some themes, such as migration caused by climate change, refugee flows, undocumented migration, and diaspora engagement, really need more room. Also, the views of migrants, which were shown via diverse real-world experiences, really need to be studied more in depth through ethnography and narratives. Oral histories, participatory action research, and community-based scholarship are all important methods for making more accurate and inclusive narratives in future projects.

Labor migration is more than just moving people; it's also about moving dreams, skills, and connections. This is a great story about people that unites us all, no matter where we live or what policies we follow. This book shows that the migration issue in Saudi Arabia and the Gulf is deep and complicated, extending beyond just numbers or legal categories. It should be based on a strong understanding of our history, culture, identity, and the hopes we have for the future. As Saudi Arabia begins the next exciting chapter of its development journey, it's important to remember that its transformation is not only about diversifying its economy or building more infrastructure, but also about how it welcomes and includes those who come to support its vision. In the Kingdom, the future of labor migration will be molded by a sense of inclusion, fairness, and respect for each other, not only by limiting or expanding it. Towards that end, the book will hopefully be a great resource, an exciting challenge, and a motivating call to action. We invite scholars, policymakers, practitioners, and migrants themselves to join us in the next step of this journey. It will be based on empathy, backed by evidence, and driven by our shared desire to make the future better for everyone.

It is now clear that labor migration in Saudi Arabia and the rest of the Gulf is not simply about money; it is a living system of people that is connected to religious beliefs, changes in the world, and the search for progress. These trends are starting to show up in a culture that is actively trying to figure out who it is by balancing modernity and tradition, welcoming globalization while valuing cultural preservation. Policymakers in the Kingdom have a great chance to set migration rules that balance the region's economic requirements with its unique cultural and spiritual values. We ought to welcome the exciting changes that are happening as the Gulf becomes a knowledge-based economy. The workers it attracts and the skills it needs are going through a huge change. High-skilled immigrants are very important to fields like AI, fintech, healthcare, and environmental sciences since they help them flourish and come up with new ideas. The conversation around migration is about to get more interesting as it moves away from simple classifications like "expat vs. citizen" and "skilled vs. unskilled" and toward a more sophisticated, capability-based framework.

Migration governance must function effectively in a world that is constantly evolving and interconnected. As this book was getting ready to come out in 2026, tensions between the US and Israel on one side and Iran on the other side in the Gulf region escalated sharply. These erupted into a multi-directional war toward the end of the process of sending the manuscript to the publisher, when the book's primary arguments, chapter contributions, and analytical framework were already done. Making major adjustments to the volume in response to ongoing, unresolved changes was neither realistic nor helpful. Yet, it also seemed essential not to let the book appear disconnected from a rapidly changing region. This brief comment in the epilogue serves as a limited but important acknowledgment of a conflict that emerged just as the book was entering production.

The timing of this escalation itself provides insight. A major idea in this collection is that to understand migration in the Gulf, one needs to consider the broader political and economic context. Labor market demand, government policies, institutional improvements, and times of regional instability that can change plans for governments, businesses, and migrants - all affect migration systems in the GCC. From this perspective, the current war pertains to the subjects addressed above. Instead of overshadowing these challenges, it highlights the continuing significance of migration governance, labor market adaptability under uncertainty, and the impact of regional instability on involuntary displacement vis-à-vis mobility frameworks and experiences.

Although it is too soon to draw firm conclusions, the war could affect migration patterns in the GCC in several ways. In the past, rising geopolitical tensions have affected the flow of new hires, investment choices, remittance patterns, and the appeal of destination countries. Even if people are forced to shun traveling and remain stuck amidst disruption, uncertainty can still change how they would move in the future. Employers might put off hiring, migrants might put off moving, and sending states might think again about the dangers and advantages of certain places. These changes might manifest slowly, but they are very important for understanding how Gulf migration systems will change over time.

At the same time, the changes described in this book show that Gulf states are now dealing with uncertainty in a different way than they used to. Digital platforms, changes to the law, and new ways to manage workers have all made migration governance more complex, as shown in several chapters. These steps might not eliminate the effects of geopolitical crises, but they can change how people feel about those repercussions. Systems that manage worker mobility, contracts, pay, and employer control may have to be overhauled to be able to handle turbulence than they were in the past. So, this moment must examine whether the newly emerging governance frameworks, which were made parts of bigger efforts to modernize and enhance the economy, are strong enough to last the test of relevance.

The multi-directional conflicts also make us rethink how unfairly migrants are treated in Gulf labor markets. One important idea in this book is that not all migrants are the same. Their experiences differ according to sector, proficiency, legal position, nationality, and institutional safeguards. These differences become especially evident when things are uncertain. Highly trained professionals may have more alternatives to renegotiate contracts or move, whereas workers in less stable industries who make less money may be more immediately affected by an economic slowdown, delayed wages, or increased insecurity. Consequently, any rigorous evaluation of the ramifications of regional warfare must recognize this complex reality.

In a more general sense, the conflict could have an effect on the economic changes that this book is mostly about. If instability in the region affects how people invest, how the government spends money, energy markets, or efforts to diversify, it could change the need for different types of workers in GCC economies. Countries with big goals like Vision 2030 and other national projects will have to deal with uncertainty while still growing and protecting recent gains in institutions. In this way, migration is still very much connected to the bigger changes in politics and the economy.

This late addendum doesn't change the main points of the book; rather it just makes them stronger. The recent rise in violence reminds us that Gulf migration is always changing, based on history, and closely linked to changes in politics and the economy. This development is vital to highlight not because it gives a vivid image of a crisis, but because it shows how important it is at the time the book is finished. In that limited sense, this epilogue connects the book more closely to the present, but it doesn't go into the details of these oc.

This book makes a valid point: other members of the Gulf Cooperation Council (GCC) often face similar challenges with migration to those of Saudi Arabia. Standardized labor regulations, reciprocal recognition of credentials, and cooperative monitoring mechanisms are examples of regional solutions that could help keep migration systems from breaking down and make them work more effectively together. Additionally, the emergence of regional migration think tanks and academic networks presents an opportunity to align research goals, share best practices, and amplify Gulf voices in global migration discussions. We are delighted about the growth of these kinds of platforms, especially those that include researchers from the Gulf and improve scholarship in the area.

Saudi Arabia can view migration not just as a means to boost its economy, but also as a tremendous force for human development that aligns with the Sustainable Development Goals (SDGs). Migrants play a lot of different roles; they are parents, students, volunteers, and active members of their communities. Indeed, policy frameworks need to strongly promote their well-being in a broad sense, including access to healthcare, integration into the culture, and granting them legal power. Such attention will presumably stand as effective paradigms for inclusiveness, something that Vision 2030 promotes and, equally important, what the vast majority of Saudis aspire towards.

Given the major changes in migratory patterns in the Gulf since the geopolitical tensions of early 2026, it is necessary to rethink the questions that will shape future research. These changes are not just temporary; they show deeper fundamental weaknesses. What do the labor mobility corridors that connect Saudi Arabia to Asia and Africa mean for the short and medium term? Will these problems speed up the nationalization of the labor market under Vision 2030, or will they make it even more important for some sectors to rely on foreign workers? Institutional resilience is just as important: how well can the Kingdom's digitized migration governance mechanisms, especially platform-based contract management and worker mobility reforms, handle geopolitical shocks?

These changes also illustrate how migration impacts people. Uncertainty and conflict influence how migrants make decisions, assess risks, and send money home. How do migrant communities adapt across different sectors, skill levels, and nationalities? What policy adjustments should lawmakers consider to balance economic objectives with security concerns? Broadly, what do these changes reveal about the connection between migration, state capacity, and geopolitical risk in the Gulf? How might they alter our perspective on migration compared to other countries?

At the same time, these improvements bring up moral and generational issues. What moral frameworks should guide migration policy when things are unknown, and how might they be used to promote values like shared responsibility, dignity, and inclusion? What are some ways that women and younger people can have more of a say in how the future will develop and how people will move?

The study of migration in the Gulf must be grounded in scientific fervor and attuned to social reality. This means incorporating a widening circle of voices to include early-career researchers, policymakers, practitioners, migrant community leaders, and others who bring diverse perspectives, deliberately turning to questions that will shape its next phase. Foremost among them is labor migration in times of uncertainty, particularly during periods of war and protracted conflict. Such moments place migrants under acute strain, leaving sending and receiving states grappling with pressures that their existing policy frameworks were not built to handle. Alongside these urgent concerns, sustained attention is also needed to nurture migrants' sense of belonging, to examine social remittances and the wider economic effects of remittance flows, and to consider the future of the rentier-state concept as diversification advances across the GCC. The Gulf has long been a meeting point for people and economies, and the patterns of mobility that pass through it are being made and remade in our own times. The chapters presented here are just one step towards making sense of that transformation.

Index

(Diagrams and tables are given in italics)